cruelty
&
utopia

Princeton Architectural Press
37 East Seventh Street
New York, New York 10003

For a free catalog of books, call 1.800.722.6657.
Visit our web site at www.papress.com.

First published in French by CIVA in conjunction with the exhibition *cruauté & utopie, villes et paysages d'Amérique latine* presented at the CIVA in Brussels from May 22 to October 5, 2003. Curator: Jean-François Lejeune, Curatorial Team: Christophe Pourtois, Director; Nathalie Filser, Director of Exhibitions; Marcelle Rabinowicz, Director of Production; Caroline Vermeulen, Production Assistant; Marie Maeck and Géraldine Govaerts, Assistants; Communication: Véronique Moerman, Nagat Daaouag, Administration: Marcelline Bosquillon, Scenography and Installation: R&R Studios, Roberto Behar, and Rosario Marquardt, Technical Coordination: Albert Cauderlier

For CIVA:

Sponsors: Communauté française Wallonie-Bruxelles, Commission communautaire française de la Région de Bruxelles-Capitale, Loterie Nationale, Invicta, Maertens, Sigma Coatings, B Group, La Libre Belgique, Radio Contact, Travhydro, Graham Foundation for Advanced Studies in the Fine Arts

Graphic Design: Dominique Cabanac, Wysiswyg; Giampiero Caiti, Millefeuilles
Editor: Jean-François Lejeune
Coordination: Nathalie Filser, Marcelle Rabinowicz, Caroline Vermeulen, Christophe Pourtois
Assistants: Marie Maeck, Géraldine Govaerts, Marcel Paquet
Copy Editing: Marleene Sholod
Translations: Accents sprl-bvba

For Princeton Architectural Press:

Publication of the English edition has been supported by the University of Miami School of Architecture.

Project editor: Nicola Bednarek

Special thanks to: Nettie Aljian, Janet Behning, Megan Carey, Penny (Yuen Pik) Chu, Russell Fernandez, Jan Haux, Clare Jacobson, John King, Mark Lamster, Nancy Eklund Later, Linda Lee, John McGill, Katharine Myers, Jane Sheinman, Scott Tennent, Jennifer Thompson, Joseph Weston, and Deb Wood of Princeton Architectural Press —Kevin C. Lippert, publisher

Library of Congress Cataloging-in-Publication Data
Cruauté & utopie. English.
  Cruelty & utopia : cities and landscapes of Latin America / Jean-François Lejeune, editor.
— 1st ed.
      p. cm.
  First published in connection with an exhibition at the CIVA in Brussels, May 22–Oct. 5, 2003.
  Includes bibliographical references.
  ISBN 1-56898-489-8 (alk. paper)
  1. Architecture—Latin America. 2. City planning—Latin America. I. Title: Cruelty and utopia.
II. Lejeune, Jean-François. III. Centre international pour la ville, l'architecture et le paysage.
IV. Title.

NA702.C7813 2005
720'.98'091732—dc22

                                                                                    2004015433

Printed in China

cruelty & utopia

cities and landscapes of latin america

CENTRE INTERNATIONAL POUR LA VILLE,
L'ARCHITECTURE ET LE PAYSAGE
INTERNATIONAAL CENTRUM VOOR STAD,
ARCHITECTUUR EN LANDSCHAP
THE INTERNATIONAL CENTRE FOR URBANISM,
ARCHITECTURE AND LANDSCAPE
CIVA

PRINCETON ARCHITECTURAL PRESS, NEW YORK

AUTHORS

Eduardo Baéz
Architect and urbanist. Vice-director of FONSAL, public agency of historic preservation of Quito (Ecuador). Lives in Quito.

Rebecca E. Biron
Professor of Hispanic Literature at the University of Miami. Author of Murder and Masculinity: Violent Fictions of Twentieth-Century Latin America *(Nashville: Vanderbilt University Press, 2000). Lives in Miami.*

Edward R. Burian
Architect and author of Modernity and the Architecture of Mexico *(Austin: University of Texas Press, 1997). Lives in Tucson, Arizona.*

Lauro Cavalcanti
Architect and Doctor of Social Anthropology. Director of the Museu do Paço Imperial (Rio de Janeiro). Curator and editor of Quando o Brasil era moderno *(Rio de Janeiro: Aeroplano editorial, 2001). Lives in Rio de Janeiro.*

Carlos E. Comás
Architect and Professor of Architecture at Universidade Federal do Rio Grande del Sul. Author of La casa latinoamericana moderna: 20 paradigmas de mediados de siglo xx *(Naucalpín, Mexico: Gustavo Gili, 2003). Lives in Porto Alegre.*

Carol Damián
Professor of Art History at Florida International University. Author of The Virgin of the Andes: Art and Ritual in Colonial Cuzco *(Miami Beach: Grassfield Press, 1995). Lives in Coral Gables.*

Keith L. Eggener
Professor of Architectural History at the University of Missouri-Columbia. Author of Luis Barragan's Gardens at El Pedregal *(New York: Princeton Architectural Press, 2001). Lives in Columbia, Missouri.*

Carlos Fuentes
Mexican novelist, short-story writer, playwright, critic, and winner of the Cervantes Prize (1987). Ambassador of Mexico in Paris (1995–1997).

Robert A. González
Professor of Architectural History at Tulane University. Editor of AULA: Architecture and Urbanism in the Americas. *Lives in New Orleans.*

Adrián Gorelik
Professor of Architectural History at Universidad Nacional de Quilmes. Author of La grilla y el parque: Espacio publico y cultura urbana en Buenos Aires, 1887–1936 *(Buenos Aires: Universidad Nacional de Quilmes, 1998). Lives in Buenos Aires.*

Hervé Hasquin
Professor of History at the Free University of Brussels. Minister-President of the Government of the French Community Wallonie-Bruxelles. President of the Board of Trustees of CIVA.

Felipe Hernandez
Professor at the School of Architecture of the University of Liverpool. Author of various essays on globalization and architecture in Latin America. Lives in Liverpool.

Enrique Larrañaga
Architect and Professor at Universidad Simon Bolívar (Caracas). Author of Casa Americana: Single-family Houses in Latin America *(Basel: Birkhaüser, 2003). Lives in Caracas.*

Jacques Leenhardt
Doctor in Social Sciences and Professor at the Institut des Hautes Etudes, Paris. Author of many books including Les Amériques latines en France *(Paris: Gallimard, 1992) and* Dans les jardins de Burle Marx *(Arles: Actes Sud, 1997). Lives in Paris.*

Jean-François Lejeune
Architect and urbanist. Professor of Architecture and Urban History at the University of Miami School of Architecture. Author of The Making of Miami Beach: The Architecture of Lawrence Murray-Dixon, 1933–1942 *(New York: Rizzoli, 2001) and* The New City—Modern Cities *(New York: Princeton Architectural Press, 1996). Lives in Miami Beach.*

Carlos Martins
Art historian. Director of Coleção Brasiliana in São Paulo. Curator of various books and exhibitions including O Paisagem Carioca *at the Museu de Arte Moderna in Rio de Janeiro. Lives in Rio de Janeiro.*

Olívia de Oliveira
Architect and Doctor in Architecture. Author of Lina Bo Bardi: Built Work *(Barcelona: G. Gili, 2002). Lives in Lausanne, Switzerland.*

Fernando Pérez Oyarzún
Professor of Architectural History at Universidad Católica de Santiago de Chile. Author of many books including Le Corbusier y Sudamérica: viajes y proyectos *(Santiago: Ediciones Arq, 1991). Lives in Santiago, Chile.*

Christophe Pourtois
Director of the CIVA in Brussels, coauthor of books on architecture and landscape.

Roberto Segre
Professor of Architecture and Architectural History at Universidade Federal de Rio de Janeiro. Author of many books on Havana and Latin America, including Havana: Two Faces of the Antillan Metropolis *(Chichester, U.K.: Wiley, 1997). Lives in Niteroí/Rio de Janeiro.*

Eduardo Subirats
Professor at New York University. Author of various books on artistic avant-gardes and globalization in Latin America, including El continente vacío: la conquista del Nuevo Mundo y la conciencia moderna *(Madrid: ANAYA & Mario Muchnik, 1994). Lives in Princeton, New Jersey.*

SCIENTIFIC COMMITTEE

Eduardo Baéz, Carlos Baztán Lacasa (Madrid), Edward R. Burian, Lauro Cavalcanti, Jorge Czajkowsky (Rio de Janeiro), Carlos Eduardo Comás, Marcelo Carvalho Ferraz (São Paulo), Carlos Alberto Fleitas (Miami), Victor Jímenez (Mexico City), Enrique Larrañaga, Carlos Martins, Maria Mercédes del Carrión (Quito), Roberto Segre, Magdalena Zavala Bonachea (Mexico City)

LENDING INSTITUTIONS AND INDIVIDUALS

Argentina
- Archivo Amancio Williams (Buenos Aires), Claúdio Williams

Brazil
- Casa Lúcio Costa (Rio de Janeiro), Maria Elisa Costa, Julia Peregrino
- Coleção Brasiliaña/Fundação Estudar (São Paulo), Carlos Martins
- Instituto Lina Bo e P.M. Bardi (São Paulo), Yannick Bourguignon, Graziella Bo Valentinetti
- Museu Lasar Segall/IPHAR (São Paulo), Denise Grinspum

- Museu de Arte Moderna (Rio de Janeiro), Claudia Calaça
- Museus Castro Maya/IPHAR (Rio de Janeiro), Vera de Alencar
- Burle Marx & Cia Ltda (Rio de Janeiro), Haruyoshi Ono, Maria de Fátima Gomes de Souza
- Instituto Moreira Salles (São Paulo), Odette Vieira, Sergio Burgi
- Museu de Arte Brasileira/FAAP (Rio de Janeiro), Izabel Branco Ribeiro

Ecuador
- Museo del Banco Central del Ecuador (Quito), Oswaldo Morejón, Juan Ortiz
- Museo Nacional de Arte Colonial/Casa de la Cultura Ecuatoriana (Quito), Carlos Yánez
- Centro Cultural Metropolitano (Quito), Maria Elena Machuca
- Fondo de Salvamento del Patrimonio Cultural del Municipio Metropolitano (Quito), Carlos Pallares
- Fundacion Guayasamín (Quito), Pablo Guayasamín
- Museo de la Ciudad (Quito), Enrique Vasconez, Maria Mercédes del Carrión
- Colección Oswaldo Viteri (Quito), Oswaldo Viteri

Germany
- Vitra Design Museum (Weil-am-Rhein), Isabel Serbeto

Mexico
- Galerías La Granja (Mexico City), Santiago González
- Museo Casa Estudio Diego Rivera y Frida Kahlo (Mexico City.), Magdalena Zavala Bonachea
- El Colegio Nacional (Mexico City)
- UNAM/DGPA (Mexico City)
- Coordinación Servicios de Información Universidad Autonoma Metropolitana, Azcapotzalco (Mexico)
- Víctor Jímenez (Mexico City)
- Dirección de Arquitecture/INBA (Mexico City)
- Museo de Arte Moderno (Mexico City.), Luis Martín Lozano, Judith Gomez del Campo
- Fundación Juan Rulfo (Mexico City), Clara Aparicio de Rulfo, Víctor Jímenez

Spain
- Museo de América (Madrid), Paz Cabello Carro
- Comunidad de Madrid, Dirección General de Archivos, Museos y Bibliotecas, Consejeria de las Artes, Carlos Baztán Lacasa
- Archivo General de Indias (Seville), Magdalena Canellas Añoz
- Museo del Ejército (Madrid), José A. Rivas Octavio, Salvador Nadales

United States
- The Edward R. Burian Collection of the Art and Architecture of the American Southwest and Mexico (Tucson)
- Carol Damian Collection (Miami)
- Archives and Special Collections, Otto G. Richter Library, University of Miami (Coral Gables), Craig Likness, Rochelle Pienn
- Carlos Fleitas, Architect (Miami)
- Jay I. Kislak Foundation (Miami Lakes), Arthur Dunkelman
- Cuban Heritage Collection, University of Miami (Coral Gables), Esperanza de Varona
- The Detroit Institute of Arts (Detroit)

Switzerland
- Barragán Foundation (Birsfelden), Federica Zanco, Elena Formia

Venezuela
- Faculdad de Arquitectura y Urbanismo, Universidad Central de Venezuela (Caracas), Azier Calvo, Giuseppe Giannetto, Maria Teresa Novoa de Padrón
- Fundación Villanueva (Caracas), Paulina Villanueva

Belgium
- Bibliothèque Royale de Belgique (Brussels)
- Musées Royaux d'Art et d'Histoire de Belgique (Brussels), Anne Cahen–Delhaye, Sergio Purin
- Bibliothèque de l'Université de Liège (Liège), Carmelia Opsomer
- Bibliothèque René Pechère – CIVA (Brussels), Gaspard Jedwab
- Guy Van Beeck (Brussels)

From the Other Side (2002), installation by Chantal Akerman
- Chantal Akerman (Brussels)
- Galerie Marian Goodman (Paris)
- Firthstreet Gallery (London)
- Coproduction: Chemah IS, Corto Pacific, Centre Georges Pompidou (Paris)
- Courtesy of Arte France, AMIP, RTBF
- Philippe Bouychou

Special thanks:
- Béatrice Van Hemeldonck, Ambassador of Belgium in Ecuador
- Mentor Villagomez, Ambassador of Ecuador in Belgium
- Juan Carlos Sanchez Troya, Consul of Ecuador in Belgium
- Carlos Fuentes (Mexico City)
- Editions Gallimard (Paris)
- Houghton Mifflin Publishers (Boston)
- Fabien de Cugnac (Atelier d'Image)
- Paul Coppens, John Hallam (Sigma)
- Marc Maertens, Frank Eulaers, Frank Granger (Maertens Transports)
- Isabelle Eeckman (Invicta)
- Michel Provost, Laurent Kaisin (B Group)
- Travhydro
- José Luis Escudero (Intercommunication, a.s.b.l.)
- Elizabeth Plater-Zyberk, Dean, University of Miami School of Architecture

[Unknown painter], *The Meeting of Cortés and Moctezuma*, oil on canvas, second half of seventeenth century (painting number three in the cycle of eight). © Jay I. Kislak Foundation, Miami Lakes.

[Unknown painter], *The Conquest of Tenochtitlán*, oil on canvas, second half of the seventeenth century (painting number seven in the cycle of eight). © Jay I. Kislak Foundation, Miami Lakes.

TABLE OF CONTENTS

Dionisio Alcedo Herrera, *Ciudad de Quito*, ink on paper, 1734. © Archivo General de Indias, Seville, Inv. A.G.I., MP Panamá, 134.

FOREWORD

HERVÉ HASQUIN

Before all else I ordain ... that the layout of the roads running north, south, east, and west be marked out. I also ordain that four adjoining lots on four streets in the middle of the plan be designated as the city square. I also ordain that two lots be reserved in the most appropriate place near the square for the building of the church, which should be dedicated to Santiago. We will choose Santiago as our patron saint and intercessor, and I vow that we shall celebrate his feast day by saying his vespers and his missa solemnis, *in conformity with the land and its disposition. And we shall also celebrate it with bulls, when there are bulls, and with jousting, javelin-throwing, and other amusements. ... I also ordain that four lots be reserved near the square, one for the city hall, another for the public jail, and the others for city offices.* [1]

From the very beginning of the discovery and conquest of America, the Spanish Crown undertook to found a network of towns and villages that would assure its claim on the recently conquered territories, symbolically, militarily, and economically. The breathtaking speed with which the conquest swept over the American islands and continent thus fully coincided with the accelerated development of a new urban form and confirmed, with each stage, the strength of this action and of the founding process as a resource and means to grant permanence to a mere military act of occupation. The foundation of towns and cities consolidated the conquest and, at the same time, gave a clear institutional form to the population policy decreed by the king.

A dense urban network enabled the Spanish Crown to dominate and control the vast American territories. From those same entities, the so-called civilizing mission of evangelization and indoctrination of the native peoples developed and spread. The instructions that Christopher Columbus received already mentioned the advantages of founding towns. The firm and persistent political intention to populate the American islands and continent would take shape in the decades that followed. The saying "*Quien no poblare, no harà buena conquista*"[2] (He who does not populate will not make a successful conquest) paraphrases perfectly the ideology of the Spanish empire and the practices of the *conquistadores* in implementing the colonization. The foundation of towns was the concretization of a complex program representing sundry ambitions of which the obvious ultimate goal was "to re-create Spain on each occasion, a Christian Spain."[3]

Quito and numerous other Latin American cities share this heritage and still maintain its traces within their urban structure and fabric. The exhibition and the book produced by the International Centre for Urbanism, Architecture and Landscape (CIVA) emphasize the many dimensions of the process of foundation and development during five centuries in a selection of emblematic cities: Havana, Mexico City, Buenos Aires, Caracas, Quito, and Tijuana in Spanish America; Rio de Janeiro and São Paulo in the former Portuguese colonies. Architecture, urbanism, art, and history project themselves into the twentieth century, allowing visitors and readers to fully apprehend the rich cultural reality blending European and American sources and creations. ∎

1. Records of Foundation, 21-XI-1527, in: Jorge García Granados, ed., *Libro viejo de la fundación de Guatemala y papeles relativos a D. Pedro de Alvarado* (Guatemala, 1934), 24. [Translation Jean-François Lejeune]

2. Quoted from Francisco Domínguez Compañy, *Política de poblamiento de España en América: la fundación de ciudades* (Madrid: Instituto de Estudios de Administración Local, 1984), 13.

3. Jaime Salcedo Salcedo, *Urbanismo Hispano-Americano, Siglos XVI, XVII y XVIII: El modelo urbano aplicado a la América española, su génesis y su desarrollo téorico y práctico* (Santafè de Bogotá: Pontificia Universidad Javeriana, 1996), 47ff.

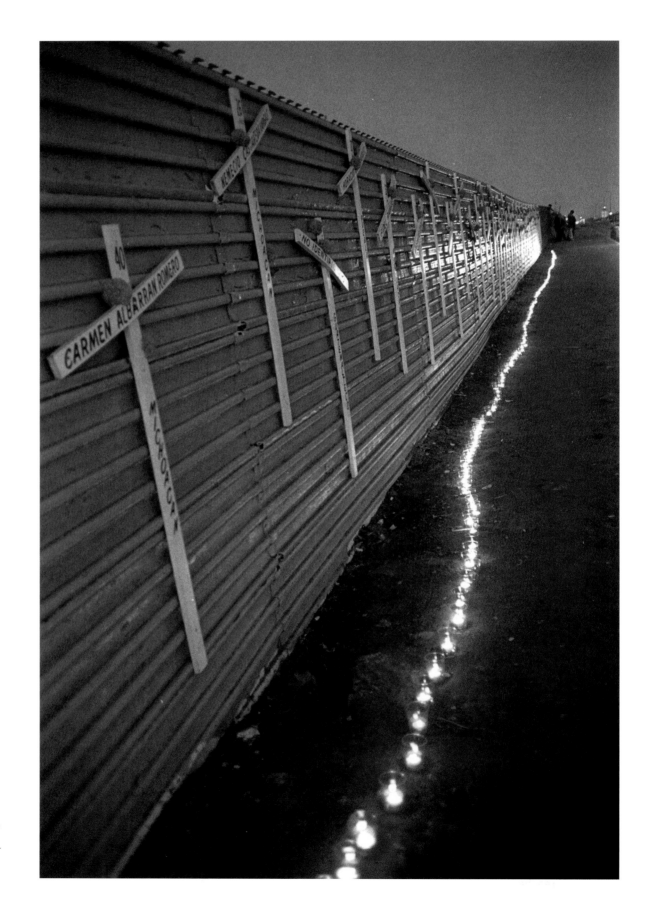

Airport area, Tijuana, 2000.
On November 1, *Fiesta de los Muertos*
(Day of the Dead), view of the ceremony
held for the Mexican men and women
who died while attempting to cross over
the Mexico/USA border. Photo Patrick
Bard. © Patrick Bard/ Editing.

FROM THE CITY OF THE CAESARS TO THE DEMYSTIFIED CITY

CHRISTOPHE POURTOIS

To cross the City [of the Caesars] required many hours along stone-paved streets laid on the banks of a large blue lake. The stone buildings were sumptuous, with their Spanish-style roofs. Nothing equaled the magnificence of its temples covered in solid silver.[1]

We usually forget that modernism came into being in a world framed by colonialism, where visions for improvement and innovation overlapped with and often caused brutal destruction. In the colonial world as elsewhere, modernism was, and remains, at once a universal ambition, a transnational operation, and myriad local variations.[2]

In 1764, James Burgh, a moralist writer of Scottish origin, published a work entitled *An Account of the First Settlement, Laws, Form of Government and Police, of the Cessares, a People of South America in Nine Letters.[3]* In a distant part of Austral-America, Patagonia, settlers from the poor and lower classes, selected for their willing characters and austere ways, had constructed perfectly laid out and rational cities in accordance with the geometrical model fashionable since the Renaissance and codified in America under the Laws of the Indies.[4] Set in abundant countryside under calm skies, these cities were under the rule of a wise government that protected a self-sufficient economic system and maintained absolute isolation from the rest of the world. Their inhabitants led a simple life, in a state of perfect equality. Two-and-a-half centuries after Columbus's discovery, Burgh had based his utopian novel, heavily influenced by Puritanism, on historical events that had given rise to the first American-born myth: the *Ciudad de los Césares.[5]*

In 1529, a small company under the command of Captain Francisco César set out to find an unknown site replete with mines rich in gold and silver. César came back a few months later and described incredibly rich lands that had been named after him. This event, contemporaneous with the destruction of the Inca Empire, gradually disappeared from the field of history and was integrated into the mythical realm of a collective imagination. Numerous costly expeditions led by "white Caesars" were launched in vain until late in the eighteenth century to search for the mythical city.

The word *utopia* derives from two Greek words, *eútópos* and *oútópos*, meaning "good place" and "no place," respectively. Utopian writings have reflected this ambiguity, being sometimes visions of good and possibly attainable social systems and at other times fantasies of a desirable but unattainable perfection. In this context, America has held from its origin, first in the eyes of the Europeans and later in those of the very Americans, "the two basic ingredients of utopia—space and time: a territory where to settle and a history with a past to recuperate or a future where to project oneself with ease."[6] 1492 was the genesis of a new historical time; America, the apparently unlimited space where many of the failed European hopes could materialize. From the Golden Age of Hesiod and Seneca to the Amazons to the Fountain of Youth, classical and medieval myths were reincarnated in the New World. Yet, the utopian America that had to be was systematically crushed under the real one—the America of conquistadors, cruel administrators, and other inquisitors. This "pulsation between utopia and reality"—a constant of Latin American history since the Conquest—reached a new apex in the seventeenth century with the establishment of alternatives to imperial domination, such as the Jesuits' missions; before and after the Wars of Independence when it

1. For more on the City of the Caesars, see Juan Martín Biedma, *Crónica histórica del lago Nahuel Huapí* (Buenos Aires: Emecé Editores, 1987), and Emilio B. Morales and Nahuel Huapí, *Descripciones históricas y geográficas* (Buenos Aires: Talleres gráficos argentinos, 1929).

2. Gwendolyn Wright, "Building Global Modernisms," *Grey Room* 07 (Spring 2002): 125.

3. James Burgh, *An Account of the First Settlement, Laws, Form of Government and Police, of the Cessares, a People of South America in Nine Letters* (London: J. Payne, 1764).

4. See the English translation of the *Ordinances for the Discovery, the Population and the Pacification of the Indies, enacted by King Philip II of Spain in 1573* on pages 18–23 of this book.

5. Fernando Ainsa, *Historia, utopía y ficción de la Ciudad de los Césares: metamorfosis de un mito* (Madrid: Alianza Editorial, 1992).

6. Fernando Ainsa, *De la Edad de Oro a El Dorado—Génesis del discurso utópico americano* (Mexico City: Fondo de cultura económica, 1992), 10. The author is indebted to Ainsa for the development of this introduction.

7. Ainsa, *De la Edad de Oro a El Dorado*, 204.

8. Joaquín Torres-García, *La ciudad sin nombre* (Montevideo: Sur, 1941).

acquired a more political and egalitarian content to help establish the new nations; and in the last century, within the programmatic content of the nationalist revolutions.[7]

The waves of immigrants who left Europe between 1865 and World War I also helped reinvigorate the "foundational spirit" of the Promised Land; Latin America returned to be space and time of utopia. The myth of the yet undiscovered city vanished with the colonization of its southernmost regions. It was replaced by the modernist belief that a "new city for a new man" could be created—note the case of Brasilia. More pragmatically, hopes of redemption and new life shifted to the capitals and large cities where, since the 1940s, immense and chaotic peripheries have been growing around the original nuclei. Traditional means of representation—whether journalistic, novelistic, cinematic, or cartographic—are less and less able to embody these conurbations; they have become *ciudades sin nombres*, to paraphrase Joaquín Torres-García.[8] At the same time, the migration of vast numbers of the poor toward the great northern neighbor continues, as if the City of the Caesars had been miraculously transported to the United States. Unfortunately, this mirage often turns out to be cruel. ∎

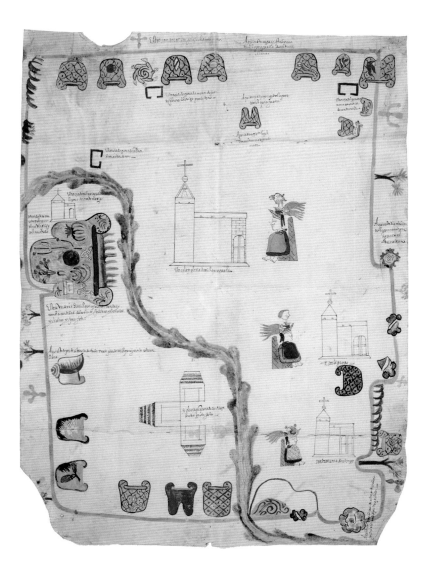

Relación Geográfica [Geographic Relation] of Misquiahuala (Atengo), México, ink on paper, October 18, 1579. © Benson Latin American Collection, University of Texas at Austin.

REFLECTIONS ON SPAIN AND THE NEW WORLD

CARLOS FUENTES

Reprinted with permission from
Carlos Fuentes, *The Buried Mirror:
Reflections on Spain and the New World*
(Boston: Houghton Mifflin, 1992).

On October 12, 1492, Christopher Columbus landed on a small island in the Western hemisphere. Against all evidence, he had put his wager on a scientific hypothesis and won: since the Earth is round, one can reach the east by sailing west. But he was wrong in his geography. He thought that he had arrived in Asia. His desire was to reach the fabled lands of Cipango (Japan) and Cathay (China), cutting short the route along the coast of Africa, south to the Cape of Good Hope, and then east to the Indian Ocean and the Spice Islands. It was not the first or the last Occidental disorientation. In these islands, which he called the Indies, Columbus established the first European settlements in the New World. He built the first churches, and the first Christian masses were celebrated there. Finding a domain empty of the Asian wealth that he had hoped for, he invented and reported back to Spain the discovery of great richness in forests, pearls, and gold. Otherwise, his patroness, Queen Isabella, might have thought that her investment (and her faith) in the highly inventive Genoese sailor had been misplaced.

More than offering gold, Columbus offered a vision of the Golden Age: these lands were Utopia, the happy place of the natural man. He had come upon the earthly paradise and the noble savage. Why, then, was he immediately forced to deny his own discovery, attack the people he had so recently described as "naked, unarmed, and friendly," hunt them down, enslave them, and even send them back to Spain in irons? In fact, young women who were taken prisoner in Cuba all died before they even reached Spain.

At first Columbus did step into the Golden Age. But very soon, through his own doing, the earthly paradise was destroyed and the formerly good savage was seen as "fit to be ordered about and made to work, to sow and to do aught else that may be needed." Ever since, the American continent has existed between dream and reality, in a divorce between the good society that we desire and the imperfect society in which we really live. We have clung to utopia because we were founded as a utopia, because the memory of the good society lies in our origins, and also at the end of the road, as the fulfillment of our hopes.

Five hundred years after Columbus, we celebrated the quincentennial of his voyage—undoubtedly one of the great events of human history, a turn in events that heralded the arrival of the modern age. But many of us in the Spanish-speaking parts of the Americas still wonder whether there is anything to celebrate. A glance at the Latin American republics would lead us to reply in the negative. Whether in Caracas or in Mexico City, in Lima or in Buenos Aires, the fifth centennial of the "discovery of America" found us in a state of deep, deep crisis: inflation, unemployment, the excessive burdens of foreign debt, increasing poverty and illiteracy, an abrupt decline of purchasing power and standards of living. A sense of frustration, of dashed hopes and lost illusions. Fragile democracies menaced by social explosion.

The present crisis throughout Latin America demonstrates the vulnerability of our political and economic systems, which have come crashing down around our heads. But it has also revealed something that has remained standing, something that we were not acutely aware of during the decades of economic boom and political fervor following World War II, something that, in the midst of our misfortunes, has remained on its own two feet. And that is our cultural heritage—what we have created with the greatest joy, the greatest gravity, and the greatest risk. This is the culture that we have been able to create during the past five hundred years, as descendants of Indians, blacks, and Europeans in the New World.

The crisis that has impoverished us has also put the wealth of our culture back in our own hands and forced us to realize that there is not a single Latin American, from the Rio Grande to Cape Horn, who is not an heir to each and every aspect of our cultural heritage. It ranges from the stones of Chichén Itzá and Machu Picchu to modern Indian influences in painting and architecture. From the Baroque art of the colonial era to the contemporary literature of Jorge Luis Borges and Gabriel García Marquéz. From the multifaceted European presence in Latin America—Iberian, and through Iberia Mediterranean, Roman, Greek, and also Arab and Jewish—to the singular, and suffering, black African presence. From the caves of Altamira to the graffiti in East Los Angeles. And from the earliest immigrants across the Bering Strait to the latest undocumented workers crossing the U.S. border at Tijuana–San Diego.

Few cultures in the world possess a comparable richness and continuity. In it, we Spanish Americans can identify ourselves and our brothers and sisters on this continent. That is why we find it so striking that we have been unable to establish a comparable economic and political identity. I suspect that this has been so because all too often we have sought or imposed on ourselves models of development that are scarcely related to our cultural reality. For this reason, a rediscovery of cultural values can give us, with luck and effort, the necessary vision of cultural, economic, and political convergences. Perhaps this is our mission in the coming century.

This book is therefore dedicated to a search for the cultural continuity that can inform and transcend the economic and political disunity and fragmentation of the Hispanic world. The subject is both complex and polemical, and I will try to be evenhanded in dealing with it. But I shall also be passionate about it because it concerns me intimately as a man, as a writer, and as a citizen of Mexico, of Latin America, who writes in the Spanish language.

Searching for a guide through this divided night of the soul of the Hispanic world, I found it near the site of the ancient Totonac ruins at El Tajín, in Veracruz, Mexico. Veracruz is the native state of my family. Its capital has been the port of entry for change, and at the same time the abiding hearth of Mexican identity. Veracruz is a city that holds many mysteries. The Spanish, French, and North American conquerors have entered Mexico through it. But the oldest cultures—the Olmecs to the south of the port city, dating from 3,500 years ago, and the Totonacs to the north, 1,500 years old—are also rooted here.

In tombs surrounding the religious sites of these native peoples, mirrors have been found, buried, ostensibly, to guide the dead through the underworld. Concave, opaque, polished, they contain the spark of light in the midst of darkness. But the buried mirror is not only an Amerindian occurrence. The Catalonian poet Ramón Xirau has titled one of his books *L'espil soterrat,* (The buried mirror), recovering an ancient Mediterranean tradition not far removed from that of the ancient Amerindians. A mirror looking from the Americas to the Mediterranean and back.

On this shore are the slate-black pyrite mirrors found at the pyramid of El Tajín, an astounding site whose name means "lightning." In its Pyramid of the Niches, rising 82 feet on a base of 115 square feet, 365 square windows open out, symbolizing, of course, the days of the solar year. Created in stone, El Tajín is a mirror of time.

On the other shore, Cervantes' Knight of the Mirrors does battle with Don Quixote, attempting to cure him of his madness. The old *hidalgo* has a mirror in his mind, reflecting everything that he has ever read, which, poor fool, he considers to be the truth.

Diego Rivera, *Dream of a Late Sunday Afternoon in the Alameda Central*, mural on transportable support, 1947–48. © Museo Mural Diego Rivera, INBA, Mexico City. At the center of the work, Diego Rivera painted the Calavera Catrina (Death), elegantly dressed, with the Plumed Serpent, an essential mythical representation of the pre-Hispanic culture of Mexico. The Catrina is a figure originally created by José Guadalupe Posada (1851–1913), the most important engraver in the history of Mexican art and an important inspiration for the Mexican painter. Rivera dedicated his mural to this great artist, who is seen here taking the arm of the Catrina. To the left, Rivera depicted himself with Frida Kahlo, who wears a traditional red Mexican dress.

Nearby, in the Prado Museum of Madrid hangs a painting by Velázquez in which he pictures himself painting what he is actually painting, as if he had created a mirror. But in the very depth of his canvas, yet another mirror reflects the true witnesses of the work of art: you and I.

Perhaps the mirror of Velázquez also reflects, on the Spanish shore, the smoking mirror of the Toltec god of night, Tezcatlipoca, as he visits the god of peace and creativity, Quetzalcoatl, the Plumed Serpent, to offer him the gift of the mirror. On seeing himself reflected, Quetzalcoatl identifies himself with humanity and falls, terrified.

Does he find his true nature, both human and divine, in the House of Mirrors, the circular temple of the Toltec pyramid at Teotihuacán, or in the cruel social mirror of Goya's *Caprichos*, where vanity is debunked and human society cannot deceive itself as it gazes into the mirror of truth? You thought you were a dandy? Look, you are truly a monkey.

Mirrors symbolize reality, the sun, the earth, and its four corners, its surface, its depths, and all of its peoples. Buried in caches throughout the Americas, they also cling to the bodies of the humblest celebrators in the Peruvian highlands or in the Mexican Indian carnivals. As the people dance, with scissors hanging from their legs and arias and bits and pieces of mirrors embedded in their headdresses, they now reflect the world, salvaging this reflection of their identity, which is more precious than the gold they gave Europe in exchange.

Are they not right? Is not the mirror both a reflection of reality and a projection of the imagination? ■

Felipe Guaman Poma de Ayala, *Decapitation of Tupac Amaru*, Lima, Peru, 1615. From Guamán Poma de Ayala, *Primer nueva coronica i buen gobierno*, manuscript at the Copenhagen Royal Library. © Copenhagen Royal Library.

Oswaldo Guayasamín, untitled lithographs, undated. From Pietro Martire d'Anghiera, *De orbe novo decades* [1516], facsimile edition (Alicante: Galería y Ediciones Rembrandt, 1984). Courtesy Special Collections University of Miami Richter Library. Published in 1530 and first translated into English in 1555, Peter Martyr's (1457–1526) book is based upon documents from various discoverers, including Columbus, and provides vivid and unique descriptions of the temples, towns, and ways of life of the New World before their destruction. The Ecuadorian painter and muralist of Andean descent, Oswaldo Guayasamín (1919–1999), illustrated this rare edition. His art reflects his strong championship of pre-Columbian civilization and of the underprivileged.

TRANSCRIPTION OF THE ORDINANCES FOR THE DISCOVERY, THE POPULATION, AND THE PACIFICATION OF THE INDIES, ENACTED BY KING PHILIP II, THE 13TH

This English translation is reprinted with permission from *The New City*, volume 1 (Foundations) (University of Miami School of Architecture, 1991): 19–33. It is based upon the Spanish facsimile edition, *El Ordén que se ha de Thener en Descubrir y Poblar, Transcripción de las Ordenanzas de descubrimiento, nueva población y pacificación de las Indias dadas por Felipe II, el 13 de Julio de 1573, en el Bosque de Segovia, según el original que se conserva en el Archivo General de Indias de Sevilla* (Madrid: Ministerio de la Vivienda, 1973).

To the Viceroys, presidents, magistrates, and governors of our new Indies and to all those others concerned let it be known: That in order that the discoveries and new settlements and pacification of the land and provinces that are to be discovered, settled, and pacified in the Indies be done with greater facility and in accordance with the service to God Our Lord, and for the welfare of the natives, among other things, we have prepared the following ordinances.

1. No person, regardless of state or condition, should, on his own authority, make a new discovery by sea or land, or enter a new settlement or hamlet in areas already discovered. If he were found without our license or approval by those who had our power to give it, he would face a death penalty and loss of all his possessions to our coffers. And, we order to all our Viceroys, magistrates, and governors and other justices of the Indies, that they give no license to make new discoveries without previous consultation with us and only after having obtained our permission; but we do consent that in areas already discovered, they can give license to build towns as necessary, adhering to the order that in so doing they must keep to the laws regarding settlements in discovered lands, and then they should send us a description.

2. Those who are in charge of governing the Indies, whether spiritually or temporally, should inform themselves diligently whether within their districts, including lands and provinces bordering them, there is something to be discovered and pacified, of the wealth and quality, and of the peoples and nations who inhabit there; but do this without sending to them war personnel nor persons who can cause scandal. They should inform themselves by the best means available; and likewise, they should obtain information on the persons who are best suited to carry out discoveries, and with those who are best fit for this purpose, they should inform themselves by the best means available; and likewise, they should confer and make arrangements, offering them the honors and advantages that justly, without injury to the natives, can be given them, and, before carrying out what has been arranged or has been learned, give narratives to the Viceroy and the magistrates and also send them to the Council, which, after looking at the case, will issue a license to proceed with the discovery, which should be carried out in the following order.

3. Having made, within the confines of the province, a discovery by land, pacified it, and subjected it to our obedience, find an appropriate site to be settled by Spaniards, and if not, by the vassal Indians so they be secure.

4. If the boundaries of the settlement are populated, utilizing commerce and ransom, go with vassal Indians and interpreters to discover those lands, and with churchmen and Spaniards, carrying offerings and ransoms and peace, try to learn about the place, the contents and quality of the land, the nations to which the people there belong, who governs them, and carefully take note of all you can learn and understand, and always send these narratives to the Governor so that they reach the Council [of the Indies].

5. Look carefully at the places and ports where it might be possible to build Spanish settlements without damage to the Indian population.[1]

13. Persons who participate in discoveries, whether by land or by sea, should take possession, in our name, of all lands and provinces they might reach and, upon setting foot on to land, perform the necessary ceremonies and writs, thus providing public evidence and faithful testimony.

14. Once the discoverers arrive at newly discovered provinces or lands, together with the officials, they should name each land, each province, and the mountains and principal rivers they might encounter as well as the settlements and towns they might find or that they may begin.[2]

NEW SETTLEMENTS

32. Before discoveries are duly recognized, no new population settlements are permitted, whether in the discovered areas or in those still to be discovered; but in those parts which are already discovered, pacified, and subjected to our mandate, population settlements, both

1. **6–12** These ordinances provide guidelines for discoveries that are made by sea.

2. **15–31** These ordinances instruct the Spaniards on the formal issues of encountering, greeting, educating, and punishing the native Indian population.

OF JULY 1573, IN THE FOREST OF SEGOVIA, ACCORDING TO THE ORIGINAL MANUSCRIPT CONSERVED IN THE ARCHIVO GENERAL DE INDIAS IN SEVILLE.

of Spaniards and of Indians, should be ordered having permanence and giving perpetuity to both groups as specified in the fourth and fifth books [of the Laws of the Indies], especially in those parts dealing with population settlements and with land allotments.

33. Having populated and settled the newly discovered area, pacified it, and subjected it to our mandate, efforts should be made to discover and populate adjacent areas that are being discovered for the first time.

34. In order to populate those areas that are already discovered, pacified, and under our mandate, as well as areas that might be discovered and pacified in the course of time, the following sequence should be adhered to: choose the province, county, and place that will be settled, taking into consideration the health of the area, which will known from the abundance of old men or of young men of good complexion, natural fitness and color, and without illness; and in the abundance of healthy animals of sufficient size, and of healthy fruits and fields where no toxic and noxious things are grown, but that it be good climate, the sky clear and benign, the air pure and soft, without impediment or alterations and of good temperature, without excessive heat or cold, and having to decide, it is better that it be cold.

35. And they should be in fertile areas with an abundance of fruits and fields, of good land to plant and harvest, of grasslands to grow livestock, of mountains and forests for wood and building materials for homes and edifices, and of good and plentiful water supply for drinking and irrigation.

36. And that they should be populated by Indians and natives to whom we can preach the gospels, since this is the principal objective for which we mandate that these discoveries and settlements be made.

37. And they should have good access and outlet by sea and by land, and also good roads and passage by water, in order that they may be entered and departed easily with commerce, while bringing relief and establishing defenses.

38. Once the region, province, county, and land are decided upon by the expert discoverers, select the site to build a town and capital of the province and its subjects,

without harm to the Indians for having occupied the area or because they agree to it of good will.

39. The site and position of the towns should be selected in places where water is nearby and where it could be deviated to better service the town and the neighboring properties; where the materials that are essential for building can be found; as well as the lands for farming, cultivation, and pasture, so as to avoid excessive work and cost, since any of the above would be costly if they were far.

40. Do not select sites that are too high up because these are affected by winds, and access and service to these are difficult, nor in lowlands, which tend to be unhealthy; choose places of medium elevation that enjoy good winds, especially from the north and south, and if there were mountains or hills, these should be in the west or in the east, and if there should be a need to build in high places, do it in areas not subjected to fogs; take note of the terrain and its accidental features and in case that there should be a need to build on the banks of a river, it should be on the eastern bank, so when the sun rises it strikes the town first, then the water.

41. Do not select sites for towns in maritime locations because of the danger that exists of pirates and because they are not very healthy, and because they do not make people able to work and cultivate the land, nor is it possible to instill in them these habits. Unless the site is in an area where there are good and principal harbors, among these, select for settlement only those that are necessary for the entry of commerce and for the defense of the land.[3]

89. The persons who were placed in charge of populating a town with Spaniards should see to it that, within a specified term assigned for its establishment, it should have at least thirty neighbors, each one with his own house, ten cows, four oxen or two oxen and two young bulls and a mare, and it should have a clergyman who can administer sacraments and provide the ornaments to the church as well as the necessary implements for the divine service; if this is not accomplished, they should lose everything already built or formed and they will incur a fine of a thousand gold pesos.

3. 42–88 These ordinances dictate the legislative, legal, and fiduciary regulations.

TRANSCRIPTION OF THE ORDINANCES FOR THE DISCOVERY, THE POPULATION AND THE PACIFICATION OF THE INDIES, ENACTED BY KING PHILIP II, THE 13TH

90. The aforesaid stipulations and territory should be divided as follows: separate first the land that is needed for the house plots of the town, then allocate sufficient public land and grounds for pasture where the cattle that the neighbors are expected to bring with them can obtain abundant feed, plus another portion for the natives of the area. The rest of the grounds and territory should be divided into four parts: one is for the person in charge of building the town, the other three should be subdivided into thirty lots for the thirty neighbors of the town.

91. Land and boundaries for a new settlement cannot be given nor taken at a seaport nor anywhere where it can ever be redundant and detrimental to the Crown because such sites will be reserved for us.

92. We define a neighbor as the son, daughter or children of a new settler or his relatives to and beyond the fourth degree that have different households and families and, if they are married, each of them has his own household.[4]

100. Those who should want to make a commitment to building a new settlement in the form and manner already prescribed, be it of more or less than thirty neighbors, it should be of no less than ten, should be awarded the authorization and territory in accordance with the prescribed conditions.

101. If there is no person with the duty to select a site for a new settlement and there are enough married men who agree to create a new settlement wherever they are directed to locate it, as long as they are no less than ten married men, they can do it and will be given land and boundaries accordingly and they will have the right to choose among themselves mayors and yearly councilmen.

102. Having chosen a site for a new settlement, as a colony, a frontier town, a town proper, a district seat, or a village, the Council and the governor of the Indies will not be satisfied by the mere fact of possession and continuity of rule and order from the start and will make them responsible for its development.

103. After the governor established a new settlement with a city directed by a mayor or a magistrate, the city or people who settle it will enlist each of the persons who had registered or comes to register for the new settlement, and the person responsible for the town must select urban lots, farm, and pasture lands for the person willing to populate the town, who shall receive the amount of peonías and caballerías on which he is willing and able to build as long as no one is awarded more than five peonías nor three caballerias if given the latter.

104. A peonía is an urban lot that is fifty feet wide and one hundred feet deep, land that will yield one hundred fifty-six bushels of either wheat or barley, fifteen bushels of corn, land sized for two days of plowing for a vegetable garden, land sized for eight days of plowing to plant trees in dry land, and pasture land for ten fertile sows, twenty cows, five mares, one hundred sheep, and twenty goats.

105. A caballería is an urban lot that is one hundred feet wide and two hundred feet deep, and the rest is equivalent to five peonías which is land that will yield seven hundred and eighty bushels of wheat or barley for bread, seventy-eight bushels of corn, land sized for ten days of plowing for a vegetable garden, land sized for forty days of plowing to plant trees in dry land, pasture land for fifty fertile sows, one hundred cows, twenty mares, five hundred sheep, and one hundred goats.

106. The caballería, both the urban lots and the pasture and farm lands, should be clearly marked and surveyed in a defined area; and the peonías, both the urban lots and farm lands, shall be marked and divided, and the pasture land will be common to all.

107. Those who accept settlement in the caballerías and peonías must build on their urban lots and live in their homestead and select the planting cycle of their farmlands and plant them and populate the pastures with cattle within the assigned time period and shall declare what will be accomplished within each period or they will lose their lots, lands and a monetary fine for the state, and must publicly accept these terms by way of a bond.

108. Those who have homestead on the caballerías and have committed to plough them and populate them with livestock can convene with workers that they will help them for construction, plough and pasture, taking

4. **93-99** These ordinances deal with various topics ranging from town officials to nearby mines and taxes on items carried along to start a new town.

into account their mutual obligations so that the settlement will be easier to implement and the soil ploughed and pastured more easily.

109. The governor who authorizes the settlement of a new town or concedes rights for an existing town to be populated anew, by means of his own authority or by making a request, should ascertain that those who have made a commitment to settle in a new town comply with the taking of seat in a proper manner. This should be done with great diligence and care. Also, the magistrates and Council procurer should initiate due process against the settlers who are bound up by a specified term and who have not complied with it to make them meet the terms, and those who might have left should be prosecuted, seized, and brought back to the town in order that they comply with the terms of settlement, and if they were in another jurisdiction, a requisitioning order should be issued in order that justice be done under penalty.

110. Having made the discovery, selected the province, county, and area that is to be settled, and the site in the location where the new town is to be built, and having taken possession of it, those placed in charge of its execution are to do it in the following manner. On arriving at the place where the new settlement is to be founded—which according to our will and disposition shall be one that is vacant and that can be occupied without doing harm to the Indians and natives or with their free consent—a plan for the site is to be made, dividing it into squares, streets, and building lots, using cord and ruler, beginning with the main square from which streets are to run to the gates and principal roads and leaving sufficient open space so that even if the town grows, it can always spread in the same manner. Having thus agreed upon the site and place selected to be populated, a layout should be made in the following way:

111. Having made the selection of the site where the town is to be built, it must, as already stated, be in an elevated and healthy location; be with means of fortification; have fertile soil and with plenty of land for farming and pasturage; have fuel, timber, and resources; have fresh water, a native population, ease of transport,

access and exit; and be open to the north wind; and, if on the coast, due consideration should be paid to the quality of the harbor and that the sea does not lie to the south or west; and if possible not near lagoons or marshes in which poisonous animals and polluted air and water breed.

112. The main plaza is to be the starting point for the town; if the town is situated on the sea coast, it should be placed at the landing place of the port, but inland it should be at the center of the town. The plaza shall be rectangular, and should have at least one and a half its width for length inasmuch as this shape is best for fiestas in which horses are used and for any other fiestas that should be held.

113. The size of the plaza shall be proportioned to the number of inhabitants, taking into consideration the fact that in Indian towns, inasmuch as they are new, the intention is that they will increase, and thus the plaza should be decided upon taking into consideration the growth the town may experience. The square shall be not less that two hundred feet wide and three hundred feet long, nor larger than eight hundred feet long and five hundred and thirty feet wide in average. A good proportion is six hundred feet long and four hundred wide.

114. From the plaza shall begin four principal streets, one shall be from the middle of each side, and two streets from each corner of the plaza; the four corners of the plaza shall face the four principal winds, because in this manner, the streets running from the plaza will not be exposed to the four principal winds, which would cause much inconvenience.

115. Around the plaza as well as along the four principal streets which begin there, there shall be portals, for these are of considerable convenience to the merchants who generally gather there; the eight streets running from the plaza at the four corners shall open on the plaza without encountering these porticoes, which shall be kept back in order that there may be sidewalks even with the streets and plaza.

116. In cold places, the streets shall be wide and in hot places narrow; but for purposes of defense in areas where there are horses, it would be better if they were wide.

117. The streets shall run from the main plaza in such manner that even if the town increases considerably in size, it shall not result in some inconvenience that will make ugly what needed to be rebuilt, or endanger its defense or comfort.

118. Here and there in the town, smaller plazas of good proportion shall be laid out, where the temples associated with the principal church, the parish churches, and the monasteries can be built, in such manner that everything may be distributed in a good proportion for the instruction of religion.

119. For the temple of the principal church, parish, or monastery, there shall be assigned specific lots; the first after the streets and plazas have been laid out, and these shall be a complete block so as to avoid having other buildings nearby, unless it were for practical or ornamental reasons.

120. The temple of the principal church, where the town is situated on the coast, shall be built in part so that it may be seen on going out to sea and in a place where its buildings may serve as a means of defense for the port itself.

121. Next, a site and lot shall be assigned for the royal council and the city hall and for the custom house and arsenal, near the temple, located in such a manner that in times of need the one may aid the other; the hospital for the poor and those sick of non-contagious diseases shall be built near the temple and its cloister; and the hospital for the sick with contagious diseases shall be built in such a way that no harmful wind blowing through it may cause harm to the rest of the town. If the latter be built in an elevated place, so much the better.

122. The site and building lots for slaughterhouses, fisheries, tanneries, and other business which produce filth shall be so placed that the filth can easily be disposed of.

123. It shall be of considerable convenience if those towns that are laid out away from seaports, inland, be built if possible on the shore of a navigable river, and attempts should be made to place the town on the side from which the cold north wind blows and that buildings that cause filth be placed on the side of the river or sea below the town.

124. The temple in inland places shall not be placed on the square but at a distance and shall be separated from any other nearby building, or from adjoining buildings, and ought to be seen from all sides so that it can be decorated better, thus acquiring more authority; efforts should be made that it be somewhat raised from ground level in order that it be approached by steps, and near it, next to the main plaza, the royal council, the city hall and customs houses shall be built. These shall be built in a manner that would not embarrass the temple but add to its prestige. The hospital for the poor who are not affected by contagious diseases shall be built near the temple and near its cloister, and the hospital for contagious diseases shall be built in an area where the cold north wind blows, but arranged in such a way that it may enjoy the south wind.

125. The same plan shall be observed in any inland place without shore, taking considerable care to ascertain the availability of those conveniences that are required.

126. In the plaza, no lots shall be assigned to private individuals; instead, they shall be used for the buildings of the church and royal houses and for city use, but shops and houses for the merchants should be built first, to which all the settlers of the town shall contribute, and a moderate tax shall be imposed on goods so that these buildings may be built.

127. The other building lots shall be distributed by lottery to the settlers, commencing with the lots closer to the main plaza, and the lots that are left shall be held by us for assignment to those who shall later become settlers, or for the use that we may wish to make of them, and so that this may be ascertained better, the town shall maintain a plan of what is being built.

128. Having made the plan of the town and having distributed building lots, each of the settlers shall set up his tent on his plot if he should have one. For this purpose the captains should persuade settlers to carry them, and those who did not bring one should make their huts of easily available local materials, so that they may have shelter, and everyone as soon as possible shall make a palisade or ditch encircling the plaza so that they not be harmed by Indians or natives.

129. Within the town, a commons shall be delimited, large enough that although the population may experience a rapid expansion, there will always be sufficient space where the people may go to for recreation and take their cattle to pasture without them making any damage.

130. Adjoining the commons there shall be assigned pasture ground for the work oxen and for the horses as well as for the cattle for slaughter and for the usual number of cattle that the settlers must have according to these Ordinances, and in a good number so they can be admitted to pasture in the public lands of the Council; and the rest of the adjoining land shall be assigned as farm lands, which will be distributed by lottery in such a number that the farm lots would be as many in number as the lots in the town; and if there should be irrigated lands, lots shall be cast for them and they shall be distributed in the same proportion to the first settlers according to their lots; the rest shall remain for ourselves so that we may assign it to those who may become settlers.

131. In the farmlands that may be distributed, the settlers should immediately plant the seeds they brought with them and those they might have obtained at the site; to this effect it is convenient that they go well provided; and in the pasture lands, all the cattle they brought with them or gathered should be branded so that they may soon begin to breed and multiply.

132. Having planted their seeds and made arrangements for the cattle in such number and with good diligence in order to obtain abundant food, the settlers shall begin with great care and efficiency to establish their houses and to build them with good foundations and walls; to this effect they shall go provided with molds or planks for building them, and all the other tools needed for building quickly and at small cost.

133. They shall arrange the building lots and edifices placed thereon in such a manner that when living in them they may enjoy the winds of the south and north as these are the best; throughout the town arrange the structures of the houses generally in such a way that they may serve as defense or barrier against those who may try to disturb or invade the town, and each house in particular shall be so built that they may keep therein their horses and work animals and shall have yards and corrals as large as possible for health and cleanliness.

134. They shall try as far as possible to have the buildings all of one type for the sake of the beauty of the town.

135. The faithful executors and architects as well as persons who may be deputed for this purpose by the governor shall be most careful in overseeing that the above ordinances be executed; and they shall hurry in their labor and building so that the town may be completed in a short time.

136. If the natives should resolve to take a defensive position toward the new settlement, they should be made aware of how we intend to settle, not to do damage to them nor take away their lands, but instead to gain their friendship and teach them how to live civilly, and also to teach them to know our God so they learn His law through which they will be saved. This will be done by religious, clerics, and other persons designated for this purpose by the governor and through good interpreters, taking care by the best means available that the town settlement is carried out peacefully and with their consent; but if the natives still do not want to concur after having been summoned repeatedly by various means, the settlers should build their own town without taking what belongs to the Indians and without doing them more harm that it were necessary for the protection of the town in order that the settlers are not disturbed.[5]

148. The Spaniards to whom the Indians are entrusted should seek with great care that these Indians be settled into towns, and that, within these, churches be built so that the Indians can be instructed into Christian doctrine and live in good order. Because we order you see to it that these Ordinances, as presented above, be incorporated, complied with, and executed, and that you make what in them is contained be complied with and executed, and never take action or move against them, nor consent that others take action or move against either their content or form, under penalty of our Lord.[6]

Dated in the Forest of Segovia, the thirteenth of July, in the year fifteen hundred and seventy-three, I the King; the Licenciado Otalaza; the Licenciado Diego Gasca de Alazar; the Licenciado Gamboa, the Doctor Gomez de Santillán.

5. **137–147** These ordinances deal with the conversion of the native Indian population.

6. This last ordinance deals with the issue of *encomienda*, a medieval institution that was initiated in Spain during the *Reconquista*. In America, it started with Columbus and lasted until the mid-1700s. Through this system, Indians were "entrusted" to the colonials as conquest bounty in exchange of their services. It is a form of slavery that obliged the Indians to forced labor.

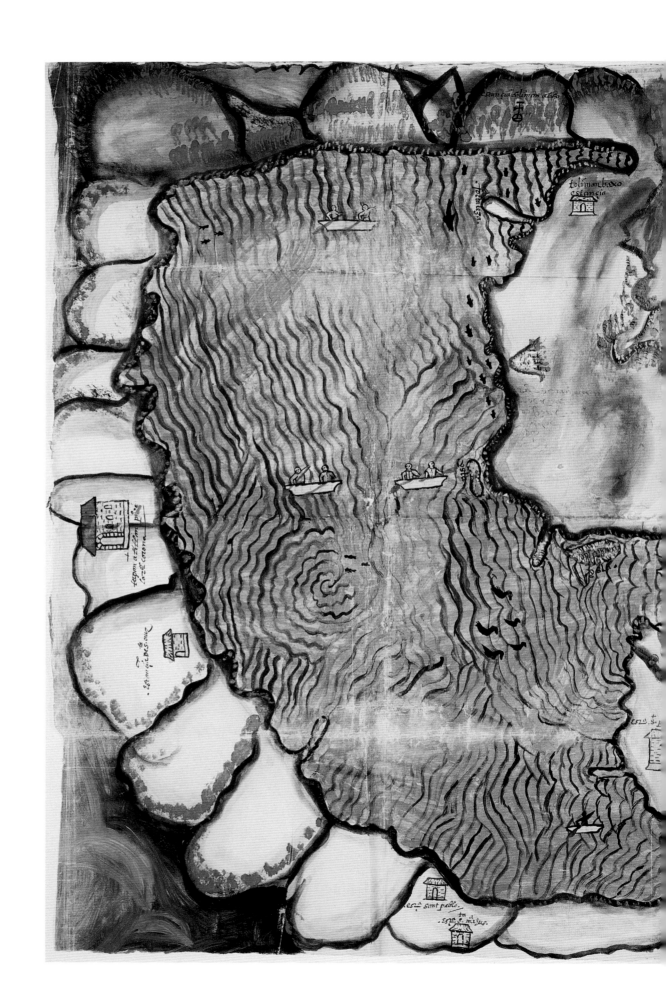

Relación Geográfica de Atitlan (Geographical relation of Atitlan), Santiago, Guatemala, manuscript, ink on paper, Feb. 8–27, 1585. © Benson Latin American Collection, University of Texas at Austin.

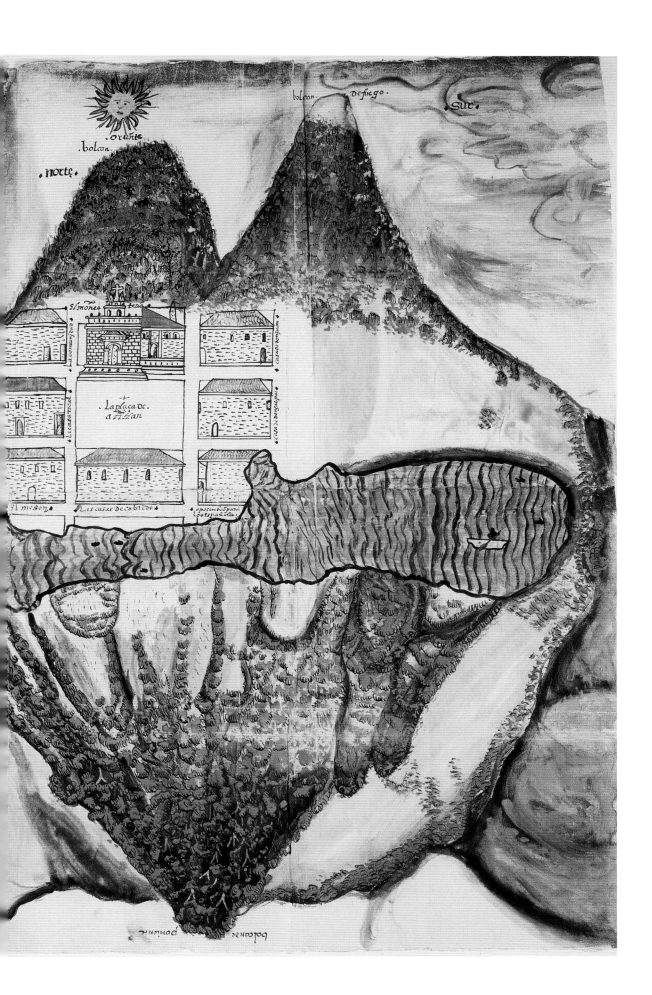

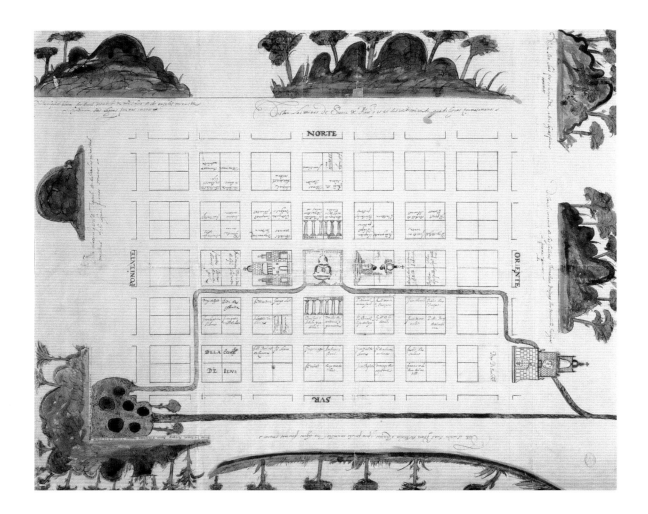

Juan Gutiérrez de Léon, *Plan of the City of Concepción, Mexico*, manuscript, ink on paper, 1603. © Archivo General de Indias, Seville, Inv. A.G.I. MP Mexico, 51.

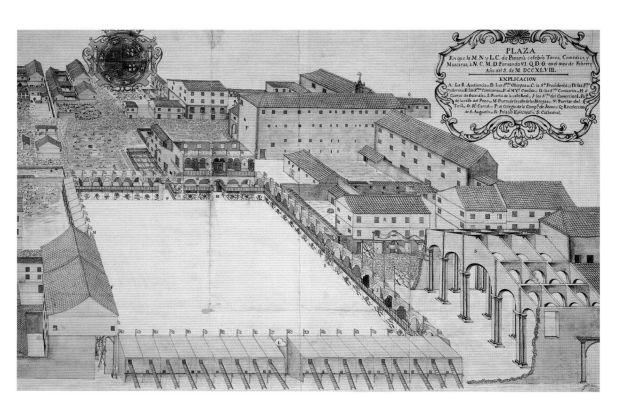

[Unknown artist], *Panama, Plaza Mayor, during a Celebration (Bulls, Comedies and Masks), the Month of February 1748*, ink on paper, 1748. © Archivo General de Indias, Sevilla, Inv. A.G.I. MP Panamá, 299.

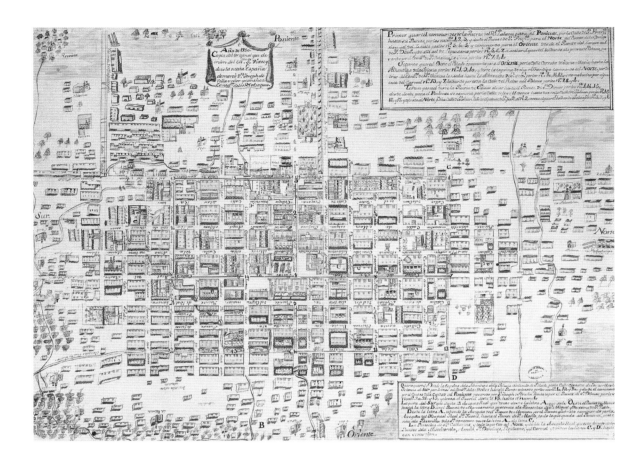

José de Villaseñor y Sánchez, *Plan of the City of Mexico*, ink on paper, 1750.
© Archivo General de Indias, Seville, Inv. A.G.I. MP Mexico, 178.

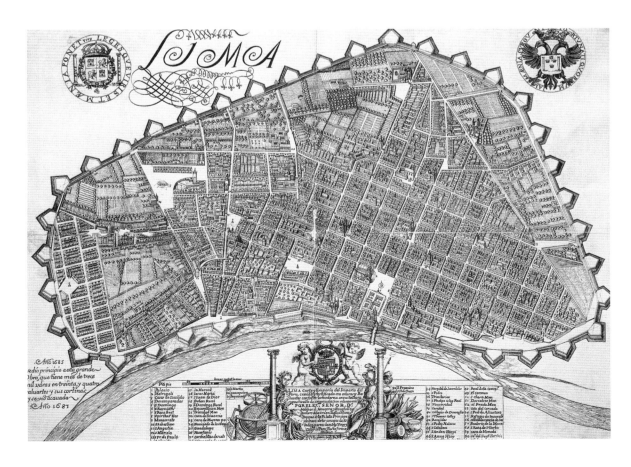

Father Pedro Nolasco, *Fortification of Lima, Peru*, ink on paper, 1687.
© Archivo General de Indias, Seville, Inv. A.G.I. MP Peru y Chile, 13.

[Unkown artist], *Plan of the New Foundation of San Felipe y Santiago, Cuba*, ink on paper, eighteenth century. © Archivo General de Indias, Seville, Inv. A.G.I. MP Santo Domingo, 512.

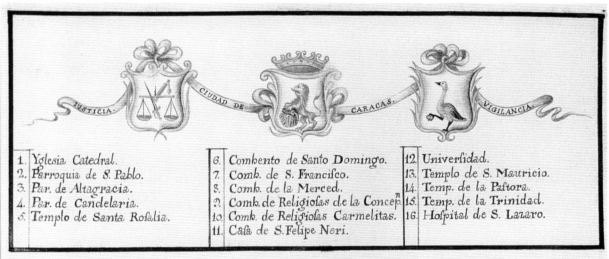

JUSTICIA. CIUDAD DE CARACAS. VIGILANCIA.

1. Yglesia Catedral.	6. Combento de Santo Domingo.	12. Univerſidad.
2. Parroquia de S. Pablo.	7. Comb. de S. Franciſco.	13. Templo de S. Mauricio.
3. Par. de Altagracia.	8. Comb. de la Merced.	14. Temp. de la Paſtora.
4. Par. de Candelaria.	9. Comb. de Religioſas de la Concep.^{n}	15. Temp. de la Trinidad.
5. Templo de Santa Roſalia.	10. Comb. de Religioſas Carmelitas.	16. Hoſpital de S. Lazaro.
	11. Caſa de S. Felipe Neri.	

Plan de la Ciudad de Caracas, con divicion de sus Barrios.

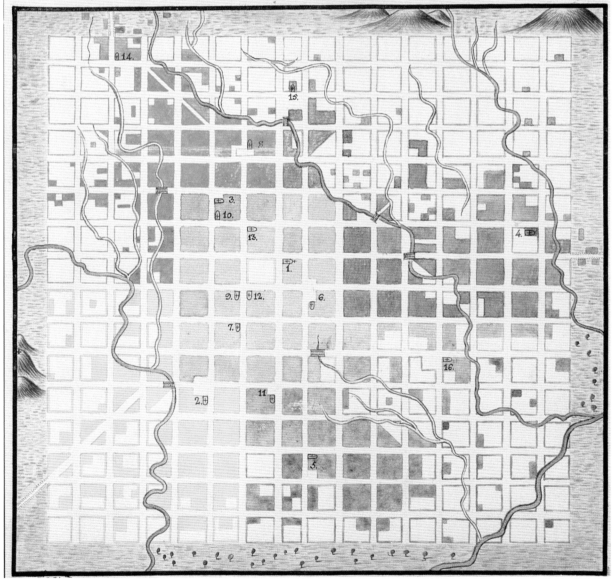

Joseph Carlos de Agüero, *Plan of the City of Caracas with its Division in Neighborhoods*, ink on paper, 1775.
© Archivo General de Indias, Seville, Inv. A.G.I. MP Venezuela, 180.

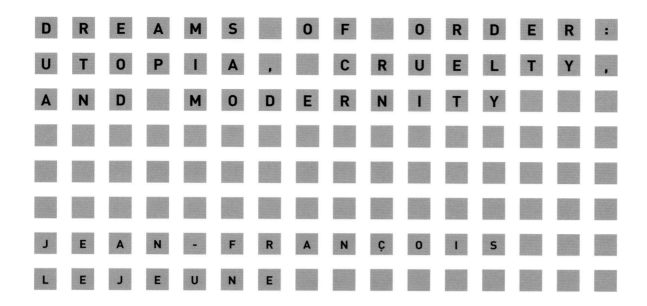

DREAMS OF ORDER: UTOPIA, CRUELTY, AND MODERNITY

JEAN-FRANÇOIS LEJEUNE

To found a city. I found a city, he founds a city—it was a verb that could be conjugated. [1]

America is a mystery, a dense tangle of founding myths and utopian longings, desert and forest. [2]

One of the most distinct attitudes of Latin American architects and planners toward urbanism is an undiminished faith in the Ideal Community. No matter how woefully short all projects fall of their goals, there persists something of the pioneer's dream of a new Civitas Dei *in the wilderness.* [3]

On February 14, 1615, from the Peruvian Andes, Felipe Guaman Poma de Ayala (1532–1616) wrote King Philip III of Spain that he had just completed *Primer nueva corónica y buen gobierno* (The First New Chronicle and Good Government). Poma's autograph manuscript—first unearthed in 1908 by Richard A. Pietschmann—had two main purposes: to give the king an account of ancient Andean history from the beginning of time through the reign of the Incas, and to inform the monarch about the deepening crisis in Andean society. The author petitioned the sovereign to undertake legislative reforms aiming at recognizing the physical and moral rights of the indigenous populations and eradicating the harm of colonial exploitation, disease, and miscegenation: the "good government" had to be led by the born-Andean population on the basis of Andean institutions. The 398 full-page line drawings that accompanied the text, written in Spanish with occasional sections in Quechua, suggest that he considered the graphic description to be the most direct and effective way of communicating his ideas to the king. Between pages 1000 and 1087, under the title "Este reino y sus ciudades y villas" (This kingdom and its cities and towns), forty plates offered a first extraordinary panorama of Peruvian and Latin American urbanization. With the exception of Riobamba (the only city shown as a chessboard), Poma represented the cities as plazas, often surrounded by grandiose nature. He drew these squares in perspective, sometimes encircled by walls, sometimes open, but always bounded by the main church, the city hall, and large houses. Cuenca, Arequipa, Potosí, or Panama thus appeared as the clones of the "Divine City" or "Heavenly Jerusalem" in the Apocalypse of Saint John, which Poma also rendered as a large geometric square (*La ciudad del cielo*, plate 952). [4] Grid pattern and *plaza mayor*, urban order amid wilderness, perspective and open city, destruction and reconstruction, utopia and reality: these were the elements that Poma emphasized in his drawings—that is, the very criteria and contradictions underlying the urban modernity and the process of wanton globalization that the Spanish Crown imposed on the new territories.

1. Alejo Carpentier, *Los pasos perdidos* [1953] (Mexico City: Cia. General de Ediciones, 1959) [author's translation]; in English, *The Lost Steps* (New York: Knopf, 1967).

2. Roberto Fernandez, "Desert and Selva: from Abstraction to Desire. Notes on the Regionalist Dilemma in Latin American Architecture," *Zodiac* no. 9: 154.

3. Sybil Moholy-Nagy, *Carlos Raúl Villanueva and the Architecture of Venezuela* (New York: Praeger, 1964), 93.

4. Poma's manuscript, now in the Royal Library of Denmark (Gl.kgl.S.2232, 4°), was not published until 1936 in Paris (by Paul Rivet). The best facsimile version can be found at: http://www.kb.dk/elib/mss/poma/; Also see Richard Kagan, *Urban Images of the Hispanic World 1493–1793* (New Haven: Yale University Press, 2000), 125ff.

Left page:
Antonio Ramírez Montufar, *Construction of the Cathedral of Santiago de Los Caballeros de Guatemala* [now Antigua, Guatemala], oil on canvas, 1678.
© Galerías La Granja, Mexico City.

5. Miguel Rojas-Mix, *La plaza mayor* (Barcelona: Muchnik Editores, 1978), 9–10.

6. For a balanced analysis see: Jaime Salcedo Salcedo, *Urbanismo Hispano-Americano, Siglos XVI, XVII y XVIII: El modelo urbano aplicado a la América española, su génesis y su desarrollo téorico y práctico* (Santafè de Bogotá: Pontificia Universidad Javeriana, 1996); Graziano Gasparini, "The Spanish-American Grid Plan, an Urban Bureaucratic Form," *The New City–Foundations*, vol. 1 (1991): 6–17.

Three centuries later, in his book *La plaza mayor*, the exiled Chilean sociologist Miguel Rojas Mix described how, lost in the confusion of the German medieval streets of Cologne, he understood what was the essential condition of being an "American" in space: the presence, both physical and symbolic, of a checkerboard of streets organized from a central square:

The topography [of Cologne] had nothing to do with the "mental topography" that I attributed to any urban layout. When dropped in one of "my" cities, and in whatever street, I knew with certainty that I would cross parallel streets to the right and to the left, that, behind or ahead of me, all of them were perpendicular and that, right in the centre, I would find the plaza de armas *flanked by the cathedral. Here, the fact that I was an American revealed itself in clearly urbanistic terms.*[5]

Why, how, and by whom were the checkerboard and the central square established as the fundamental pattern of Latin American urbanization? Given the absence of primary explicative source materials, historians have long been forced to make assumptions and elaborate theories that often contradict one another. The most recent scholarship and interpretation—generated from Latin America itself—suggest that the conceptual framework of the Latin American city was a fluctuating synthesis of four main influences: the new foundations in Spain during the medieval *Reconquista*; the theories of the Renaissance and the Ideal City; the expression of a rational will of Roman-imperial inspiration; and, finally, the encounter with the pre-Columbian cities and civilizations.[6]

ROMAN INFLUENCE AND MEDIEVAL FOUNDATIONS

As Richard Kagan writes in *Urban Images of the Hispanic World*, the fundamental difference between the *urbs* (the city as architectural entity) and the *civitas* (the city as community) dates back to Thucydides and the Aristotelian vision of the *polis* as a community where citizens live happily and in accord with law and justice. Inspired by Roman political philosopher Cicero (106–43 B.C.) and redefined seven centuries later by Isodore of Seville (560–636) in his encyclopedic *Etymologiae*, this concept dominated the Spanish Middle Ages and the vision of the Ideal City during the Renaissance.[7] During his long reign (1252–84), Alfonso X the

7. Kagan, 19–44.

Left
Felipe Guaman Poma de Ayala, *Ciudad de los Reyes*, Lima, Peru, 1615. From Felipe Guamán Poma de Ayala, *Primer nueva corónica y buen gobierno*, manuscript at the Copenhagen Royal Library. © Copenhagen Royal Library.

Right
Felipe Guaman Poma de Ayala, *Riobamba*, Peru, 1615. From Felipe Guamán Poma de Ayala, *Primer nueva corónica y buen gobierno*, manuscript at the Copenhagen Royal Library. © Copenhagen Royal Library.

Wise consolidated the antique heritage by establishing the *Siete Partidas* as the main code of Spanish law. This pioneering text resembles an encyclopedia while reflecting the three cultures present at the court—Catholic, Jewish, and Arab. It established Roman law as the legal basis of the Iberian monarchy and was to exert an enormous influence on the foundations and the administrative habits of the New World.

Historian Daniel Stanislawsky, for his part, asserted that "the idea that it was possible to found a city according to a plan laid out in advance was unknown to the Spanish."[8] Yet, during the *Reconquista*, the Spanish leaders founded a series of cities breaking with the Muslim organic tradition. They went back to the model of the antique city, in particular the *castrum* of the Roman armies with its *cardo* and *decamanus*. The new towns were laid out as an irregular chessboard and had a central

François-Auguste Biard, *Amazonian Indians Adoring the Sun God*, oil on canvas, c. 1860. © Coleção Brasiliana/ Fundação Estudar, São Paulo.

square at the intersection of the axes. Among them were Petra on the island of Majorca (c. 1300), Puerto Real (1488), and Santa Fe de Grenada (1491), founded during the siege of the Andalusian city and experienced by various future stakeholders of the conquest. In spite of its medieval character, the conceptual image of the new town was probably a source for the first American foundations.[9]

In this perspective, it is pertinent to talk about an Iberian "pre-Renaissance." In 1384–85, a period of crisis in the process of the *Reconquista*, the Catalan monk Francesc Eiximenis (1327–1409) proposed a theoretical model of the city, based upon a regular grid pattern with a spacious central plaza of square dimensions and additional symmetrically laid-out smaller squares. By doing so, he anticipated by about a century the plans of the Ideal City drawn up by the Italian theoreticians of the Renaissance Leone Battista Alberti, Antonio Filarete, and Francesco di Giorgio Martini. It is thus through Florence, Rome, and Naples (as a political and intellectual exchange center with Spain) that the *città ideale* would return to Spain and influence Hispano-American cities: a geometrically laid-out city, based on the discovery of perspective and symmetrically organized around a central square integrating the different powers and institutions.[10]

8. Daniel Stanislawsky, "Early Spanish Town Planning in the New World," *Geographical Review* (January 1947): 94.

9. Gasparini, 6–17.

10. Francesc Eiximenis, *Dotzè llibre del Crestià* [1384–85, first edition in Valencia, 1484] (Barcelona: Edicions 62, 1983). See also Ruth Eaton, *Ideal Cities: Utopianism and the (Un)built Environment* (New York: Thames & Hudson, 2002); Carlo Giulio Argan, *The Renaissance City* (New York: G. Braziller, 1970).

THE CULTURE OF PERSPECTIVE

After the setback of the trading posts set up by Christopher Columbus (1451–1506) in Hispaniola, Francisco de Bobadilla asked Nicolás de Ovando to found cities based on the Castilian model. On August 5, 1502, he drew up the plan of the first European city of the New World, Santo Domingo. Far from reflecting the "harshness of a first try," the town plan displayed, in spite of the distortions imposed by the geography, the invariants of Spanish American planning: firstly, the *plaza mayor* generating the network of streets—in this case, a block left empty and partially occupied by the cathedral placed parallel to the square—and, secondly, the checkerboard pattern as basic geometrical figure—here made of well-ventilated straight streets opening up on the sea and the river.[11] Contrary to Santa Fé de Grenada, it is the square as "urban void" that organized two couples of streets in two equivalent directions. Yet, it was not the plan that most

11. Erwin W. Palm, *Los monumentos arquitectónicos de la Española, con una introducción a América* (Santo Domingo, 1955). The reference is in Stanislawsky, 95.

View of Santo Domingo, undated, sixteenth century. From: Arnoldus Montanus, *De nieuwe en onkekende weereld* (Amsterdam: J. Meurs, 1671). Courtesy Special Collections, University of Miami Richter Library.

Juan de Siscara, *Plan of the Primitive Plaza de Armas de La Habana* [with parish church and the fortress of La Fuerza], ink on paper, 1691. © Archivo General de Indias, Seville, A.G.I., MP Santo Domingo, 96.

12. Quoted in Palm, 61, from Alexander Geraldinus, *Itinerarium ad Regiones sub Aequinoctiali* (Roma, 1631).

13. Quoted in Palm, 61, from Gonzalo Fernández de Oviedo y Valdés, *Sumario de la natural historia de las Indias* [1515–1527] (Madrid: Editorial Summa, 1942).

14. Erwin Panofsky, *Perspective as Symbolic Form* (New York and Cambridge: Zone Books, 1991); Joseph Rykwert, *The Idea of a Town: The Anthropology of Urban Form in Rome, Italy and the Ancient World* (Cambridge: MIT Press, 1988); Leonardo Benevolo, *The Architecture of the Renaissance* (Boulder: Westview Press, 1978), 430.

impressed the first visitors but the "modernity" of its streets in the spirit of the Renaissance. Walking along the Calle de las Damas, the first street of the New World, remains as impressive today as it was for the first humanist bishop, Alessandro Geraldini. At his arrival in 1519, he wrote, "The streets are so straight and so broad that they outrun even the Florentine streets."[12] Oviedo y Valdés underlined this view:

All houses of Santo Domingo are built of stone like in Barcelona; and the town is much better laid out than Barcelona, because the streets are more even and much wider, and without comparison much more straight; because, as it was founded in our times, in addition to the opportunity and to the plan of its arrangement for its foundation, it was traced with rule and compass, and all the streets of one dimension, facts that demonstrate its superiority in respect to all the other populated places that I have visited.[13]

It is this *Idea of a Town*, this culture of *Perspective as Symbolic Form* that places Hispano-American cities, from Santo Domingo onward, at the center of Renaissance modernity. As Leonardo Benevolo put it:

It would be a mistake to consider the American experiments as marginal episodes in the history of architecture; they were not only quantitatively the most remarkable schemes realized in the sixteenth century, but were also in some ways the most significant, because their characters depended more upon the cultural concepts developed at this time, and less upon the resistance put up by the environment.[14]

After the foundation of Santo Domingo, the seven cities created in the following years by Diego Vélazquez on the island of Cuba were based on the same principles that Ovando set up in Hispaniola: Baracoa, Bayamo, Trinidad, Sancti Spiritus, Havana, Puerto del Principe, and Santiago represented "in the Caribbean and in America at large the last program of urban creation inspired by the concept of 'collective memory' of the motherland."[15] With their irregular grid and their small blocks, these plans and those of the first coastal cities of Mexico—Veracruz and Campeche—were still distant from the strict geometric diagram that was to rule the foundations subsequent to the conquest of the Aztec and Andean worlds. The constricted Caribbean sites usually made the establishment of a clear checkerboard impossible. Regular plans and straight streets had to distort and adapt to difficult coastlines and other obstacles such as hills and marshes. The central plazas were already more or less square in proportion, but their dimensions remained small and practically medieval. Well-known explorers and writers visiting Havana, such as Alexander von Humboldt (1769–1859), criticized the streets as "too straightforward," "too narrow," and "badly laid-out." Yet, we have to gainsay this accusation and assert, as did the pioneer of magical realism in Latin American literature, Alejo Carpentier (1904–80), that this layout potentially "expressed the wisdom of its creators who sought to protect themselves from the sun and the violent rains at all times."[16] In the drawing showing the city at the end of the sixteenth century (1567), the *plaza de armas* clearly stands as the starting point of the first rectilinear streets edged by urban "huts" or *bohíos*. It opens on the bay and features the Renaissance-type fortress of La Fuerza on one of its sides. A comparison with the same part of the city on the plan of 1691 illustrates the increasing urbanity of the streets now lined with patio houses. Alongside the bay, the artist showed the ceiba tree under which the first mass had been celebrated: in so doing he raised the tree to the symbolic dimension of a monument.

THE FIRST INSTRUCTIONS OF POPULATION

The Instructions of Population of 1513 marked the second phase of colonization. Enacted in Valladolid at the attention of Pedrarías Davila, who was to land in Panama the following year, they lay down the foundations of the populating doctrine:

Having seen all the things that are necessary for the settling of the site, and having selected the most appropriate site which can provide the most things that are necessary for the people, the lots shall be distributed to build the houses; and they shall be allotted according to the quality of the settlers; and they shall be given order; in such a way that having created the lots, the town must look ordered in the space left to the plaza, the location of the church, and the order of the streets, because the new towns or settlements that are ordered at their inception will remain ordered with little effort and cost, while the others will never be ordered.[17]

The same instructions were reissued in 1521 to Francisco de Garay for the population of the Amichel province in Mexico and to Hernán Cortés in June 1523. Charles V would confirm and reinforce them three years later. Common to all, the repetition of the word "order" clearly reflected the will of the Spanish government to proceed on a coordinated and bureaucratic development during the continental phase of the conquest.

The founding surveyor or *alarife* who eventually defined the practice of urban design on the American territory was Alonso García Bravo, the greatest planner of the colonization. First, he laid out Panama La Vieja (1519) on the basis of the 1513 regulations. The same year, he was with Hernán Cortés (1485–1547), who ordered him to draw up the plan of Vera Cruz. He took part in the conquest of Tenochtitlán, and in 1521, he went on to establish the plan of Mexico City (1521) on the ruins of the Aztec capital.[18] A few years later, he planned Oaxaca and Santiago de los Caballeros de Guatemala—two foundations of 1527 that, with their perfect gridiron plan, marked a turning point in the definition of urban form in America. From then on, the Ordinances for Population—of 1526, 1543, and the Laws of the Indies of 1573—were to rule the official act of foundation: the imposition of the Christian faith in a pagan world and the designation of the city as a perfectly sacred and geometrical space. As Gabriel Guarda wrote:

The ceremony of foundation possessed in itself very antique roots and, with its character of spiritual nature, could be connected with the theme of the creation of sacred space: the hierofanía, *with its sources in the Orient and in Rome, later taken over by Christianity and the basis of all ceremonies of this type in medieval Europe.*[19]

15. Felipe Préstamo, "Las siete villas de Velázquez," in F. Prestamo, ed., *Cuba: Arquitectura y urbanismo* (Miami: Ediciones Universal, 1995), 99–117; Maurice Halbwachs, *On Collective Memory* (Chicago: University of Chicago Press, 1992).

16. Alejo Carpentier, *La Ciudad de las Columnas* (Barcelona: Ed. Lumén, 1970), unpaginated.

17. Quoted in Edwin Palm, *Los orígenes del urbanismo imperial en América* (Mexico City: Instituto Panamericano de Geografía e Historia, 1951).

18. Manuel Toussaint, *Información de meritos y servicios de Alonso García Bravo, alarife que trazó la ciudad de México* (Mexico City: Impr. Universitaria, 1956).

19. Gabriel Guarda, *Historia urbana del Reino de Chile* (Santiago de Chile: Ed. Andrés Bello, 1978), quoted by Salcedo Salcedo, 57.

Havana, city and port (1567) during the first decades of the sixteenth century, manuscript, ink on paper (1767). © Archivo General de Indias, Seville, A.G.I., MP Santo Domingo, 4.

THE ENCOUNTER OF PRE-COLUMBIAN SPACE

20. Plan of Tenochtitlán by Hernán Cortés, in "Praeclara Ferdinandi Cortéssi de Nova maris Oceani Hyspania Narratio" (The clear relation of Hernán Cortés about the New Spain of the Atlantic Ocean), 1524; Erwin Palm, *Tenochtitlán y la ciudad ideal de Dürer* (1527) (Paris: Musée de l'homme, 1951).

21. Aldo Rossi, *The Architecture of the City* (Cambridge: MIT Press, 1982).

22. Letter by Hernán Cortés, 1522, quoted by Francisco de la Maza, *La ciudad de Cholula y sus iglesias* (México: Instituto de Investigaciones Estéticas, UNAM, 1959).

23. Graziano Gasparini, *Formación urbana de Venezuela, siglo XVI* (Caracas: Editorial Armitano, 1992), 38ff.

24. Barbara E. Mundy, *The Mapping of New Spain: Indigenous Cartography and the Maps of the Relaciones geográficas* (Chicago: University of Chicago Press, 1996).

Cortés had a stroke of genius when he decided to select Mexico City as the capital of the empire. By rebuilding Tenochtitlán, he could take advantage of the sophisticated administrative and economic network put in place by the Aztecs. His second letter of 1524 to Charles V included the only contemporary Western-style "representation" of Tenochtitlán—a view that went around the globe and whose monumental and geometrical character, never seen before, may have influenced the late Renaissance vision of the Ideal City, in particular Albrecht Dürer's (1471–1528).[20] What is certain is that the discovery of the city and of its large and orderly spaces must have coincided with and reinforced the desire for order dear to the Renaissance.

Indeed, the urban diagram of Tenochtitlán appearing in Cortés' letter is clearly visible in the reconstruction plan by Alfonso García Bravo: the two main axes intersecting in the center and continuing across the surrounding lagoon; the orientation of the checkerboard and the elongated rectangular form of the blocks; the immense space occupied by the Spanish plaza that coincided with the Aztec market on the edge of the ceremonial center; and, among other similarities, the market square of Tlatelolco. As Aldo Rossi put it, the layout of a city "as an urban fact" is unlikely to disappear.[21] Although the religious center had been destroyed, that was not necessarily the case in other areas: the heaps of ruins unavoidably slowed down the reconstruction, but they must also have oriented it. In this city in transition, the surviving houses of the Indian *caciques* had to coexist with the half-ruined temples, with Cortés' enormous fortress (on the location of Montezuma's old and new palace—today the National Palace), the original and modest cathedral built with the stones of Aztec pyramids, and a few hundred houses inhabited by the Spanish.

Another example of urban palimpsest is Cholula, discovered in 1519, fifty miles northeast of Mexico City. "[The city] counts almost twenty thousand houses," Cortés wrote, "it is the most beautiful city I ever saw outside Spain."[22] For a long time, the present Cholula was considered a new Spanish city. However, Graziano Gasparini has now demonstrated that modern Cholula is in fact the Aztec city that the Indians had continued to inhabit in proximity to the Spanish foundation of Puebla; it was, subsequently, "the most important urban heritage of pre-Hispanic America."[23] On the one hand, the dimension of its rectangular checkerboard—more than three hundred blocks, of which many were still unoccupied before 1950—is not rational in comparison to the limited size of Spanish foundations and must thus be of Aztec origin. On the other hand, the way the plan of Cholula integrates the pre-Columbian pyramids within its grid pattern seems to be an organic phenomenon, not an operation created *a posteriori* and equally incompatible with Spanish practice. This unique synthesis can be seen in the superb *Relación geográfica de Cholula* (Geographical relation of Cholula, 1581) drawn in response—one of 167 known—to Philip II's Questionnaire of 1577 about the Spanish foundations and their population, political jurisdiction, spoken languages, geography, flora, and fauna. The plan suggestively showed the convent of Los Remedios built on top of one pyramid in an extraordinary example of urban syncretism.[24]

Could we affirm then that the discovery of Mexico created the Hispano-American city in its classical form? Yes in regard to the perfection of the grid, which would prevail in all future foundations; no in the sense that the rectangular blocks of Mexico City, Puebla, and Cholula, of Aztec origin, would

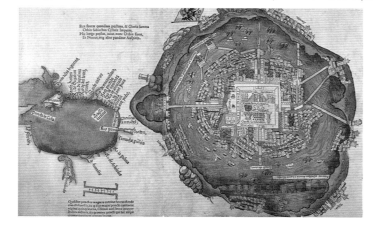

Map of Tenochtitlán, [late version, hand-colored], 1524. From the letter of Hernán Cortés, "Praeclara Ferdinandi Cortéssi de Nova maris Oceani Hyspania Narratio." © The Newberry Library, Chicago, all rights reserved.

not reappear elsewhere. In fact, it is in Oaxaca that Bravo invented the *cuadricula*, the exclusively Hispano-American model of urban grid made of large square blocks centered on a square plaza. From the founding of Quito (1532) and Lima (1533) on the same model, the perfect checkerboard spread everywhere. Hispano-American urban planning had entered a new phase; the encounter between the spatial conception of the European Renaissance with the open and geometric pre-Columbian space definitely buried all traces of medieval urbanism on the South American continent.

In Cuzco, conquered by Francisco Pizarro (1478–1541) in 1534, the Spanish largely reused the original plan of the city. The Inca stone buildings on which the adobe Spanish floors were added gave it its mythical and syncretic aspect. Nevertheless, in Cuzco as in Mexico City or Lima, the pre-Columbian heritage is best expressed in the exceptional size of the public spaces. Here, Vitruvius' definition of the square as a building-like "enclosed" space is reversed. In Mexico City (the Zócalo as the ancient Aztec market) or Cuzco (the three large adjacent squares make up for the huge Inca central square), the "cosmic" dimensions of the urban spaces, both at ground and sky level, take the upper hand; the buildings serve as foreground to gigantic nature. In the pre-Columbian cities, pyramids "echoed the sacred mountains, which, as a result, are intensified by the human will of symmetry and geometry: the power of the natural form is emulated and controlled."[25] Among all the checkerboard plans created in history (Greece, Rome, Eastern Europe, Inca Empire), the Latin American ones have the largest urban blocks; their unique dimensions must have responded, consciously or not, to the theoretical concept of cities without walls, to the immensity of the territory, and to the discovery of the Aztec and cosmic Inca vision of space.

The vertical dimension was practically absent from the early Hispanic city: the urban chessboards of Mexico, Antigua Guatemala, or Oaxaca literally thrust toward the volcanoes or, as in Buenos Aires, "spilled" like geometrical oil stains between Rio de la Plata and Pampas. They were the horizontal and modern answer to the "natural and built mountains" of pre-Columbian cities. In the painting of the *Villa Imperial de Potosí* (c. 1770), the city and its houses seem to dissolve into the mountain syncretically depicted as symbol both of the Virgin Mary and Pachamama, the Andean mother goddess. In the background, the lakes connected to the underground silver mines conjure the violent exploitation process of this proto-industrial epoch, which caused the death of hundreds of thousands of Indian workers.

View of Cholula, c. 1950. © Juan Rulfo & Carla Aparicio de Rulfo, bajo custodía de la Fundación Juan Rulfo. Photo Juan Rulfo.

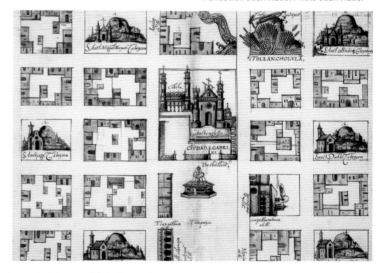

Relación Geográfica [Geographic Relation] de Cholula, Tlaxcala, México, manuscript, ink on paper, 1581. © Benson Latin American Collection, University of Texas at Austin.

A RENAISSANCE AND MEXICAN UTOPIA

When Don Antonio de Mendoza arrived in Mexico City in 1535, city development entered into a new phase. The Viceroy of New Spain was charged to enforce the interests of the Spanish state over the personal interests of the *conquistadores* and *latifundia* owners. Born in Grenada in 1492, this cosmopolitan man, who had lived in

25. Vincent Scully, *Architecture: The Natural and the Man-made* (New York: St. Martin's Press, 1991), 6–7.

26. For this whole section, see Guillermo Tovar de Teresa, "La utopia del Virrey de Mendoza," *La utopia mexicana del Siglo XVI: Lo bello, lo verdadero, y lo bueno* (Mexico City: Grupo Azabache, 1992).

Flanders, Hungary, and Germany, brought with him a library of more than two hundred books. Mendoza imposed a utopia both humanist and imperial, inspired by Alberti—a copy of his *De Re Aedificatoria* survives, annotated by Mendoza's hand (1539). In Mexico City, Mendoza extended the original plan of Bravo by tracing large and straight streets allowing the passing of horses; the *plaza mayor* was edged with arcaded palaces—a typology that would characterize numerous Mexican central squares and be codified later in the Laws of the Indies. He founded the University and created the cities of Morelia (originally Valladolid de Michoacán, it was based on Plato's seven conditions for an ideal city), as well as Guadalajara and Querétaro. All these achievements had a purely Renaissance layout based on the perfect square.[26]

To Mendoza's civil utopia (which lasted from 1535 to 1555), churchman Vasco de Quiroga (c. 1470–1565) answered with a "social" utopia founded on Thomas More, whereas the Franciscan Juan Zumárraga (1468–1548) developed a religious one articulated on Erasmus's theories. As first bishop of Mexico, Zumárraga was responsible for the destruction of the Texcoco idols and manuscripts. Yet, his actions demonstrated the contradictions of that time

Plan of the City of Panamá on Its New Site, manuscript, ink on paper, 1673. © Archivo General de Indias, Sevilla, A.G.I., MP Panamá, 84.

[Anonymous], *Villa Imperial de Potosí*, oil on canvas, Potosí, Bolivia, c. 1770. © Museo del Ejército, Madrid.

as he also created, with Mendoza, the Colegio de Tlatelolco, where the reformist Bernardo de Sahagún was a teacher. He gave this institution a progressive curriculum that emphasized language learning—a tool of pacification and mutual comprehension according to Zumárraga—and that prepared young natives for leadership responsibilities. As auditor of Mexico, Vasco de Quiroga founded the hospital-village for Indians in Santa Fé outside the capital. In Michoacán, he developed various ideal Indian communities where locals received instruction in religion but also in the arts and crafts and in the fundamentals of self-government. Quiroga described their working in his *Ordenanzas*, literally adapted from More's *Utopia* (1516).

With the rise of Protestantism, Europe and the Renaissance spirit entered a time of crisis. 1571 marked the arrival of the Inquisition in Mexico and the decline of the Tlatelolco College. The Jesuits would eventually resume the theme of the "ideal and innocent" Indian city in the vast program of missions—called *reducciones*—they established in Paraguay, Argentina, and in southern Brazil. The reduction of São Miguel (1756)—today in ruins, like all the other missions—is a paradigmatic example of Jesuit planning: a large square faced the church, while parallel lines of modest houses constituted a primitive but methodical checkerboard.

THE LAWS OF THE INDIES, 1573

Lúcio Costa, *Sketch of Igreja do Carmo in Diamantina*, c. 1922. © Casa Lúcio Costa, Rio de Janeiro.

Enacted in 1573 by Philip II, the "Ordinances for the Discovery, the new Population, and the Pacification of the Indies" constitute one of the most remarkable documents of modern urbanism, a Hispanic utopia of the Ideal City. Indeed, out of 148 ordinances, the 52 articles that specifically refer to the urbanization process—site selection, layout, plan, square, location of the main buildings—confirmed what had become common practice in the Indies: the open checkerboard plan generated from the *plaza mayor* as political and social center. As established by law, those principles met the three criteria that, according to Pierre Lavedan, synthesize the urban principles of the Renaissance: first the organic connection between all parts of the city and the subordination to a clearly established center; second, the monumental perspective; and, third, the "program."[27] Moreover, this ideal city as *urbs* was also conceived as *civitas*. To that effect, the other ordinances deal with Indians' rights, protection from slavery, education, punishment, and conversion to Catholicism. In theory at least, the times of cruel discovery and colonization were over, and a new humanistic phase of administration and population was to follow. The debates about the validity of the conquest and the rights and identity of the Indians (the dispute of Sepúlveda versus Las Casas) had calmed down, and, in this perspective, the Laws of 1573 clearly reflected the moderating influence of Bartolomé de las Casas (1474–1566).[28] Spain thus had the opportunity to implement one of the main goals of the Renaissance, almost impossible to carry out in Europe: to create a city as one creates an authentic project, perfect in its form and in its physical and symbolic order.[29] Historians have often minimized the importance of these laws, arguing that hundreds of cities, including the future capitals, were founded prior to 1573. They certainly have a point, but it minimizes the fact that the laws merely extended the scope of the previous Instructions; moreover, those critics rarely take into account the fact that the original urban cores were still sparsely inhabited and built. The great merit of the Ordinances of 1573 is that they stabilized an urban form still in its infancy and clarified the conditions allowing its consolidation. These texts gathered both concepts and experiments that, turned into laws and put into practice, allowed the development of both architectonic unity and urban density, two major attributes of Latin American urbanity. Another criticism highlights the contradictions between the laws and reality: for instance, they prescribed the

27. Pierre Lavedan, *Histoire de l'urbanisme: Renaissance et temps modernes* (Paris: Henri Laurens, 1941), 34; Dora Crouch et al., *Spanish City Planning in North America* (Cambridge: MIT Press, 1982).

28. Lewis Hanke, *All Mankind is One: A Study of the Disputation between Bartolomé de Las Casas and Juan Ginés de Sepúlveda in 1550* (DeKalb: Northern Illinois University Press, 1974).

29. See in particular: *El Sueño de un ordén: la ciudad hispanoamericana* (Madrid: CEHOPU, 1989); Javier Aguilera, *La plaza en España e Iberoamérica: el escenario de la ciudad* (Madrid: Ayuntamiento de Madrid, 1998).

30. Catherine Wilkinson-Zerner, *Juan de Herrera: Architect to Philip II of Spain* (New Haven: Yale University Press, 1993).

31. Richard Kagan, *Spanish Cities of the Golden Age: The Views of Anton van den Wyngaerde* (Berkeley: University of California Press, 1989).

32. Catherine Wilkinson-Zerner, 164. This quote applies particularly well to Latin American cities.

Javier Alvarez, *View of Mexico City*, oil on canvas, c. 1850. © Museo de América, Madrid.

Father Rodrigo Ménendez, Plan of the convent of Santo Domingo, Lima, 1681. From Juan Ménendez, *Tesoros verdaderos de las Indias* (Rome, 1681).

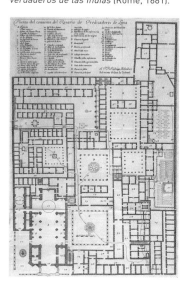

plaza mayor as a rectangle of Vitruvian proportions (2:3), whereas the squares actually built were almost all square. Yet, the difference between the work built and the work on paper was not unusual in Renaissance time: as in Andrea Palladio's *Four Books of Architecture* (1570), the Laws of the Indies combined the ideal with the real, the immaterial perfection of the Neo-Platonic vision of the world and the real construction of the city. Their architectonic precision and the direct quotations from Vitruvius and Alberti often suggested that, behind the hand of the king, the personality of a major architect could be discerned. No material evidence exists, but Catherine Wilkinson-Zerner argues that the architect of the Escorial, Juan de Herrera (1530–1597), was the co-author of the urbanistic aspects of the laws.[30] In the 1560s, extensive planning became a priority for Philip II, who embarked upon modernization of the cities and of their infrastructures, still strongly tinged with medievalism and Arab culture. Population censuses, the systematic description of the Spanish cities by Anton Van den Wijngaerde, and the Indies Questionnaire (that led to the Geographical Relations) date back to this time.[31] This program was carried out, for example, during the reconstruction of the *plaza mayor* in Valladolid—which Zerner asserts to be a "standardized" model for the Laws of the Indies—in 1561. More importantly, it was implemented with the construction of the Escorial, whose geometrical order and representative abstraction may have influenced the spirit of the Laws. Herrera's economic and moral vocabulary offered the means "to underline the king's virtues and to transpose them into the heroic scale of the urban environment. Simplicity became virtuous and virtue was monumentalized."[32] The pragmatism of the Ordinances confirmed the fact that the square is the main monument of the city, its emptiness contrasting with the visible hierarchy of power embodied by the temples or the rulers' palaces dominating the utopian European treatises. Indeed, no royal statue stood at its center until the Independence, when monuments to Simón Bolívar and other liberators would be erected. Likewise, the absence of a strong concept of fortification—in sharp contrast with the Italian treatises—led Sigfried Giedion to write that the Hispano-American city, for which the Laws envisaged a constant and open extension, constituted "the real invention of the modern city."[33]

33. Sigfried Giedion, *Space, Time and Architecture: The Growth of a New Tradition* (Cambridge and London: Harvard University Press, 1941).

34. See the illustration in this book, 27.

CONSOLIDATION AND SYNCRETISM

During the seventeenth and eighteenth centuries, Latin American cities experienced a consolidation process under the auspices of the Laws of 1573 and an increasingly interbred society. The urban cores solidified and a "mineral" city with compact streets, walls, and squares arose, relegating nature to the majestic patios. The urban blocks, originally divided up into four very large parcels, were split up: the houses, once isolated on their lots, grew side by side with party walls on lots that decreased in size as the density increased. The courtyard house, developed step by step and with successive additions, became widespread, whereas richer households built full-fledged palaces designed on the antique or Renaissance model; indeed, Mexico City became known as the "city of palaces." Its flat roofs around its many courtyards created the image of a horizontal city at the foot of volcanoes, a scene skillfully depicted by the artists of the nineteenth century. The major convents set up in the neighborhoods around the *plaza mayor*, forming genuine cities inside the city. Organized around large patios, they served as college, church, or hospital, such as the convent of San Francisco in Quito, or the convent of Santo Domingo and others in the axonometric view of the *Fortificación de Lima* (1687) by Pedro Nolasco.[34]

During the Baroque era, the public spaces of Antigua Guatemala, Quito, Lima, La Paz, or Guadalajara were no longer "empty spaces waiting for a form, but genuine places designed to accommodate various shapes,

35. Mario Sartor, "Types et modèles urbains dans l'Amérique espagnole entre le XVIè et le XVIIè siècle," in *La ville régulière: modèles et traces* (Paris: Picard, 1997), 95.

36. See the illustration in this book, 26 (bottom).

Top
Casimiro Castro, *The City of Mexico Seen from a Balloon*, lithograph, c. 1855.
© Museo de América, Madrid.

Bottom
Pedro Gualdi, *Southeastern View of the Panorama of Mexico City*, c. 1840.
© Museo de América, Madrid.

according to a conception of the urban space and the act of celebration that the ephemeral Baroque was able to illustrate—perusing the rites of death, the triumphal entrances, and both sacred and profane exaltations—for a new and political production of social consensus."[35] This society of theater and entertainment was beautifully represented in a perspective drawing showing the construction of the new *plaza mayor* in Panama (1748). After its destruction by a hurricane, Panama was relocated and refounded on the basis of the Laws of the Indies: in a rare occurrence, four streets emerge from the center of the square. While some parcels still lie fallow, a series of tents, both commercial and decorative, already establishes the urban contours of the square, bound to become a meeting and entertainment place. Inevitably, this view recalls Vitruvius and his description of the Roman forum as an "open-air building" intended for games and, here, the *corrida*.[36]

A painting by Antonio Ramírez Montufar, *Construcción de la Catedral de Guatemala* (1678), reflects a similar yet ambiguous "urbanity." Ramírez confronts the spectator with the diversity and complexity of the local reality. He shows the musicians beating time to work; various ethnic groups at work such as the Spanish or Creole stonemasons, the Indian porters, and other bricklayers in action on the scaffoldings; the objects and the tools of that time; and the roofs of the temple, with their multiple domes reminiscent of the Arab-Andalusian structures

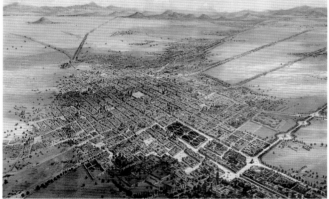

37. María Concepción Amerlinck de Corsi, "Construcción de la catedral de Guatemala" in *Los Siglos de Oro en los Virreinatos de América 1550–1700* (Madrid: Museo de América, 1999), 163–66 [see p. 30].

38. Kagan, *Urban Images of the Hispanic World*, 141.

39. Carlos Venegas Fornias, *La urbanización de las muralles : dependencia y modernidad* (Havana: Ed. Letras Cubanas, 1990).

whose design was imported from Spain.[37] Hundreds of people cross paths in all directions: the bishop in his coach; the civil authorities observing and legitimizing the work from the arcades of the town hall. Several clergymen, students, ladies with their children, knights and their black squires transit on foot. Indians of both genders and all ages sell their wares; the painter depicts their clothes with an almost ethnographic precision. Altogether, the great number of races, human activities, and particularities make of this vision a genuine "human comedy," even if the aim of the painting is to glorify the fact that "the new temple—the 'miracle of America' in the words of a local observer—was essentially a municipal effort, the product of a *civitas* essentially dedicated to God's service."[38]

MODERNIZATION IN HISPANIC AMERICA AND BRAZIL

Until the end of the eighteenth century, cities were socially and economically under the undemocratic yoke and monopolistic control of the richest families and the Spanish Crown. The physiognomy of the Baroque era changed little and presented an atmosphere of urban monotony only alleviated by the singularity of the central square as the focal point of an increasingly multicultural socialization and of the religious buildings such as monasteries and universities. With the exception of Mexico City, where the first public park of Hispanic America (la Alameda) was established at the end of the sixteenth century, the late-Baroque city did not provide many tree-planted spaces and promenades.

It is the growing influence of the French *lumières* and the success of a new type of public space—the Champs d'Elysées in Paris; and the Paseo del Prado and the Botanical Garden in Madrid by Ventura Rodriguez and Juan de Villanueva (1776–1783)—that gave the impulse to renovate the city. During the first decades of the nineteenth century, *paseos* were built in Havana, San Juan de Puerto Rico, Lima, Bogotà, Mexico City, and many urban centers. These long and shaded promenades extended the main streets and were often established outside the city walls. Far from being pale imitations of the French boulevards, the *paseos* formed an urban typology specific to Hispanic countries with a high degree of formal inventiveness, as witnessed in the Paseo de la Reforma in Mexico City or the Paseo del Prado in Havana, linked to a botanical garden like the one in Madrid. The Cuban capital city grew with such inevitability that the walls were destroyed in 1863. Following the example of Vienna (1858), a "ring" was built. Prestigious places of business, theaters, cafés, and Spanish clubs would establish themselves along its edges and squares in the following decades: for the first time, the center of gravity had moved away from the colonial center—a phenomenon that would be repeated in Havana and other Latin American cities.[39]

Frédéric Mialhe, *Theater of Tacón and Paseo de Isabel II* (today Paseo del Prado and Paseo Martí), Havana, lithograph, c. 1840. © Museo de América, Madrid.

After 1850, the urban system became more complex and more functionally organized. Following the example of Paris, new public buildings and spaces were built, such as theaters, commercial galleries, parks, and train stations. Everywhere, the *plaza mayor* was transformed into a densely planted garden, adorned with memorials. The language of the Beaux Arts system and its eclectic vocabulary, symbol of modernity and "civilization," extended to architecture, urban infrastructure, and the design of public spaces and gardens. Overall, these changes resulted not only from the integration of the major Latin American cities in the global economic system, but also reflected the massive waves of European immigration in the late nineteenth and early twentieth centuries.

The same was true of Brazil. This country entered the international scene with the arrival in 1808 of the Portuguese court, who were fleeing attacks by Napoleon I. Between 1532 and 1600 the Portuguese had founded

seventeen urban centers, all of them on the coast, with the exception of São Paulo de Piratininga. Here again, what can be called the "collective memory" played a prominent role. In contrast to Spanish cities, these trading posts never had an experimental function. Most of the time, the settlers sought to reproduce a model reminiscent of the topography of Lisbon or Porto. The upper part of the town was primarily residential, whereas the lower neighborhoods were more commercial. Urban layouts varied according to the site but tended to form an irregular checkerboard distorted by the local topography, such as in Rio de Janeiro. Public buildings were scattered in a sparsely constructed city; the monumental location of the churches was particularly remarkable as they were placed on the highest sites like acropolises.

In Rio de Janeiro, the French influence dated back to 1810 (the city became the capital of the Portuguese empire in 1815) and the arrival of the *mission française* and its leader, architect Grandjean de Montigny (1776–1850).[40] From then on, the new aristocracy and, later, the bourgeoisie were determined to get rid of the colonial symbols and to give the city a new, neoclassical image before embracing eclecticism at the end of the century:

The faith in the civilizing character of eclectic architecture, in its capacity to modify the living habits of a society wedged in the past becomes the hegemonic discourse, amply transmitted by the illustrated periodicals and other important newspapers. At the heart of this discourse, the number one enemy was colonial architecture— its houses and other buildings considered backward, ugly, non-hygienic, badly lighted and ventilated: all adjectives that were not limited to architecture but to the general urban state of the capital, Rio de Janeiro.[41]

Between 1890 and 1935, this bourgeois modernizing utopia set up infrastructures, erected new buildings, and designed urban promenades and vast public parks; it even founded new cities, a tradition that had been interrupted. The project for a new federal capital city in Brazil—the future Brasilia—was launched during the nineteenth century. Likewise, in 1897, Aarão Reis drew up the plan of a new capital city for the state of Minas Gerais, Belo Horizonte. Its checkerboard, punctuated with squares and crossed by large avenues and diagonals, closely resembled the plan of Washington, D.C. In 1880, French engineer Pedro Benoit used a similar and

[Anonymous], *View of the City of Salvador* [de Bahía], oil on canvas, undated [befpre 1868]. © Coleção Brasiliana/ Fundação Estudar, São Paulo.

40. *Grandjean de Montigny, 1776–1850: un architecte français à Rio* (Paris: L'Académie, 1988).

41. Cláudia Thurler Ricci, thesis manuscript (2002), "L'eclettismo come simbolo di modernità e civilizzazione a Rio de Janeiro (Brasile): l'opera de Adolfo Morales de los Rios," unpaginated.

Donat-Alfred Agache, View of the proposed business center on the site of the former Castelo Hill, Rio de Janeiro, 1929. From Donat-Alfred Agache, *Cidade do Rio de Janeiro, extensão, remodelacão, embellezamento* (Paris: Foyer brésilien, 1930). Courtesy Special Collections, University of Miami Richter Library.

Lúcio Costa, Perspective of the project for the Federal University of Rio de Janeiro, 1936. From Lúcio Costa: *Registro de uma vivência* (Rio de Janeiro: Empresa das Artes, 1986). Also see illustration p. 177, top.

42. On this period, see Artura Almandoz Marte, *Planning Latin America's Capital Cities 1850–1950* (London: Routledge, 2002); Jaime Benchimol, *Pereira Passos: um Haussmann tropical* (Rio de Janeiro: Prefeitura da Cidade do Rio de Janeiro, 1990).

43. Letter from Le Corbusier to the Minister of Education Capanema, quoted in Marcelo Ferraz, ed., *Lina Bo Bardi* (Milano: Charta, 1994), 276 [author's translation].

strictly geometric plan—a Beaux-Arts update of the Renaissance ideal city scheme—to found the new city of La Plata in Argentina. In Buenos Aires, the Avenida de Mayo was opened across the colonial fabric (1884), and the French landscape architect Joseph Bouvard tried, with mitigated success, to create Haussmanian diagonals (1907); in Rio, the mayor Pereira Passos sliced open the Avenida Central (1905), a large boulevard that would become a showcase of grand eclectic buildings, like the Museo de Bellas Artes by Adolfo Morales de los Rios (1858–1928). Pereira Passos was also responsible for the construction of the waterfront Avenida Beira Mar, which opened up the Guanabara Bay to modern transport while highlighting its extraordinary landscape.[42]

Yet, in Brazil as in all of Latin America, this reforming momentum often remained limited to the surface of things. A mask of modernity concealed both the lack of thorough reforms (urban, social, and institutional) and the considerable disparities remaining between the cities and the still feudal countryside. In Brazil, for example, the *favelas* appeared during the first decades of the twentieth century. It was the beginning of an urban form and typology in total opposition to both colonial urbanism and the modernist vision of the city, and whose apparent freedom and modernity seduced Le Corbusier. Fascinated as he was by the colonial cities and their vernacular white patio houses, he firmly rejected the modernizing and eclectic vision of the elites. Moreover, for him, the colonial squares, in contrast to the public spaces of northern Europe, still remained the real stage for urban life. In a letter to the Minister of Education Capanema regarding Salvador do Bahía, Le Corbusier wrote:

Mister Minister, do not order the construction of theaters with stages and seats, but leave open the squares, the streets, and the gardens of the city. Have them build wooden platforms and benches, accessible to all, and the Brazilian people will occupy them, improvising as always with their natural elegance and intelligence. [43]

THE CITY AS LANDSCAPE

The French landscape architect Jean-Claude Nicolas Forestier (1861–1930) arrived in Havana in 1925. It was the first of the three stays that would enable him to develop the master plan of the metropolis and to design its most prestigious and popular public spaces in collaboration with local architects. Like Le Corbusier in in Brazil and Argentina, he studied the city scientifically from an airplane in order to apply, on a metropolitan scale, the relationship with the landscape and the territory, which he had used in his private and public garden projects in Morocco, Paris, Seville, and Barcelona: "the science of gardens to the benefit of Civic Art."[44] He respected the colonial center, turned the Paseo del Prado into an urban "living room," proposed a new civic center, and endeavored to give peripheral districts a logical layout. Likewise, he made the university one of the best campuses outside the United States—a genuine acropolis, reached by a majestic staircase linking the university portico to the foot of the hill in direction of the Caribbean Sea.

His most essential contribution remains the system of parks and avenues he proposed to control the rapid expansion of the city and to emphasize its natural surroundings. Contrary to Buenos Aires, where he had proposed a similar concept in 1924, the design for Havana was in great part implemented. The Malecón was the climax of this method of highlighting the landscape: more than four miles long, the pedestrian and automobile promenade along the bay and the sea was conceived as the metropolitan facade to the former colonial city and its modern neighborhoods. It was embellished by a succession of viewpoints, esplanades, commemorative monuments, and geometrically delineated gardens.

Like Forestier, Donat-Alfred Agache (1875–1934) was a member of the *Société française des urbanistes* created in 1911 to promote a new urbanism (or Civic Art) that would be at once classical and modern, formal and scientific, and would blend the tradition of the Beaux-Arts with the modern concepts of Camillo Sitte, Raymond Unwin, and Eugène Hénard.[45] His comprehensive plan for Rio de Janeiro in 1929—known as Plan Agache—was a stunning and ambitious document, even if some of his monumental visions for the development of the bayfront were quite incompatible with the morphology and the character of the city. Paradoxically, it is one of the projects most open to criticism—the leveling of the Castelo hill to make place for a new business center—that would give Le Corbusier, Lúcio Costa, and others the opportunity to design the major modern projects of that era, such as the Ministry of Education and Health (1937–43). At the regional scale, Agache and his team laid the foundations of the modern Rio: they worked out the communication network through the complicated geography, established a modern port, and led the typological transformation of Copacabana and Ipanema into high-density mixed-use neighborhoods.[46] A vast system of parks embraced the rain forests dominating the city, the seashores, and the beaches. As in Havana, the plan created an exceptional and unique synthesis between the natural and the man-made, "the modern city as a form of landscape."

A few years later, from Santa Fé de Bogotá, where he directed the planning department from 1935 to 1943 after designing the plan of Santiago (1933), the Austrian Karl Brunner-Lehenstein (1887–1960) wrote in his *Manual de Urbanismo*:

The final objective—the beauty of the city—depends as much on the consideration given to nature as to the architecture that must be present. The natural beauty of plants and trees and a rational architecture devoid of exoticism and based on order give a sense of proportion to plastic urban beauty.[47]

44. Bénédicte Leclerc, "La Science des Jardins au Service de l'Art Urbain," *Pages-Paysages* no. 2 (Paris, 1989); Jean-François Lejeune, "The City as Landscape: Jean Claude Nicolas Forestier and the Great Urban Works of Havana, 1925–1930," *Journal of Decorative and Propaganda Arts* 23 (Cuba): 151–85.

45. David K. Underwood, "Alfred Agache, French Sociology, and Modern Urbanism in France and Brazil," in *Journal of the Society of Architectural Historians* (June 1991): 130–66.

46. Donat-Alfred Agache, *Cidade do Rio de Janeiro, extensão, remodelacão, embellezamento* (Paris: Foyer brésilien, 1930).

47. Karl Brunner-Lehenstein, *Manual de Urbanismo* (Bogotá, 1938–40); Carlos Morales and Mauricio Pinilla, "Karl Brunner, Architect and Urbanist," *The New City*, Volume 1 (1991), 34–39.

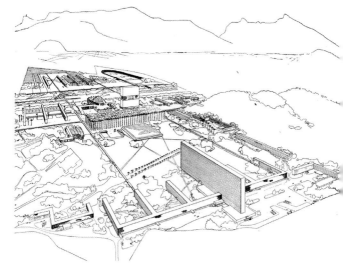

Le Corbusier, Perspective of the project for the University City of Brazil, Rio de Janeiro, 1936. From *Le Corbusier et Pierre Jeanneret, Œuvre complète, 1934–38* (Zurich: Éditions H. Girsberger, 1953).

UNIVERSITY CITIES: THE LAST UTOPIAS

48. Hugo Segawa, "Rio de Janeiro, México, Caracas: University Cities and Modernities 1936–1962," Fifth International DOCOMOMO Conference, Stockholm, Sweden, September 16–18, 1998, unpaginated.

49. Carlos Raúl Villanueva, *Textos escogidos* (Caracas: Universidad Central de Venezuela, 1980), 99. [author's translation].

In developing countries grappling with rapid urbanization and structural social inequalities, the foundation of new public universities was seen as a means to compensate for the lack of an independent education system and research tradition, but also to advance a modernization and emancipation project that would spur a social, cultural, and scientific revival. Between 1930 and 1965, the new university cities of Mexico, Rio de Janeiro, Caracas, Bogotá, Panama, and other capitals were conceived as urbanistic and social laboratories. Genuine cities inside the city, they represented "means of occupying as yet non-urban empty spaces on an unprecedented magnitude and organizing expansionist vectors for the cities."[48] Moreover, the urbanism, the architecture, and the integration of the visual arts that characterized these campuses became metaphors of the fever for social, aesthetic, and political modernity that gripped the continent during that period.

As for North America, the creation of cities in the midst of wilderness was a fundamental theme in its urban history. In its purest form, the North American campus—free from the constraints and the reality of the city, from which it always stood at a respectful distance—was the fruit of the eighteenth-century European Enlightenment and one of the greatest American contributions to the history of urban form. The model of reference was the campus of the University of Virginia (1817–26), founded and designed by Thomas Jefferson (1743–1826), third president of the United States, as a modern *polis*, an ideal city where architecture and nature, body and spirit could blossom in perfect harmony, sheltered from the dangers of urban life.

The quality of campus design declined sharply after WWII in the United States. Unexpectedly, it is in Latin America that the campus resurfaced in the history of modern architecture. In Caracas and Mexico City, for instance, architects and urbanists succeeded in maintaining the utopian spirit of the campus and, at the same time, integrating the principles of the International Congress for Modern Architecture (CIAM). Once again, it is the relationship with the landscape that underlined the formal conception and interpretation of these ideal places where, at least in theory or for the duration of one's education, the inequalities of the "real" city had to be reduced or erased altogether.

It is well known how much the geography of American cities and landscapes influenced the evolution of Le Corbusier's thought. Yet, paradoxically, this new vision did not inspire the bible of modernistic urban planning—the Charter of Athens (1933)—which treated the landscape as an undifferentiated field. By contrast, the modern architects and town planners of Latin America continued not only to exploit this American paradigm but renewed it by shedding a modern light on the pre-Columbian and colonial roots. On the university campus of Caracas, for instance, Carlos Raúl Villanueva (1900–1975) reinterpreted the colonial vocabulary: the "covered walks" crisscrossing the campus recalled the arcades of the colonial center, and the narrow passages between the buildings of the Humanities Complex were reminiscent of its narrow streets. On the other hand, he criticized sharply the colonial grid plan as an authoritarian device, misused by speculation, which led him to the radical design of the *plaza cubierta* (covered plaza):

The sign of authoritarian possession represented by the grid did not escape the common fate of myths.... The wealth of relations brought in by the evolution of society does not permit to be restrained in such simplistic forms. The summarizing value of the plan of the Conquest period must give way to the organic plan, structured into neighborhood units whose structure and conformation reflect the social wealth of the human relationships they contain.[49]

Luis Barragán, *El Ziggurat*, perspective for the center of the new town of Lomas Verdes, Mexico City, 1964. Photo Armando Salas Portugal. © Fondation Barragán, Birsfelden.

Likewise, on the campus of Mexico City, Mario Pani and Enrique del Moral demonstrated the validity and seductive power of the modernistic concepts by associating them with the urban tradition of Teotihuacán and Monte Albán. However, it is in the two projects for the Federal University of Rio de Janeiro, never implemented, that Le Corbusier and Lúcio Costa achieved the scenographic integration of nature and architecture. On the panoramic site of Quinta de Boa Vista, Le Corbusier organized the campus around the Square of the Thousand Palm Trees, while Costa structured it along a monumental arcaded square and a majestic pedestrian avenue colonnaded with six rows of royal palms.For Costa, to be modern implied a perfect knowledge of the past. It was the necessary condition to reinterpret it.[50]

Apart from the university cities, the last utopian works of the 1940s–1960s reveal the same inventiveness in the vision of the "city as landscape:" among them, the parks and gardens of Roberto Burle Marx, the Gardens of El Pedregal by Luis Barragán and the public housing ensembles of Mario Pani in Mexico City, the monumental ensemble of Pampulha by Oscar Niemeyer, and, last but not least, the new Brazilian capital, Brasilia, planned by Costa. There is one last project deserving our attention, that of Lomas Verdes, a planned but unrealized city for 100,000 inhabitants to the northwest of Mexico City (1964–73). In the center of a site consisting of four hills, Luis Barragán imagined the most beautiful and most poetic urban complex of South American modernism: at its center a majestic axis, defined by two symmetrical rows of high-rise parallel bars, climbs up a hill, which is crowned with a golden cube-shaped church in a hermetic and metaphysical vision that brings to mind Bruno Taut's concept of the *Stadtkrone*.[51] As seen in his red and blue perspective drawing, Barragán realized the poetic and surrealist synthesis of urban pre-Columbian tradition, vernacular colonial language, and pure European modernism. The drawing resonates with Carlos Fuentes' words:

But when all is said and done, what Rivera, Kahlo, and all the artists of the Mexican Revolution were really discovering, without fully realizing it, was that Mexico had an unbroken, generous, all-encompassing culture in which the past is always present. On this basis we should be able to create an inclusive, not an exclusive, modernity. This, I believe, is the true goal of Latin America, a continent that cannot hope to be explained without its Indian, Black, and European (Mediterranean, Iberian, Greek, Roman, Arab, Jewish) roots.[52]

Lasar Segall, *Favela I*, ink on paper, 1954–55. © Museu Lasar Segall, São Paulo.

50. Lúcio Costa, *Registro de uma vivência* (São Paulo: Empresa das Artes, 1995).

51. Vittorio Magnago Lampugnani, "Luis Barragán: Urban Design and Speculation" in: Federica Zanco, ed., *The Quiet Revolution* (Milan: Skira, 2001); Bruno Taut, *Die Stadtkrone* (Jena: E. Diedrichs, 1919).

52. Carlos Fuentes, introduction to: *The Diary of Frida Kahlo: An Intimate Self-Portrait* (New York: Abrams, 2001), 19.

MODERNITY, GLOBALIZATION, AND CRUELTY

Modernity—or the desire for modernity—is destructive and, in this sense, implacable and cruel. Its fundamental goal is to willingly destroy an existing order and replace it with a new one. Thus, any project defined as a project tending toward modernity implies a globalization process, whose intrinsic tendency is to destroy local particularities. The Spanish conquest of the New World was the first form of globalization in America; the orderly checkerboard plan epitomized the rational organization of the territory combined with forced evangelization. Baroque art and architecture, while being the triumphant expression of this process, were at the same time a subtle means of resistance to it. The second wave of globalization following movements of independence marked in fact the continuation of the colonial status quo. Behind the modernizing French influence, both artistically and politically, national and liberal elites continued to act as internal colonial powers by further rejecting native and Indian cultures.

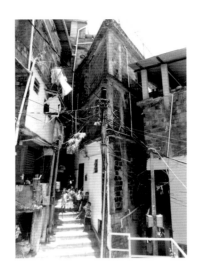

Street of a *favela*, Rio de Janeiro, c. 2000. © Fundação Bienal de São Paulo, Biennale de Venezia, 2002. All rights reserved.

In the 1930s, the myth of progress and technological modernization took over. On the one hand, Latin America became a stronghold of the European-based architectural and urban modernity that would often be brutal and destructive; on the other hand, its architects invented an "other" modernity, which blended the international and the local, nationalism and tradition, with modernity. In contact with the social, cultural, and geographic reality of the Americas, functional and technological purism transformed into a more subtle modernism, more sensual, linked to the popular and artisanal cultures, and conscious of the cosmic reality of the territory.

The last phase of globalization has been under way since the end of WWII. The military dictatorships that arose in the 1960s–1980s went hand in hand with the end of urban experiments and idealisms. Corruption, real estate speculation, the almighty automobile, and the growing influence of the North American model led to the devastation of the colonial centers and to the sprawling extension of the cities and their hinterlands. This globalization has two major effects: on the one hand, a massive internal migration toward the vast conurbations, accompanied by the exponential rise of social disparities and the creation of urban ghettos, either very rich or very poor often juxtaposed in an unpredictable and surprising manner as in Rio de Janeiro; on the other hand, the exodus of both high and low classes toward a better life in the United States—Miami, Los Angeles, San Diego. It is this contrast that distinguishes the opus of two Belgian contemporary artists in contact with Mexico. Francis Alys's videos and paintings frame a dynamic reflection on urban densification and concentration of poverty, epitomized by the *ambulantes* invading the public spaces and privatizing them for their own survival. Chantal Akerman's movie and installation *From the Other Side* (2002) plunges the spectator into the dangerous and cruel flight of the Mexicans toward the promised lands of Arizona, Texas, and California.

Faced with these individual solutions to a global crisis, is a revival of the collective and globalizing utopias—even in forms that would question the parameters of modernity that dominated the first half of the 1900s—possible or even desirable at the onset of the twenty-first century? Or should the much needed response be to generate "partial utopias," working within the interstices of the existing Latin American conurbations, which, today, are not only beyond all control but also indefinable in their totality. These partial utopias make use of the landscape and geography, like Alberto Kalach's *Lakes Project* to rebuild part of the hydrologic system that existed around Mexico City, and the strategy for new public spaces implemented in Rio, Bogotá, or Curitíba. They also aim at creating new "spaces of liberty" like Bo Bardi's *cidadela de liberdade* at the Sesc Pompeia in São Paulo or the *projetos favela bairro* developed by the municipality of Rio since 1995 in order to turn the *favelas* into genuine cities and neighborhoods.[53]

Today, the poetic and syncretic vision of Jorge Amado's *favelas* in Marcel Camus's *Orfeu Negro* (1950) has given way to the terrifying reality of *Cidade dos Deus* (Fernando Meirelles, 2003). Yet, behind the ugliness, the cruelty, and the violence, one can discover extraordinary cities within the city in complete opposition to the system of "learned" architecture and urban planning, either colonial or modern. *Favelas* are in a process of constant flux: "they never stop growing (first horizontally, now vertically) and, thus, are never fixed down as traditional cities, planned or not." The planned city, tree-like, is firmly planted in a roots-system that gives it its image of order; the organic or partially planned city is a city-shrub that functions on a radicular system, neither simple nor orderly. As for the *favela*, "it can be seen as a city-lawn responding to a rhizomic system of great complexity."[54]

This is far removed from the Spanish gridiron and the utopias of the Renaissance. Paola Berenstein Jacques compares the Brazilian *favelas* to "cruel labyrinths" where kites fly as signals for the drug lords, who are seen as the new "Minotaurs" chased after by Theseus/policemen. Having killed the Minotaur, Theseus celebrated his victory by dancing. After all, the samba was born in the *favelas*.[55]

53. "The Lakes Project," *Praxis—Mexico City: Projects for the Megacity* (New Orleans: Praxis, 2001); Rodolfo Machado, *The Favela-Bairro Project: Jorge Mario Jureguí Architects* (Cambridge: Harvard Graduate School of Design, 2003); *Rio Cidade: O urbanismo de volta ás ruas* (Rio de Janeiro: Prefeitura de Rio de Janeiro, 1996).

54. From the essay "Estética das favelas," (unpaginated manuscript), partially published in English: Paola Berenstein Jacques, "The Aesthetics of the Favela: The Case of an Extreme," *Transforming Cities, Design in the Favelas of Rio de Janeiro* (London: AA Publications, 2001).

55. Paola Berenstein Jacques. On this conclusive section, see in particular Gwendolyn Wright, "Buildings Global Modernisms", *Grey Room* 07 (Spring 2002): 124–34.

Center of Havana, hand-colored photograph, 1995. © Photo Irene Sperber, Miami Beach.

Lúcio Costa, *Pilot Plan of Brasilia* [competition drawing], ink on paper, 1957. © Casa Lúcio Costa, Rio de Janeiro, all rights reserved.

49

QUITO: CITY AND LANDSCAPE BETWEEN UTOPIA AND REALITY

EDUARDO BAÉZ

The City of Quito is located at the foothills of the very high Mount Pichincha, famous for its ancient eruptions of rock and fire, leaving the town center relatively flat but for a small inclination. It looks like a truly striking amphitheater, as seen from a hill that runs alongside the town. From this spot one can appreciate the majestic view of Quito in its entirety. From all these places one can see the buildings arranged in this beautiful amphitheatre shape that would handsomely stand its ground in Europe, as readers will tell by the descriptions that I will faithfully and directly put to you.[1]

Gaetano Osculati, *We are Angels, We Come from Heaven and We Ask for Bread*, engraving, 1847–54. Milan, Tipografi Editori, 1854, from *El Regreso de Humboldt* (Quito: Museo de la Ciudad, 2001).

Thus observed the Jesuit Mario Cicala—who traveled from Messina, Italy, to the Province of Quito, South America, in August 1741. Thirty years later in Viterbo, Cicala wrote a detailed description of the area that currently encompasses Colombia and Ecuador. This vision, which must have been that of hundreds of Europeans enticed to the American continent by illusion and adventure, reveals the wonderful merger that exists in Quito between the second Inca capital, the Spanish foundation (the original core of the city), and the virgin nature of its surroundings. Historians tell us that the origin of Quito goes back to the territorial and military extension of the Inca empire, when the Incas were looking for lands with a more benign climate and found a fertile and tranquil area to safely settle and store their treasures. The splendor of the town can be ascertained by these words reported by Cieza de León: "Huayna Cápac had ordered more than five hundred loads of gold and more than a thousand loads of silver as well as many gems and fine clothes to be brought to Quito."[2]

The place where Quito was founded is a small, flat plateau of about five hundred acres, carved in places by deep gorges (*quebradas*) stretching from the slopes of Mount Pichincha. Three great gashes cut through the original settlement: the San Diego gorge, next to the monastery of the same name; Manosalvas, which crossed the Plaza de Santo Domingo; and Jerusalém, down from El Placer, which housed the Inca Baths: *Spanish conquistadors who came to Quito from the South, from Peruvian lands, had heard of the Inca Huayna Cápac's "House of Pleasure,"... a place that housed the Inca Palace, an enormous body of buildings including military quarters, swimming pools and gardens and which Spaniards called "El Placer," translating the Inca word. The complex was burned down by Rumiñahui, and the name has been preserved to this day in the place now occupied by water reservoirs.[3]*

1. Mario Cicala, *Descripción histórica topográfica de la provincia de Quito de la Compañía de Jesús* (Quito: Biblioteca Aurelio Espinos Pólit, 1994).

2. Quoted in Jorge Salvador Lara, *Memorias del Ñaupi Quito* (Quito: Ediciones Quitumbe, 2002).

3. Jorge Salvador Lara, *Memorias*. The destruction of the Inca city was the result of Spanish attacks and of the self-defense arson tactics of the Indian leader Rumiñahui.

Left page
Eruption of the volcano Pichincha seen from the city of Quito, October 5, 1999.

4. The names of 204 founders are engraved on the walls of the cathedral. See: Vicente Llamazares Martín, *Quito* (Madrid: Ediciones de Cultura Hispanica, 1989).

5. José Gabriel Navarro, "Contribuciones a la Historia del Arte en el Ecuador," *Boletín de la Academia Nacional de Historia*, volume 1 (Quito: Editions Salesiana, 1925).

6. José Gabriel Navarro, "Las formas arquitectónicas europeas en la arquitectura hispanoamericana," *Boletín de la Academia Nacional de Historia* (Quito: Ediciones Prensa Católica, 1959).

7. Jorge Salvador Lara, *Memorias.*

8. José María Gonzalez de Valcárcel, *Restauración monumental y puesta en valor en ciudades americanas* (Barcelona: Editions Blume, 1977).

9. Ernesto La Orden Miracle, *Elegio de Quito* (Madrid: Ediciones de Cultura Hispánica, 1975).

10. Padre Agustín Moreno, *Fray Jodoco Rique y Fray Pedro Gocial, apóstoles y maestros franciscanos en Quito* (Quito: Ediciones Abya-Yala, 1998). A monument, inaugurated in 1934, recalls the location of the first planted wheat; the long bas-relief on the facade of the Legislative Palace includes Father Rique as one of the five founding fathers of modern Ecuador.

11. Sebastiano Serlio, *Tutte le opera di architettura*, Book III, plates CXLVI and CXLVII (Venezia, 1540). The five first books were published between 1537 and 1551.

This small plateau, at an average altitude of 9,380 feet, is surrounded by minor hills that serve as lookouts and give Quito a singular landscape: south is El Panecillo ("the small bread"), a small round hill about 650 feet high; the foothills of Pichincha and San Juan stand to the west, and to the east lies Itchimbía hill. Climbing to any of these elevations, a walker suddenly faces an incredible view of long mountain ranges that frame the famous "Avenue of Volcanoes," in the words of Alexander von Humboldt: Cayambe to the northeast, Antisana in the eastern range, the majestic Cotopaxi to the south, and, further on, the Tungurahua and Chimborazo peaks, all summits culminating above 14,500 feet. On the slopes of the hills that surround Quito are traces of the old Inca Trail, a sinuous path through hills and mountains that linked the natives with the Inca South.

On August 28, 1534, Captain Sebastián de Benalcázar officially founded the city of San Francisco de Quito on behalf of Francisco Pizarro.[4] The Spaniards traced the city plan as an almost perfect grid, centered on the *plaza mayor*, where the main church, the governor's house, and the houses of important *conquistadores* were built.[5] On all sides of the plaza, the blocks were square and about 300 Castilian feet wide; each block was divided into four original lots, so that each house faced two streets. The first houses were generously sized and provided for comfortable living, with interior patios, gardens, and large yards for animals. The plan reflected the first ordinances of population decreed by Charles V in 1523, but, as in Tenochtitlán and Cuzco, it seems that the Spanish layout closely followed the urban traces of the destroyed Inca city.[6] According to Jorge Salvador Lara:

Many believe that Quito's old quarter grid layout is the work of the Spaniards. The fact is that Benalcázar took advantage of the paths originally set for the Inca town, using the three Inca roads as the starting point. Baudin was the first to recognize this fact when he described how the original Inca town resembled a grid, with narrow and stone-made streets crossing at right angles.[7]

Over the next four decades, the plan became more complex and two other squares took shape in conjunction with the construction of the large monasteries: the Plaza San Francisco, which dominated the city from a small elevation and faced the convent of the same name; and the Plaza San Domingo, sloping toward the church and the entrance gate of the city from the southern valley. This apparently simple layout had to accommodate the topography and, in particular, avoid the ravines (*quebradas*). The utopian model of the grid encountered a landscape and a cultural space that were almost impossible to imagine in the most insensate dreams. The encounter was a first manifestation of the "magic realism" that characterizes the culture of Latin America in its physical, social, and cultural aspects. For José María González de Valcárcel, the Spanish American town "is not, as has erroneously been said on occasions, a provincial carbon copy of an European town. Its essential features are sometimes as diverse as its adaptation to the surrounding area is perfect."[8]

Likewise, in the description of Ernesto La Orden Miracle:

In a corner of the Guayllabamba dale a small gorge opens up, hidden on the very hillside of the Pichincha peak. In this green hole our grandfathers built Quito, on the ruins of the Inca city. No city had ever been built on such a tormented ground: the perfect grid with spacious plazas and straight and wide roads. It was planned almost from the air. Hidden aqueducts rode the sides of the hills and there are differences in levels of one hundred meters among the eight or ten built-up blocks.[9]

Rafael Salas, *Landscape of the City of Quito, Ecuador*, oil on canvas, 1860. Photo Galo Valencia. © Archivo Histórico Banco Central, Quito.

Luis Cadena, *Plaza de San Francisco de Quito* (with the traditional Indian market, El Tlanquil), oil on canvas, 1881. © Museo de la Ciudad, Quito.

Frederic Edwin Church, *Cotopaxi*, oil on canvas, 1862. © The Detroit Institute of Arts, Detroit.

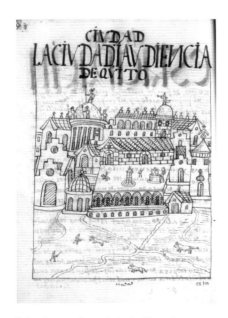

Felipe Guaman Poma de Ayala, *City and Audience of Quito*, 1615. From Guamán Poma de Ayala, *Primer nueva coronica i buen gobierno*, manuscript at the Copenhagen Royal Library. © Copenhagen Royal Library.

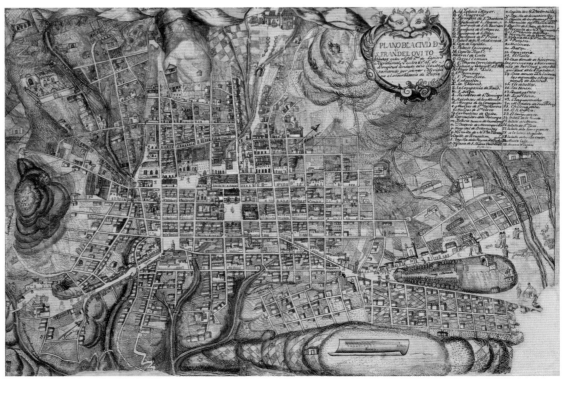

Juan Pio Montufàr, *Plan of San Francisco de Quito*, ink and watercolor on paper, undated (nineteenth century). © Centro Cultural Metropolitano, Quito.

JODOCO RIQUE, A FLEMISH BUILDER IN QUITO

To come to America was to realize a dream, whether driven by ambition, adventure, or religious zeal, as was the case of the Belgian Franciscan monks who arrived in Quito to convert the natives and expand the Christian kingdom. Joos van Rijcke van Marselaer (1498–1578), known in Spanish as Jodoco Rique, was a Flemish priest from Mechelen who studied in Leuven and joined the Franciscan Order in Ghent. In 1532, Jodoco Rique attended the General Chapter of his Order and was granted permission to travel to the West Indies. With his mate, Johann de Clerck Van Hove, he left the Ghent monastery and headed for Bruges, where they were joined by Friar Pieter (Pedro Gosseal), the nurse, and Friar Simon. On their way to Peru, they heard of the foundation of Quito and the possibility of establishing a large monastery. They arrived in December 1534, the first Franciscan monks in the fledgling town. On January 25, 1535, they laid ground for the church and the convent of San Francisco. During the thirty-five years he spent in Quito, Rique was not only a great builder; he was also an educator, pacifist, and entrepeneur. The Flemish friar is warmly remembered in Quito as the founder of the Franciscan Order and one of the first to preach the gospel to the natives. He is also credited with bringing European wheat to America and founding the first brewery in the region.[10]

Calle El Panecillo, Quito, engraving, 1881.
© Archivo Histórico Banco Central, Quito.

An edition of the *Books of Architecture* by Sebastiano Serlio (1475–1554), translated into Castilian by Francisco de Villalpando and annotated by Jodoque Rique's hand, suggests that the Italian theoretician was a major source for the works accomplished by the Flemish friars at the Convent of San Francisco. The facade on the square and the atrium that precedes it—a platform, 300 feet long with twelve gates—clearly reflect the Renaissance influence. Most remarkable is the circle-shaped staircase with the thirteen concave and ten convex steps that link the plaza to the plinth. First used by Donato Bramante in the courtyard of the Belvedere at the Vatican, the staircase was also illustrated in Serlio's work.[11] In contrast, the church (whose design is also attributed to Rique) formed a hybrid gothic-Renaissance structure, covered with a magnificent wood ceiling in Mudejar style. The complex, comprising three churches, thirteen cloisters, and patios, was completed in the seventeenth century. It is one of the most important and richest monuments of Latin America.

The Inka Road. Photo Jorge Juan Anhalzer. From *Quito desde el aire* (Quito: Imprenta Mariscal, 1997), all rights reserved.

During the sixteenth and seventeenth centuries, thanks to its status as Royal Audience and its flourishing textile industry, Quito grew in size and population. Between 1580 and 1583, the Spanish Francisco de Berrera, master builder of the cathedral of Puebla de Los Angeles (Mexico), sojourned in Quito. He laid out the plans of the convents of San Agustín and Santo Domingo. Other buildings rose, like the Compañia, a large urban complex founded by the Jesuits in the vicinity of the Plaza Mayor. In 1650, Quito counted two hundred blocks, seven squares, and 2,500 houses. Thirty-five hundred resided in the city, not including the Indians, the Creoles, women, and children: in total, twenty thousand persons.

12. See Edward Dolan, *Green Universe: The Story of Alexander von Humboldt* (New York: Dodd, Mead, 1959).

13. Alexander von Humboldt, *Cosmos: A Sketch of a Physical Description of the Universe* (London: H. G. Bohn, 1849–58).

The epidemics, the earthquakes (in 1698, 1704, and 1755), the social and political instability, the echoes of Tupac Amaru's rebellion of 1781, and, primarily, the expulsion of the Jesuits in 1767 all contributed to dramatically slow the growth of the city and its hinterland during the eighteenth century. The limits of the city did not change, even if construction and re-construction proceeded, providing to some extent an alternative to the textile and agricultural crisis.

FROM HUMBOLDT TO CHURCH

14. On Humboldt's travel: *El regreso de Humboldt* (Quito: Museo de la Ciudad, 2001); Alexander von Humboldt, *Vues des Cordillères, et Monuments des Peuples Indigènes de l'Amérique* (Paris: F. Schoell, 1810).

At the start of the nineteenth century, with help from both his family and the Spanish Crown (a crucial grant from Charles IV), the German naturalist Alexander von Humboldt (1769–1859) embarked on a five-year journey across Latin America.[12] With the French botanist Aimé Bonpland (1773–1858), he traveled to Cuba, from Caracas to the Orinoco, and from Bogotá to Trujillo (Peru), a road that led them to Quito in 1802, before bringing them back to Mexico (1799–1804). On his return to Europe, Humboldt devoted more than twenty years to the publication of his research, a task that he completed mostly in Paris. His written and illustrated corpus, scientific but also imbued with fable and mystery, transmitted to the European world the "re-discovery" of the equatorial lands, the immersion within a sublime but dangerous landscape, the perception of costumes and people, the climate, the flora and fauna, but also the "cosmic" vision of the Andes:

It is that part of the surface of our planet where nature, within a minimal space, gives birth to a great variety of impressions. In the colossal mountains of Cundinamarca [Colombia], Quito and Peru, crisscrossed by deep valleys, man can observe all families of plants and all the stars in heaven.[13]

Selection of insects in Guyaquil. From Edward Whymper, *Travels amongst the Great Andes of the Equator* (New York: Scribner's Sons, 1892).

Hanging of slaves, engraving, 1837. From *Costumes de Colombie* (Paris: Fermín Didot Editeurs, 1837).

Humboldt climbed all the volcanoes around Quito, studied the pre-Columbian sites, visited colonial cities, and observed the way of life and trade, the simplicity of commercial negotiations, and the existence of the *tianguis*—a sort of primitive market form seen in squares, of which the most outstanding in Quito was the one in San Francisco.[14] Like his scientific predecessors—including Charles-Marie La Condamine (1701–1774), Alejandro Malaspina (1754–1810), and José Celestino Mutis (1732–1808)—Humboldt commissioned painters and other artists to produce the drawings and engravings that filled the European cabinets and salons. Reality, in this rationalist century, went well beyond the fiction of the first chroniclers of the Indies and their exegeses. For Humboldt, the task of the modern landscape painter was to bring to light the genuine characteristics of a terrestrial region. Among the artists he influenced, German Johann Moritz Rugendas (1802–1858) travelled and painted extensively in South America; likewise, Frederic Edwin Church (1826–1900) became one of the most important American Hudson River School painters. He made several journeys in the 1850s in the footsteps of Humboldt: he produced stunning views of the Andes, among which are the two versions of the eruption of the Cotopaxi (1863).[15] Later, the English writer and journalist H. G. Wells (1866–1946) published his famous short story "The Country of the Blind," in which he portrays his idea of an exotic country: "Three hundred miles and more from Chimborazo, one hundred from the snows of Cotopaxi, in the wildest wastes of Ecuador's Andes, there lies that mysterious mountain valley, cut off from all the world of men, the Country of the Blind."[16]

Humboldt and the other explorers of the period were the pioneers as well as the main disseminators of the "idea of America" in Europe. Their writings and images—including paintings, engravings, measured drawings

Top
Father Leonardo Deubler and Venancio Gaudolfi, Facade of the church of the Compañia (Jesuit Order), 1722–65, Quito.

Bottom
[Jodoco Rique], Staircase to the church and convent of San Francisco, inspired by Sebastiano Serlio, Plaza de San Francisco, Quito, c. 1550. Photo from *Quito Patrimonio* (Quito: Editorial Municipal, 2000).

Top
Ceiling of the patio of the convent of San Francisco, Plaza de San Francisco, Quito, sixteenth century.

Bottom
Oswaldo Viteri, *Some Silent Penitent* (Algún penitente silencio), collage of fabric and paper on canvas, undated (second half of twentieth century). Photo Galo Valencia. © Archivo Histórico Banco Central, Quito.

15. Günter Metken, "The Heart of the Andes: From Humboldt's Kosmos to the Paintings of Frederic Edwin Church," in Jean Clair, ed., *Cosmos: From Goya to De Chirico, from Friedrich to Kiefer—Art in Pursuit of the Infinite* (Milan: Bompiani, 2000), 33–40.

of archaeological remains and of the flora and fauna—documented a variety of natural, social, and political topics, but all portrayed the customs and traditions of this faraway land, where two civilizations mixed both violently and gently. An engraving published in Paris in 1837 by Fermín Didor shows emphatically not only the clothing, but also the culture, the condition of slavery, and the way of life of the various population groups in America, including a native man carrying on his naked back a man dressed in European attire.

SYNCRETISM: THE SCHOOL OF QUITO

16. H. G. Wells, *The Country of the Blind and Other Stories* (London: T. Nelson, 1913); quoted in "El Ecuador inventado," supplement to the daily *El Comercio de Quito*, October 2002.

17. Damián Bayón, *History of South American Colonial Art and Architecture: Spanish South America and Brazil* (New York: Rizzoli, 1992).

The most obsessive mission of religious orders in America was to convert the locals to Christianity, and the most didactic way of doing so was through paintings and the use of symbols and images as preaching methods. From the sixteenth century onward, the American native was forced to blend, socially and culturally, two opposite worlds. He had to replace the living nature of his natural habitat with the representation of foreign ideologies, incomprehensible to him. In order not to lose the bases of his culture and values, he built a synthesis, a syncretic vision in which the two worlds and systems of values would be able to meet.[17]

It was then that the Latin American Baroque style exultantly emerged as the culminating expression of a religious, natural, cultural, and social syncretism. In Quito as in many other cities, an abundance of indigenous and foreign artists—engravers, painters, masons, draftsmen, stucco carvers, gold gilders, sculptors—appeared on the scene and spontaneously formed what historians call the "School of Quito." Natives from Quito were recruited by religious orders as "art soldiers" who, together with evangelical groups, received instructions from priests and were encouraged—gently or harshly—to copy images that came from Spain. It is surprising to observe, for example, the lack of light shown in certain religious paintings of the sixteenth and

Edward Ender, *Alexander Von Humboldt and Aimé Bonpland in Their Hut in the Jungle*, oil on canvas, c. 1850.
© Berlin-Brandenburgische Akademie der Wissenschaften, Berlin.

seventeenth centuries that, although they were made in Quito, where the equatorial sun penetrates every door and window, depicted dark medieval-like rooms and effigies of saints descending from the heaven under a storm.[18] Art in Quito remained profoundly propagandistic and European:

The conquest was both military and spiritual. The colonial period was characterized by the co-existence of two European powers: the Spanish Crown and the Catholic Church. This ambivalence marked the orientation of a whole grand epoch, where a series of paradoxical situations developed affecting mainly the fine arts as the predominant formal cultural language that showed a duality of concepts: a pseudo-feudal mystical ideal, rigid and archaic, and a Renaissance technique in continuous renovation and opening.[19]

Bernardo de Legarda, *The Immaculate Virgin*, sculpture in polychrome wood, seventeenth century. Photo Galo Valencia. © Archivo Histórico Banco Central, Quito.

The indigenous landscape and context did not particularly motivate artists during the colonial period, forcibly and obsessively occupied as they were in religious paintings devoted to catechism, crucial for the conversion of Americans. Miguel de Unamuno synthesized this observation with the verdict: "Spain conquered America with Jesus Christ blows."[20] From the second half of the seventeenth century onward, local artists slowly but steadily incorporated their own language, customs, and vision. Among the main figures, Miguel de Santiago (1626–1706) stands out as one of the greatest painters. His *Procession during the Drought* (1699–1706) depicted, for the first time in Ecuadorian art, the extraordinary natural context of the city: the Pichincha volcano, the Panecillo, and a minimalist view of the urban skyline.[21] Other great artists were the painter Fray Pedro Bedón (1556–1621) and, especially, the sculptors Manuel Chili, Caspicara, and Bernardo de Legarda (1699–1773). The last transcended the Baroque tradition with his "aerial" sculptures of the Immaculate Virgin (*Virgén apocalíptica*)—"dancing" virgins perched over a crescent moon, with silver wings, and holding down a dragon.

In architecture, the sixteenth-century churches displayed, beyond the Renaissance sources already mentioned, the traces of the Moorish culture imported from southern Spain—in particular, the wooden Mudejar ceilings in the convents of Santo Domingo, San Fernando, and San Francisco. These traits continued even during the Baroque period, which, in Quito, was a fusion of Spanish, Italian, Flemish, and German influence. Here, the Baroque was expressed in a singular manner, mixing elements from nature, fauna, and flora: the six Salomonic columns of the facade of the Compañia are decorated with raisin grapes; under the Moorish-style ceiling, the altar, pulpit, and chapels create a gold leaf exhibit of foliage, vines, fruits, birds, and caryatids. At the church of San Agustín, hidden indigenous deities like the Sun God surfaced on the front wall. Quito was all about *mestizaje*—the Spanish term that represents the union of the white man and the Indian, the European and the American, the vision of a world of scientific and cultural progress against the cosmic vision of peoples who could rely only on the wealth of their natural and symbolic environment.

18. Musée Filanbanco, *Tesoros artísticos: selección, prólogo y comentarios de Agustín Moreno Proaño* (Quito: Guayaquil,1983).

19. Ximena Escudero, *América y España en la escultura colonial Quiteña, historia de un sincretismo* (Quito: Ediciones Banco de los Andes, 1992).

20. Filoteo Samaniego, "Humboldt y el paisaje cósmico de los Andes," *El regreso de Humboldt*.

21. Nancy Moran de Guerra y Alfonso Ortiz Crespo, *Los Siglos de Oro en los Virreinatos de América 1550–1700* (Madrid: Museo de América, 1999), 338–39.

22. Jorge Benavides Solís, "Quito en la memoria," in *Quito* (Madrid: Ediciones de Cultura Hispanica, 1989), 23.

REPUBLICAN OPENING AND PROGRESS

The social and economic depression, the libertarian aspirations that were shaking the continent, and the rise of a dominant class that became more and more independent from Spanish protection were the antecedents of the uprising of August 1810 that gave to the city the glorious epithet of *"Luz de América"* (lighthouse of America). Twelve years later, the victorious battle of the Cerro against Spanish troops opened the way to independence. Quito became the capital of Ecuador in 1825.[22]

Alexander von Humboldt, *Geography of Plants in the Tropics*, engraving, 1803. © Stadtmuseum Berlin, Berlin.

23. Eduardo Galeano, *Memoria del fuego* (Mexico City: Siglo Veinteuno Editores, 1982), 243.

24. Eliecer Enríquez, quoting the German Jesuit Joseph Kolberg in *Quito a través de los siglos* (Quito: Imprenta Municipal, 1938).

25. Luciano Andrade Marín, *Notas históricas sobre el parque de la Alameda* (Quito: Archivo Histórico del Banco Central, 1996).

Miguel de Santiago, *Procession during a Drought*, oil on canvas, Quito, 1699–1706. © Museo del Santuario de Nuestra Señora de Guapulo, Quito.

The nineteenth-century European concept of progress penetrated then, in a curious way, the small city of 60,000 residents (census of 1861). Progress went hand in hand with a new homogenizing and globalizing trend, whose roots were in Paris and London. Traditional art forms—both indigenous and Spanish colonial—and manifestations were increasingly criticized and repressed. In 1867, Ecuador took part in the Universal Exposition in Paris: *The catalogue [of the exhibition] exalts the Ecuadorian artists who, even if they can't be called original, attempt at least at reproducing, with remarkable fidelity, the masterworks of the Italian, Spanish, French, and Flemish school.*[23]

These trends embraced the symbols of modernity coming from Europe and definitely rejected all rural and Indian elements that had made up the country until then. Between 1850 and 1870, major public edifices were built in the Beaux-Arts eclectic manner: the Palace of the Archbishop, the Palace of Justice, and the Governmental Palace. This European influence accelerated under President Garcia Moreno with the construction of the Astronomical Observatory, the new Panopticon/Penitentiary, the Teatro Sucre, the School of Arts and Crafts, and the Polytechnic School. Nevertheless, this architectural "globalization" encountered some problems linked to transportation, communication, and availability of materials and technology: "the upper floors [of the Quito residences] attempt to imitate European elegance...yet, the cost is incredibly high, given that, with the exception of carpentry, literally everything has to be imported from Europe."[24]

In 1892, Antonio Flores became president. On the northern edge of the colonial center he established the Alameda, a triangular park *à la française*, designed by landscape architects Fusseau and Santoliva. The beautiful gardens, ordered around a lagoon whose waters came directly from the Pichincha, then hosted the Exposition of 1892, an important event that was to promote Ecuadorian products in anticipation of the Expositions of Madrid and Chicago on the four hundredth anniversary of the discovery.[25] Quito finally entered, half a century after the first European industrial exposition, into modernity. At the same time, the triumph of the liberal revolution of 1895, guided by General Eloy Alfaro, turned upside down the antiquated socioeconomic structures of the country—conservative, clerical, and based on the latifundium model—that had persisted since the Republic and had maintained the people in misery and ignorance.[26]

On June 5, 1908, the first locomotive linked Quito to Guayaquil, the main port on the Pacific Ocean. Commerce and industry flourished; education and communication developed; ideas and capital circulated better. The first signs of a new wave of "globalization" intent to transform the still rural city into a metropolitan center inspired by Haussman's Paris emerged around that period: buildings were reconstructed in the Beaux-Arts manner; boulevards and new neighborhoods expanded the city to the north (Boulevard 24 de Mayo, Avenida Colombia); market squares were progressively transformed into French-style parks for relaxation and promenade (Plaza de San Francisco, Plaza Grande or Mayor). On the centenary of the first shout of Latin American independence (August 1909), a grandiose monument was inaugurated at the center of the Plaza Grande, a work of two Italian artists, Durini and Minghetti.

Top
Royal Passage, Quito, 1915. Photo Ignacio Pazmiño. © Archivo Histórico Banco central, Quito.

Bottom
Calle Guayaquil, Quito, 1926. Photo Remingio Norona. © Archivo Histórico Banco central, Quito.

26. Paúl Aguilar, *Quito: arquitectura y modernidad* (Quito: Museo Municipal Alberto Mena Caamaño, 1995). See also Rubén Moreira, "Eclecticismo e historicismo en la arquitectura de comienzos de siglo en Quito," in *Revista del CAE* (Quito, 1998).

During the 1910s and 1920s, the modernization of the infrastructure and the city's public life accelerated. Tramway lines now circulated between the center and the northern districts; Italian-born architect Giacomo Radiconcini designed the Pasaje Baca, the Teatro Capitol, and the first cinema, the Art Nouveau Variedades built in front of the Teatro Sucre. Likewise, Francisco Durini built the Pasaje Central (like the Baca, a local version of the Milanese Galleria) and the headquarters of the Banco Central.[27]

URBAN EXPANSION AND PRESERVATION

Avenue 10 de Agosto, c. 1940. Photo Gottfried Hirtz.

Like all Latin American capitals, Quito grew exponentially from the 1930s: in 1922, the city counted 80,000 residents; it had 209,000 in 1950, and reached over a million in 1990. At the same time, the urban area went from approximately 9.5 square miles in 1960 to more than 70 in 1990. The northern districts now stretch over more than 15 miles, yet the sprawl has remained relatively well contained in width between the two ranges of mountains that define the valley. The modern cultural and business center as well as the middle-class residential neighborhoods have grown north of the Alameda at the location of the first suburbs of the city; museums, theaters, grand hotels, and skyscrapers are now located along and between two main axes, Avenida Colón and Avenida Amazonas, although new American-like centers are developing further to the north. The historic core has emptied of its well-to-do residents and polarized as institutional center and indigenous marketplace: employees and sidewalk vendors take it over during the day; it is mostly empty and lifeless at night. To the south of the Plaza de Santo Domingo, poor and self-made indigenous neighborhoods have taken over the hills: this "improvised" city has become landscape at the end of the Avenue of the Volcanoes.

Paradoxically, the historic center has recently gained a renewed cultural and symbolic value at the geographical center of a linear city that nowadays extends more than thirty miles in the north-south direction. Declared World Heritage of Humanity by UNESCO in 1978, it is now the place of various operations of historic preservation and rejuvenation: its main squares and monumental complexes have been restored and a slow rebirth is currently repositioning the core of the city as cultural center for the whole of the population.[28] In spite of its social, economic, and urban problems, metropolitan Quito remains more than ever the result of a fusion between utopia and reality, the tangible and the intangible; a marvelous coexistence of urban and rural, city and landscape; the dream of an order and the quest of the unreal in unknown but fascinating regions; a syncretic vision between the global and the local, intermingling two cultures; the mutation of customs and the adaptation of the ordinary to the admirable, of the banal to the substantial. ∎

27. Rubén Moreira, *Eclecticismo e historicismo.*

28. On the program of historic preservation in Quito (buildings and public spaces), see for instance: *Recuperando la historia* (Quito: FONSAL, 2002).

Ramiro Jácome, *Procession for the First Barrel of Oil, Quito*, oil on canvas, undated (second half of twentieth century), Centro Cultural Metropolitano, Quito.

Night view of the Plaza Santo Domingo with monastery and church of Santo Domingo in the foreground, and the self-built indigenous neighborhoods over the hills in the background, 2002. Photo Jean-François Lejeune.

CITY AND LANDSCAPE IN THE CONSTRUCTION OF BRAZIL

CARLOS MARTINS

Nineteenth-century travelers were intellectually prodigal in relation to Brazil; they left a significant number of records—both narratives and images—that were the result of diligent work in observing, researching, and understanding. Not only various official missions and expeditions, but also innumerable artists and dilettantes were moved by curiosity to experience the adventure of the tropics. This precious legacy has provided us with a series of reflections on the construction of the landscape as well as the image of the country.

Brazil, today a country of continental dimensions, was colonized "little by little, on foot, step by step, both along the coast as well as inland. These adventurers were the ones that formed the first urban centers. Only three of these centers became cities: Salvador (1549), Rio de Janeiro (1565), and Filipéia de Nossa Senhora das Neves (1584), the present-day João Pessoa."[1] This picture of early times is an indication of the circumstances that guided the occupation of the land, according to "the spirit of the Portuguese domination . . . which was less concerned with building, planning, or laying foundations, than in exploiting the easy riches that were all available there for the taking."[2]

In the beginning, the coastal centers served to protect the overseas territories of Portugal and facilitate the flow of products from the land. The large landowners lived in the countryside and came to town for holidays and celebrations. Only government workers, officials, and merchants lived in the cities, along with the poorest sectors of society. Until the mid-eighteenth century, rural life was a privilege and "the natural and social landscape was marked by the predominance of the plantation over the city, which was a mere appendage of the former. The plantation was linked to the idea of nobility and was the place for permanent activities, to the side of the empty cities—an extreme manifestation of ruralism, due to the intent of the colonists and not to an imposition of the surroundings," as Antônio Cândido mused.[3]

The Portuguese settlements of the era consisted of simple gatherings of contiguous or neighboring dwellings, laid out freely or along narrow streets and alleys that wound about in accordance with the topography of the land. Not infrequently, they were little more than rural centers that were more densely settled. Religious and administrative buildings occupied a privileged position. Contrary to the recommendations of the Spanish Laws of the Indies, the gridded pattern was not legally prescribed, even if it was sometimes used when there were no natural obstacles. For Sérgio Buarque de Holanda, "Routine and not abstract reason was the principle that guided the Portuguese, in this as well as in so many other expressions of their colonizing activity."[4] And he adds, "The city built by the Portuguese in America is not a mental product; it is insufficient to disturb the scene of nature, and her silhouette is intertwined in the line of the landscape."[5]

Alessandro Ciccarelli, *Rio de Janeiro*, oil on canvas, 1844. © Coleção Brasiliana, Fundação Estudar, São Paulo.

Left page:
Detail of Ciccarelli, *Rio de Janeiro*.

1. Maria Helena Flexor, "Núcleos urbanos criados por Pombal no Brazil do século XVIII," in Denise B. P. Machado, ed., *Anais do IV Seminário de História da Cidade e do Urbanismo* (Rio de Janeiro: UFRJ/PROURB, 1996), 602.

2. Sérgio Buarque Holanda, *Raízes do Brasil* (São Paulo: Companhia das Letras, 2002), 95.

3. Quoted in Sérgio Buarque Holanda, *Raízes do Brasil*, 16.

4. Ibid., 109–110.

5. Ibid.

Hercule Florence, *View of Santarém from the West*, watercolor on paper, 1828. © Russian Academy of Sciences, Moscow.

Salvador exemplifies this affirmation. In the most important city of the colony and, until 1763, its administrative center, the day-to-day life was equally wanting in greater vitality. Only in the nineteenth century would it become a rich trading center. Founded on the eastern side of the great bay of Todos os Santos, "its terrain is so uneven, and particularly to the west, the escarpment so steep, that along the beach there is only space for a single principal street, cut in the middle by some alleys; the other part of the city rises in terraces, the largest of which occupies the mountainous ridge of the promontory, at an elevation of 100 to 200-plus feet above the littoral."[6] Eduard Hildebrandt (1818–1868), a German artist with a romantic and adventurous spirit, traveled in various countries of the world and was in Brazil in 1844. He sensitively captured the vibrant, poetic atmosphere of the city, the sea view, and its interaction with the landscape, calling attention to its busy port as well as its most important buildings.[7]

The discovery of precious minerals stimulated a new strategy for occupying the Brazilian territory. In the process of moving inland, urban centers began to appear or assume importance, and their presence became determining factors in the development of the various regions. Ouro Preto, founded in 1698 and former capital of the State of Minas Gerais, owes its origin to the discovery of gold. The city grew with the demands of this new productive activity and began to accumulate wealth and power. It spread out, noble and aristocratic, over the undulating hills of the Itacolomi mountain range, as seen in the luminous watercolor by Thomas Ender of 1817.

The Treaty of Madrid (1750), which ratified the plan drawn up at Tordesillas to divide Spanish and Portuguese colonies, triggered a series of actions by the Portuguese government to protect and even expand its territory in America. The reign of Dom José I (1750–1777) was crowned by the polemic policies of its minister, the Marquis of Pombal, who developed programs of economic, social, administrative, judicial, and political reorganization. It was Pombal who extended the actions aimed at establishing the borders and maintaining the unity of Brazil, which was elevated to viceroyalty status in 1763. Part of this strategy was the creation of planned urban centers, some of them starting from already existing settlements, spontaneously formed in the previous centuries and now redesigned or urbanized. Inherent in

6. Johann Baptiste von Spix and Carl F. P. Martius, *Viagem pelo Brasil, 1817–1820* (São Paulo: EDUSP, 1981), vol. 3, 143–44.

7. See Gilberto Ferrez, *The Brazil of Eduard Hildebrandt* (Rio de Janeiro: Distribuidora Record de Serviços de Imprensa, 1989).

the regular layout pattern used in these centers was the concept of order. The cities imposed themselves as instruments of domination and power. Santarém, on the right bank of the Tapajós River, was born out of those Pombaline policies. The watercolor of Frenchman Hercule Florence (1804–1879), a member of the Langsdorff Expedition, shows the simplicity of this planned settlement. The presence of many boats is already an indication of Santarém's importance, reiterated in many narratives that described a village whose "location guarantees it will be rapidly flourishing and opulent, with the progressive settlement of those regions."[8]

In the absence of formally trained officials, the urbanists, engineers, architects, and master workmen of that process were the magistrates and captains-general themselves. Only later was it possible to count on the presence of specialized labor, artisans, and tools for public and private works. The slaves were always the builders.

8. Spix and Martius, *Viagem pelo Brasil*, 98.

THE TRAVELER'S GAZE

During the three centuries of Brazil's colonial history, few travelers registered the peculiarities of the urban centers and their interaction with the landscape. Their greater concern was with the description of strategic situations; the urban fabric was frequently represented under monotonous or homogeneous graphic forms, and the landscape was simplified. Added to these records were scattered notes from scientific missions or surveying commissions for setting boundaries and for territorial defense organized by the Portuguese Crown. The great and important exception is the work of the Dutch in the Brazilian Northeast, with outstanding paintings by Frans Post and Albert Eckhout executed during the occupation of the territory by the West Indies Company between 1630 and 1654.

The gaze of the travelers of the first decades of the nineteenth century was very different: their attitudes and interests transformed radically, and concurrently so did Brazil in its search for self-affirmation as a nation-state. After a long period during which the Portuguese Crown forbade free access by foreigners, this immense territory was finally opened to the world theater, with the transfer of the court of Lisbon to Rio de Janeiro in 1808. With the opening of the ports to friendly nations, diplomatic, commercial, artistic, and scientific missions immediately appeared on the scene.

The nineteenth century was, without a doubt, the century of explorations dedicated to learning about the Earth, and Brazil, for so long present in the European imagination, offered a strange reality. Its great territorial extension and the rich diversity of its natural resources presented an immense variety of unique

Eduard Hildebrandt, *Panorama of Bahía*, watercolor on paper, undated. © Staatliche Museen zu Berlin, Berlin.

9. Daniel Pedro Müller, *Ensaio d'un quadro estatístico da província de São Paulo ordenado pelas leis municipais de 11 de abril de 1836 e 10 de março de 1837* (São Paulo: Governo do Estado, 1978); introduction by Honório de Sylos, 12.

10. Ana Maria de Moares Belluzo, *O Brasil dos viajantes* vol. 3 (São Paulo: Metalivros, 1994), 11

landscapes. In the process of growth and organization, the cities and villages adapted to nature in a flexible and peculiar manner. Based on a survey of the population in 1797, according to Honório de Sylos, Rio de Janeiro had 50,000 inhabitants; Salvador, 45,600; Recife, 30,000; São Luís do Maranhão, 22,000; and São Paulo, 7,300.[9] The population of the country, made up of different European ethnic groups, native Brazilians, Indians (considered "savages"), and the massive presence of African slaves, was a stimulating mosaic of human and social diversity.

The reconnaissance missions were primarily responsible for the collection, preparation, and abundant production of publications that covered an entire universe of studies and interests—plants of different species, animals of all families, samples of the most varied minerals, maps and routes, diaries of journeys, topographical and landscaping views, ethnographic objects, and more. Additionally, it was impossible to count the number of people who landed at Rio de Janeiro, arriving from Europe and even the United States. In this complex universe of investigation and research, it was not uncommon to encounter a commercial interest in obtaining new goods and values for the enrichment of the economy and cultural life of those countries.

In their repertoire the travelers brought the current aesthetic and scientific concerns, and their outlook reflected their knowledge and vision of the world. These included the consecrated canons of neoclassicism in addition to the new propositions set forth by the romantic movement, and the recent teachings of Alexander von Humboldt on the representation of nature from the artistic-physiognomic point of view—diversity must be carefully observed and its various components duly contextualized. According to Ana Maria de Moares Belluzzo, the landscape of the "knowledge of nature and its demystification" was associated with that of "the Edenic myth and the worship of nature" in the construction of an image for this unknown world that was being unveiled. The author furthermore points out that "the appearance of a landscape of Brazil is due, above all, to the aesthetic-scientific perception that was, in the last analysis, derived from the model of Humboldt."[10]

FROM HUMBOLDT TO DEBRET

Humboldt (1769–1859), the great German scientist and thinker, took part in the pioneer expedition in America between 1799 and 1804. He traveled through many countries, from Cuba to the Andes; yet he did not study Brazil, as the Portuguese Crown prevented him from entering the country. After his return to

Europe, and for more than three decades, he published work that impressed, touched, and stimulated a Europe anxious for new paths in the arts and sciences. Yet his presence was felt indirectly in Brazil, through the Austrian Mission and the Langsdorff Expedition. The Austrian Mission was made up of a group of scientists, and, for a short time, included the artist Thomas Ender (1793–1875). In the context of this grand undertaking, the German naturalists Johann Baptist von Spix and Carl Friedrich von Martius carried out the most important research, traveling throughout the interior of the country for three years, eventually reaching the Amazon. The many publications produced when they returned to Europe make up a complex work that reveals the extension and variety of the universe they studied.

Schmidt, *View of the Morro de Santa Teresa, Rio de Janeiro*, bodycolor on paper, c. 1837. © Museu Imperial, Coleção Paul Geyer, Rio de Janeiro.

Between 1822 and 1829, Baron of Langsdorff, the consul-general of Russia in Rio de Janeiro and a man of great empirical and inquiring spirit, organized another expedition of similar orientation—that is, also based on Humboldt's point of view. Johann Moritz Rugendas (1802–1858) documented the first trip to Minas Gerais; the second trip, which concentrated on the fluvial routes into the interior and reached the Amazon, included the Frenchmen Aimée-Adrien Taunay and Hercule Florence, who were responsible for the visual records of this genuine adventure, which culminated in the madness of Langsdorff. The precious set of collections, paintings, drawings, and notes that were sent to the Russian Academy of Sciences only came to public attention one hundred years later.[11]

Praised by Humboldt as a master of the art of reproducing the physiognomy of nature, Rugendas was in Brazil twice, from 1822 to 1825 with Langsdorff, and again from 1845 to 1846. Using notes made on this first trip, he published *Voyage pittoresque dans le Brésil*. The wallpaper that Jean Julien Deltil designed for the manufacturer Zuber from lithographs of Rugendas's book created an immense, curious, and fanciful panorama for the decoration of bourgeois residences. It is in this period that the panoramas gained wide acceptance, being used in diverse ways as another form of representing distant places and events.[12]

At that moment in time landscape painting was equally stimulated by the nascent concept of "nation-states" and their search for a proper cultural identity. Brazil, seeking a place in the union of nations, chose its capital, Rio de Janeiro, as the city-symbol of the empire. For Margarida Souza Neves, "in the process of inventing Brazil as a unity, the city of Rio de Janeiro, by the Additional Act of 1834, was made distinct and

11. Boris Nikolaevich Kommisarov and Johann Moritz Rugendas, *Expedição Langsdorff ao Brasil 1821–1829. Rugendas. Taunay. Florence* (Rio de Janeiro: Edições Alumbramento, 1998).

12. Johann Moritz Rugendas, *Voyage pittoresque dans le Brésil* (Paris: Engelmann & Cie, 1835); Kommisarov and Rugendas, *Expedição Langsdorff ao Brasil*. On the wallpaper, see Bernard Jacqué, "Panoramic Wallpaper," in *Brasiliana: A Collection Revealed, Coleção Brasiliana* (São Paulo: Fundação Rank-Packard / Fundação Estudar, 2000), 106–19.

Jean Julien Deltil, from Johann Moritz Rugendas, *Views of Brazil*, wood engraving and painting on paper, printed wallpaper by the Fabrique de Papiers Peints Zuber, Rixheim, France, c.1830. © Coleção Brasiliana, Fundação Estudar, São Paulo.

13. Margarida Souza Neves, "A cidade e a paisagem" in Carlos Martins, ed., *A Paisagem Carioca* (Rio de Janeiro: Rio Arte, 2000), 27.

14. Jean-Baptiste Debret, *Voyage pittoresque et historique au Brésil* (Paris: Firmin Didot Frères, 1834–39). On the French Mission, see: *Afonso de Taunay, A missão artística de 1816* (Rio de Janeiro: Ministério da Educação e Cultura, 1956); Adolfo Morales de los Rios, *Grandjean de Montigny e a evolução da arte brasileira* (Rio de Janeiro: Empresa a Noite, 1941).

separate from the province of Rio de Janeiro, to become the Neutral Municipality of the Court; the image of city-capital was consolidated, not only as the headquarters of the government and the administration of the empire, but above all, as the representation of the entire Imperial State, to dramatize its projects and monumentalize its identity."[13]

The French Artistic Mission came to collaborate with the formation of this new nation through the establishment of the Academy of Fine Arts in Rio de Janeiro. The academic teaching of art and architecture was part of a "civilizing" process proposed by the Portuguese court for the Brazilian territories. In 1816, Nicolas Antoine Taunay, Jean-Baptiste Debret, architect Grandjean de Montigny, and others arrived, led by Joachin Le Breton; they were recognized and respected masters who, nevertheless, had lost prestige in post-Napoleonic France. Despite facing a series of difficulties in the execution of their duties in Brazil, they were able to affirm themselves through their teaching activities—creating disciples and followers—as well as through the production of their own works. On his return to France, Debret (1768–1848) published the justly famous *Voyage pittoresque et historique au Brésil*.[14]

MEMORIES, RECORDS, AND TRACES

Diversity and scale were distinct elements in the representation of the Brazilian landscape. "In his attitudes toward the new terrains, sights and vegetation," Dawn Ades wrote, "the reporter-traveler sought a new domain, a new control over the vast and the unknown. It is worth noting, for example, the predominance of panoramic views that simultaneously impress us with the scale and with the precision of the topographic details."[15] Nestled between the hills of the Atlantic rain forest and the beautiful reflecting pool formed by the Guanabara Bay, Rio de Janeiro was by far the most represented landscape of all Brazilian cities: its streets and squares, its houses and churches, all provided valuable records of everyday life. Views exploring the relationship between architecture and nature were taken from various existing strategic points, allowing the observer to admire the wonderful extension of the landscape. The whimsical relief of the mountains and the presence and serenity of the bay and the city that imperceptibly slip into the scene under a radiant sky are elements presented from the widest variety of angles by hundreds of artists who came to Brazil from various locations and under the most diverse circumstances throughout the nineteenth century. The works presented here—by Alessandro Ciccarelli, Emil Bauch, H. Schmidt, and Nicolas Antoine Taunay—reveal significant expressions of the documentary and symbolic relation of the landscape of Rio de Janeiro, its different neighborhoods and landmarks. Together, they show a universe in kaleidoscope, with multiple facets of a landscape that unfolds in interpretations of reality.

Other regions of the country also attracted the interest of travelers, not only for the diversity of nature, but for the peculiar features and specific characteristics of the villages and cities. It was on the outskirts of São Paulo that Prince Dom Pedro proclaimed independence in 1822, but the city would only attain prominence as an urban center during the nineteenth century, with the affirmation of coffee in the national economy. The Frenchman Arnaud-Julien Pallière, working in the Court since 1817, was charged with recording the views of cities in the provinces of Rio de Janeiro, São Paulo, and Minas Gerais. The artist's panorama of São Paulo is taken from the banks of the Tamanduateí River and shows the Piratininga plateau, where the city was located, representing in a simple way its main churches and groups of houses.

15. Dawn Ades, "Os Artistas viajantes, a paisagem e representações do Brasil" in Carlos Martins, ed., *O Brasil Redescoberto* (Rio de Janeiro: Paço Imperial, 1999), 17.

Thomas Ender, *Vila Rica* (now, Ouro Preto), watercolor on paper, undated (1817–18). © Akademie der Bildende Künste, Vienna.

São Luís do Maranhão was a large center for the production and exportation of cotton. Joseph Léon Righini, unlike other travelers, remained for many years in the regions of the north and the northeast, eventually dying in Belém do Pará. Righini's painting of São Luís do Maranhão showed the city in the background, almost as a pretext for presenting the varieties of vegetation in the foreground, emphasizing the twisted aerial roots of the trees and bushes characteristic of regions with a great variation in the tides.

Belém secured for itself the position of principal port on the commercial route for medicinal products from the Amazon basin. Righini also presented a broad panorama of Belém do Pará, where the facades of the dwellings next to the river were described from an almost scientific documentary viewpoint. However, the composition acquired a spectacular dramatic effect with the presence of a whirl of clouds, the vestiges of a threatening storm that had just struck—a daily occurrence in this region.

Thus, over the course of the nineteenth century, the scientific, poetic, and creative gaze of the travelers crisscrossing the country of Brazil produced an abundance of iconographic material—from simple notes of an affectionate attitude or records of topographic landscapes to exemplary expressions of the picturesque and the sublime. In the search for an understanding of this unknown world, they defined a landscape and an image of Brazil that, throughout the years, would be assimilated by the Brazilians as a vision of themselves. Today, these memories, records, and traces continue to awaken feelings of dignity and nostalgia.[16] ■

16. See Carlos Martins, *Brasiliana: A Collection Revealed.*

Arnaud-Julien Pallière, *Panorama of the City of São Paulo Seen from the Rio Tamaduatei*, watercolor on paper, 1821–1822. © Coleção Beatriz e Mario Pimanta Camargo, São Paulo.

Joseph Leon Righini, *View of San Luis de Maranhão*, oil on canvas, 1863. © Coleção Brasiliana, Fundação Estudar, São Paulo.

Emil Bauch, *Entry of the Barra de Rio de Janeiro Seen from Santa Teresa, Rua Aprazivel*, oil on canvas, 1859. © Museus Castro Maya, Rio de Janeiro.

Nicolas Antoine Taunay, *Church of Glória, Rio de Janeiro*, oil on canvas, 1824. © Museu Imperial, Coleção Paul Geyer, Rio de Janeiro.

Joseph Leon Righini, *Panorama of Belém after the Rain*, oil on canvas, 1879. © Museu Imperial, Coleção Paul Geyer, Rio de Janeiro.

THE VIRGIN OF THE ANDES

CAROL DAMIAN

Incipit Litania in lauden B.M.V. (Litany in praise of the Blessed Virgin Mary)

Ave María Filia Dei Patris	*Ora pro nobis*
Ave María Mater Dei Filii	*Ora pro nobis*
Ave María Sponsa Spiritus Sancti	*Ora pro nobis*
Ave María Templum Trinitatis	*Ora pro nobis*
Sancta María	*Ora pro nobis*
Sancta Dei Genitrix	*Ora pro nobis*
Sancta Virgo Virginum	*Ora pro nobis*
Sancta Mater Christi	*Ora pro nobis*
Quem Tu peperisti	*Ora pro nobis*
Mater Purissima	*Ora pro nobis*
Mater Castissima	*Ora pro nobis*
Mater Inviolata	*Ora pro nobis*

Andean people worshiped Pachamama or a regional version of an Earth Mother long before the arrival of the Spanish. Although it is impossible to calculate the longevity of this belief with exactitude, praise to Pachamama is still spoken in the lore of oral tradition, and the historical significance of the deity is evident in the descriptions of native culture and religion found in the Spanish Chronicles. Despite Spanish attempts to destroy belief in Pachamama and Inca efforts to requalify her status within the rights of noble descent, she survived and remained an essential deity. It is this Earth Mother deity who is revered in her new syncretic reality as the Virgin Mary in the Andes. The Virgin became the synthesis of the many cults and sites dedicated to ancient deities associated with the earth, nature, and revered personalities such as Pachamama, Copacabana, the Moon called Quilla, and the Inca Queen, or Coya.

The enshrining of Mary in the Americas may be seen at one level as an extension of a process already well under way in Spain, where images of the Virgin had been steadily gaining in devotional popularity since the twelfth century. In the colonial situation, Mariolatry was particularly pervasive. The image of the Virgin Mary became the most effective means for the indigenous people to disseminate their own sacred imagery.[1]

1. On the theme of this essay, see Carol Damian, *The Virgin of the Andes: Art and Ritual in Colonial Cuzco* (Miami: Grassfield Press, 1995). This essay focuses on the syncretic image of the Virgin Mary in the Andes, but it is possible to adopt a similar methodological and aesthetical approach to study other images and iconographic symbols associated with other cultural groups such as Aztecs and Mayas.

Left page:
Luis Nino, *Our Lady of the Victory of Malaga*, oil on canvas, region of Potosí Bolivia, c. 1735. © Denver Art Museum, Denver, Colorado, Collection Frank Barrows Freyer.

The production of religious art in Cuzco and the Andean region incorporated artisan sectors from the Spanish, mestizo, and indigenous communities. The School of Cuzco was dependent on the organization of workshops and guilds capable of producing great quantities of painted, sculpted, and architectural decoration. This guild system involved extended families and a variety of combinations of apprentices and masters from the Spanish and indigenous populations. The work was commissioned by Spanish and native patrons for religious, private, and commercial purposes. Perhaps most significantly, this system addressed the needs of a biracial population and two distinct systems of religious beliefs. The religious images produced in these workshops, particularly the image of the Virgin Mary, were also the result of two distinct systems of artistic development—European and Andean. The native artist mastered both.

THE VIRGIN MARY, PROTECTRESS OF THE SACRED LANDSCAPE

The paintings of the Virgin from the Andes are unique combinations of a multitude of symbolic themes. However, the one consistent feature that appears as a dominant stylistic and iconographic trait is the triangular shape of the Virgin's dress, a reference to the shape of a mountain and her role as Pachamama, the Earth Mother. So pervasive is this trait among images produced in Quito, Cuzco, and Potosí, that it appears not only on canvases, but on murals and statues as well. Considering the most popular images of the Virgin with their many variations, the constant reference to Earth Mother and the abiding love of the people in the Americas become evident.

The Virgin dressed as a mountain pays tribute to the Andean landscape and the spirits that dwell within and overlook every aspect of daily life. Her image in the shape of a mountain, or as protector of the earth and its sacred sites and cities, inspired the most characteristic works of the Andean artists. To look at the Andean images of the Virgin is to look at a complex of symbols and concepts. The shape of her dress; the dress itself, with its golden ornamentation and rich array of flowers and jewels; the offerings of Andean flora and fauna that accompany her; the landscape of natural and architectural forms; the presence of feathers as a decorative addition; and the numerous attributes, including the Moon, all contribute to the image of the Virgin as a distinct product of her environment, both natural and spiritual.

Typical representations describe Mary in the wide mountain, or bell-shaped, dress associated with Pachamama. Pachamama is a comprehensive deity, worshiped on numerous levels and in numerous manifestations as the protector of the crops and miners, and giver of life for more than two thousand years. Pachamama and her agricultural counterparts became identified with particular iconographic attributes related to fertility rituals, as well as astronomical and calendrical cycles. These included ritual dressing, feathers, solar radiances, birds, and offering objects. She represents the physical world, paired with (and in certain opposition to) the sun. Thus, everything on Earth and in it is, or is sustained by, Pachamama. She does not have concrete form as a human deity. Her force is contained within the earth—a rock in the field, a river stream, or a mountain. The Spanish chroniclers stated repeatedly that: "They worship the Earth because they say it was their mother and they had to make her form and her offerings; and they also said she was the mother of fire, and corn and other seeds and the sheep and cattle, and the *chicha*."[2] For this reason, "they worshiped the summits of all peaks and mountain passes, and offered maize and other things," as their Mother, the Earth.[3] One Andean legend portrays her all-encompassing nature by describing

2. Cristobal de Molina, "Cosas Acaescidas en el Peru [1535]," in Francisco Esteve Barba, ed., *Biblioteca de Autores Españoles: Cronicas Peruanas de Interes Indigena* vol. 209 (Madrid: Atlas, 1968), 76. The *chicha* is a fermented drink made from corn.

3. Cristobal de Molina, "An Account of the Fables and Rites of the Incas [1535]," Clements R. Markham, ed., *Narratives of the Rites and Laws of the Incas* (London: Hakluyt Society, 1873), 59.

the sexual/reproductive parts of her body as Lake Titicaca, her torso as Quito, her heart as Cuzco, and her mouth as Lima. The entire Andean world of the Inca was contained within Mother Earth.[4]

The mountain was a metaphor for life and existence in the Andean world. The extraordinary reverence for the Earth was manifested in shrines throughout the Andean territory. Worship of the Earth was the most persistent of Andean rituals, from the simple *paga a la tierra* (pay the Earth), where something (usually *chicha*) is offered to the Earth before every agricultural and significant activity, to the placement of stones and other ritual objects on roadside locations and grand pilgrimage shrines, often in inaccessible and isolated locations. It was also the most difficult to identify, eradicate, or replace. Within a twenty-mile radius of the city of Cuzco, the capital of the Inca Empire, the archaeologist John Howland Rowe counted 350 Earth shrines in the Spanish Chronicles descriptions, most of them along the *ceques*, the ritual lines of demarcation and procession.[5]

The image of the Virgin as the mountain is evident in those works that actually describe her as or in the mountain. One of the best known paintings—a striking example of illustrating the Virgin as the mountain, worshiped within the context of a royal Inca and Christian presence—comes from Alto Peru. In *La Virgen María con el Cerro de Potosí* (The Virgin Mary with the Mountain of Potosiama), the face and hands of the Virgin are actually within the conical shape of the mountain of Potosí. In the celestial level above, God the Father, Jesus Christ, and the Holy Ghost hold a crown over the mountain peak (her head). Within her mountain/gown are roads, trees, and animals, with native people going about their daily activities. The native people are totally integrated within the landscape beneath the protection of the mountain. The landscape is transformed into a ritual of humankind and nature.

The landscape of the Andes is seldom hospitable. The mountainous areas are rocky and prohibitive. Rocks are part of the sacred landscape of the mountains, their villages, and the *wak'as* of special significance.[6] The *Our Lady of Cocharcas under the Baldachim* is portrayed as a statue on a pedestal. She holds a bent candle, a particularly distinct Andean object associated with the devotion to the miraculous statue of the Virgin of Cocharcas, a village in the province of Andahuaylas near Ayacucho. This is an Andean interpretation of the European veneration of the Virgin of Candlemas. The uniqueness of the landscape and the details that surround her are characteristic of the Cuzco School and their pantheistic love of nature with its flowers and birds, the creations of Pachamama. The compatibility of man and nature is dependent on the beneficence of Mother Earth. The Virgin Mary is intimately identified with the Andean countryside in paintings of numerous titles with mountain-shaped dresses and flora, fauna, and local identities, which are distinctly Andean, not Spanish.

[Anonymous], *The Virgin Mary of the Mountain of Potasiama*, oil on canvas, eighteenth century. © Casa Nacional de la Moneda, Potosí, Bolivia.

4. Robert Randall, "La Lengua Sagrada," *Alppanchis* XIX, no. 29–30 (1987): 267.

5. See John Howland Rowe, "Inca Culture at the Time of the Spanish Conquest," in Julian H. Steward, ed., *Handbook of South American Indians* (Washington, D.C.: Smithsonian Institution Press, 1946), vol. 2, 183–230; Michael J. Sallnow, *Pilgrims of the Andes* (Washington, D.C.: Smithsonian Institution Press, 1987); and R. Tom Zuidema, *The Ceque System of Cusco: The Social Organization of the Capital of the Inca* (Leiden: E. J. Brill, 1964). These three works describe the *ceque* system.

6. A *wak'a* (*huaca*) is a native Andean god; a sacred being or spirit, often thought of as an ancestor. It can be materialized in a multitude of forms, such as hills, caves, mountains, rocks, and mummies, and is now associated with the archaeological artifacts of the Andes.

THE ICONIC SYNCRETISM

Throughout Latin America, there are images associated with particular places and miraculous events, many of them originating in Spain, and with their arrival in the Americas, they took on new meaning. One of the most popular and recognizable of these is the Virgin of Guadalupe, associated with Mexican indigenous lore, but revered in the Andes as well. Devotion to the Virgin became official in 1757, when she was declared

[Anonymous], *Our Lady of Cocharcas under the Baldachin*, oil on canvas, School of Cuzco, Peru, c. 1765. © Brooklyn Museum of Art, New York.

patroness of all Spanish dominions in the New World. According to ancient records, it was in December 1531 that the Virgin of Guadalupe appeared to a poor Indian at Tepeyac, a sacred hill northwest of Mexico City, which held the sacred shrine dedicated to Tonantzin, the Mother Goddess of the Mexica.[7] The catastrophic flood of 1629 in Mexico City—and the intervention of the Virgin of Guadalupe who "rescued" the city from destruction—strengthened her importance. For the Inca descendent Guamán Poma, the apparition of the Virgin took place "for the benefit of the Indians"; at the same time, the miracle became a symbol of the importance and grandeur of the city. This double function can be read in the famous anonymous painting, today conserved in the Basilica of Guadalupe in Mexico City and titled *Traslado de la imagén de la Virgen de Guadalupe a la primera ermita y primer milagro* (The transportation of the image of the Virgin of Guadalupe to the first hermitage and the first miracle).[8]

This concept of "oneness" with the land is also symbolized in images of the Virgin of the Pilgrims from Cuzco. They wear shepherd's hats and are dressed in gowns profusely decorated with flowers. For the Spaniards, the broad-brimmed shepherd's hat also relates ideologically to the Virgin as La Divina Peregrina (Sacred Pilgrim) and La Virgen de Mercedes (Virgin of Mercy). Both of these concepts can also be easily related to the conquered and displaced people of the Andes. Sacred pilgrimage is an essential aspect of Andean religion. The people make pilgrimage journeys to sacred locations—mountains, rocks, or caves—to pay tribute to the nature spirits who dwell there and leave offerings while pledging their servitude to the spirit of the land. The Virgin of Mercy combines all of these elements: she is agricultural protectress, pilgrim, and humble servant. She wears a dress that is a tapestry of floral brocade patterns and golden details and borders. In becoming a carpet of flowers and golden jewels, she symbolizes the beneficence of Mother Nature.

The symbolism of the golden objects identified as Inka insignias takes on new meaning in the painting of *Our Lady of the Victory of Malaga* (c.1737) by the indigenous artist Luis Nino. She commemorates a Spanish event but is depicted in the characteristic lavish style of Alto Peru. The Virgin stands beneath an elaborate European Baroque arch decorated in sculptural relief profusely ornamented in patterns of gold. Her crown and radiant halo display the native artist's metallurgical skills. She also wears the flat triangular gown of gold and tapestry brocade tooled in gold-stenciled *estofado* so elaborate that the Christ child is lost in its patterns. The interesting semicircular design on the bottom of her dress contains references to the moon. Its abstract form would appear to have been inspired by the *tumi*, the ceremonial knife of the Inca and pre-Inca peoples. As a decorative device within the patterns of the dress of the Virgin of Malaga, the *tumi* relates to the moon and to Mary as the victorious Queen of Heaven and Queen of the Andes. When the form of the *tumi* is turned upside down, it resembles a flower bud, specifically of the *ñukchu lily*, the sacred flower of the Inca. The compressed, flat patterning of the entire arrangement of figure and decorative devices reveals other solar forms including the radiant aureole behind her crown and the semicircular, crescent form above her shoulders. Within the masterful application of gold leaf and *estofado* patterns, the artist repeats the circular and semicircular forms of the moon to produce a composition of great elegance and complexity

7. Stafford Poole, *Our Lady of Guadalupe: The Origins and Sources of a Mexican National Symbol, 1531–1797* (Tucson: University of Arizona Press, 1995). The Aztecs were also called "Mexicas" from the mystical name of Lake Texcoco.

8. Felipe Guamán Poma de Ayala, *El primer nueva corónica y buen gobierno* [1615], critical edition by John V. Murra and Rolena Adorno (Mexico City: Siglo Veintiuno, 1988). Also see the integral facsimile version at http://www.kb.dk/elib/mss/poma/.

[Anonymous], *Our Lady of Lake Titicaca*, oil on canvas, School of Cuzco, Peru, eighteenth century. © Private collection,

[Anonymous], *The Transportation of the Image of the Virgin of Guadalupe to the First Hermitage and First Miracle*, oil on canvas, Mexico, c. 1650. © Museo de la Basilica de Guadalupe, Mexico.

9. See the illustration on page 59.

that is as much a tribute to Mary as it is to Coya, the Inca queen. Her association with the moon is also significant and descended from European imagery based on the Immaculate Conception and her apocalyptic references.

Our Lady of the Victory of Malaga is but one interpretation of Mary's connection with the symbolism of the moon. Her image is more often conflated with lunar imagery than any other and her presence on or floating above a crescent moon appears in statuary as well as in paintings, and as elegant European derivations as well as indigenous interpretations. In Quito, the most important school of sculpture artists produced the most remarkable of these images. The statues were objects of devotion found in churches and private chapels; statue paintings abound throughout the Americas and take on numerous shapes, especially because they replicated the mountain and could act as hiding places for indigenous fetishes. As such, their iconography became increasingly complex and identified with costumes and the ancient rituals of dressing.⁹

The first Catholic parish was established in Cuzco in the sixteenth century and was dedicated to the Virgin of Bethlehem, who the people affectionately call *La Mamacha Belén* (The mother Belén). She is represented in Cuzco paintings with the baby Jesus and as a royal, queenly figure. Surrounded by cherubs, angels, and saints, she wears a crown and holds a royal scepter in her right hand, the symbol of authority. The baby Jesus, dressed in an identical bell-shaped gown and crown, disappears amid the elaborate patterns of its brocade. The regularity of the floral/brocade pattern is unique to the Cuzco School in its geometric stylization, reminiscent of the *tocapu* patterns of Inca textile design. Flat patterning is distinctive of the Cuzco School and of the two-dimensional planar tendencies of pre-Hispanic art in the Andes. The decorative flat-relief designs resemble the relief work on ancient temples and idols in the complexity of its patterns. The Andean artist may have attempted to imitate European techniques of stylization for the representation of his Andean/Christian goddess, but not to the exclusion of his own heritage of visual signs and symbols. Knowledge was conveyed through these signs. The arrangement of patterns, the positioning of objects, the sign of the new moon—all contribute to the image as more than what appears as a stiff, archaic representation of the Virgin and Child.

To view the image of the Virgin Mary as part of the structure of ideological sign systems of Andean ritual objects imparts new meaning to its form and function. The earliest Andean artifacts reveal that the people had used certain iconographic traits—including appendages, fangs, wings, circles, and vegetation—to describe the idols of ancient ritual. Subsequent culture areas included these distinctive elements in their own ritual iconography, while developing their own regional variants. Finally, the Inca appropriated specific Andean symbols and developed their own vocabulary of ritual iconography. The language of Andean ritual was thus well established by the time of the arrival of the Spanish. The native artists continued to maintain its efficacy by incorporating it into Christian imagery.

For example, the dress of the Virgin Mary is often decorated with elaborate brocade patterns that are reminiscent of Inca *tocapus*, the symbolic glyphs that indicate a hierarchical reference to the elites in Inca society. Although no clear decipherment of these signs and symbols has been made, it is safe to assume that the symbols portray more than mere decorative values. Felipe Guaman Poma de Ayala (c. 1613–15) illustrated the headpieces and shields of authority as well as 150 designs of circles, triangles, dots, and Zs embroidered on the garments of the Inca nobility in his effort to identify and preserve the distinctive traits associated with the heritage of the Inca.

[Anonymous], *The Virgin of Mercy*, oil on canvas, School of Cuzco, Peru, eighteenth century. © Collection Ronna Hope Katzin, Fort Lauderdale, Florida.

The tendency to abstraction found so frequently in the shapes and designs on the dress of the Virgin is found in Poma's drawings and reappears in an ideogram from the text of Don Juan de Santacruz Pachacuti-yamqui, a design especially significant to a discussion of sacred landscapes and cityscapes. The Virgin stands between two trees that represent the mother and father of Manco Ccapac, the first Inca, with the fruit of the trees symbolizing future generations of Incas. The three squares are the "emblems of the house of his fathers whence he descended."[10] The central one is inscribed with a rhomboid surrounded by four circles (Tawantinsuyu, Empire of the Four Quarters). In the center of the rhomboid there is another square with a circle, which may be the symbol for the city of Cuzco itself. The circle would be the symbol of the Temple of the Sun from which the *ceques* radiate.

Images of the Virgin and Child are particularly endearing to the people of Latin America. Her representation as a sentimental and maternal queenly figure adorned with flowers and jewels elevates the Virgin to that of a queen and the Child becomes a miniature king. She may hold lilies (Christian symbols of purity and the flower of the Virgin), the rosary, and/or a candle. Both the Virgin and Child always wear elaborate brocade dresses, often with garlands of pearls secured by jeweled flower broaches. The swags of pearls are characteristic of the *Virgin of the Rosary of Pomata*. Pearls were Spanish symbols of perfection, greatly admired as jewels of great beauty and luxury. They were also prized ornaments for Andean idols dressed by pre-Hispanic coastal peoples and were buried in elite tombs as accompaniments to the mummies.

The *Virgin of the Rosary of Pomata* combines a number of interesting iconographic attributes: jewels, a mountain-shaped gown, and, quite distinctively, feathers. The use of feathers in images of the Virgin Mary was unique to Cuzco. They were particularly associated with the Virgin of Pomata and can be found in her crown and that of the Child Jesus. The original meanings of the use of feathers are important to the understanding of the cultural content of the Cuzco School. Regarding the Spanish contribution, there are

10. Juan de Santacruz Pachacuti-yamqui, "An Account of the Antiquities of Peru" (c. 1620), in Clements R. Markham, ed., *Narratives of the Rites and Laws of the Yncas*, (London: Hakluyt Society, 1873), 77.

Illustration in text:
Don Juan de Santacruz Pachacuti-yamqui, c. 1620. Drawing from Juan de Santacruz Pachacuti-yamqui, "An Account of the Antiquities of Peru" (c. 1620), in Clements R. Markham, ed., *Narratives of the Rites and Laws of the Yncas* (London: Hakluyt Society, 1873).

Spanish images of the Virgin of the Pilgrims wearing a wide-brimmed felt hat with a feather, in the European style of pilgrimage hats; moreover, feathers may have been worn in the hats of the conquistadors. On the other hand, while feathered crowns are not found in the royal iconography associated with the Virgin as Queen of Heaven in European representations, it is significant to note that feathers were long associated with ritual objects in the Andes and represent royalty in Inca iconography.

The Virgin of the Andes relates to the spirits of the mountains. Added to the mountainous shape of her dress, the feathers also place her in a royal Inca context, affirming the Inca appropriation of Earth Mother for their own aggrandizement. Birds, flowers, the mountains, and bounty of the Earth are all associated with the symbolism of the sacred landscape. The significance of Mary as an Andean deity only reinforced the love of the native peoples for the Christian Virgin and for nature. She became the synthesis of all that they adored.   ■

[Anonymous], *Virgin of Bethlehem*, oil on canvas, School of Cuzco, Peru, eighteenth century. © Banco de Crédito del Perú, Lima, Peru.

[Anonymous], *Virgin of the Rosary of Pomata*, oil on canvas, School of Cuzco, Peru, eighteenth century. © Convento de Santa Catalina, Cuzco, Peru.

WRITING AND CITIES

EDUARDO SUBIRATS

One of the most extraordinary introductions to the history of Latin American architecture is given in a book that, while it cannot be considered a history book, does not deal with architecture either. It deals with the peculiar social and political condition of intellectuals in this geopolitical region. The book is entitled *La Ciudad Letrada* (The lettered city), and its author was one of the most distinguished Latin American literary critics of the twentieth century, Angel Rama.[1]

"Lettered," in the literal sense of the word, means a cultivated person, educated in the humanities. However, it would be wrong to mistake the circumstances that surround this literary and political character, which originated in the Iberian cultural universe, with the humanistic tradition related to the modern concept of *homme de lettres*. In the Castilian and Spanish American language, "lettered" predominantly means lawyer, or one with a degree in law; it means "a person of law." In the Latin American context, it also implies a long-established, dusty colonial institution. It summarizes the identity of writing and power in the legal and theological system of colonization. Hernán Cortés legitimized his conquest of Tenochtitlán by being a Christian of clear lineage and a virtuous hero, but also as a "lettered" man. The political administration in viceroyalty was thus mainly a task for *letrados*.

The modern Latin American writer and intellectual that Rama examined in his essay of literary critique is an heir of this colonial legacy: someone who considers literary activity as the institutional power inextricably linked to the traditional practice of writing. However, Rama refers to a *ciudad letrada*—a "lettered city"— and this concept may be considered as an allusion to the city as literary Parnassus, as community of men and women devoted to literature. This is not so. The "lettered city" is rather the city conceived according to the rigor of writing; the city inexorably built according to the writing of law; cities planned according to rules, aims, and means laid out in written form by the colonial power; and cities constructed as legal, theological, and architectural devices adapted to the conversion needs of the indigenous, dispossessed, and rootless mass, to their mobilization as slave and semi-slave labor, and to their administrative and ecclesiastical control. Such cities have a rectangular layout, with absolutely straight streets, rigidly structured around a central square that organizes and represents in its architecture the legal and political systems of Monarchy and Church. These are cities such as colonial Mexico City, Oaxaca, or Lima.

These features of Baroque colonial cities also share a central aspect of Latin American cities of the twentieth century. They define axiomatically the post-colonial metropolis under their function of mobilizing

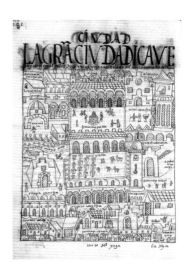

Felipe Guaman Poma de Ayala, *Cuzco*, 1615, Peru. From: Guamán Poma de Ayala, *Primer nueva coronica i buen gobierno*, manuscript at the Copenhagen Royal Library. © Copenhagen Royal Library.

1. Angel Rama, *The Lettered City* (Durham: Duke University Press), 1996.

Left page:
Oscar Niemeyer, Ministries under construction, 1958–60, Brasilia. Photo Marcel Gautherot. © Institut Moreira Salles, São Paulo.

Stone of the Twelve Angles, wall of the former palace of Inka Rocca (Hatun Rumiyoc), Cuzco. Photo César Paternosto. From *The Stone and the Thread: The Andean Roots of Abstract Art* (Austin: University of Texas Press, 1996).

2. William Niño Araque, "Villanueva, Momentos de lo Moderno," in *Carlos Raúl Villanueva: Un moderno en Sudamérica* (Caracas: Galería de Arte Nacional, 1999), 23ff.

3. See Stefan Zweig, *Brazil: A Land of the Future* (Riverside, CA: Ariadne Press, 2000). The *bandeirantes* were gangs of colonists from the São Paulo region who continuously crisscrossed the inland territories of Brazil in search for riches (cattle, gold, slaves, etc.). Their dynamic culture of brutality and plunder is said to be, paradoxically, at the roots of the entrepreneurial spirit of the modern São Paulo and citizens, *paulistas*. *Sertão* is the Brazilian term for the deep interior of the country.

4. On Brasilia see for instance: Norma Evenson, *Two Brazilian Capitals: Architecture and Urbanism in Rio de Janeiro and Brasília* (New Haven: Yale University Press, 1973); James Holston, *The Modernist City: an Anthropological Critique of Brasilia* (Chicago: University of Chicago Press, 1989).

the industrial and post-industrial mass of people and goods. They show a conception of space subordinated to global and local administrative and economical imperatives. Last but not least, this historical perspective of colonial cities inside the modern metropolis allows us to discern some profound aspects of the so-called urban and architectural utopia of Latin America in the twentieth century.

The most eloquent expression of these modern urban projects in Latin America is Brasilia, the federal capital politically conceived by Juscelino Kubistchek, and designed by Lúcio Costa, Burle Marx, and Oscar Niemeyer. Less than fifty years after its foundation, the planned city of Brasilia now functions as a "historic center," which is now threatened by chaotic and unplanned expansion. Other "new" cities like Belo Horizonte in Brazil (planned in 1894 and inaugurated in 1897) or Monterrey (a village until the 1880s and now the third largest city in Mexico) expand constantly, like most Latin American cities, with no real pattern or plan. Yet, there is, at least, one more and equally impressive example of a political capital that fulfilled the criteria dictated by the European modern movement under the different Latin American environmental and political conditions: the projects of Carlos Raúl Villanueva for Caracas. The synthesis of formal rationalism and Baroque plasticity, classicism and functionalism of its architecture and urban interventions constitutes a model of classical proportions. However, Villanueva's architecture is deeply entrenched in local cultures; it is inserted in a city that already possessed its own social and architectural history. If this was not enough, this architecture and urbanism show a reflective relationship with the social, historical, and physical reality of Caracas.[2]

On the contrary, Brasilia reveals in a pure state the convergence of the industrial rationality of European modernism at the beginning of the twentieth century and the characteristics of the Latin American colonial and post-colonial cultures. Its political project was a penultimate heroic deed of the conquering spirit of the *bandeirantes*. It is an example of an industrial civilization abruptly inserted within the wild *sertão*.[3] Its layout, its legal and urban structure follow the basic patterns of the Iberian colonial city: a geometrical order of the city in the middle of nowhere, with a mixture of military rigidity and missionary rationality that already subjugated the Baroque architects. In terms of organization and performance Brasilia is the reflection of the secularized ideas of colonial mercantilism and salvationism transferred first to the modern, secular, and positivist discourse of "order and progress" and, secondly, reformatted under the stylistic concepts of the international functionalism of the postwar decades. It is an ideal space, an abstract and complex design, projected according to the bureaucratic rationality of a city-state that was politically conceived as a machine of gigantic proportions aimed at the undefined exploration and exploitation of natural and human resources of a virtually unlimited national territory. Brasilia is an archetype of the "lettered city."[4]

Whether they are colonial capitals founded upon fair laws or modern cities with a functional layout, one can only understand the whole civilizing magnificence of these lettered cities if one contemplates their reverse side. The reverse side of colonial cities is the massive destruction of the symbolic and urban order of civilizations and old American cities, the systematic plundering of their resources and the consequent liberation of a massive slave labor force. The reverse side of the post-colonial megalopolis is the human mass symbolically hybridized and socially disintegrated that is extended without boundaries along the infra-urban periphery. The reverse side of cities founded by writing and law encompasses the unnamed massive

Lúcio Costa, Night view of the central axis of Brasilia, 1958–60. Photo Marcel Gautherot. © Institut Moreira Salles, São Paulo.

settlements—*favelas, ranchos*—that are currently populated by most of the economically, environmentally, and militarily displaced people of Latin America.

These dehumanized suburbs continue to expand as a material refutation of the colonial and modern civilizing dreams. Yet, as at the time of the Conquest, there have been powerful reasons to deny their existence or ignore them as false problems. From the perspective of the colonial rationality, outside or before the legal "order of writing," there was only the dark kingdom of an age with no history, of cities with neither name nor law. It was a sort of arbitrary universe vaguely mistaken for a diabolic state of nature or for an "empty continent."[5] Therefore, the foundational condition of the American colonial city built more geometrically was a geographically and culturally empty space, with neither past nor memories. If this space was not effectively populated, it was emptied and militarily evacuated until it was reduced to virtually nothing. The old Lima is an example of a city built on a deserted moor. Mexico was a city built on the ashes of Tenochtitlán. All modern cities, with no exception, are based on one of these two principles. Brasilia is but one example. Its layout is extended along the infinite and empty horizon of the *sertão*. But its foundation was preceded by the destruction of the *cerrado* forest and the eradication of the indigenous settlements that populated it.[6]

This destructive principle is both functional and symbolic. It enables the installation of technical and urban tools of civilization and modernity as if they came from heaven. At the same time, it excludes and hides its devastating human and environmental consequences. Its contemporary urban and architectural expression are the *favelas*, the shantytowns, and other areas of subhuman infra-habitation and suburban territorial

5. Eduardo Subirats, *El continente vacío: la conquista del Nuevo Mondo y la conciencia moderna* (Madrid: ANAYA and Mario Muchnik, 1994). Also see Joaquín Torres Garcia, *La ciudad sin nombre* (Montevideo: Sur, 1941).

6. The *cerrado* is a type of vegetation in central Brazil, characterized by dense low trees and a gramineous soil.

occupation generated by successive waves of indigenous, African, and mixed-race crowds to the center of industrial production, through a continuous process that started with the gold and silver mines of Potosí and keeps renewing itself in the *maquilas* (factories) of Tijuana, Mexico.

RATIONALITY AND SENSUALITY OF FORMS AND SPACES

The American colonial city did not incarnate only the written order of the law. The writing was not just the means of an alienated and alienating power. It was also a sacred writing. It meant the book, the Gospel. It represented the symbolic and spiritual order of a messianic hope. This transcending promise of salvation was also reflected in the urban order of the city, and in the theological and architectural design of the church that crowned it as its spiritual center. It was constructively laid out as a functional and rational instrument of concentration and vigilance of the converted and colonized indigenous population. However, as time went by, it also became a Baroque church. It was a church conceived as a space, at once imaginary and marvelous. Its architecture was elevated as the sublime spectacle of the miraculous and mystic transfiguration of human existence, of the suppression and overcoming of the terrestrial contingencies of the city in a virtual kingdom of the redeemed. It was a sensually dynamic space, full of ornaments, inhabited by voluptuous angels and virgins, intoxicated by sacred voices and music, inebriated with incense and color. It was an architecture that crowned the functional order of the colonial city as the representation of the City of God.

The Baroque mysticism, sensuality, and sense of spectacle provided American capitals and colonial cultures with a specific and unmistakable character. In the post-colonial age these Baroque and neo-Baroque aesthetics were largely extended in poetry and architecture under multiple variations and names, in the full sense of a national identity. The same messianic transcendence, a sensuality of similar characteristics, and the same fascination for performance distinguish many of the most remarkable examples of literary, plastic, and architectural modernism. In the modern and secular city, the representation of transcendence and glory adopted the classical and enlightened criteria of arts and humanities. The colonial city as representation of divine order was transformed into the modern spectacle of civilization.

Brasilia also constitutes a great paradigm in this respect. Its "Pilot Plan"—conceived by Lúcio Costa in 1957—did not just include its monumental avenue punctuated by the never-ending uniformed and monotonous parade of prismatic ministries, built "à la Le Corbusier."[7] It did not just end in the archaic icons of power and death—its pyramid and its dome, its antenna-obelisk or its mausoleum—inspired by the classicist models of imperial cities of Europe and United States. Brasilia is, on the one hand, an expression of functionality born in the German expressionist ateliers, in the Bauhaus, and in the Cartesian features of Le Corbusier, adapted to the geographic amplitude and administrative imperatives of colonial expansion and modern industrialism. On the other hand, it is the combination of this colonial functionality with the sensual and mystic rhythms of the bossa nova, of the African religious and artistic expressions of Bahía and Rio de Janeiro, of the formal purity that distinguishes the architectural spaces and the design of pre-colonial Amazonian cultures, and the plasticity of samba. Lúcio Costa repeatedly said, at the end of his life, that Brasilia was a "romantic city." It is indeed a carnival fantasy, a glass and concrete chimera, a city of dreams. It is where, one day, politics met poetry, under the popular clamor of a national democratic celebration.

Here I would like to posit a hermeneutical reading that tries to understand the artistic and architectural work from its functional integration in a civilizing process, either colonial or post-colonial, either modern or post-modern. But, at the same time, it is an aesthetic interpretation. It is a reading that apprehends the artistic work according to its formal and expressive intentions, and to its spiritual transcendence. As a consequence, it tries to assimilate this transcendence into a virtual kingdom of beauty that the Baroque age formulated through the architectural, poetic, and musical representation of a divine city in another world and that the modern secular spirit has suggested as Ideal City (città ideale) and as space of social transformation.

In the friezes and griffins of Baroque Mexican facades, for example, one can detect an identifiable writing, inserted in the *Mudejar* tradition of the Spanish Baroque, which gave the virtuous Nahuatl or Mayan architects and craftsmen the possibility to express their own conception of space and sometimes even show

7. See A. Buchmann, *Lúcio Costa: o inventor da cidade da Brasília, centenário de nascimento* (Brasília: Thesaurus Editora, 2002). Brasilia was inaugurated in 1960.

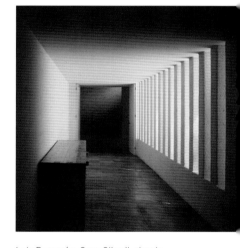

Luis Barragán, Casa Gilardi, view in direction of the pool, Mexico City, 1975–77. Photo Armando Salas Portugal. © Fondation Barragán, Birsfelden.

Alberto da Veiga Guignard, *Imaginary Landscape*, oil on canvas, 1950. © Collection Angela Gutiérrez, all rights reserved. Guignard painted the landscape of Ouro Preto (Minais Gerais) and its Baroque eighteenth-century churches in a style that recalls the expressionist abstraction of Torres García and Xul Solar.

pictographic elements that belonged to their destroyed artistic heritage. The spiritual and transcendent value of this Baroque ornament cannot be separated from the details of the artistic form, even or precisely within its most individual expressive aspects. The kinetic reiteration of geometrical patterns or the multicolor vibrancy that the ornamented facades of Taxco and Zacatecas exert on our retina—these bodily sensations tell us more about the works than the academic interpretation of linguistic moments and technical means.

Likewise, in front of such modern architecture as the Rufino Tamayo Museum (1981), designed by Teodoro González de Léon and Abraham Zabludowsky in Mexico City, we immediately recognize the abstract and intensively dynamic language that has characterized, among others, the great architecture of German expressionism, from Erich Mendelsohn to Bruno Taut and Hans Scharoun.[8] Yet the proportioned monumentality of the staircases of the Tamayo Museum, its inclined planes that limit outer space and, at the same time, lead us to ramps and inner spaces, its geometrical flights and its massive volumes, all transport us immediately to the clear geometrical surfaces, the ramps and staircases, of ceremonial Aztec or Zapotec architecture. The aesthetic pleasure that accompanies our physical movement through the inner spaces of this museum becomes more intense inasmuch as it allows us to circulate in the middle of spaces, symbols, and memories of different ages and cultures.

The religious architecture of the Minas Gerais in Brazil was a recreation of the Baroque models of the Counter-Reformation in Rome. However, the real surprise comes from its orchestration in an exuberant landscape of soft hills on whose summits their crystalline plans and elevations are set like perfect diamonds, silhouetted as counterpoints to the rural horizons of the high mountain ranges of the region. The inner spaces of these churches, which rarely fail to convey the sense of welcome and community particular to the evangelic cults, are equally surprising. A great deal of their ornaments, paintings, and sculptures is

8. Paul Heyer et al., *Mexican Architecture: The Work of Abraham Zabludovsky and González de León* (New York: Walker and Co, 1978).

the work of popular artists, mostly anonymous, who left in geometrical volumes and in the deeply expressive forms of their carvings, the mark of African artistic traditions that arrived in Brazil with slave trafficking. The rough textures of old wood, the whitewashing and the mosaics, the vibrant shine of gold and the strong color contrasts provide these inner realms with a secret mystic atmosphere, related to the African religious cults that borrowed the Catholic liturgy of the Baroque.[9]

This spiritual appropriation and the consequent transformation of space, sculpture, and painting that it entails, explains the ideal adaptation of these Baroque churches to the popular culture of towns such as Salvador de Bahía or Ouro Preto.

The same process of recreation, synthesis, and linguistic transformation distinguishes the great modern architectural works of Latin America. Luis Barragán is one of the important names that must be mentioned in this context. His characteristic orthogonal spaces, his virtuous orchestration of filled and empty volumes, the constructive use of color in big, rectangular, carved surfaces, and the enclosure of vegetal forms under the strict aesthetic order of plans and elevations, are usually interpreted as Mexican variations of the aesthetical program of the European neoplasticism. Yet the great mural surfaces, free from ornaments, also constitute a distinct feature of Catholic monastic architecture. Barragán himself referred to his fascination for the never-ending walls of convents in Spanish medieval towns. Likewise, the orthogonal organization of space, the geometrical construction according to strict numeric codes, and the empty volumes are common features of pre-colonial monasteries. Undoubtedly, Barragán managed a difficult negotiation between the different symbolic meanings that the right angle, the numeric proportions, and the geometrical plans have had in the Zapotec mysticism, in the Christian monastic discipline, and in the Cartesian asceticism of painter Piet Mondrian and architect Jacobus Johannes Pieter Oud. The experience of quietness, concentration, and inner rigor that, at times, as for his example in his own house, reaches an oppressive extent, cannot be separated from these cultural memories.

Just to add another distinguished example, the original borrowing of international styles and the free-willed transfiguration of its rationalist languages in forms and spaces of exalted dynamics and sensuality is shown in one of the most flamboyant and constructive elements of modern Brazilian architecture: staircases. No one who has visited the Itamaraty Palace (1959–67), an architectural jewel of Brasilia by Oscar Niemeyer and Roberto Burle Marx, can forget the generous and elegant proportions, the powerful ascending movement, and the lightness of its central staircase. Before one touches the first step, one feels visually transported upward. Once again, we find here a Baroque feature that appears in a series of very well-known and celebrated staircases in seventeenth- and eighteenth-century Roman palaces. But the staircases also represent a modern feature that appears at its best in the Parque Güell (1900–14) of Antonio Gaudí, or in the Salzburg Festspielhaus (1920) project by Hans Poelzig, in the Glasshaus (1914) by Bruno Taut, and always with an emphatic iconographic meaning. From an aesthetic viewpoint, the staircase is a dynamic element of space transformation. Its symbolic function is to suspend gravity and transform constructive material in ascending movement and energy. Beginning with the biblical texts, the staircase has been one of the most important mystic symbols.

The monumental hall of Itamaraty is symbolically defined by the presence of earth and water that unite, without discontinuity, the outer and inner space of the palace. The staircases are the mediation between

9. See Edward Sullivan, *Brazil: Body and Soul* (New York: Guggenheim Museum, 2001); Damían Bayón, *History of South American Colonial Art and Architecture: Spanish South America and Brazil* (New York: Rizzoli, 1992). On Baroque interiors, see for instance Lúcio Costa's sketch of Diamantina (page 39).

Lina Bo Bardi, Poster for the film *Bahía of all Saints* (Bahía de todos os santos, José Hipolito Trigueirinho Neto, 1960), 1960. © Instituto Lina Bo e P.M. Bardi, São Paulo.

Church of Bom Jésus de Matosinhos with the statues of the twelve prophets by Brazilian sculptor Aleijadinho, 1800–5, Congonhas, Minas Gerais, Brazil. Photo Marcel Gautherot. © Institut Moreira Salles, São Paulo.

these elements and the grand hall upstairs; however, here this central and upper space of the palace is not a room but an open patio and a hanging garden. It is Niemeyer's legendary quotation of the Babylonian gardens. In its design, Roberto Burle Marx drew a subtle dialogue between the sensuality of Arabic gardens and the hermetic order of the Japanese landscape. But, in fact, this hanging garden is a celebration of the Amazonian exuberance.

In the Museu de Arte Moderna in Rio (Affonso Eduardo Reidy, 1953–68), the staircase also plays an exciting role. It breaks, with its spiral ascending movement, the aesthetic rigidity of the Modulor, to which young Brazilian architecture paid tribute more for the freedom of movement that it allowed than for the industrial intransigence that it tried to impose. Reidy conceived these stairs, divided into a sensually curved segment and a segment of rigorous orthogonal rhythms, as a path of initiation toward the kingdom of beauty—the theme of the museum. Another staircase, by João Vilanova Artigas and this time built like the immense ascending ramps of the pre-colonial American monumental architecture, assumes a central role in the School of Architecture and Urbanism of the University of São Paulo (1961). Such a ramp—the architects of the city always say—was to be used by the gods!

Finally, I would like to remember the time when Lina Bo Bardi showed me, with a mixture of modesty and naughtiness, a note signed by Niemeyer's own hand in which he thanked her with lovely words for her marvelous staircase in the Solar de Unhão, the colonial wharf for slave trafficking in Salvador de Bahía, which she transformed into a museum of popular culture and a place of memory.[10]

SOCIAL, ECOLOGICAL, AND IDENTITY CRISES

Bo Bardi liked to communicate the immense happiness that signaled her arrival in Brazil. She spoke with enthusiasm about its exuberant landscapes and the fascination that she immediately felt for its expressions of popular culture. She confessed willingly how she was seduced by the expressive freedom of the young architects that she met at the beginning of her new life: Niemeyer, Burle Marx, Reidy, Levi, Vilanova Artigas, and others. That freedom tied her definitively to Brazil. Bo Bardi told me that she left post-fascist Italy with two "bags." The first was the architecture of European avant-garde before World War II, under whose spirit she had been trained. The second was a deception. Despite or due to her experience of fascism, Bo Bardi believed in the urgency to reconsider that willingness of rupture and renovation that had inspired European artists and intellectuals of the Gropius generation, of German expressionism, and the first years of Italian futurism. But in the immediate postwar Europe the young architect did not feel the freedom that was essential to generate a project that would truly rejuvenate society or to articulate a new architecture. "Brazil gave me that freedom," she always said. And she underlined it with the awareness of the immense obstacles that she had encountered in her career, from the tanks used by the incoming military dictatorship to shut down her exhibition of popular art in Bahía (April 1964) to the usual mediocrity of the academic world.

However, Bo Bardi's architecture did not only grow within the context of Brazilian architectural expressionism represented by Reidy, Niemeyer, Vilanova Artigas, or Mendes da Rocha. Her architectonic and formal language can only be understood by taking into account her proximity to Brazilian popular cultures and memories and, particularly, the African spiritual universe of Bahía. Likewise, her work is a direct reflection of her close friendship with the intellectual and artistic bohemia that materialized in the *Vanguardia Tropicalista* of its capital, Salvador de Bahía and included such remarkable names as film director Glauber Rocha, singer Caetano Veloso, poet and songwriter Waly Salomão, and poet and anthropologist Antonio Riserio.[11] She used to describe Latin America as a cultural family characterized by a poetic and socially innovative imagination, an architecture integrated into popular expressions, and a "free" intelligence. In contrast to this sensual world, what suffocated her in postwar European and North American architecture and in its succession of "neo-styles" and "post-movements" was its trivial identification with technological and political power, its childish obedience to market rules, its empty formalism.

It is important to underscore these particular circumstances, as they suggest how and why innovative architectonic proposals from a formal, technological, and civilizing point of view have been generated in Latin America. They help to better understand the critical experiments and models for the present that point toward a better future. I will summarize briefly the significance of these projects in regard to three major concerns of the twenty-first century: environmental destruction, elimination of cultural memories, and the broad phenomenon of social disintegration in the contemporary megalopolis.

10. On Lina Bo Bardi, see Olívia de Oliveira's essay and notes in this book. On Artigas, see João Masao Kamita, *Vilanova Artigas* (São Paulo: Cosac & Naify Edições, 2000). On Niemeyer, see *Oscar Niemeyer: a Legend of Modernism* (Frankfurt/Boston: Birkhäuser, 2003).

11. See Burnes Saint Patrick Hollyman, *Glauber Rocha and the Cinema Nôvo: A Study of his Critical Writings and Films* (New York: Garland, 1983); Caetano Veloso, *Tropical Truth: A Story of Music and Revolution in Brazil* (New York: Alfred A. Knopf, 2002); Antonio Risério, *Avant-garde na Bahía* (São Paulo: Instituto Lina Bo e P. M. Bardi, 1995); and Larry Crook and Randal Johnson, *Black Brazil: Culture, Identity, and Social Mobilization* (Los Angeles: University of California, Los Angeles, 1999).

Detail of a bas-relief of the Temple to the Sun, Palenque, Mexico, 1935. Photo Germaine Wenziner. © Musée Royaux d'Art et d'Histoire, Cinquantenaire, Brussels, no. IAM 87.1.104.

12. On Porto, see Alexander Tzonis and Bruno Stagno, *Tropical Architecture: Critical Regionalism in the Age of Globalization* (New York: Chichester, 2001); and Ricardo Castro, ed., *Rogelio Salmona* (Bogotá: Villegas Editores, 1998).

13. The experimental architectural group Las Gaviotas, in Colombia, is another example of an architecture that responds to this formal, ecological, and social dimension. See their eco-hotel in Marsella, *Escala* vol. 28, no. 168 (1995): 73–75.

14. Rafael López Rangel, *Diego Rivera y la arquitectura mexicana* (Mexico City: Dirección General de Publicaciones y Medios, 1986); *Diego Rivera Museum-Anahuacalli* (Mexico City: Organizing Committee of the Games of the XIX Olympiad, 1970).

Lina Bo Bardi, Museum of Popular Art of Salvador de Bahía, view of the complex of Solar do Unhão with the new square overlooking the sea, 1959. © Instituto Lina Bo e P. M. Bardi, São Paulo.

As for the first theme—the conservation of environmental habitats—two architects, the Brazilian Severiano Porto and the Columbian Rogelio Salmona, must be mentioned.[12] Porto's architecture is particularly relevant in his experiments with construction materials adapted to the surrounding conditions of the Amazonian region. He also developed a series of traditional technologies with modern means and socially and environmentally responsible objectives. Interestingly, Porto's and Salmona's works accommodate these technological and functional innovations under a repertoire of original formal solutions that, at the same time, keep a close dialogue with the traditional architectural languages of the region. Nevertheless, I would like to point out that architectural experiments of forms of habitat and territorial occupation that are socially, culturally, and environmentally friendly, capable of restoring memories, habitats, and traditional forms of life in the areas threatened by post-industrial colonialism, today constitute a wide and diversified trend in all Latin America (particularly in the Amazon and the central states of Mexico). This research includes a wide range of strategies, from the restoration of historical centers and the recovery of old craft traditions, to the development of environmentally sustainable technologies and an innovative formal repertoire.[13] The obstacles encountered by these architects are, of course, considerable. The enormous economic and political power of the construction industry has a tendency to silence and abandon these modern experiences, giving them a marginal place. Furthermore, the architectural critique tends to ignore them because they infringe upon the linguistic boundaries of the corporative fetishism that characterizes the representation of architecture and urbanism within the cultural industry.

The second example is related to the restoration of cultural memories successively threatened by colonization and globalization. In this context one of the most original architectural structures of Latin America comes to mind: the Anahuacalli museum by Diego Rivera and Juan O'Gorman. It is a work relatively unknown by Latin American and international architectural critics. It is, obviously, a highly controversial project. To begin with, it is difficult to erase the sight of this singular monument from one's mind. The building is perceived as an impressive black cubic mass of basalt in the middle of a landscape of volcanic lava. Located in a poor and remote southern suburb of Mexico City, it rises in a gesture of painful solitude. Its expressionist facades offend the visitor, like a cry of agony or a prophetic curse.

The functions of this monument constitute another singular aspect. The Anahuacalli (1944) was conceived as museum and mausoleum at the same time; therefore, it accommodates an important archaeological collection. Its walls are literally filled with beautiful artistic works of pre-Columbian crafts, but they are not exposed under the sterile principle of an archaeological taxonomy and even less with the mercantile intentions of a design exhibition. The objects exhibited in this museum are not quotes of an academically formed memory, but they constitute a testimony of the destruction and death of the pre-colonial Mexican civilizations. The Anahuacalli is a museum that reinterprets the constructive elements of Aztec and Mayan temples. The Anahuacalli is an authentic museum and temple of the holocaust of the historical civilizations of the Americas.[14]

It is a unique building, not only because it is the only one with such a specific intention, but also because it raises the memory of destruction, and, at the same time, the memory of the resistance of the American people to that destruction. Here Diego Rivera and Juan O'Gorman recall the destruction of early American civilization under the affirmative sign of beauty: the beauty of the past, and, here in particular, of Mayan and Aztec pottery. They do so, last but not least, by celebrating the socially responsible modern art that occupies the central and symbolically privileged space of this architecture. The easel of Diego Rivera exhibited in the main hall could not be a more potent icon.

However, apart from these symbolic values, the Anahuacalli fulfills a "manifest" function as a reflection on the architectural form. Both Rivera and O'Gorman criticized the overlapping of international fashions and styles in Latin American towns and cities. They saw as a result of this process the disintegration of the urban footprints of memory and their related collective identities. Both artists attacked the inferiority and mediocrity that was hidden under these sanctioned languages. Instead they defended and defined a concept of architectural form rooted in the reflection of the enclosed cultural memories.[15]

None of these architectonic experiments—whether Diego Rivera's or the previously mentioned works by Porto and Salmona—should be relegated to a "regional" category. First, they are not so clearly grounded in the traditions and lifestyles of local historical communities. Second, and more importantly, the problems they pose—the colonization of historical languages, the destruction of the urban fabric, and the environmental destruction of the cities—are the most global crises that threaten humankind in the twenty-first century. In fact, the technical redefinition of architecture from the point of view of environmental balance and the redefinition of its spaces on the basis of historical languages are closer to the universal categories formulated by Vitruvius or Karl Friedrich Schinkel than the Cartesian intransigence of Le Corbusier or Gerrit Rietveld, and the commercial obsession of postmodernism. Therefore, both architects represent a formal, technical, and civilizing alternative at the same time.

The third and last theme relates to the integration of architecture in the socially, aesthetically, and environmentally degraded urban fabric of the Third World; and, conversely, the integration within the architectonic project of the multiethnic and multicultural wealth that distinguishes these mega-cities. Under this theme I would like to consider the most important urban complex designed by Lina Bo Bardi: the Centro Cultural CESC Pompeia in São Paulo (1977).

Functionally speaking, the center is an entertainment space that accommodates a cultural center, a library, exhibition halls, art galleries, and two theaters. At the formal level, Bo Bardi's project is, as I have already mentioned, the result of several decades of work about expressions of Brazilian popular culture. In this context it is important to underline that her concept of "popular"—and in general what in Latin America is called popular art, music, and culture—are as far from the European fascist populisms of the 1930s as from the industrial elements of North American pop culture. This difference goes back to a partially failed attempt of Christian conversion of the colonized populations, and to an incomplete process of industrial and post-industrial rationalization. Finally, the typological definition of Bo Bardi's cultural center and museum also breaks the classical tradition that defined the museum as a place of trophy, and its contemporary translation into computer-designed architecture, whose aseptic

Diego Rivera and Juan O'Gorman, Anahuacalli Museum, Coyacán, Mexico City, 1944. From *Diego Rivera Museum-Anahuacalli* (Mexico City: Organizing Committee of the Games of the XIX Olympiad, 1970).

15. Ida Rodríguez Prampolini, Olga Sáenz, Elizabeth Fuentes Rojas, eds., *La palabra de Juan O'Gorman* (Mexico City: UNAM, 1983), 136-sq, 204.

Lina Bo Bardi (curator), View of the exhibition NORDESTE Museum of Popular Art of Salvador de Bahía, 1963. © Instituto Lina Bo e P. M. Bardi, São Paulo.

16. See *Cidadela da liberdade* (São Paulo: SESC, Instituto Lina and P. M. Bardi, 1999).

spaces literally seize and sequester works of art under their spiritually dead dimension of fetishist artifact.[16]

To the contrary, the CESC Pompeia is founded on the integration of the popular cultures that have been abruptly displaced from their rural context to the megalopolis and were later marginalized by industry and cultural bureaucracies. To represent this objective, Lina Bo Bardi designed a series of highly meaningful spaces. To begin with, she used the most common architectonic element in the megalopolis of the Third— and of the First—World: the industrial ruins (here a former factory of kerosene barrels). Secondly, she symbolically transformed these spaces of human sacrifice and urban desolation into a play, recreation, and pleasure area. Formally, this transformation takes place under a series of architectural languages that combine rhythms and motives of German expressionism and Italian futurism with traditions of carpentry and construction in exposed brick, citations of industrial engineering, and variations around Latin American traditional culture. Under this polyphony of different languages and spaces there is a dialogue between the popular party and the erudite culture, between the museum as memory place and the public square, between the library and the sport fields. It is something similar to a *Gesamtkunstwerk*, a "total work of art" but without the stilted style that Richard Wagner gave to the term with his operas, and with a transparent social democratic projection.

Night view of São Paulo, 1997. Photo Juca Martins. © Institut Moreira Salles, São Paulo.

THE LETTERED CITY

I would like to conclude with the beginning: the lettered city, the city rationally planned, with a theological hierarchy and invigilated according to a functional and rational rigor. I would like to conclude with the terminal evolution of this lettered city. Nowadays, whether they admit it or not, most Latin Americans live in megalopolises akin to Mexico City or São Paulo that are socially, environmentally, and culturally unsustainable. They contemplate the boundless extensions of highly populated suburban areas, subject to the rigor of infra-poverty and globally planned moral degradation. These are authentic "anti-cities" where the order of law means violence and where the act of writing accompanies a sustained regression to post-human forms of life.

The privileged place of this other writing on cities—or rather the writing of the anti-city—has been the Latin American novel of the twentieth century. It is *El Señor Presidente* by Miguel Angel Asturias, the story of Guatemala beset by violence, corruption, and de-humanization. It is Comala, the city of the dead born in the imagination of Juan Rulfo in his novel *Pedro Páramo*: a town transformed into hell and inhabited by men and women reduced to agonizing specters. It is also the combination of poetic intensity and extreme misery of Chimbote, narrated by Jose Maria Arguedas, an illegal and abandoned suburb in the inhospitable and never-ending periphery of Lima. Or it is a city such as Asunción described by Roa Bastos in *Yo, el Supremo*, a city that crumbles from inside under the effect of despotism and violence.[17] ■

17. Miguel Angel Asturias, *El Señor Presidente* (New York: Atheneum, 1964); Juan Rulfo, *Pedro Páramo* (New York: Grove Press, 1959); Roa Bastos, *I, the Supreme* (New York: Knopf, 1986); José María Arguedas, *El zorro de arriba y el zorro de abajo*, in J.M. Arguedas, *Obras Completas* vol. 5 (Lima: Editorial Horizonte, 1983).

Le Corbusier, New urban structure for Rio de Janeiro, pencil on paper, 1929. © Fondation Le Corbusier.

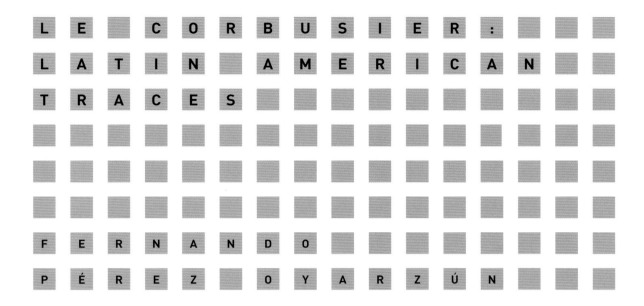

LE CORBUSIER: LATIN AMERICAN TRACES

FERNANDO PÉREZ OYARZÚN

At an early stage in his career, Le Corbusier (1887–1965) perceived that Africa, Asia, or America could offer significant opportunities for his architecture. After achieving worldwide recognition, his failure in international competitions, like those for the Palace of the Nations in Geneva (1927–28) and the Palace of the Soviets in Moscow (1931), restricted the possibilities to test his architectural ideas in the field of large-scale public commissions. In fact, some of those opportunities would not come for him in Europe until the reconstruction process following World War II. Thus, he made continuous and numerous trips around the world to disseminate his architectural ideas and—perhaps more importantly—to attain professional opportunities. But beyond those undisputed pragmatic motivations, travel and contact with remote places offered Le Corbusier a privileged occasion for reflection and for nurturing his sensibility with new materials and ideas. The formative travels of his youth were in some way prolonged by each new significant voyage taken in his maturity. Fernand Léger's advice to the influential historian Paulo Prado to propose Le Corbusier to design a new Brazilian capital in 1926 speaks clearly to the professional aims of his Latin American connections.[1] The enthusiasm that French poet Blaise Cendrars conveyed to him about the continent referred more clearly to the theoretical and artistic ones, but both were frequently mixed and interconnected.[2] The remote and the exotic represented for him both inspiration and professional opportunity.

Latin America seems to have been particularly significant for Le Corbusier in terms of architectural expectations. "Under such light, architecture will be born," he stated at the end of *Précisions sur un état présent de l'architecture et de l'urbanisme*, a book that looked at the continent as a promised land for architecture.[3] South America was able to stimulate his imagination with the power of its geography, as well as a place with enough cultural tradition to understand his classical and poetic approach to modernity, and enough openness to accept his innovations.[4] It was also a place where the need for new institutions and monuments matched the political will or the economic power to bring them about. Time proved those expectations false, but the master's intense activity, including travels, contacts, studies, and projects, lasted for more than three decades, always in the hope of getting significant commissions.

Why did Le Corbusier attribute such an important role to South America, both for himself and for the development of modern architecture? One explanation could come from his personal position among modern architects. He did not feel much at home with either the German group of the Neue Sachlichkeit or

1. Cecilia Rodríguez dos Santos et al., *Le Corbusier e o Brasil* (São Paulo: Tessela projeto, 1987), 41.

2. Le Corbusier, *Précisions sur un état présent de l'architecture et de l'urbanisme* [1930] (Paris: Editions Vincent, Fréal et Cie., 1960), 19–20; in English: *Precisions on the Present State of Architecture and City Planning* (Cambridge: MIT Press, 1991), 19–20.

3. Ibid., 19.

4. Ibid., 245.

Le Corbusier on board the *Lutecia* sailing to Europe, 1929. © Fondation Le Corbusier.

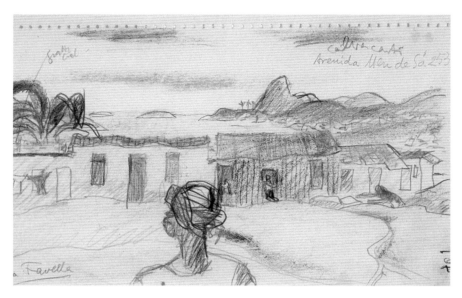

Le Corbusier, Sketch of *favelas*,
pencil on paper, Rio de Janeiro, 1929.
© Fondation Le Corbusier.

with the Soviet architects. North America—which he was already planning to visit—represented for him a more pragmatic position, which privileged "the violence of business and the preeminence of production."[5] The idea of "latinity," which he used to describe South American culture, pointed to something he felt familiar with and which appeared to be receptive to his message.

On the other hand, the first contact Le Corbusier had with South America in 1929 happened at a particular moment of his life. He had reached a stage of maturity in his professional career, expressed in architectural works such as the Villas Stein (1927) and Savoye (1928–29). In his forties, he had already earned a worldwide reputation and the first volume of his *Oeuvre complète* was about to be published; on the personal side he was about to marry Ivonne Gallis. Thus, his first trip to South America is associated with a turning point both in his private life and his career. In architectural terms this would be expressed by the Errazuriz House in Chile, a commission he received in Buenos Aires in 1929, and the first of a series of projects exhibiting a new sensibility toward materials and tradition.[6] This new responsiveness would expand to his drawings and paintings, which would more frequently register human bodies and exotic types.

SOUTH AMERICAN EXPERIENCES

Le Corbusier's journey of 1929 was a major travel experience, lasting a couple of months, which was rather exceptional for him. It inaugurated three decades of contacts that included seven other trips: five to Colombia and two to Brazil, all of which were connected with professional commissions. Travel was always more than a practical opportunity in Le Corbusier's life. It played a formative role in his youth and, to a certain extent, remained important throughout his life. It was a source of commissions and, at the same time, of a vital experience that nurtured his sensibility and imagination. What were those experiences from the 1929 visit that would be prolonged in later voyages and contacts?

One of the main objectives was contacting eventual patrons. They could be enlightened aristocrats and intellectuals like Victoria Ocampo in Argentina, Paulo Prado in Brazil, or Matías Errazuriz, who was living in Buenos Aires as Chilean ambassador to Argentina. They could be politicians, like Minister of Education Gustavo Capanema, who played such an important role in his 1936 Brazilian stay, or the minister Zuleta Angel, whom he met in the U.S. in 1947 and who would be primarily responsible for the commission of the Bogotá plan.[7] But it was also the common people, especially of exotic type, who drew Le Corbusier's attention when he met them in Brazil and in Paraguay. He portrayed them in some of his sketches and spoke about them in the travel notes included in *Précisions*.

Nevertheless, it was his encounters with the geography and the landscape—both man-made and natural—of South America that most deeply affected Le Corbusier's sensibility. The experience of the "natural"—which had been a part of his youth and was now amplified by American magnitude—allowed him to

5. About Le Corbusier's travel to the USA in 1935, see Mardges Bacon, *Le Corbusier in America* (Cambridge: MIT Press, 2001). "Violence des affaires… la production à outrance," *Précisions*, 245.

6. Christiane Crasemann Collins, "Le Corbusier's House Errazuriz. A Conflict of fictive Cultures," *Harvard Architecture Review*, v. 6 (1987): 38–53.

7. Pedro Bannen, "Bogotá-Colombia: Cinco viajes y un plan para una ciudad latinoamericana" in Fernando Pérez Oyarzún, ed., *Le Corbusier y Sudamérica: viajes y proyectos* (Santiago de Chile: Ediciones Arq, 1991), 72–85, and Rodrigo Cortes, "Bogotá 1950, plan director de Le Corbusier," in Oyarzún, *Le Corbusier e Sudamérica*, 86–97.

experience a new version of the "sublime." Some of the most inspired pages of his travel diary are those devoted to the natural landscape. The power and scale of the Argentinean pampas and rivers, the red plateau around São Paulo, and the dancing geography around Rio de Janeiro were enthusiastically described in *Précisions*, and their sheer power of suggestion emphasized by the vision from above. Thanks to the experience of flying, which Le Corbusier enjoyed in Latin America perhaps for the first time in his life, his admiration for the plane—formerly seen as a metaphor for the "well posed problem"—became a real and poetic experience, revealing the less rational side of his personality. This aerial view, with its sense of totality, even inspired him to develop the conceptual "law of the meander" to explain the complexities of the creative process.[8]

It is precisely the impact of this Latin American experience that explains the internal tension within the book *Précisions*, published in 1931. The unusually long series of lectures given in Buenos Aires gave Le Corbusier the opportunity to summarize and evaluate his own thinking, which had not been exposed in such a comprehensive way since *Vers une architecture*, of 1922. This prophetic message, which Le Corbusier brought with him as intellectual baggage in the tempered version of his early maturity, was now confronted by the freshness of his South American experiences. The formative experience of his youth, as described in his *Voyage d'Orient*, deepened during his South American stay, revealing the complexities of his understanding of modernity and tradition.

POETRY AND INFRASTRUCTURE

It is a well-known fact that Le Corbusier did not succeed in his professional expectations to get commissions in Latin America: the Errazuriz house (1930) was never built; Victoria Ocampo gave the commission for her own "modern" house to the more conventional yet talented Argentinean architect Alejandro Bustillo (1889–1982); his schemes for the Ministry of Health and Education and the project for a University City in Rio de Janeiro (1936) were not accepted and were later commissioned to Brazilian architects; his plans for Buenos Aires (1938) and Bogotá (1947–52), although developed, were never implemented.[9] As for his project for the French Embassy in Brasilia, it was interrupted by his death.[10] It is almost ironic that the only commission finally built was the Curutchet House in La Plata (1949–55), whose owner (a provincial physician interested in the design of surgery instruments) he never met.[11]

In lack of built works, the lessons of this Latin-American experience are best understood and studied through the series of sketches of 1929 published one year later in *Précisions* and later in his *Carnets*. They illustrate Le Corbusier's complex way of observing, analyzing, and reconstructing reality in the form of an architectural or urban proposal.[12] They range from the aerial vista made during his flight from Buenos Aires to Asuncion del Paraguay, to the *favelas* in Rio de Janeiro, to a fazenda (plantation) and the landscape of the outskirts of São Paulo. However, it is to the studies of urban projects for Buenos Aires, Montevideo, São Paulo, and Rio de Janeiro (following the route of his 1929 trip) that he gave the most attention in the *Oeuvre complète*.[13]

The basic components of these schemes are virtually the same: the diagram of one or two grand avenues leading to, or directly associated with, the construction of big, linearly built inhabitable volumes. Halfway between building and urban plan—thus quite distant from the traditional Beaux-Arts "master plan"—those

8. Adnan Morshed, "The Cultural Politics of Aerial Vision: Le Corbusier in Brazil (1929)," *Journal of Architectural Education*, 55, no. 4 (2002): 201–10.

9. Carlos Eduardo Comas, "Prototipo e monumento, un ministerio, o ministerio" *in Projeto* 102: 136–149. See also Rogerio Castro Oliveira, "Dos Proyectos por una Ciudad Universitaria: *las modernidades electivas* de Le Corbusier y Lucio Costa" in Oyarzún, *Le Corbusier e Sudamérica*, 128–41.

10. Jorge Francisco Liernur and Pablo Pschpiurca, "Precisiones sobre los proyectos de le Corbusier en la Argentina, 1929–1949" in *Summa* 243: 40–55; Wren Strabucchi and Juan José Ugarte, "La Embajada de Francia en Brasilia: una interpretación del proyecto" in Oayrzún, *Le Corbusier e Sudamérica*, 160–69.

11. Alfonso Corona Martinéz, "Algunas observaciones sobre la casa Curutchet en La Plata, y el rol de las casas particulares en la obra de Le Corbusier" in Oayrzún, *Le Corbusier e Sudamérica*, 148–55.

12. Le Corbusier, *Carnets (Sketchbooks)* (Paris: Herscher, Dessain et Tolra, 1981–82); see in particular, vol. 1, 1914–1948, Carnet B-4.

13. Le Corbusier and Pierre Jeanneret. *Oeuvre complète de 1929 à 1934* (Zürich: Les Editions d'architecture, 1964).

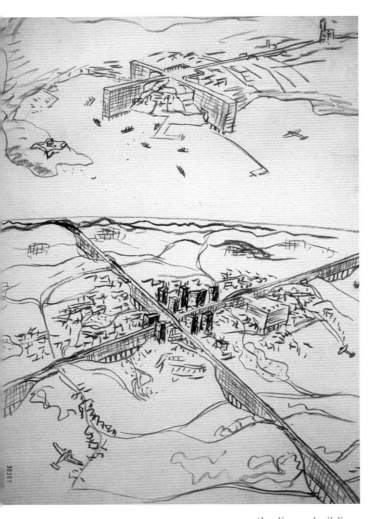

Le Corbusier, Perspectives showing the freeways/bridge/building in Montevideo (top) and São Paulo (bottom), ink on paper. © Fondation Le Corbusier.

sketches showing a combination of gigantic blocks and suspended freeways were seen by Le Corbusier as a way of domesticating the Latin American territory and imposing architectural order on its cities.

For Buenos Aires, he conceived a large platform built out over the Rio de la Plata and facing the city center. Five cruciform skyscrapers, 650 feet tall, reflected the dark surface of the river and created a super-scaled urban facade visible to travelers arriving by transatlantic liners or by air at the new airport to be built close to the towers over the river. Providing a vertical landmark against the horizontal extension of the pampas under the Argentinean sky, the towers were thought to house a business center and be the starting point of a freeway leading to the interior of the country. This powerful image would remain as the origin of the Buenos Aires Plan, developed ten years later in collaboration with the young Argentinean architects Jorge Ferrari Hardoy (1914–1977) and Juan Kurchan.

In the proposals for Montevideo, São Paulo, and Rio, a new conceptual connection was forged between the building and the automobile: the suspended freeway ("seascraper" or "landscraper"), on the roof of a linear building and adapting to the changing topography, traced a new and vigorous sign over the city and the territory. Taking advantage of the sloping terrain, the traditional main street of Montevideo was extended at a constant height over the harbor, generating a pier-like building that descends 250 feet below the roadway. The study for São Paulo derived from the enormous diameter of the city and the complex circulation system that made it difficult to enter. Le Corbusier's proposal assumed the Roman town plan diagram: a *cardo* and a *decumanus* created an artificial topography of territorial scale. Here, the linear buildings were explicit references to the Roman aqueducts, as in Segovia.

In Rio de Janeiro, the building/viaduct transformed into dancing and sinuous strips reflecting the exuberant geography of the city. Three hundred and thirty feet high, carried on 100-foot-high pilotis, they crossed the city from part to part and connected it over the bay to the city of Niteroi. The scheme—and its multiple variations realized in the following trip of 1936—keenly addressed one of the city's problems: how most fluidly to connect its different sectors, separated by a chain of ridges and bays. As in Montevideo and São Paulo, the artificial horizontality of the suspended highway was to establish both an urban and geographical facade; the roof became an imposing mirador, which makes the experience of driving a car as exhilarating as that of flying—something Le Corbusier had experienced in those days.[14]

AMANCIO WILLIAMS AND OTHER DISCIPLES

Among those who made up the international crew who regarded the atelier of Rue de Sèvres as a kind of alternative graduate school of architecture, Latin Americans were perhaps the largest group. From Roberto Matta (1911–2002), a young Chilean architect who arrived at the atelier in the early 1930s and later became well-known as a painter, to Guillermo Jullian de la Fuente, another Chilean who was part of the latest group in the 1960s, Le Corbusier's atelier attracted some of the most gifted Latin American architects of those three

14. See Yannis Tsiomis, *Le Corbusier: Rio de Janeiro 1929, 1936* (Paris: Centro de Arquitetura e Urbanismo do Rio de Janeiro, 1998).

decades. These included also Roberto Dávila (1899–1971) from Chile; Teodoro González de León and Pedro de la Mora from Mexico; Jorge Ferrari Hardoy, Juan Kurchan from Argentina; Justino Sierralta from Uruguay; Germán Samper from Colombia; Augusto Tobito Acevedo from Venezuela; Roberto Waceham from Peru; and Roberto de Carvalho from Brazil. Some of them, like the Colombian Rogelio Salmona, eventually rebelled against the master. Others, like the Chilean Emilio Duhart Harostegui, let his influence appear in their later work, as happened in his project for the United Nations Headquarters in Santiago (1960–66). Almost all of those disciples went back to their respective countries and played a significant architectural and cultural role. A literal formal influence may not always be recognizable in their work, but given the role that most of them assumed in their respective countries, the concealed or evident presence of Le Corbusier lay behind a significant part of Latin American modern masterpieces.

Yet, not all of those who received, and often interpreted in original and personal ways, the master's ideas were part of the atelier of the Rue de Sèvres. Distant disciples like Brazilian Lúcio Costa, Oscar Niemeyer, and Affonso Eduardo Reidy owed to Le Corbusier the inspiration of their early work, yet they developed their respective works with great autonomy, giving birth to one of the most influential Latin American architectural movements of the twentieth century. It is perhaps in the work of Affonso Eduardo Reidy (1909–1964) that some of those seminal ideas of the late 1920s are most obvious. His linear housing schemes for Pedregulho (1947–52) and São Vicente (1952), along with others like Conjunto Residencial das Catacumbas (1951), elaborated on sinuous linear schemes tightly connected with geography; they included elevated streets and promenades, and sometimes bridged over important arteries. His proposal for Aterro e Parque do Flamengo (1953–62) in collaboration with Roberto Burle Marx recalls the fluent mobility that Le Corbusier dreamt of for

Amancio Williams, Project for an airport on the Río de la Plata, ink on paper, Buenos Aires, 1944–45. © Archivo Amancio Williams.

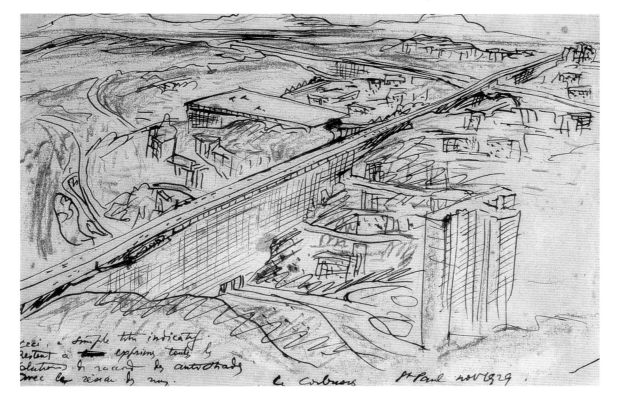

Le Corbusier, São Paulo (general view with elevated freeway), ink and pencil on paper, 1929. © Fondation Le Corbusier.

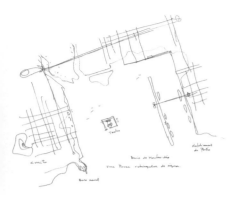

Paulo Mendes da Rocha, Urban proposal for the Bay of Montevideo, Uruguay, 1998. From Paulo Archias Mendes da Rocha et al., *Mendes da Rocha* (Barcelona: GG, 1996).

15. George Bonduki Nabil, Carmen Portinho et al., *Affonso Eduardo Reidy* (São Paulo: Editorial Blau, Instituto Lina Bo e P. M. Bardi, 2000); Paulo Archias Mendes da Rocha et al., *Mendes da Rocha* (Barcelona: GG, 1996). On the role of Burle Marx, see Jacques Leenhardt's essay in this book.

16. *Amancio Williams* (Buenos Aires: Archivo Amancio Williams, 1990).

17. In "Raçoes da Nova Architectura" (1934) Lucio Costa did a lucid interpretation of the historic situation of modern architecture and the role played by Le Corbusier. See Lúcio Costa, *Razones de la nueva arquitectura y otros ensayos* (Lima: Embajada del Brazil, 1986).

Alfonso Eduardo Reidy, Perspective of the Conjunto Residencial das Catacombas, Lagoa Rodrigo da Freitas, Rio de Janeiro, Brazil.

the Rio de Janeiro coast. Likewise, a recent project for Montevideo's harbor by Paulo Mendes da Rocha (1998) makes evident to what extent this poetic approach to large-scale, geographic schemes persists among Brazilian architects. Superseding the form of the bay, Mendes da Rocha turns it into a water plaza, conceived as the port's core. A theater located on an island gives a festive and poetic touch to the scheme.[15]

In the case of Argentinean Amancio Williams (1913–1989), Le Corbusier's ideas were probably received through books and periodicals. Having studied engineering and trained as a pilot, Williams embodies the figure of the modern architect even more thoroughly than Le Corbusier himself. Although Williams did not always recognize the explicit influence of the master upon him, he admired Le Corbusier and cultivated a long relationship with him. Two of his works exhibit this particular stimulus. The scheme for the Buenos Aires Airport (1944–45) developed with elegance and originality Le Corbusier's own version of 1929. Later in his career, Williams's utopian project "The City Which Humanity Needs" (1974–89) reinterpreted the theme of the long curvilinear building. He transplanted Le Corbusier's concept for Rio de Janeiro into the flat Argentinean landscape: a huge ribbon-like building, a fifteen-story mega-structure that could infinitely unfold over the Pampa.[16]

Another—and less mentioned—side of Le Corbusier's gravitation toward Latin American architectural culture is his theoretical and poetic presence. Except in works by a few like Lúcio Costa, the real complexity of Le Corbusier's ideas was not always assimilated in Latin America.[17] The great majority of his followers reduced him to a simplified version of his iconography or to a vague defense of architectural innovation. The Valparaíso School and the Borchers Studio, both in Chile, were other exceptions to this attitude. They saw Le Corbusier as a particular option within the realm of modernity, an option that enabled to connect architecture with art and poetry and was not merely the expression of technical progress.

The Valparaíso School emerged in the early 1950s under the leadership of architect Alberto Cruz Covarrubias and poet Godofredo Iommi (1917–2001). More than an iconography or the expression of technical progress, they took from Le Corbusier his vision of architecture connected with art and culture, and his method of registering reality through drawing and sketches. Except for an early tendency to use white cubic shapes, the more complex and organic forms of the Valparaíso School—as they can be seen in the Open City—do not resemble Corbusian forms.[18] Nevertheless, their proposed dialogue between poetry and architecture, their connection with painters and sculptors, and above all their way of departing from observations of the urban reality—which seeks to capture what they call "the structure of acts"—point to Le Corbusier as their source of inspiration.

During his student years, Juan Borchers (1910–1975) made a very systematic investigation of Le Corbusier's work, which would be reflected in his early architectural projects. Later on, a great part of his amazing theoretical production would emerge from a critical reference to the master's ideas. This is well demonstrated by the attention that he paid to the Modulor and to the alternative proportional system that he developed in his book *Meta Arquitectura*.[19] In the case of the Copelec Building in Chillán (1960–64), Chile, he brought the forms and methods of the late Le Corbusier to a new state of complexity.[20]

THE LEGACY OF SOUTH AMERICA

The development of Le Corbusier's thoughts cannot but be compared with Picasso's: clearly identifiable stages appear in succession, but traces remain from earlier stages that do not disappear completely. Le Corbusier's South American studies represent the emergence of a new sensibility toward urban thought, as

Amancio Williams, *The City that Humanity Needs*, ink and watercolor on paper, Buenos Aires, Argentina, 1974–89. © Archivo Amancio Williams.

coduños de Valparaiso :
coduños de Valparaiso mirando el mar a través de los arboles:
lo que tanto se buscaba.
el mar a través de los arboles
la ola y la hoja

18. The School of Valparaíso finds its origin in the re-founding of the School of Architecture of the Universidad Católica de Valparaíso by the young architects Cruz, Iommi, and others. In 1970, they started to plan and build the *Ciudad abierta* (Open City), an utopian project to serve as an experimental construction camp for the new school. See Rodrigo Pérez de Arce and Fernando Pérez Oyarzún, *Valparaíso School: Open City Group* (Montréal: McGill-Queen's University Press, 2003).

19. Juan Borchers, *Meta Arquitectura* (Santiago de Chile: Mathesis Ediciones, 1975); and Juan Borchers, *Institución Arquitectónica* (Santiago de Chile: Ed. Andrés Bello, 1968).

20. The Copelec Building, an electrical cooperative in the south of Chile, was the result of the collaboration between Borchers, the Chilean Isidro Suarez, and the Spanish Jesun Bermejo.

21. It is certainly not a coincidence that the first version of the Algiers project was published in the pages immediately following his Latin American sketches, in the second volume of the *Oeuvre Complète*, 138–43.

the Errazuriz House does in the realm of architecture. The sketches for Buenos Aires, Montevideo, São Paulo, and Rio de Janeiro marked the way in which Le Corbusier, enthused by his Latin American experience, proceeded to gradually abandon his former urban repertoire (still apparent in the Buenos Aires sketch) to explore a new formal language—a language less associated with the establishment of a rational catalogue of a "city for three million inhabitants" and closer to a phenomenological approach to geography and landscape.

Le Corbusier developed these schemes in the following years, as in his projects for the University City and the Ministry of Health and Education (1936) in Rio de Janeiro, or in the development plans for Buenos Aires (1938, with Ferrari and Kurchan) and Bogotá (1947–52). But it is perhaps in his 1930 Plan Obus for Algiers that the elements of the South American urban sketches achieved a more accomplished state of maturity: the mega-buildings, the viaducts, the freeways elevated on top of towers, and the prismatic skyscrapers terminating the system by the coast, all are there. But more important than the use of a new repertoire is a new urban attitude toward the existing city: the new scheme is superimposed on top of the existing urban fabric, therefore not asking for new land or complete *tabula rasa* as in the Plan Voisin for Paris. Beyond the possible economic opportunity of inventing a non-existing site, the proposal for Algiers can be interpreted as a kind of urban "collage" in which old and new attempt a kind of dialogue.[21]

Many South American traces can thus be recognized in Le Corbusier's life and work. They speak to his presence on the continent and about the complex relationships he maintained with it for three decades. But they also speak of the connections between modern architecture and peripheral cultures. The influence of the "rusticity" of the Errazuriz House and the typological reinvention at the Curutchet House are well known. Likewise, it is not by chance that some of the most important pieces of modern architecture and city design, at least in terms of scale, happened to be built in peripheral and even remote places: Chandigarh (where he developed the concept of urban block elaborated for Bogotá), Dacca, and even Brasilia are good examples, as were the projects for Algiers that were never built.

It is not only that those countries provided, for historical and practical reasons, the opportunities that Europe was not able to offer. It was modern architecture itself that, aspiring to universality, had, from its beginnings, a permanent impulse for global dissemination. The idea of influence is not able to explain, by itself, the complexities of this phenomenon: some significant chapters of modern architectural history took place in those peripheral locations. Being that Latin America is one of them, the knowledge of that chapter of history is fundamental to understanding the cultural range and scope of modern architecture. ■

Le Corbusier, Sketch for the Administration City on the Río de la Plata, Buenos Aires, pencil on black paper, 1929. © Fondation Le Corbusier.

SPACES OF HYBRIDIZATION: THE HOUSE OF THE ARCHITECT

FELIPE HERNANDEZ

Luis Barragán,

Lina Bo Bardi,

Juan O'Gorman,

Oscar Niemeyer,

and Carlos Raúl Villanueva

The house an architect builds for himself may be considered in general a manifestation of his aspirations, a kind of witness, a confession of his aims, a holograph in which one can not only examine the visible text but also graphically trace the secret motives of his text and the deep-running roots of the poet's inspiration.[1]

Latin American cultures are understood today as dynamic, heterogeneous, and complex formations with discontinuous histories, whose different components maintain an intangible struggle for survival and identification. During the past fifty years, cultural theorists have aimed to reveal those areas of conflict where the very fractures of Latin American cultures can be found, and where diverse and often hostile sociocultural groups clash while attempting to negotiate their differences. The complexity of this kind of dynamics has been revealed in the fact that there exist numerous areas of tension, not only between Latin America and the world cultural centers (the "world cities" in the words of Fernand Braudel) but also within Latin America itself. As a result, ruptures and violent tensions characterize the processes of cultural formation in Latin America, which become apparent in its neighborhoods, urban spaces, and buildings.

The notion of hybridization has certainly reached its highest point within contemporary cultural theory, especially in relation to debates of identity formation, post-colonialism, and globalization. It is not surprising that the hybridization debate has also been appropriated within architectural circles to theorize the effect that these phenomena have had on cities and buildings. It caught the interest of architectural theorists in the early 1980s, but, in most cases, it was used in a reductive fashion only to describe architectural works that combine different materials, forms, and/or architectural referents. For example, Wladimir Krysinski, in his essay "Rethinking Postmodernism: With Some Latin American Excursus," uses the notion of architectural hybridization to describe the work of so-called postmodern architects like Michael Graves, Aldo Rossi, and Robert Venturi.[2] The hybrid dimension of their work, according to Krysinski, depends only on the fact that these architects mix various architectural languages, historical referents, and different systems of coding in their buildings. In his discourse, he never transcends the limits of architectural form and aesthetics.

Chris Abel is another theorist who elaborates on the notion of hybridity. In his book *Architecture and Identity*, Abel dedicates an entire section to the notion of hybridization. The chapter, entitled "Living in a

1. Ernesto Rogers, *The Architectural Review* (1954). Quoted by David K. Underwood, *Oscar Niemeyer and the Architecture of Brazil* (New York: Rizzoli, 1994), 78.

2. See Wladimir Kryzinski, "Rethinking Postmodernism: With Some Latin American Excurses," in Robert Young, *Latin American Postmodernisms* (Amsterdam and Atlanta: Rodopi, 1997).

Left page
Luis Barragán, Barragán House, view of the terrace patio, Calle Francisco Ramírez 14, Mexico City, 1947–48. Photo Armando Salas Portugal. © Foundation Barragán, Birsfelden.

3. Chris Abel, *Architecture and Identity* (Oxford: Architectural Press, 1997), 166. Abel's approach is different from that of Krysinski in that he is aware of the enormous potential of the notion of hybridization despite the fact that he decides not to engage in similar areas of inquiry.

4. Néstor García Canclini, *Hybrid Cultures: Strategies for Entering and Leaving Modernity* (Minneapolis: University of Minnesota Press, 1985).

5. See Felipe Hernandez, "On the Notion of Architectural Hybridization in Latin America" in *The Journal of Architecture*, vol.7, no. 1 (London and New York: Routledge, 2002): 77–86.

Luis Barragán, Ortega/Barragán House, Calle Francisco Ramírez 20, Mexico City, 1940–43. Photo Armando Salas Portugal. © Foundation Barragán, Birsfelden.

Hybrid World," discusses mainly the fusion of different architectural referents in southeast Asia with particular attention to the mixing of Islamic and classical architectural features in some colonial buildings in Malaysia. Although Abel suggests that the notion of hybridization has larger political implications than those explored in his book, and that there are plenty of possibilities for future theoretical elaboration within architectural theory and practice, his idea of hybridization remains reductive. It is clear that for Abel, hybridization is the offspring of the direct fusion between two predecessors. As he himself puts it:

The hybrid architecture shown here is therefore offered, not only as an example of what individual architects have achieved in the past, but also as a more general metaphor for other possible future hybrid culture-forms. It is possible, therefore, to look upon such architecture as representing the product of a creative process of cultural interaction, which, while being associated in these cases with colonialism, might also be produced out of other sorts of global interactions, and other, less destructive cultural balances of power; in short, wherever two or more vital cultures meet and produce their hybrid offspring.[3]

In Latin America, architects and architectural theorists appropriated the notion of hybridization at the beginning of the 1990s following the success of Nestor Garcia Canclini's book *Hybrid Cultures: Strategies for Entering and Leaving Modernity*.[4] Colombian architect Carlos Rueda, for example, has elaborated on the notion of hybridization since it first appeared in the Latin American arena. However, like many other Latin American architects and theorists, he ignores the political potential that is intrinsic to the notion of hybridization. Because he seems uninterested in its subversive implicit capacity, his use of the notion—to describe or carry out superficial analyses of built architectural objects—is not only reductive but also of little political efficacy.[5] It therefore appears that the notions of *hybridity* and *hybridization* have been thoroughly mistaken within architectural circles as they serve only to describe architectural works that combine different forms, materials, or decorative motifs. It could, therefore, be easily affirmed that in the early 1990s, the terms hybridity and hybridization became merely fancy words that replaced the term *eclectic*, or *eclecticism*, so common in art history and architectural theory to describe the phenomenon of the mixing of styles.

In order to overcome this theoretical impasse, it must be ascertained that hybridization has two different but correlated dimensions: hybridization as a permanent process and hybridity as a result. As a permanent process, hybridization produces results that may manifest synthetic characteristics, like a fusion of different elements into one, as in the case of Canclini's discussion of artisan works or in the examples of Krysinski, Abel, and Rueda. However, the elements that give rise to these results need to be part of a permanent and unending process of hybridization that occurs in a different cultural dimension. In other words, hybrid synthetic manifestations imply the existence of another dimension in which synthesis never occurs, in which different elements remain apart, and, perhaps, not in a harmonious coexistence but in a permanent struggle for survival. Hybrid fusions, or hybrid static manifestations, can therefore only be obtained if, in a different dimension, the struggle among their constitutive elements never ends. Otherwise, hybridization would lead to the end of all permanent processes of cultural and architectural becoming. For this reason, attention will be drawn to that other dimension where differences remain unresolved and coexisting in an antagonistic relationship. At that level, hierarchical structures that support claims for cultural superiority can be, at least theoretically, eliminated.

6. For this reason, it is somewhat ironic that today they all are classified as Latin American modernists, which is, after all, a vague and misleading title.

THE INCOMMENSURABILITY OF DIFFERENCE

In spite of their aesthetic differences, the houses that Luis Barragán, Juan O'Gorman, Carlos Raul Villanueva, Oscar Niemeyer, and Lina Bo Bardi designed as personal residences between 1947 and 1954 belonged to an ambitious architectural and cultural agenda. These architects firmly believed, some more militantly than others, that the architecture they produced responded to the needs of their still unstable nations. On the one hand, the governments of Mexico, Venezuela, and Brazil, as well as most Latin American nations, began to advocate modernization. This, to some extent, implied the deletion of an indigenous historical past and the adoption of European and North American social, cultural, and political models. On the other hand, the nationalist movements, opposed to the "developmentalist" official agendas, called for the recuperation of a lost indigenous past that the other group wanted to erase. Regardless of the fact that both movements sought to erase a shameful colonial past, their means and aspirations were opposed. The search for a national identity, therefore, developed between these two extremes, a situation that could not but engender tensions and conflicts. In many cases, antagonism led to popular revolts and violent incidents. Within these difficult conditions, the above-mentioned architects attempted to overcome these ideological positions and to demonstrate, through their urban and architectural work, what a modern and hybrid national culture should be.[6]

Given their character of private dwellings, the houses that Barragán, O'Gorman, Villanueva, Niemeyer, and Bo Bardi designed for themselves could not have the sociopolitical and cultural impact of their larger and public projects. However, they bring about an outstanding opportunity to explore the notion of architectural hybridization. Whereas their architectural forms differ and sometimes conflict, they all combine attributes of European and North American modernity—the influence of Le Corbusier is clearly visible—with architectonic elements borrowed from the national cultures. This synthesis led to distinctive and fascinating architectures and spaces, inseparable from the specificity of their context. Moreover, these residences have one particularity that makes them unique in the history of architecture of these decades. From their inception, Barragán, O'Gorman, Villanueva, Niemeyer, and Bo Bardi, integrated in their modern forms and interiors a cocktail of furniture and works of art from modern, colonial, or vernacular origins. As in Lúcio Costa's sketches of the Casa Fontes (1931) and other residences, modern furniture by European designers such as Le Corbusier, Arne Jacobsen, or Mies van der Rohe shared their space with Louis XV and vernacular chairs and cabinets. Likewise, the works of artists like Josef Albers, Jean Arp, Alexander Calder, Mathias

View of Calle Francisco Ramírez, with the Ortega/Barragán House (foreground) and the Barragán House (background), 2002. Photo Jean-François Lejeune.

Goeritz, or Joan Miró, to mention only a few, were often juxtaposed with religious colonial imagery and indigenous artisan work.[7]

CASA BARRAGÁN AT CALLE RÁMIREZ 14

Barragán's second house (1947–48)—like his first residence, Casa Ortega (1940–43), on the same street—contains, for example, numerous religious motifs such as crosses, angels, and representations of the Annunciation. These share the room with bull skulls and paintings by Josef Albers. Other rooms are furnished in an almost minimalist fashion with only vernacular chairs and tables, and indigenous pagan imagery. One of the most paradigmatic spaces, due to the coexistence of radically different objects, is the one that shares the entry and the stair landing. It contains the famous "gold canvas" given by Mathias Goeritz to Barragán as a present; the walls are painted in bright colors, the steps are finished in stone, and a cantilevered table supports a modern telephone, a folkloric doll, and a rustic Oriental lamp. All of these contrasting elements are contained in a house that is made of reinforced concrete, with concrete block used for the main walls, and commercial pine beams to support the roof.[8]

7. One must emphasize the importance of the trips that Lúcio Costa made in the 1920s throughout the cities and villages of Minais Gerais (in particular, Diamantina) for the development of his theoretical thinking and of his built work; see in particular Lúcio Costa, *Lúcio Costa, registro de uma vivência* (São Paulo: Empresa das Artes, 1995); Lúcio Costa, *Aleijandinho* (Rio de Janeiro: Museu de Arte Moderna, 1978).

8. Federica Zanco, ed., *Luis Barragán: The Quiet Revolution* (Milan: Skira, 2001).

Luis Barragán, Barragán House, interior, Calle Francisco Ramírez 14, Mexico City, 1947–48. Photo Armando Salas Portugal. © Foundation Barragán, Birsfelden.

The layout of the house is very sophisticated, and the resulting spatiality is extremely elegant. The use of straight lines and angles as well as double heights for the social spaces and studios is very liberating and relates to modern architectural principles. Yet, there is an almost medieval demarcation of areas so as to keep servants away from the view of guests and the owner. The ground floor is dedicated to social activities, the middle floor contains all the private spaces, and the top floor is dedicated to servants. On that floor, the servants do not have views of the backyard, which is exclusively for the contemplation of Barragán and his guests. Servants have tiny windows looking into a small terrace dedicated to them and separated from Barragán's own terrace, or with views into the drying area of the laundry. A staircase that does not have access to the middle floor, where the bedrooms are, unites the servants' quarters with the kitchen, where they perform their daily duties away from the main social areas, a fact that emphasizes the division between higher and working classes. In this way, what seems to be a liberating spatial arrangement and a display of wealth and intellectuality is, at the same time, a traditional house that reinforces class division and segregation. Not only can we see a contrast—and, perhaps, a conflict—in the coexistence of artisan work with modern art, or in the use of materials such as reinforced concrete and volcanic tiles, but also in the attitude toward society. The plans of the house combine an elegant modernist language with a colonial, almost medieval, distribution of spaces. In this way, despite its uniqueness and extraordinary architectural quality, Barragán's house at Calle Rámirez 14 reveals the incommensurable differences, characteristic of Latin American cultures.

Luis Barragán, Barragán House, entry hall, Calle Francisco Ramírez 14, Mexico City, 1947–48. Photo Armando Salas Portugal. © Foundation Barragán, Birsfelden.

9. Victor Jímenez, *Juan O'Gorman: principio y fin del camino* (Mexico City: Círculo de Artes, 1997), 31. Quoted in Antonio Luna Arroyo, *Juan O'Gorman, Autobiografía, antología, juicios críticos y documentación exhaustiva de su obra* (Mexico City : Cuadernos Poulares de Pintura Mexicana Moderna, 1973).

CASA O'GORMAN

The house of Juan O'Gorman (1949–53) has generally been considered the antithesis of Barragán's. O'Gorman's house is not only different on the exterior, which shows an amazing combination of materials, forms, imagery, and symbolism; it is also distinct in the approach to architecture and notions of national culture. At the time when he designed his house, he maintained that the true identity of Mexican people resided in the recovery of a lost pre-Columbian Mexican past. Therefore, he did not own a collection of modern abstract art, which he and his friends of the nationalist movement—like Diego Rivera—dismissed as characteristic of a decadent bourgeoisie, hence by no means Mexican. Carved out of the volcanic terrain of El Pedregral, "the house is formed from a lava cave and architectonic elements that harmonize with the forms of the natural rocks."[9] Likewise, the mosaics of natural colored stones that clad the walls function as metaphors of the local flora. O'Gorman dedicated the house to Ferdinand Cheval and his Palais idéal (Hauterives, France, 1890–1924) and made constant references to Antonio Gaudí and Frank Lloyd Wright, who inspired the "organic" vision of his latest works. The house displayed nonetheless a rationalist arrangement of spaces, which contrasts with the organic forms; likewise, modernist details, like the cantilevered steps of the staircase, emphasized a certain degree of ambiguity between materials and methods of construction.

Juan O'Gorman, Personal house, interior staircase, Mexico City, 1949–53. From Clive Bamford Smith, *Builders in the Sun: Five Mexican Architects* (New York: Architectural Books Publishing, 1967), all rights reserved. Also see illustration on p. 221 of this volume.

Overall, O'Gorman's house is evidence of the conflicting attitudes toward architecture during the mid-twentieth century in Mexico. Its architect, for example, designed several Corbusian functionalist houses and schools in and around Mexico City before he turned fiercely against this kind of architectural approach. Barragán, for his part, was no stranger to Le Corbusier's works (as witnessed in the series of modernist apartment buildings he built in the 1930s), but his eager interest in Mexican colonial and vernacular

architectures always prevailed over other influences. His latest work is known for the juxtaposition of platonic volumes and eroded stone walls and his use of bright colors taken from popular architecture. Whereas Barragán advocated an architecture of abstract and pure forms, O'Gorman called for a "realistic architecture" that would establish harmony between man and the land that he/she inhabits. The rivalry between Barragán and O'Gorman brought to the fore the fractures and contesting positions that existed—and continue to exist—within the Mexican nation, and the impossibility of "totalizing" national cultures.

Carlos Raúl Villanueva, Caoma House, Calle La Florida, Caracas, 1951–52. Photo Paolo Gasparini.
© Fundación Villenueva, Caracas.

VILLANUEVA: CASA CAMOA AND CASA SOTAVENTO

Carlos Raúl Villanueva built his modern house, Camoa (1951–52), in La Florida, a residential neighborhood in Caracas made up of Victorian villas and colonial architecture. He built it with a reinforced concrete frame and hollow brick for the walls. Instead of bright colors, he used white in keeping with the principles of the International Style and with his own modernist approach to architectural practice. Villanueva also had a large collection of artworks and a diversity of furniture. In the living room, for example, there are chairs of several styles and origins, as well as religious motifs and colonial Madonnas, together with paintings by Piet Mondrian, Joan Miró, and Laszlo Moholy-Nagy, sculptures by Jean Arp, and mobiles by Alexander Calder. The neutrality of the modern white house allows for the coexistence of all these objects without major conflict. In that way, the artworks and furniture create a peculiar spatiality that conveys an uncommon feeling of harmony. Yet there is also a sense of tension because synthesis never really occurs. Different elements and objects share the same physical space, but remain apart in a struggle for differentiation.[10]

Carlos Raúl Villanueva, Sketch for the Sotavento House, Carabellada, 1957.
© Galería de Arte Nacional, Caracas.

10. Sibyl Moholy-Nagy, *Carlos Raúl Villanueva and the Architecture of Venezuela* (New York: Praeger, 1964); Paulina Villanueva, *Villanueva en tres casas* (Caracas: Universidad Central de Venezuela/Fundación Villanueva, 2000).

Another kind of tension is found in Villanueva's Sotavento beach house in Caraballeda (1957). Here, Villanueva was faced with the severe climatic conditions of Venezuela's Caribbean coast. In order to respond to the tropical climate, Villanueva sought for inspiration in Hispanic colonial architecture, from which he appropriated the use of timber louvers and pergolas that diminish the intensity of the local light while allowing for natural ventilation. However, since the house was again made of a concrete frame, Villanueva also used fixed concrete screens that are reminiscent of the architecture of Le Corbusier, and which contrast with the lightness and elegance of the movable louvers. The Sotavento house creates fantastic spaces where the traditional and the modern coexist. This is seen not only in the use of differing materials and a broad repertoire of architectural solutions but also in the way the house is inhabited. The main functional spaces of modern living (kitchen, toilets, bedrooms, and game room) are arranged around a main social area where swinging hammocks reveal other aspects of life that contrast with the rationality of modern architecture. The architecture of Villanueva shows how different and contrasting elements are re-codified and gain new significance through their coexistence without necessarily ever synthesizing. Villanueva's work challenges architects to reassess the notion that the presence of differences and contradictions is a sign of failure.

Carlos Raúl Villanueva, Sotavento house, Carabellada, 1957–58. Photo Paolo Gasparini. © Fundación Villenueva, Caracas.

NIEMEYER: CASA NAS CANOAS

Oscar Niemeyer's house in Gávea, Rio de Janeiro (1953), shows a different approach to modern architecture. It makes evident the conflict between rationalist and organic architecture, as well as the heroic impulse of the architect and, perhaps, of Brazilian architecture altogether. The house is located on a plateau in the middle of an aggressive canyon surrounded by wild and endemic vegetation. The layout of the top floor responds to nature; there are no straight lines or angles. At the center of the composition, a huge granite rock penetrates both the house and the swimming pool; it rises from the earth as a miniature echo of the Serra do Mar that dominates the house and its garden. To the thin concrete roof that seems literally to float above ground without any support, Niemeyer opposed the chthonic forces of a geology that becomes quasi-mythological. The result is a very "liquid" space that seems to have no barriers to separate the inside from the outside, or enclose the distant views. Here, too, mixed furniture and objects—straight-lined modernist pieces, polished materials, plastic, Thonet chairs, and an Empire-style sofa—contrast with the fluidity of organic space. To a colonial wooden statue of the Virgin in the living room correspond the abstract but classical statues of Alfredo Ceschiatti in the garden.

Here Niemeyer inverses the Corbusian principles that he used in his previous residence, the Lagoa House (1942), or Lina Bo Bardi in her own Glass House. The pilotis have disappeared. The house is brought back to the earth, into the earth. A straight staircase—of which one side descends directly along the granite rock—leads to the lower level that contains the bedrooms and service spaces. Here, the whole space becomes rectilinear and respects a strict functionalist arrangement. The house presents a tension between the plastic forms of the top floor and the linearity of the private level on the one hand, and between the curved walls of the top and the quality of a substantial variety of modern furniture on the other. Likewise, Niemeyer defies the axiom that the integration with nature must be achieved though formal mimesis or the use of natural materials:

Canoas is Niemeyer's first great utopia synthesis, a highly personal statement that sought to "neutralize" the basic philosophical distinction between art as something created and artificial and nature as something to be harnessed by technology. The ultimate paradox is that this compelling image of neutralization—the house's near total reconciliation of art and nature—is achieved by subtly manipulating the modern techniques that Niemeyer seeks to deny.[11]

11. Underwood, *Oscar Niemeyer*, 86. On the house, also see Gilbert Luigi, *Oscar Niemeyer: une esthétique de la fluidité* (Marseille: Parenthèses, 1987).

Oscar Niemeyer, interior of Canoas House, Gávea, Rio de Janeiro, 1953. Photo Jean-François Lejeune, 2001.

12. See Esther da Costa Meyer, "After the Flood: Lina Bo Bardi's Glass House" in: *Harvard Design Magazine*, no. 17 (Hard/Soft, Cool/Warm) (Fall/Spring 2002); *Casa de Vidro—The Glass House 1950–51* (São Paulo: Instituto Lina e P. M. Bardi, Editorial Blau, 1999).

Oscar Niemeyer, Canoas House, Gávea, Rio de Janeiro, 1953. Photo Marcel Gautherot. © Institut Moreira Salles, São Paulo.

BO BARDI: CASA DE VIDRO

Lina Bo Bardi, Glass House, view of the living room, São Paulo, 1951. Photo Pedro Ribeiro. © Instituto Lina Bo e P. M. Bardi, São Paulo.

Lina Bo Bardi's personal house, or *Casa de Vidro* (Glass House), seems also to subscribe to the heroism that characterized Brazilian architecture in the 1940s and 1950s. The house was built in 1951 in a new suburban development known as Jardin Morumbí.[12] Despite being located on the slope of a hill overlooking the valley and the sprawling city in the distance, the house was also elevated on thin pilotis. As one enters the property from below and ascends the steep slope, the house seems to be detached from the ground. It establishes a radical separation between the natural surroundings and the artificiality of architecture, an attitude that recalls Le Corbusier in the 1920s. However, the penetration of nature through the central patio reconciles this separation. This central void and the stairway that links the house to the garden under the pilotis creates not only a visual but also a tactile connection between nature and architecture in a way that is reminiscent of the contemporary work of Alvar Aalto.

The interior of the house is decorated with an enormous variety of furniture, lamps, paintings, statues—and objects of popular art—a "mélange" to which Lina and Pietro never stopped adding over the years. A priori, this mix of furnishings would appear to threaten the simplicity and elegance of its architecture. In fact, it reflects Bo Bardi's personal interest in juxtaposing elements from different contexts so as to unveil the tensions that exist between them. In other words, Bo Bardi experimented with the coexistence of diverging elements in order to introduce new values and significance to architecture. Yet, the coexistence of these architectural referents and motifs conceals a potential conflict, a conflict that is not material but socio-cultural. Bo Bardi's house was built on the grounds of an old preserve of Brazilian forest where local people gathered for recreation and where some poor people lived. Her house was the first to be built in the area, but others followed soon after. Paradoxically, for an architect who dedicated most of her career to the rescue and re-evaluation of popular life and art, Lina Bo Bardi's Glass house brought to light the inescapable antagonism between Brazilian dominant social classes and the minorities.

A RHIZOMIC RELATION

The personal residences of Lina Bo Bardi, Luis Barragán, Carlos Raúl Villanueva, Oscar Niemeyer, and Juan O'Gorman reveal not only the juxtaposition of different architectural and decorative elements, but also the complex hybrid condition of the sociocultural context in which they were inscribed.[13] Contrary to what many architectural theorists believe, it is my contention that there is no fusion of sorts in the houses that these five architects designed for themselves. On the contrary, the houses reveal a tension between different architectural languages, referents, and motifs. Furniture and decoration contribute to accentuate this sense of difference and conflict rather than facilitate fusion or harmonic coexistence. Indeed, what appears to be a physical fusion in concrete, brick, clay, wood, or any other material these houses are made of, remains culturally separated and maintains an intangible struggle for survival that is never reconciled in the building. Instead, different elements establish a rhizomic relation.[14] As in the analogy established between the orchid and the wasp in various writings by Deleuze and Guattari, these different components reaffirm their independent identities while at the same time achieving new values and significance in their relation with others. Accordingly, the architectural significance of the houses of Barragán, O'Gorman, Villanueva, Niemeyer, and Bo Bardi does not reside in the synthesis of these different languages and elements, but in the very conflicts that their coexistence reveals. In other words, if we consider the above houses as examples of a hybrid architecture, it is not because they combine different materials, architectural referents, furniture, and art works, but because they emerged, exist, and remain intangibly connected to a vast, complex, hybrid sociocultural formation that is Latin America. ■

13. More should be said in the context of this essay on the sociopolitical context of the works. See for instance Zeuler Lima and Sandra Vivanco, "Culture Translated and Devoured: Two Brazilian Museums by Lina Bo Bardi," in Felipe Hernandez, ed., *The Journal of Romance Studies 2*, no. 3 (2002): 45–60. Most modernizing urban and architectural projects, such as those designed by Villanueva (El Paraíso in Caracas) and Niemeyer (Brasilia), were based upon the assumption that cultures and nations in Latin America were homogeneous, or, if not, could be homogenized through the construction of urban infrastructure, by improving educational structures, and by promoting industrialization. Yet, these projects had the opposite effect. Instead of homogenizing the nation, they did eventually make visible the complex sociocultural reality of all Latin American nations.

14. "Rhizome": in botany, horizontal, underground plant stem capable of producing the shoot and root systems of a new plant. This capability allows the parent plant to propagate vegetatively (asexually) and also enables a plant to perennate (survive an annual unfavourable season) underground (From *Encyclopaedia Britannica*, 2003).

Lina Bo Bardi, Sketch for the Glass House, ink on paper, São Paulo, 1951. Photo Pedro Ribeiro. © Instituto Lina Bo e P. M. Bardi, São Paulo.

MARVEL, MONSTER, MYTH: THE MODERN CITY IN LATIN AMERICAN LITERATURE

REBECCA E. BIRON

If Latin American cultural identity evokes vast landscapes and a vibrant indigenous present, the region's economic survival and global relevance depend on processes intimately wedded to urbanization: technological modernization, governmental centralization, and European aesthetic conventions. Obviously, a number of large urban centers already enjoyed long histories in America before foreign explorers and conquistadors stumbled upon them in the sixteenth century. However, the idea persists into this new century that Europeans introduced "civilization" in America by founding the colonial cities. Today, indigenous traditions are still primarily coded as rural, while European-style modernization is primarily labeled as urban. Thus, the rural/urban distinction continues to characterize Latin America as much as does the indigenous/European distinction.

Whenever Latin American artists and writers highlight the rural/urban divide in their work, or whenever they focus exclusively on urban scenes and urban social issues, they evoke this tension. It is indeed difficult to avoid dichotomy. On the one hand, images of shiny urban magnificence and futurism highlight by contrast the backwardness and primitivism of so-called pre-modern, or anti-modern, rural traditions; on the other hand, images of urban decadence, cultural imitation, and social alienation emphasize the purity, autochthony, and sense of community to be found in idealized rural landscapes. In spite of that inevitable either-or relationship, the most compelling twentieth-century Latin American writers tackle urban themes from a different angle. Rather than attempting to decide whether the region is more European or more autochthonous, they strive to understand and represent cities as sites where definitions of modernity can be complicated, for Latin Americans and non-Latin Americans alike. By focusing on cities as crucibles for the simultaneously seductive and repulsive, productive and destructive, grand and banal nature of modernity itself, they disavow the notion that the modern belongs to any given continent or culture. They posit that it appears only in the most contradictory and hybrid sites of intense human interaction, differentiation, and imagination. The large cities of Latin America are those sites.

Twentieth-century Latin American literary attempts to describe the city move freely between realist depictions of urban scenes to the staging of modernity as a quintessentially urban construct. They combine physical mapping with psychic fantasy to show how large cities embody the ironies of modernity. By considering carefully how some major authors have rendered the largest cities (Rio de Janeiro, Buenos Aires, Mexico City), it is critical to discern these writers' complex relationship to the idea of the city, whether it is featured as a

1. Nestor García Canclini, "Las cuatro ciudades de México" in Nestor García Canclini and Miguel Angel Aguilar, eds., *Cultura y comunicación en la ciudad de México*, vol. I (Mexico City: Universidad Autónoma Metropolitana, Iztapalapa, Grijalbo, 1998), 109. [Author's translation].

2. José Vasconcelos, *La raza cósmica* [1925] (Mexico City: Editorial Planeta, 1999), 67–68. [Author's translation]. In English: *The Cosmic Race: A Bilingual Edition* (Baltimore: John Hopkins University Press, 1979).

primary character in its own right or as a setting teeming with metaphor and symbol. In a lecture series presented in Buenos Aires in the late 1990s, Nestor García Canclini distinguished the basic modes of urban representation, insisting on the intertwined elements of actual and imagined space in our experience of cities: *Above all, we should think of the city simultaneously as a place in which to live and as a place to be imagined. Cities are made of houses, parks, streets, highways, and traffic signs. But they are also made of images. Those can be the maps that invent and give order to the cities. But novels, songs, films, print media, radio, and television also imagine the meanings of urban life. The city becomes dense with heterogeneous fantasies. The urban center designed to function, laid out on a grid, escapes that design and multiplies itself through individual and collective fictions.*[1]

In accordance with Canclini's observation, the literary citations I have chosen to consider here blend physical description—the multiple maps that "invent" and "organize" cities—with individual experience and desire—the "heterogeneous fantasies" that constitute our urban imaginary. I have organized the texts according to three general perspectives that emerged in the course of the twentieth century in work by major Latin American urban authors: the modern city seen as a marvel of human achievement and design, the mega-city seen as monstrous deformation of that design, and the global city seen ironically as a new myth of cultural inclusion and access.

THE MODERN CITY AS MARVEL

This image reflects a dream of progress and the perpetually new. The dream, however, includes a strong foreboding. In spite of its celebration of presentism and technological conveniences, it also signals the losses and dangers that accompany the privileging of fantasy and novelty over history and tradition. José Vasconcelos, Roberto Arlt, and Jorge Luis Borges represent a variety of modes of marvel at the city in the 1920s and 1930s: awed wonder and celebration, angry class resentment, and hyper-fictional free play.

The travelogues of Mexican educator, philosopher, ambassador, and writer José Vasconcelos (1882–1959) serve as fascinating examples of how pro-modern desire controls representations of the Latin American city. Vasconcelos traveled in the 1920s and the 1930s. His comparative descriptions of the most remarkable aspects of Rio de Janeiro and Buenos Aires merit consideration. He relies on stereotypes of Brazil and Argentina to find what his preconceived notions had prepared him to see. He highlights the visual liveliness of the houses and sidewalks of Rio, pointing to the way in which the colors of the modern city reflect the ocean that kisses it:

Sidewalks decorated with pieces of granite in symmetrical designs, white and pink, that evoke the old Portuguese style; modern houses made for the luxury market fill eight or ten streets that meet around a grand boulevard. In the display windows you see brooches set with diamonds of petrified light, of tourmaline greens, blues, maroon, clear like a drop of water, bluish like the ocean; this is part of the fantastic Brazil, come true right before our eyes.[2]

Visually, Rio lives up to this early twentieth-century tourist's image of Brazil as a place shining with well-planned, "symmetrical," yet fantastic urban design. Curiously, however, Vasconcelos does not comment

much on the city's inhabitants. His references to Portuguese influences relate to the distant past, but he does not attempt to discuss the Luso-Afro-Brazilian present. He privileges the city as a type of art installation, organized to please the eye, and not to disturb the viewer with difficult social issues.

In contrast to his focus on the physical structures and colors of Rio, Vasconcelos's description of Buenos Aires turns on his own sexual appreciation of the women there:

A stroll down Calle Florida at twelve is a drama of repressed desire; the limitless pain of not being a God, able to summon to a gay dance of love all the amazing beauties who pass by in cars or who circulate along the sidewalks, with their Andalucian way of walking, in which their hips undulate with lines that imitate music. . . . Maybe monogamous love is a thing of villages. In the big cities you cannot remain faithful, and if you don't betray through deed, you betray through thought; terrifying abandonment of souls that cannot rely with certainty on even one other soul, because we all have inside us a thirst for novelty and beauty, the source of betrayal of the deepest affections.[3]

Here Vasconcelos is beside himself with desire. Not only is he taken with the women on Florida Street because they move, for him, with the sensuality of Spanish women, but he leaps to conclusions about the modern city's effect on faithfulness in general. Musing that monogamy may be possible only in small towns or villages, he finds that modern cities cause infidelity. The city itself, he asserts, forces "us" to betray our

3. Vasconcelos, *La raza comica*, 148–49.
[Author's translation].

121

Florida Street between Córdoba et
Viamonte, Buenos Aires, 1936. Photo
Horacio Coppola, from *El Buenos Aires de
Horacio Coppola* (Valencia: IVAM,
Generalitat Valenciana, 1996).

Carnival in Rio de Janeiro, ca. 1950. Photo
Marcel Gautherot. © Institut Moreira
Salles, São Paulo.

most deeply held commitments because it responds so graciously to our "thirst for novelty and beauty." As opposed to the anonymous, sensual intimacy created by the narrow Florida Street, Vasconcelos also finds "novelty and beauty" in the combination of broad avenues and spaces where one can sit and observe the traffic as in Avenida de Mayo:

The Avenida de Mayo is something else altogether; it is a wide, cosmopolitan boulevard, full of hurried and crowded traffic, not of strollers, but of people on their way to work; the long, wide street extends in direction of the Legislative Palace, lined with massive, five and six-story buildings; on the wide sidewalks, some small trees and, every now and then, outdoor café tables, so the locals can enjoy being on the street. Sometimes this one detail is enough to indicate hospitable cities, cities for walking.[4]

He contrasts this inviting urban design to the rush of New York or London, which he considers to be barbaric and anything but "novel and beautiful." It would seem that, whether describing constrained physical spaces or wide, long boulevards, Vasconcelos is predisposed to grant Buenos Aires superior status in the realm of cities that claim to be modern. He establishes clear criteria for judging the truly modern city: it must move him to desire and to reflection. It must be anonymous and fast-paced, but it must allow him plenty of time for comparative rural/urban analysis, and the peaceful consumption of sights and sensations.

For the Mexican visitor Vasconcelos, Rio dazzles the eye and Buenos Aires addles small-town values. In both cases, the traveler's pleasant fantasy governs his assessment of the urban situation. For Argentinean Roberto Arlt (1900–1942), on the other hand, Buenos Aires's gleaming buildings and wide boulevards underscore class differences and the gritty reality of poverty that modern architecture glosses over. In a trilogy of urban novels, *El juguete rabioso* (The Mad Toy, 1926), *Los siete locos* (The Seven Madmen, 1929), and *Los lanzallamas* (The Flamethrowers, 1931), Arlt follows disenfranchised characters as they plot ways to overcome poverty and disillusionment in the very city about which Vasconcelos will later write, "Buenos Aires is our Paris, the capital of our America."[5] From Arlt's point of view, this location of the "high modern" center of Latin America in Buenos Aires denies the other city, the one that after 1920, "could be discovered in the emergence of a working-class and popular culture, formed under the influence of cinema and radio and organized by a rapidly developing cultural industry."[6]

Erdosain, the main character of *Los siete locos*, wanders the city streets seeking solace from the anguish of having minor debts he knows he cannot repay. While he appreciates the architectural accomplishments of his city, the buildings and walls he passes ultimately just remind him of his excluded status:

He walked through the solitary sections of Arenales and Talcahuano streets, by the corners of Charcas and Rodríguez Peña, in the intersections of Montevideo and Quintana Avenue, appreciating the spectacle of those streets of magnificent architecture, forever denied to the poor and the unlucky. His feet, on the white sidewalks, crunched the fallen banana leaves, and he fixed his gaze on the oval glass of the grand windows, made opaque by the whiteness of the curtains inside. That was a different world within the filthy city he knew, a different world for him, who now felt his heart beat with a slow and heavy rhythm.... Stopping, he observed the shiny, luxury garages, and the green cypress canopies of the gardens, defended by walls with identical cornices, or thick wrought-iron strong enough to block a lion.... And he was six hundred pesos and seven cents in debt![7]

4. Ibid., 149. [Author's translation].

5. Ibid., 206. [Author's translation].

6. Beatriz Sarlo, *Jorge Luis Borges: A writer on the Edge* (London: Verso, 1993), 15.

7. Roberto Arlt, *Los siete locos*, in *Obras*, Vol. I (Buenos Aires: Editorial Losada, 1997), 178. [Author's translation]. In English, *The Seven Madmen* (Boston: D. R. Godine, 1984).

8. Jorge Luis Borges, "Cuaderno San Martin" [1929] in *Obras completas*, 1923–1972 (Buenos Aires: Emecé Editores, 1974), 81. [Author's translation].

9. Ibid.

10. Ibid.

11. On the concept of *barrio* or neighborhood, see Adrián Gorelik's essay in this book.

Arlt's characters lead with their class resentments, seeing the city through hostile eyes. As the complex plots show, by accusing Buenos Aires itself as the cause of their lack of access to wealth, these characters misdirect their energy. Rather than actively engage in class struggle and the challenge of economic structures, they invest their energies in developing fantasies of access to upper-class privileges. Although, for Arlt, Buenos Aires does not necessarily entrap his characters, it definitely symbolizes their economic marginalization by literally refusing to open its doors to them.

Arlt's characters gaze at Buenos Aires on a vertical axis; they are at the bottom, and the unattainable enjoyment of the city's modern benefits is beyond their reach, like the new high-rise office buildings. Jorge Luis Borges's (1899–1986) characters, in contrast, gaze on a horizontal axis, more related to time and a north-south grid than to class distinction and upward mobility. Unlike Arlt's characters, they are not seduced by the empty promise of modernization as a class-equalizing vehicle. Nor are they attracted like Vasconcelos by the city's reflection of their own desire for novelty. Instead, for Borges, Buenos Aires opens itself to its inhabitants' fantasy of romantic heroism, a fantasy apparently available to everyone. Borges's most famous lines concerning his hometown conclude an early poem ostensibly about the history of its founding. In "La fundación mítica de Buenos Aires" (*Cuaderno San Martín*, 1929), the young poet questions the idea of origins:

And was it along this torpid muddy river that the prows came to found my native city?[8]

He continues to shake the founding myths with conditional verb forms and with words like *pensar* (to think) or *suponer* (to suppose) rather than *saber* (to know). He fights for the honor of locating the first encampment of explorers in his own neighborhood, Palermo:

On the coast they put up a few ramshackle huts, and they slept uneasily. This, they claim, was in the Riachuelo, but this is a fable concocted in La Boca. It was a full city block and in my neighborhood: in Palermo.[9]

The poem continues by painting beloved scenes of life in the poet's barrio, implying by the contiguity of verses the anachronistic thesis that the founders of Buenos Aires had themselves named the streets after nineteenth-century political figures, played the famous Argentine card game of *truco*, and had listened to tangos while smoking tobacco together. Seeing the historical foundation of the city as coterminous with his own romantic, twentieth-century experience of it, Borges concludes:

Hard to believe Buenos Aires had any beginning: I see it to be as eternal as air and water.[10]

In this negation of the city's historical origin, Borges reveals a profoundly ambivalent relation to its modern status as well. It is firmly situated in the author's present and in his presence in the sense that this poem insinuates that the essential Buenos Aires is to be found in Borges's barrio.[11] However, the city's essence also transcends the present and any specific locale in that the poet judges it "eternal:" neither of the present nor of the past. In any case, Buenos Aires for Borges remains Buenos Aires "for Borges." That is, the poet's self-conscious desire ("I deem it . . . ") for his city to be identified wholly with his own corner of it (Palermo) or wholly with the very elements of air and water that retain primacy over the city's own, extra-textual existence.

In his later prose work, Borges will continue to depict modern Buenos Aires more as a necessary and pleasurable projection of authoring consciousness than as a setting for plots. For Borges, the city grants its residents a sense of mastery over physical space as well as over individual dream-space. Wide boulevards easily connect the efficient concentration of people and services inside the city to the free, open spaces outside the city. Traveling back and forth affords Borges's characters the opportunity to play in the borderland between dream and reality.

In the short story "El Sur," for example, the city, or, more specifically, the journey from Buenos Aires to the *campo* (the countryside), induces a sense of omnipotence and release. After suffering a serious head injury and undergoing an operation in Buenos Aires, the librarian Juan Dahlmann looks forward to convalescing at his family's estate in the south. Reading between the lines of the story, Dahlmann's journey away from the city and toward a romanticized gaucho knife-fight that will kill him is actually an elaborate fantasy he develops as he dies in a sanatorium on Ecuador Street in Buenos Aires. The narrator carefully selects vocabulary and uses third-person to ensure that we cannot know the difference for sure, but we are invited to try to distinguish between the real death and the fantasy death. The fantasy begins with irony when Dahlmann thinks he is traveling through Buenos Aires on his way to the train station:

Reality favors symmetries and slight anachronisms: Dahlmann had arrived at the sanatorium in a hackney coach and now a hackney coach was to take him to Constitution Station. The first fresh tang of autumn, after the summer's oppressiveness, seemed like a symbol in nature of his rescue and release from fever and death. The city, at seven in the morning, had not lost that air of an old house lent it by the night; the street seemed like long vestibules, the plazas were like patios. Dahlmann recognized the city with joy on the edge of vertigo: a second before his eyes registered the phenomena themselves, he recalled the corners, the billboards, the modest variety of Buenos Aires. In the yellow light of the new day, all things returned to him. Every Argentine knows that the South begins at the other side of Rivadavia. Dahlmann was in the habit of saying that this was no mere convention, that whoever crosses this street enters a more ancient and sterner world. From inside the carriage he sought out, among the new buildings, the iron grille window, the brass knocker, the arched door, the entranceway, the intimate patio.[12]

The city transmogrifies into a familiar old house that Dahlmann knows so intimately he can remember each element before riding past it. When he does open his eyes to the real city, he peers beyond the new buildings, not really seeing them, in search of that which he desires. We do not know if he finds it. The only verb used is *buscaba* (he was searching).

Whereas Vasconcelos seeks the new temptations of the modern city, and Arlt's characters face urban barriers to class mobility, Borges's Dahlmann finds the old and the familiar in an imagined space that conforms to his fantasy. In all three cases, though, significant loss accompanies the urban travelers' desire. However imaginatively, Vasconcelos enters the realm of betrayal by reveling in Buenos Aires's promise of multiple lovers. Arlt's characters become criminals who travel through the city in futile pursuit of wealth and power. Dahlmann travels out of Buenos Aires, with its new buildings that obscure the traditional houses he longs to see, only to face his own death. The physical characteristics of Buenos Aires as well as Rio de Janeiro (for Vasconcelos) and Buenos Aires (for Borges) serve as metaphors for the narrators' or

12. Jorge Luis Borges, "El Sur," in *Ficciones* (Buenos Aires: Emecé Ediciones, 1996), 526. [Author's translation].

protagonists' inner states. In Vasconcelos's case, his own desire to be made modern leaves him vulnerable to the cities' enticements. In Borges's case, the modern city's lack of history (or its eternal nature) leaves it vulnerable to its inhabitants' dreams. The miracle that the modern city really offers, then, is the creative and moral freedom necessary to fantasize fully.

THE MEGA-CITY AS MONSTER

This trope appears later in the century, when mass migrations from rural zones to urban centers overwhelm the relatively stable structures of post-colonial cities. José Luis Romero defines the changes introduced in Latin America by the *ciudad masificada* (the massified city) after 1930, under the effects of economic destabilization provoked by the Wall Street crash, and later by World War II:

The contours of the habitat changed; ways of life and ways of thinking became massified. As they became massified, some cities that underwent rapid and intense growth began to show a transformation of their urban physiognomy: they stopped being cities in the strict sense, and turned into a juxtaposition of disconnected and anonymous ghettos.[13]

Regarding Mexico City in particular, by far Spanish America's most populous city, Nestor García Canclini traces to 1980 the origins of the three main processes that prompt the restructuring of urban spaces up to the last decade of the century: economic recession and the subsequent loss of hope for betterment among the city's inhabitants; the shrinking of industry and the concomitant growth of informal and illegal economies; and an increase in violence.[14] In relation to this dispersal of urban energies away from collective projects and planned modernization, García Canclini also addresses the problems faced by writers. After this period, Mexican authors can no longer present a coherent image of their capital city : "The narrations that the urban experience organized in the historic-territorial city destructure themselves when the megalopolis becomes incomprehensible."[15] He rightly accepts Juan Villoro's view that, though Carlos Fuentes seemed to include all aspects of the city in his 1958 novel, *La región más transparente* (When the Air is Clear), it is no longer possible for any single writer to do so.[16] The most innovative current literary as well as anthropological representations of Mexico City have accepted the fractional nature of their subject. As García Canclini's work shows, they have incorporated the city's atomization into sophisticated new methodologies for describing and analyzing it.

The opening section of Carlos Fuentes's novel reaches high levels of poetic delirium as the protagonist, Ixca Cienfuegos, invites us to hurl ourselves into the city that permeates everything from earth to the heavens, from the present to the past, from the material to the imaginary:

Come, let yourself fall with me into the lunar scar of our city, city scratched by sewers, crystal city of vapor and mineral frost, city witness to all we forget, city of carnivorous cliffs, city of immobile pain, city of immense brevity, city of the motionless sun, city of long burning, city of slow fires, city up to its neck in water, city of playful lethargy, city of black nerves, city of three umbilical scars, city of yellow laughter, city of twisted stink, city rigid between air and worms, city ancient in lights, old city nested among birds of omen, new city next to sculptured dust, city reflection of gigantic heaven, city of dark varnish and stonework, city

13. José Luis Romero, *Latinoamérica: las ciudades y las ideas* (Mexico City: Siglo Veinteuno Editores, 2001), 321–22. [Author's translation].

14. Néstor García Canclini, "Las cuatro ciudades de México," 35. Identifying the simultaneous cultural histories that constitute the urban center, García Canclini names four cities that make up Mexico City: the historical-territorial city, the industrial city, the communicational city, and the city of multicultural hybridity. 1980 figures prominently within these categories as an important date for noting population growth (from 1.6 million in 1940, to 5 million in 1960, to 12 million in 1980, to 18 million in 2000), changes in industrial patterns (Mexico City provided 32.1 percent of the gross national product in 1940, and 48 percent by 1980), and changes in communication technologies (the massive ownership of private televisions and videocassette players in the 1980s leads to increasing time spent at home and less in public interactions).

15. Canclini, "Las cuatro ciudades," 23.

16. Canclini quotes from "Elogio de la mujer desnuda" by Juan Villoro.

Carlos Tejeda, *The City of México towards 1970*, oil on canvas, 1947. © Private collection, all rights reserved.

Judas in a street of Mexico City, Holy
Saturday, c. 1950. Photo Juan Rulfo.
© Juan Rulfo & Carla Aparicio de Rulfo,
bajo custodía de la Fundación Juan Rulfo.
Also see Rivera's painting on p. 218.

beneath glistening mud, city of guts and tendons, city of the violated defeat (that secret defeat we could never nourish by the light of day), city of submissive markets, clay flesh, city reflecting fury, city of anxious failure, city in a storm of domes, city woven with amnesia, the return to childhood, the incarnation of the pen, bitch city, hungry city, sumptuous villa, leper city of sunken rage, city. Incandescent prickly pear. Eagle without wings. Serpent of stars. Here we are. What can we do? Where the air is most transparent.[17]

Fuentes delves into and soars through a multidimensional city, converting our quotidian relationship to urban space into a flight of modernist free association. He mixes temporal shifts—*ciudad de brevedad immense* (city of immense brevity); *ciudad vieja en las luces* (city ancient in lights); *ciudad nueva junto al polvo esculpido* (new city next to sculptured dust)—with striking visual juxtapositions—*entre el aire y los gusanos* (between air and worms); *cicatriz lunar* (lunar scar). He confronts vibrant emotions—*ciudad lepra y cólera hundida* (leper city of sunken rape)—with static images—*águila sin alas* (eagle without wings).

After 1980, Mexico City can no longer be apprehended in this totalizing way. Consider the following excerpts from two Mexican fictions published around that year. The first is taken from Armando Ramírez's poetic fantasy of underclass revenge in *Violación en Polanco* (Rape in Polanco, 1980); the second from Fuentes's bourgeois coming-of-age story "El día de las madres" in his collection titled *Agua quemada* (Burnt Water, 1981):

To the right, as if heading for Santa Clara, we could see the cardboard houses climbing the hills, some already falling apart, the lizards everywhere, the lack of water, hunger in the bony bodies, the pain of sleepy women, the sickness of the stinking dogs.... We took the road to the new atzacoalco *[settlement], to where the poor folks have instituted their own whole culture, you can see the taco guys, the chicken guys, the salespeople in all those activities....*[18]

The same ads for beer, vacuum cleaners...soaps, televisions, the same squat little shacks, the barred windows, the iron curtains, the same hardware stores, repair shops, convenience stores with their freezer at the entrance full of ice and sodas, the roofs of corrugated tin, the dome of some colonial church lost amid a thousand water tanks, a stellar, smiling display of fortunate, pink, recently painted characters: Santa Claus, the blonde Model-of-the-Day, the white Coca-Cola elf with his bottle-top crown, Donald Duck; and below them the splay of millions of extras: the hawkers of balloons, chewing gum, and lottery tickets; the kids in tee-shirts and short sleeves hanging around record players, chewing, smoking, hesitating, gambling; the materialistic trucks; the navy of Volkswagens.[19]

These passages enumerate objects that signify a strangely monotonous urban diversity, where block after block of micro-cities offer the same view over and over again, and where everyone seems to perform the same actions, no matter which barrio or colonia they inhabit. The quote from Ramírez focuses on poverty in the city's outskirts. It signals the combination of privation, sad creativity, and the informal economy. But the description also highlights anonymity, the multitude, and the repetitive. This vision projects urban expansion into the farthest reaches of the Valley of Mexico. One might think of such passages as the language of the truly "sub-urban," in the sense that they describe subaltern social groups in the periphery of an urban setting, replicating the structures of the central sectors of the leviathan city.

Fuentes's passage provides a disarticulated jumble of objects, activities, advertisements, and empty icons in its efforts to depict the *ciudad masificada* as no longer poetic. It has become a screen full of

17. Carlos Fuentes, *La región más transparente* (Mexico City: Fondo de Cultura Económica, 1958), 20–21. [Author's translation]. In English: *Where the Air Is Clear* (New York: Farrar, Strauss and Giroux, 1984).

18. Armando Rámirez, *Violación en Polanco* (Mexico City: Grijalbo, 1980), 47. [Author's translation].

19. Carlos Fuentes, "El día de las madres," in *Agua quemada: cuarteto narrativo* (Mexico City: Fondo de Cultura Económica, 1981, 45–46. [Author's translation]. In English: *Burnt Water: Stories* (New York: Farrar, Straus and Giroux, 1980).

two-dimensional displays. In both Ramírez's and Fuentes's texts of the 1980s, the collections of images fill the printed page like grids fill a map or like concrete blocks fill in a wall. Commas give them regimented order, and they appear as solid paragraphs unbroken by dialogue. In addition to reflecting the city through their printed form, these lists produce mental images for readers. The continuous naming of objects observed in the urban landscape produces a film-like sensation of jumbled simultaneity, as if one were sweeping a camera across the visual field.

This descriptive method only seems at first reading to fortify urban fictions with components of Mexico City's materiality. The lists combine objects actually seen (vehicles, buildings, garbage, advertisements) with human activities that the narrators imagine as being equally material components of the city. As a result, the attempt to reinforce the presence of the real city fails in two ways. First, the mixed content of the lists reproduces a telling tension between what one literally sees and what one merely visualizes. Second, because a list of words can only be comprehended in linear succession, the very order of the words deconstructs the illusion of simultaneous access to all these sights. Therefore, the lists do not display the city so much as a desire that their own limitations paradoxically deny. They obsessively rehearse the conflict between wanting to describe the urban real and knowing that the real urban monster exceeds their grasp.

THE GLOBAL CITY AS MYTH

The idea of the Latin American global city evokes, of course, debates about how we define "world cities" and how processes of economic globalization affect urban identities, practices, and cultures. Two major Latin American cultural critics and urban chroniclers, the Mexican Carlos Monsiváis and the Argentine Beatriz Sarlo, have written extensively about the myth of how globalization brings new unities to Latin American urban centers. Both Monsiváis and Sarlo describe the ironic trajectory that representations of Latin American cities have followed in the course of the twentieth century: from modern marvel and inapprehensible monster to a feigned mastery over the monster by the sword of the international market. These thinkers mine the tension between a positive discourse on globalization, originating mainly in dominant business and political circles, and a critical popular culture.

This popular culture, according to both Sarlo and Monsiváis, consumes globally. It knows that it constitutes the city as monster even as it enjoys and suffers from the massive loss of centralized control and effective urban planning. At the same time, however, it cynically recognizes the promises of globalization as a new urban mythology. This analysis surfaces in a variety of ways when they begin to describe their home cities in the late 1990s.

The unique thing about Argentina is that its government and legislators serve the market, thinking that this is enough to produce an efficient and modern city....

The problem with the market's imposing its rules on the city in every aspect is not just the preservation of cultural elements that come from the past and are completely inert in the present. When we say "market," we refer to an expansive and generalizing form of power that takes over all spaces. Just walk down Junín Street, in front of the most famous cemetery in Argentina (Recoleta); you'll see the mix of taste and impunity with which the big restaurants have occupied the sidewalks with their awnings, their carpets of artificial grass, the publicity umbrellas and the speakers that play awful ballads in the afternoons. This is the market: a spatial metastasis, a powerful and anarchical proliferation. The market has converted the

Center of São Paulo, Marconi Street near São Luis, c. 1940. Photo Hildegard Rosenthal. © Institut Moreira Salles, São Paulo.

20. Beatriz Sarlo, 81–82. [Author's translation].

21. Carlos Monsiváis, *Los rituales del caos* (Mexico City: Ediciones Era, 1995), 248. [Author's translation].

corner of Coronel Díaz and Santa Fe into a kind of moving parking lot, clogging the traffic in a neighborhood permanently scarred by the building of the same type of shopping area that, in Buenos Aires, is invading the whole of the city center.[20]

For Sarlo, the biggest problem facing Buenos Aires is not uncontrolled population growth, not the disorder caused by rural migration to the city, and not increased density in the city center. The state's faith in the new mythology of globalization as a panacea for urban ills is in fact the problem. The cancer she describes physically and visually invades the city center with the bland, plastic, ugly signs of market-worship. The form in which the North American model of shopping centers occupies her city most effectively exemplifies this invasion.

Writing about Mexico City, Monsiváis mixes realist anecdotes with religious references to shatter the illusion that the globalized, market-driven city can even begin to be described in its vast amorphous nature. In *Los rituales del caos*, his collection of vignettes, sarcastic reveries, fictional interviews, and analytic essays, Monsiváis parodies the *Book of Revelation* to describe the apocalypse in and of Mexico City:

And I will tell of what I saw the first day of the third millennium of our Age. He who has ears, let him hear, and he who does not, let him drown in lasciviousness, in concupiscence, in drunkenness, in gluttony, in banquets, and other abominably delicious pleasures.

And I saw an open door, and I entered, and I heard archangelic sounds, like the Muzak that was heard the day of the announcement of the Final Judgment, and I saw Mexico City (that now reached Guadalajara on one side, and Oaxaca on the other), and it was not illuminated with glory and fear, but it was indeed different, more populated, with legions swaying in the abyss of each square meter, and video-clips that exhorted couples to the demographic blessing of sterility or the Eden of having single-child families, and a liter of water cost a thousand dollars, and there was a charge for putting your head in an oxygen tank for a few seconds, and in the entrances to the metro stations there were random drawings to determine who would get to ride. "No more than 15 million people per day," said one of the many signs on the metro walls that serve as chalice for the incontinent.[21]

This apocalyptic vision hyperbolizes what is already happening in Mexico City. The *ciudad masificada* has ceased fearing itself and has embraced the lack of mastery or control over the modern dream of order that opened the twentieth century. The city "limits" expand limitlessly, and a de-territorialized *Muzak* pervades even the weightiest scenes—*el Juicio Final* (Last Judgment), which could just as easily refer to the actual Apocalypse as to an official's call at a soccer game, or the outcome of some sensational rape/murder trial. Rights once considered universal and free, like access to water or oxygen, now require payment. But the people do not register this situation as negative, so long as they have the power to consume and are targets of marketing. Monsiváis concludes *Los rituales del caos* in this manner:

And at that moment I saw the apocalypse face to face. And I understood that our holy fear of the Final Judgment relies on a devilish intuition: we won't be here to witness it. And I saw the Beast out of the corner of my eye, with seven heads and ten horns, and ten crowns between its horns, and over its heads the name of blasphemy. And the people applauded and took pictures and videos of it, and recorded its exclusive

Center of São Paulo, Viaduct do Chá, near Praça Ramos de Azevedo, c. 1940. Photo Hildegard Rosenthal. © Institut Moreira Salles, São Paulo.

Xul Solar, *Pagoda*, watercolor, ink, and pencil, 1925. © Galeria de Osma, Madrid.

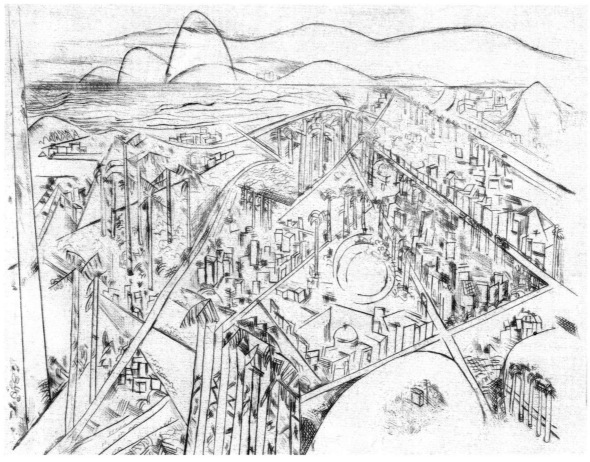

Lasar Segall, *Rio de Janeiro III*, etching, 1930. © Museo Lasar Segall, São Paulo.

22. Ibid., 250. [Author's translation].

pronouncements while, with a clarity that would later turn into a painful mist, the belated awareness came to me: the most dreadful nightmare is the one that excludes us definitively.[22]

Carlos Monsiváis's bitter humor and biting rhetoric point out the religious and mythological elements of uncritical acceptance of globalization. In agreement with Sarlo, he shows that worship of the international market leads to the abdication by the local governments of their role in genuine urban development. That abdication leads, in turn, to decay and loss of urban cultural patrimony. Still, Monsiváis ambivalently acknowledges that the rituals created by popular culture do offer some compensation, however small, for the loss of the modern dream of urban progress: at least the myth of the global city invites all the city's inhabitants to participate in the culture of consumption that will finally consume the monster. Mexico City may very well eat its own tail, but the act of "writing the city" keeps the spectacle alive indefinitely. ■

Joaquín Torres-García, two pages from *La ciudad sin nombre* (Montevideo: Sur, 1941). Collection Jean-François Lejeune. Uruguayan painter, teacher, and theorist Joaquín Torres-García (1874–1949) was a leading figure of the avant-garde in Latin America. He described *La ciudad sin nombre*, with his calligraphy and ideograms, as a fiction where "the simple characters with no human reality that populate it are there only to materialize the drama that unfolds in the contemporary world, between the ideal values of the spirit, universal and eternal, and the material interests, whether individual or collective."

Dr. Atl, *San Juan de Letrán Avenue*, atl-
colors on masonite, undated (c. 1940).

THE PEARL OF THE ANTILLES: HAVANA'S TROPICAL SHADOWS AND UTOPIAS

ROBERTO SEGRE

Havana is the city of the uncompleted, the rickety, the asymmetrical, and the abandoned. [1]

In Havana, there exists the other city, made of collapsed and anguished areas, the very city to which the promenaders arrive, armed with a facile skepticism. [2]

Two basic thrusts have triggered the evolution of Western cities: the internal, gradual socioeconomic development and the centralized decisions of the political power. At one extreme end of the spectrum of urban history, cities like London, Brussels, São Paulo, or even Los Angeles have written themselves into the history books because of their heterogeneous structure, made of a multitude of singular interventions, added and conserved over the centuries. At the other extreme, Washington, Paris, St. Petersburg, or Brasilia bear the indelible mark left by great patrons and planners, who imagined or radically altered the global structure. Havana, however, always maintained a subtle middle path between the spontaneous weaving of the urban fabric and the presence of representative icons of central authority. Although it became the Spanish Crown's "Jewel of the Antilles" or, as José Martín Félix de Arrarte called it in 1761, the "Key to the New World, Threshold to the West Indies," its main function as the fleet's warehouse, protected by stony castles, deprived her from boasting the symbolic *plaza mayor*, or main square that was the feature of colonial capitals in Latin America.[3] Rescued from that ignominy in the eighteenth century, when the Iberian Plaza Real was re-planned to be the colonial Plaza de Armas, the square remained unfinished, however, with only two sides defined by the stern-looking palaces of the Capitanes Generales (1776) and Segundo Cabo (1770). Later in the following century, the autocratic Governor General Miguel Tacón (1834–38) established the system of boulevards and promenades (the most important being the Paseo del Prado and the Paseo Carlos III) that would transform this "secret" and compact "colonial lentil"—as it was admirably described by José Lezama Lima—into an aristocratic, neoclassic city whose arcaded streets spread out to the populous areas of the periphery.[4] Havana then became the *Ciudad de las Columnas* (City of Columns) in Alejo Carpentier's appellation.[5] After 1850, the colonial walls were destroyed; in their place and within the former military zone, a "ring" was planned as an ensemble of squares, apartment blocks, and public buildings that recalled the Viennese model.[6] However, the almost fifty years of fights and battles for independence all but retarded its completion.

With the birth of the Republic in 1902, the size of Havana changed radically. The Creole bourgeoisie rejected the architectural attributes of the historic fabric. It built its new habitat and the state-representative public

1. Alejo Carpentier, *El amor a la ciudad* (Madrid: Alfaguara, 1996), 28.

2. José Lezama Lima, *La Habana* (Madrid: Editorial Verbum, 1991), 61.

3. Roberto Segre, *La Plaza de Armas de La Habana. Sinfonía urbana inconclusa* (La Habana: Editorial de Arte y Literatura, 1995).

4. Lima, *La Habana*.

5. Alejo Carpentier, *La ciudad de las columnas* (Barcelona: Editorial Lumen, 1970).

6. Carlos Venegas Fornias, *La urbanización de las murallas: dependencia y modernidad* (La Habana: Editorial Letras Cubanas, 1990).

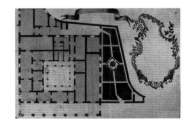

Casa de Correos, *Plaza de Armas*, ink on paper, Havana, 1785. © Servicio Histórico Militar [12184/Cuba], Madrid.

Left page: View of the Seafront Avenue (Malecón) with the monument to Maximo Gómez, Havana, 1920s. © Collection Carlos Alberto Fleitas, Miami.

7. Roberto Segre, "Havana from Tacón to Forestier" in Arturo Almandoz, ed., *Planning Latin America's Cities, 1850–1950* (London: Routledge, 2002), 193–213.

8. Albo Alvarez-Tabío, *Invención de La Habana* (Barcelona: Editorial Casiopea, 2000).

9. On Forestier see Jean-François Lejeune, "La ville et le paysage: influences et projets américains," in Bénédicte Leclerc, ed., *Du jardin au paysage urbain. Actes du colloque international sur J.C.N. Forestier* (1990) (Paris: Picard Editeur, 1994), 173–87.

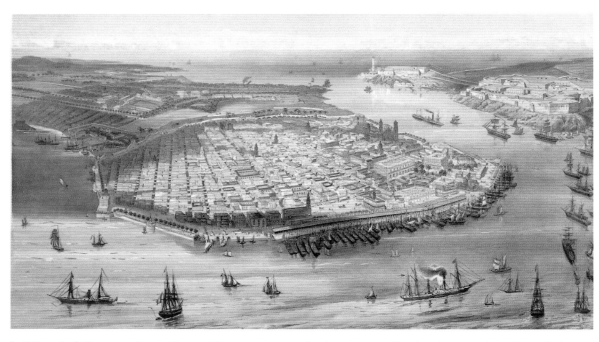

L. Asselineau, *General View of Havana from the Air*, lithograph, early eighteenth century. © Museo de América, Madrid.

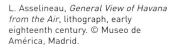

buildings in full antagonism to those of the now deceased colonial power. The iconic value of the Plaza de Armas was substituted with that of Parque Central, the nerve center of Havana life, the large planted square part of the Ring outside of the walls. The refined nineteenth-century neoclassic palaces, located in the Ring (Monserrate Street), were left behind in favor of the eclectic mansions built along the Prado and in the new peripheral district of Vedado.[7] While the government was erecting the main monuments to Republican power (such as the Presidential Palace in 1920 and the Capitol in 1929), the rich Spanish merchants showed their resilient economic power by also building luxury centers or clubs, like the Centro Gallego (1915) and the Centro Asturiano (1927). Already in 1925, places like the Parque Central, Paseo del Prado, and the Malecón formed a continuous public space where the political, cultural, and social life of "elegant Havana" unraveled, the starting point for the urban stage required by the government elite.[8]

This axis, however, was encroached by barrios (neighborhoods) of laborers from the tobacco factories located close to the new monuments. Rich landowners lived in that central area—as well as merchants and politicians—in sharp contrast with factories and workers' dwellings. The need was obvious, therefore, to create a new administrative center related to the areas of expansion of the moneyed classes. The districts of Vedado, Miramar, and Country Club were the result of that territorial expansion that implied a metropolitan vision of the city, like in Haussmann's Paris or the large North American cities (Chicago, New York, Washington). In the mid-1920s, despite new local urbanistic initiatives, including those of the architect Pedro Martínez Inclán (1883–1957), Carlos Miguel de Céspedes, then minister of public works (1925–33) during the government of General Gerardo Machado, invited the French landscape architect Jean Claude Nicolas Forestier (1861–1930) to design the first integral blueprint of Havana.[9]

Beauty and cruelty, hedonism and dictatorship, classicism and tropical landscape characterized the conformation of 1920s–1930s Havana into a "city spectacle" and "capital of fiction" (as Alejo Carpentier had it), a city oblivious to the misery and suffering that affected the workers and peasants throughout the island. On the one hand, buildings and urban spaces were modeled on the aesthetic patterns of the French culture. In an attempt to forget the Spanish ancestry of the colonial legacy, the Capitolio Nacional (national capitol), the main architectural icon of this period, assumed the cupola of Soufflot's Pantheon in Paris. On the other hand, Gerardo Machado installed an ironclad dictatorship that implacably persecuted intellectuals and left-wing militants. The Communist student leader Julio Antonio Mella, lover of the famous Italian photographer Tina Modotti, was murdered in 1929 in Mexico by Machado's henchmen.[10]

In spite of the growing economic influence of the United States, European cultural models persevered among the members of the high bourgeoisie, who belonged to a homogeneous social circle. Before the world crisis of 1929, the building euphoria that characterized the *années folles* in Havana managed to achieve a coherent landscape defined by the classical languages of many architectural showpieces—both private and public— located between the Parque Central and the lower-density neighborhoods to the west of the historic center: Vedado, Miramar, and Playa de Marianão. The sugar magnate Juan de Pedro y Baró and the landowner Enrique Conill, itinerant residents of the City of Lights, promoted their links with Paris, like the Terry family from Cienfuegos, who occupied the Châteaux de Chenonceaux. It is from there that stylistic influences from Spain, Italy, and France traveled to the mansions of Orestes Ferrara, José María Cortina, María Luisa Gómez Mena, and Pablo González de Mendoza in the Vedado district; or of Marcos Pollack and Carmen Casuso in the Country Club neighborhood.[11]

10. Hugh Thomas, *Cuba or the Pursuit of Freedom* (New York: Da Capo Press, 1998).

11. Albo Alvarez-Tabío, *Vida, mansión y muerte de la burguesia cubana* (Havana: Editorial Letras Cubanas, 1989); and Maria Lúisa Lobo Montalvo, *Havana. History and Architecture of a Romantic City* (New York: Monacelli Press, 2000).

View of the Paseo de Carlos III, Havana, 1920s. © Collection Carlos Alberto Fleitas, Miami.

12. Jean-François Lejeune, "The City as Landscape: Jean-Claude Nicolas Forestier and the Great Urban Works of Havana, 1925–1930" in T*he Journal of Decorative and Propaganda Arts 1875–1945*, no. 22 (Cuba): 150–85; Heriberto Duverger, "El maestro francés del urbanismo criollo para La Habana," in Leclerc, *Du jardin*, 221–60.

13. Roberto Segre, "El sistema monumental en la ciudad de La Habana: 1900–1930" in Roberto Segre, *Lectura crítica del entorno cubano* (Havana: Editorial Letras Cubanas, 1990), 89–113.

14. Carlos Sambricio and Roberto Segre, *Arquitectura en la ciudad de La Habana. Primera Modernidad* (Madrid: Electa España, 2000).

15. Roberto Segre, "Pedro Martinez Inclán (1883–1957). Primer urbanista cubano," in *Ciudad y Territorio. Estudios Territoriales*, no. 128, vol. 33 (Madrid, 2001): 122–25.

Rich with a vast experience of landscape and urban projects in Europe (France, Spain), Africa (Morocco), and Latin America (Buenos Aires), Jean Claude Nicolas Forestier arrived in Havana in 1925 with a team of French experts joined by Cuban architects. He flew over the city in an airplane—as Le Corbusier had done in Rio de Janeiro and Buenos Aires—to comprehend the totality of the urban structure, and enthusiastically set out on the mission for which Carlos Miguel de Céspedes had commissioned him. He designed a monumental Plaza Cívica (civic plaza), equidistant to the historic center and the districts of Vedado and Miramar; he regularized the road system with axial avenues, diagonals, and other majestic squares, neatly separating vehicles from pedestrians when possible; he conceived the general plan for the university campus and designed, in association with Raúl Otero and César Guerra, the monumental staircase that marks its entrance from the city. He simultaneously integrated nature and landscape design as integral components of the new urban development scheme: the system of parks he conceived for Havana followed the principles of North American landscape architect Frederick Law Olmsted.[12] His dedication to the design of gardens made him aware of tropical vegetation, the great need to provide shade in squares and promenades, and the value of the sinuous landscape of Havana's coastline. Forestier created a series of "urban salons" throughout the former colonial center and the new districts (the Plaza de la Fraternidad; the Paseo del Prado, which he completely redesigned; the Avenida de los Presidentes; the Malecón along the sea), alternating parterres with leafy trees, monumental palm trees (which he reintroduced in the center) and an elaborate urban décor of benches, lampposts, and pavements. He modeled the image of a classic city, a refined and elegant urban context for the relaxed pedestrian with time on his hands—both the aristocratic *flâneur* and the curious American tourist. Night and day, they could enjoy the light, the shade, the breeze, walking along promenades bordered by luxurious mansions and monumental palaces, scanning the horizon along the Malecón, or sitting idly in the bucolic gardens of the Hotel Nacional.[13]

A CONTRADICTORY MODERNITY

The Centellador lighthouse at the top of the Capitol, Havana, 1929. From *Album fotográfico de los actos celebrados con motivos de la toma de posesión de la Presidencia de la República por el General Gerardo Machado y Morales* (Havana: Secretaría de Obras Públicas, 1929). Courtesy The Wolfsonian-FIU, Miami Beach.

The modern movement arrived in no hurry in Havana. The negative effects of the 1929 world crisis and the popular uprising against Machado in 1933 opened up the history of Cuba to an opaque institutional period that lasted until the 1940s. The homogeneity of the academic system gave in to the pressure of speculative development as the city expanded to form new suburbs. New architectural codes emerged and the new Art Deco decorative elements were adopted, coming from Europe and the United States.[14] José Luis Sert (1902–1983)—who had left Franco's Spain—made a stop in Havana in 1939 on his way to New York. There he gave a lecture and met a group of young architects led by Eugenio Batista (1900–1992), who established the Cuban branch of the CIAM. Both the architectural proto-modernism as well as the new and challenging urban ideas of Forestier's Beaux-Arts system transformed the image of the city, favoring essential road networks and the increasing presence of the motorcar. In 1945, Pedro Martínez Inclán drafted the "Havana Charter," adapting the precepts contained in the "Athens Charter" to the Caribbean context.[15]

During the 1940s, and as a result of high sugar sales during World War II, the successive constitutional governments of Fulgencio Batista (1940–44) and Ramón Grau San Martín (1944–48) allocated enormous resources to public works in Havana. Squares, avenues,

Aerial view of the colonial center of Havana, with Plaza de Armas (in the middle) and the Malecón in construction, c. 1925. Photo Illa. © Collection Carlos Alberto Fleitas, Miami.

schools, and hospitals became landmarks in the public spaces of the arbitrary suburban expansion of the capital, and this within the canons of anonymous functionalism. However, it is in the 1950s that Havana's contradictory "modern" personality surfaced. Fulgencio Batista's (1901–1973) military coup of 1952 triggered political and social reactions that transformed his government into a bloody dictatorship that came to an end on January 1, 1959, with the victory of the armed guerrillas headed by Fidel Castro. A deep antagonism separated the avant-garde cultural manifestations from the financial interests of politicians, financiers, and landowners, backed by North American capital. A literary and artistic movement emerged, which identified with a small nationalist bourgeoisie who attempted to revive the historic ancestry, reinterpreted in modern terms. Its main players were writers like Alejo Carpentier, José Lezama Lima, Nicolás Guillén, and Virgilio Piñera; painters like René Portocarrero, Mariano Rodríguez, Luis Martínez Pedro, Guido Llinás, Cundo Bermúdez, Raúl Martínez, and Fayad Jamís; the musicians Ernesto Lecuona and Benny Moré; the architects Eugenio Batista, Mario Romañach, Frank Martínez, Nicolás Quintana, Antonio Quintana, and Humberto Alonso; and the ballet dancer Alicia Alonso, among others.[16]

Likewise, the dependency on the United States was felt with extreme intensity. Whereas Machado had looked toward sophisticated Paris, Batista adopted Miami's frivolous and scattered model. The government supported the mafia of the north, who invested profuse amounts in casinos and hotels, making Havana part of an axis of gambling and pleasure with Las Vegas and Miami. United States tourism became one of the main engines of the Cuban economy, and of the functional and infrastructural modernization of this "perverted Pompeii of the

16. Eduardo Luis Rodríguez, *La Habana. Arquitectura del siglo XX* (Barcelona: Blume, 1998).

17. Guillermo Cabrera Infante, *Three Trapped Tigers* (New York: Harper & Row, 1971); in Spanish: *Tres tristes tigres* (Barcelona: Editorial Seix Barral, 1983).

18. Eduardo Luis Rodríguez, *Havana Guide. Modern Architecture 1925–1965* (New York: Princeton Architectural Press, 2000). Graham Greene, *Our Man in Havana: An Entertainment* (New York: Viking Press, 1958).

Caribbean." The nerve center of the city moved once again. The Parque Central—which maintained its hegemony until the 1950s—and the Plaza Cívica, still unbuilt, were left behind in favor of the dynamism of hotels and the nightlife that appeared in Vedado (the Capri, Hilton, Saint John's, and Riviera) or toward Miramar (the Comodoro, Sans Souci, and Château Miramar).

Not surprisingly, the architectural icon of the decade was not a public building such as the Capitolio or the monumental Palacio de Justicia (1957)—a late reminder of the academic axiality of Forestier's Plaza Cívica—but the exuberant Tropicana (1951), "the world's most luxurious cabaret." Designed by architect Max Borges Recio and located in the suburban area of the Mariañao district, it marked the symbolic end of the "Havana of the *flâneur*," now substituted by the fourth "urban dimension" (to paraphrase Emma Álvarez Tabío). Cabrera Infante's realist chronicles of the period are full of white and shiny, duck-tailed convertible Cadillacs or black Oldsmobiles hurtling at high speed on the new avenues and highways.[17] The urban ritual of the *paseo* (promenade) under the leafy trees has become a thing of the past; it has been substituted by frivolous evenings in dark nightclubs (like the central Sloppy Joe's or the distant and exclusive beachside clubs), or by the beginnings of consumerist fever in the air-conditioned stores (Ten Cent, Woolworth, Sears) or the new shopping centers of La Rampa or La Copa. The celebrities of the time were Santos Trafficante, Meyer Lansky, Ernest Hemingway, Frank Sinatra, or Graham Greene.[18] The residential model shifted from the area of Vedado to Country Club; its architectural paradigm was the isolated villa built for the Schulthess family in 1956 by Richard Neutra, with a swimming pool submerged in bucolic gardens created by Roberto Burle Marx.

Jean Claude Nicolas Forestier, with Raúl Otero and César Guerra, Grand staircase of the University of Havana, 1925–30. Photo Secretaría de Obras Públicas de Cuba. © Institut Français d'Architecture (Paris, Fonds Leveau).

View of the Havana Ring with the colonial center in the foreground (La Habana Vieja), the Capitol, and the Paseo del Prado, 1920s. © Collection Carlos Alberto Fleitas, Miami.

In 1953, Fulgencio Batista's minister of Public Works, Nicolás Arroyo, commissioned José Luis Sert, Paul Lester Wiener, and Paul Schulz, urban planners and architects and members of Town Planning Associates in New York, to design a new general plan for the development of Havana, known as Plan Piloto. Under pressure from North American real estate investors, the government established the Junta Nacional de Planificación (National Planning Bureau) in 1955. Its responsibility was to coordinate various urban and tourist projects in several regions of the country: Havana, Varadero, Trinidad, and Isla de Pinos.[19] Sert, accompanied by some renowned professionals of the decade (including Mario Romañach, Nicolás Quintana, Eduardo Montoulieu, and Jorge Mantilla), put forward a proposal for a city of three million people—Havana had then only one million—covering the metropolitan region.[20] Its merit lay with the foresight of having a balanced development of the city around the bay and taking advantage of the possibilities for expansion toward virgin lands on the eastern coast, accessible via the imminent opening of the tunnel under the bay (1958). This triggered the design of ambitious, expensive residential projects by architects of international repute like the American firm Skidmore, Owings & Merrill, and the Italian Franco Albini.

In response to U.S. investors' requests to build new hotels, offices, and shopping centers, Sert's Plan Piloto wiped out most of the historic colonial center: he protected the best colonial squares, but substituted the urban fabric with a Hollywood-like reconstruction, custom-made for the American tourist and financier. Sert and his team proposed to create an artificial island on the Caribbean Sea, replete with hotels, casinos, and other pleasure palaces. They also designed, in cooperation with Gabriela Menéndez, a dream-like presidential palace that would have been located between the fortresses of the Morro and the Cabaña. It commanded an impressive view of the whole city, a transparent and clear building that contrasted with the dark and crooked political power within.

Although there has been a consensus among recent critics on the aesthetic value of the architectural output of the period, it is difficult to doubt the "naive" and "ideology-free" planning, alien to the ferocious repression against the defenders of democracy and the financial maneuvering of Batista's dictatorship that characterized this decade. The fall of the regime in 1959 showed how those metropolitan dreams collapsed like a house of cards.[21]

19. Josep M. Rovira, *José Luis Sert, 1901–1983* (Madrid: Electa España, 2000).

20. *Plan piloto de La Habana* (New York: Town Planning Associates, 1959).

21. Roberto Segre, "La Habana de Sert: CIAM, ron y cha cha cha" in *Historia Urbana*, no. 4 (Universidad Politécnica de Valencia, Valencia, 1997): 49–61.

Arroyo and Ménendez with Walton Beckett, Hilton Hotel, Vedado, Havana, 1957. © Collection Carlos Alberto Fleitas, Miami.

SOCIALIST UTOPIA AND URBAN HOPES

Beauty and cruelty went hand in hand in the history of Havana's urban and architectural symbols, which are today admired as silent witnesses to the creative capacity of politicians, urban planners, and architects. They silenced the echoes of the dungeons in the colonial castles, which forged the first monumental system in Havana. Governor Tacón's compelling opposites—the fortress of the Príncipe and the gigantic neoclassic prison—are easily forgotten when walking along the Paseos de Carlos III or the Paseo del Prado, among the ivory-like Carrara marble statues. The bulk of the Capitol or the Justice Palace, representing the all-embracing power of the repressive state, have lost their fear-inspiring presence.

Thus, with the establishment of the socialist-oriented Revolutionary Government in Cuba, the dynamics of architecture and urban planning took a full turn. In more than forty years of political continuity, no monumental

View of the Malecón, with the United States Embassy (Harrison & Abramovitz, 1953) to the left, Havana, late 1950s. © Collection Carlos Alberto Fleitas, Miami.

22. Roberto Segre, "La Habana siglo XX: espacio dilatado y tiempo contraído," in Concepción Otero, ed., *Arquitectura cubana. Metamorfosis, pensamiento y crética. Selección de textos* (La Habana: Artecubano Ediciones, 2002), 44–67.

23. Joseph Scarpacci, Roberto Segre, and Mario Coyula, *Havana. Two Faces of the Antillean Metropolis* (Chapel Hill: University of North Carolina Press, 2002).

symbol of political or civic power was built in Havana, contrary to what occurred in socialist Russia, China, and Eastern European countries.[22] The new regime assumed an essentially anti-urban attitude and policy: post-1960s Havana's representative icon is not a building, but a void, the empty space of the Plaza de la Revolución, where the political leadership and the Cuban people have been meeting for decades. Inherited from Forestier's plan, the huge square is surrounded by monumental government buildings erected during the 1950s. Yet, it has never reached a defined design. Its political role has waned since the construction, at the beginning of the twenty-first century, of the "Anti-Imperialist Tribune" on the Malecón, a covered metallic structure of dubious architectural value, located opposite the United States embassy in Vedado. This is a new center where the urban masses congregate, an expression of the love-hate relationship with the Colossus of the North.[23]

Although the functional structures of the socialist state resided in Havana, the aversion shown by the political leaders toward the capital soon became evident. During the 1970s, as a result of the rural mobilization produced by the "zafra de los 10 millones" (the 10 million harvest, a drive to produce an annual harvest of ten million tons of sugar), Fidel Castro suggested moving the government to Guáimaro in the center of the island. Ideologically, this attitude is understandable. First, there is the Marxist thesis of eliminating the contrasts between town and country that was already present in the socialist utopias

José Luis Sert and Town Planning Associates, *Plan Piloto de La Habana, masterplan for Havana*, 1955–58. From *Plan Piloto de La Habana* (New York: Town Planning Associates, 1959). Courtesy Cuban Heritage Collection, University of Miami Richter Library.

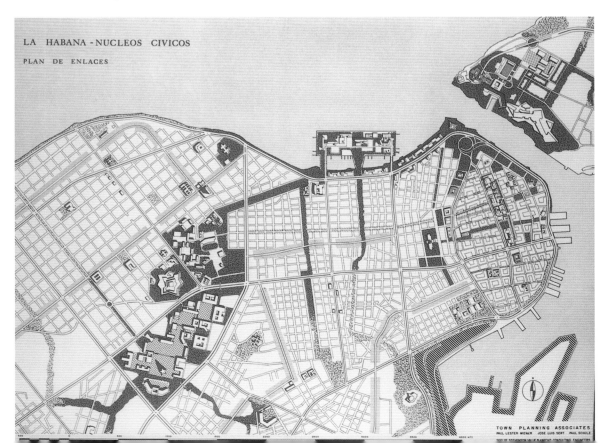

LA HABANA - NUCLEOS CIVICOS

PLAN DE ENLACES

TOWN PLANNING ASSOCIATES

of the nineteenth and twentieth centuries. Reminders of this theoretical stand are the proposals by urbanists and de-urbanists during the early years of the October Revolution.[24] Secondly, the bulk of the armed struggle against Batista took place in the mountains of Sierra Maestra, with the help of the peasants. It later spread throughout Cuba's agricultural lands, but with lesser participation of the urban sectors. Thirdly, egalitarian ideals of the *Manifiesto de la Moncada* (Moncada Manifesto) were identified with the needs and the way of life of the poorest strata of the population, mercilessly exploited throughout the centuries—the peasants. Likewise, the daily imperatives of an underdeveloped country—later subjected to the U.S. embargo—encouraged frugality, the ethos and rigor of a productive peasant life, opposing parasitism, hedonism, and the material satisfaction available in Havana, which was assumed to be a developed metropolis. Thus, for forty years, the urban townscape remained unaltered in its central areas, as most of the new buildings appeared on the periphery. The "myth of the new" prevailed on the contextual integration between the past and the present.[25]

An attempt to materialize the longed-for utopia linked to the new way of life and the creation of the "new man," as proposed by Che Guevara, was carried out during the 1960s in the so-called romantic period of the revolution. Facing the "corrupt city," inherited from the capitalist past, the natural landscape became a source of inspiration for desirable ethical and moral behavior. To live, work, and study in contact with nature would forge healthy habits and customs, and would purify the individual physically and spiritually. These new social and cultural values guided the three main public projects built by the government in that decade: the Unidad Vecinal (housing development) of East Havana; the University Campus José Antonio Echeverría; and the Art Schools Complex, which included ballet, modern dance, music, fine arts, and drama, in the barren periphery of Cubanacán, Havana.

Whereas the void of the Plaza de la Revolution represents the urban icon of "global" socialist Havana, the Art Schools Complex bears witness to the creative freedom of the

Ricardo Porro, Vittorio Garatti, and Roberto Gottardi, School for the Arts, Cubanacán, Havana, 1961. Photo Paolo Gasparini. © From John Loomis, *Revolution of Forms, Cuba's Forgotten Art Schools* (New York: Princeton Architectural Press, 1999).

24. Carl E. Schorske, *Thinking with History: Explorations in the Passage to Modernism* (Princeton: Princeton University Press, 1998).

25. Roberto Segre, *Arquitectura y Urbanismo de la Revolución cubana* (Havana: Editorial Pueblo y Educación, 1995).

Jean-Claude Nicolas Forestier, Perspective of the final project (partially realized) for the Avenida del Puerto, the Avenida del Palacio, and the Paseo del Prado, Havana, 1929. Photo Secretaría de Obras Públicas de Cuba. © Institut Français d'Architecture (Paris, Fonds Leveau).

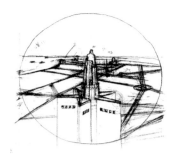

Jean Labatut, Perspective of the project for the José Martí monument, Plaza de la República, 1943. © Archives Jean Labatut, Special Collections, Princeton University Library. All rights reserved.

26. John Loomis, *Revolution of Forms. Cuba's Forgotten Art Schools* (New York: Princeton Architectural Press, 1999).

27. Roberto Segre, "Geografía y geometría de América Latina: naturaleza, arquitectura y sociedad," in *Ciudad y Territorio. Estudios Territoriales*, no. 128, vol. 33 (Madrid, 2001): 283–94.

28. Eusébio Leal Spengler, *Desafío de una utopía. Una estrategía integral para la gestión de salvaguardia de La Habana Vieja* (Havana: Oficina del Historiador de la Ciudad, 1999).

1960s. The schools came about as a result of Fidel Castro's fascination with the bucolic golf course of the Havana Country Club, a site that he decided to transform into a utopian paradise for the formation of Cuban and Third World artists. The architects Ricardo Porro (1925), Vittorio Garatti (1927), and Roberto Gottardi (1927) took on the difficult task of creating an ideal poetic environment for painters, sculptors, dancers, musicians, and actors. The site, the landscape, the quest for cultural syncretism between modernity, Spanish traditions, and African ancestry, all added to the metaphorical language of the identifying attributes of "Cubanness" and served to shape the new images of pavilions, vaults and brick domes, freely set on the topography of the land.[26] The rigid rationality of the urban grid disappeared, together with the concrete jungle and stereotyping International Style schemes. In its stead, an exuberant nature, tropical sensuality, and intellectual surrealism created free and sinuous forms, framing the fluidity of moving bodies along shaded galleries.[27]

However, this romance between culture and nature, between architecture and landscape, was left truncated when the space of productive nature was favored over the contemplative passivity of art. For almost twenty years colonial and republican Havana was abandoned to its fate on account of the supremacy of agricultural and suburban development, while the Art Schools were demonized by a so-called production-led ideology that would support an architecture with "more social contents."

At the end of the twentieth century, ruralized, reviled, and maligned Havana seems to have recuperated its historic path, framed by the beauty of its urban form and the intensity of its social life no longer reduced to the magnificence of the coastal Malecón. Its historic center is steadily re-emerging and the five Art Schools will be restored. No doubt, the contraction of four decades of history and the paralysis of all construction activity bequeathed for future generations a deteriorated metropolis. Yet, contrary to all other Latin American capitals, with the mostly intact fabric of its colonial streets, republican squares, and multiple styles, monuments, and works of art, Havana constitutes a unique urban legacy in Latin America and the Caribbean. It must be protected and preserved to continue shining as "the Pearl of the Antilles," grandiose evidence of civic art in the Americas.[28] ■

Alexandra Exter, Illustration for the manuscript by Lydia Cabrera, *Arere Marekén* [1932–33]. © Cuban Heritage Collection, University of Miami Richter Library.

Max Borges Jr., "Salon de arcos de cristal" (Room of the crystal arches), Tropicana nightclub, Havana, 1951. Photo Pepe Navarro. From Eduardo Luis Rodriguez, *Arquitectura del siglo XX* (Barcelona: Blume, 1998).

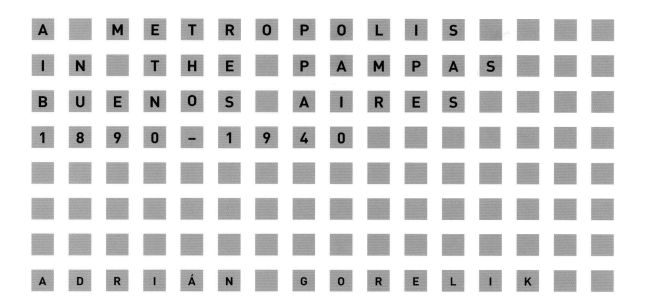

A METROPOLIS
IN THE PAMPAS
BUENOS AIRES
1890 – 1940

ADRIÁN GORELIK

One of the particularities of Buenos Aires is that you cannot see its end. [...] The Pampas does not show any obstacle. [1]

Buenos Aires is a piece of the Pampas translated into a city. This explains the construction in blocks. [...] A city is shaped repeating blocks to the infinite, with no needed boundaries. [...] The principle of repetition to the infinite, showed by nature with the Pampas, was scrupulously respected by men when they had to build the human world in front of the natural world. [2]

The traditional stories about fin-de-siècle Buenos Aires show a "European city" modernized with British loans and infrastructure, French architecture and urban criteria, Italian constructors and builders, and inhabitants from everywhere. This story is partly true; but the quotes heading this essay, by two European visitors arriving in Buenos Aires at two different times between 1890 and 1940, underscore an "American" feature of the city that enables a better understanding of the urban processes and the perception that the culture of Buenos Aires had of them: the relation of the city with the Pampas, which explained both the generalized use of the urban grid and the unlimited suburban expansion.[3]

The Buenos Aires elites were painfully aware of such features, and they tried to modify them with their European eagerness; at the end of the century, this was not easy to achieve. The never-ending perspectives of the streets of Buenos Aires; the houses with low terrace roofs that multiplied in the territory; the monotonous regularity of the plain and the atmosphere of a frontier camping site that was evoked by the provisional constructions built to host the "exotic" crowds that arrived by boat; everything transformed Buenos Aires into a formless chaos, "the ugliest city that I have ever seen of first, second and fourth order," according to Miguel Cané, a conspicuous member of that elite.[4]

According to the civilizing paradigm that ruled the second half of the nineteenth century, Buenos Aires should be the opposite of the barbarism of the Pampas, that anonymous extension responsible both for the political traditions of the *caudillismo* (from *caudillo*: a Latin American dictator) and the nomad character of Argentineans. But what became increasingly clear to the observers of the modernization process was that through the grid the city was extended along the Pampas in a process of metamorphosis rather than in a process of acculturation. The city of 1910 "had no end" because the Pampas was no longer an obstacle but

1. Georges Clémenceau, *Notes de voyage en Amérique du Sud. Argentine, Uruguay, Brésil* (Buenos Aires: Ed. Cabaut et Cie., 1911), 29. The Pampas (often called the Pampa; in Spanish, *la Pampa*) designates the vast plain extending westward across central Argentina from the Atlantic coast to the Andean foothills. The name comes from a Quechua Indian word meaning "flat surface."

2. Massimo Bontempelli, *Noi, gli Aria. Interpretazione sudamericane* [1933] (Palermo: Sellerio Editore, 1994), 68–69.

3. For a more detailed discussion of the themes in this essay, see Adrián Gorelik, *La grilla y el parque, Espacio público y cultura Urbana en Buenos Aires, 1887–1936* (Buenos Aires: Ediciones de la Universidad Nacional de Qilmes, 1998).

4. "Carta al Intendente Torcuato de Alvear desde Viena (14-1-1885)," in A. Beccar Varela, *Torcuato de Alvear. Primer Intendente Municipal de la Ciudad de Buenos Aires* (Buenos Aires: Kraft, 1926), 481.

Left page
Mario Palanti, Barolo Building, Avenida de Mayo, Buenos Aires, 1921. Postcard, private collection, Brussels.

rather a means for metropolitan expansion. For this expansion, more important than the modernizing work of Torcuato de Alvear, the first governor of Buenos Aires (1880–87) when it became the capital of the nation, was a series of transformations that happened at the end of the century and defined the future of the city for several decades.

In 1887 two districts of the province (Flores and Belgrano) were annexed to the capital city, making it four times bigger in area and one of the largest metropolitan jurisdictions in the world. Until then, the municipal district had little more than 15 square miles, with 400,000 inhabitants concentrated in only 1,300 constructed blocks. After the two districts were annexed, the city had more than 70 square miles, but in the new area there were no more than 25,000 inhabitants in a few populated blocks in the villages of Flores and Belgrano. The rest was the immensity of the Pampas abruptly incorporated into the city. If the problem of the culture of Buenos Aires had been to set the limit of civilization against the vacuum that constituted the Pampas ("the desert"), those two problems, the limit and the vacuum, were included on a scale never seen before. What were those lands that were incorporated, and how could they become a city? In the numerous answers to these questions, in the position adopted concerning the problem of expansion, the so-called modern Buenos Aires would be adequately formed.

METROPOLITAN EXPANSION AND PUBLIC REFORM

Once aware of the importance of such questions in the development of Buenos Aires, it is relevant to think about a series of urban decisions made by the public authorities at the end of the century that we can see today as a package of public actions with surprising consequences for the future. The first of such actions was the limit established for the new enlarged municipality: the "Boulevard de Circunvalación," or the current Avenida General Paz. In order to lay the boulevard, a regular and artificial line was drawn that attempted to fix an ordered figure for the new city while preserving the centrality and symmetry of the traditional city, despite the huge change of scale. The design of the boulevard repeats, like a geometrical projection in the territory, the gesture used in 1820 to design the boulevard Entre Ríos-Callao, or what Alvear tried to design with his "perimeter boulevard" project. All three cases brought to the fore the definite "idea of the city" that originated from the regularizing tradition of the nineteenth century. The Napoleonic matrix, deeply rooted in the urban thought of Argentina through the action of the Topographic Department in the nineteenth century, imagined the city renovating itself and growing in a concentric manner around its foundational core.

The whole modernizing program of Alvear—the "Argentinean Haussmann" as he was named in his time—could be explained in that tradition. It encompassed the re-qualification of the center, with the transformation of the Plaza de Mayo (the colonial plaza that concentrated the governmental and commercial functions); the layout of the late nineteenth-century central boulevard, the Avenida de Mayo, ratifying the topographic balance between the south and the north of the city; and a perimeter boulevard to regularize the border of the city and thus serve as a hygienic line for the "insalubrious" places (hospitals and cemeteries, slaughterhouses and factories) and to

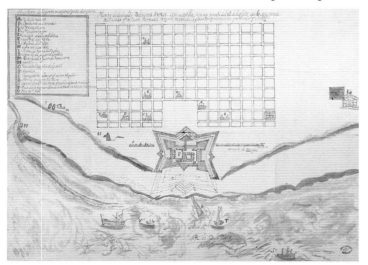

Plan of the City of Buenos Aires, ink on paper, 1708. © Archivo General de Indias, Sevilla, Inv. A.G.I., MP Buenos Aires, 38.

eventually contain the urban "organism" by defining a clear frontier with the hinterland. To change the size of the city in 1887, the public authorities responded with the reflection of that regularizing tradition, trying to cut a clear and distinct urban figure, this time by drawing an imaginative line in the middle of the Pampas. This wish for regularization was also a wish for "form," a counterpart to other transformations of the city at the end of the century that showed the power of that tradition in the urban culture of Buenos Aires. A case in point was the new port on the Rio de la Plata, Puerto Madero, which was being built at the time at the center of the fan-shaped urban figure created by the curved peripheral boulevard.[5]

The second public action was to define the way in which the new urban area was to be occupied. The usual hypothesis is that such occupation was the result of the market, the electrification and extension of the tram network, and real estate speculation.[6] In fact, the lands that were incorporated into the city were private, and the public authorities lacked the legal expropriation tools that, in a regularizing tradition, would have enabled them to keep a "green belt," thus controlling expansion. However, even with these restrictions, that urban tradition was so strong that the municipal bureaucracy, given the huge number of private urbanization proposals, reacted by rejecting one after the other. The argument presented was always the same: they needed a general public plan as a base to make decisions that would ensure "continuity" with the existing city and "regularity" of layouts in the whole metropolitan territory.

In this contradictory context—with the pressures of private interests and the resistance of public authorities who did not approve the expansion but did not have the resources to avoid it—the municipal bureaucracy finally drew in 1898, ten years after the annexation, the public plan that would define the future city. The principles of continuity and regularity resulted in a square-based and uniform grid that accurately defined, block by block, like a homogenizing mesh laid on the plain, the vast fields surrounding the traditional city up to the new boundary. The plan was published in 1904 and the private expansion process started the same year, fostered by the real estate

Luis Taso, *General View of Buenos Aires from the Río de la Plata*, print, nineteenth century. © Museo de América, Madrid.

5. Graciela Silvestri has developed these topics in her analysis of the construction of the port of Buenos Aires. See "La ciudad y el río," in Jorge Liernur and Graciela Silvestri, *El umbral de la metrópolis. Transformaciones técnicas y cultura en la modernización de Buenos Aires* (1870–1930) (Buenos Aires: Sudamericana, 1993).

6. See James Scobie, *Buenos Aires, Plaza to Suburb, 1870–1910* (New York: Oxford University Press, 1974).

Left
Plan de 1888, Department of the Engineers of the Nation, Buenos Aires. © Museo Mitre, Buenos Aires.

Right
Plan of the Public Works Department of the City of Buenos Aires (on the basis of the plan of 1898 by Engineer Carlos María Morales), 1904, Buenos Aires. © Museo Mitre, Buenos Aires.

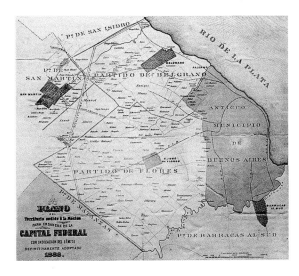

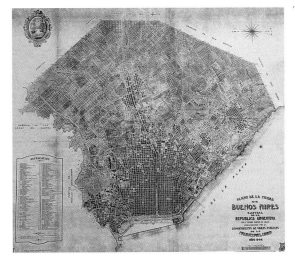

and tram networks, and guided by a public plan of streets that not only promised each of the neighborhoods emerging from those market impulses future integration in a collective layout but also offered them the public support of potential urbanism.

Finally, the third public action was the design of an embryonic system of parks that tried to shape, starting from Palermo, the first public park established in 1870, a green line encompassing the consolidated area of the city from north to south. This system of parks was projected and carried out by the municipal bureaucracy during the same years when the grid plan was being designed, but both actions show strong contradictions. The green line was planned as a hygienic border of the city, preserving its size and concentration while avoiding expansion on lands that the grid was opening to the market. However, it soon became clear that, in an unpredicted way, both actions would combine their reformist effects because, in the context of expansion, parks became meaningful public centers for the new popular neighborhoods that were being developed within the undifferentiated grid.

Obviously, this package of public actions, although not fully coherent, showed a desire for reform at the end of the century. It imagined the city as a uniform frame, which controlled the speculation process to some extent and which was able to lay the urbanistic basis for a kind of integrative social distribution. Such a concept was in strong contrast with the common Latin American practice at that time. Either out of disregard for the state, or because the state was a direct partner of the investors, or because aristocratic prejudice continued to prevail against the popular poor areas, new subdivisions in and around Latin American cities were formed devoid of regulations. Without contact with each other, they were not part of the overall picture of the future city they were forming, thus giving birth to the typical difference between the "formal" and "informal," and the "legal" and "illegal" city. Contrary to that, the existence in Buenos Aires of a public plan that not only included the existing city but also foresaw a growth that would only come about over many decades, was one of the material bases of urbanity that made possible the creation of a public space and that established in the urban form one of the key factors of future social and cultural integration.

If one looks for models for this urban reformism, one could look at the Plan of the Commissioners of New York in 1811: its grid projected the expansion of the entire island at a time when the old Dutch city was hardly developed to its limits. A Latin American example is the plan for the "Ciudad novísima" in Montevideo from 1878, when the Artigas Boulevard was laid out. In the case of Buenos Aires, the wish for reform coincided with an equal distribution of public services in the territory, brought about by the state at about the same time. These urban expressions of the process of "urban equalization" were applied in public institutions of reform, such as the school and public hospital; the same process generated the basis for the electoral reforms that took place from the beginning of the century. In this way the rational and uniform ambition of universalization of public rights, typical of the Argentinean "conservative reformism" was expressed. It tried to formalize "from above" the combination of "public space" and "market" that consolidated the modern city.

THE SEARCH FOR THE CENTER

During the following decades, the progressive occupation of this territory represented the main urban phenomenon in Buenos Aires. Oddly, contemporary observers did not regard the expansion process as the public will for urban reform but instead as the mere physical determinism of the Pampas. In 1910, looking for an explanation for such disproportion, architect Enrique Prins inconsolably described the city as a "flat land, border of the great savannah of the Pampas where nature did not offer the picturesque opportunities of hilly

Intersection of Jean Jaurès and Paraguay, in the periphery, Buenos Aires, 1935. Photo Horacio Coppola. From Horacio Coppola and Alberto Prebisch, *Buenos Aires 1936: visión fotográfica* (Buenos Aires: Municipalidad, 1936).

The "classic" diagonal: Avenue Presidente Roque Sáenz Peña, Buenos Aires, 1936. Photo Horacio Coppola. From *El Buenos Aires de Horacio Coppola* (Valencia: IVAM, Generalitat Valenciana, 1996).

7. "Arquitectura de la ciudad de Buenos Aires," in *Censo General de la Población de la Ciudad de Buenos Aires* (Buenos Aires: Compañía Sudamericana de Billetes de Banco, 1910), 374.

8. Camillo Sitte's book was published in Vienna in 1889 under the title *Der Städtebau nach seinen künstelrichen Grundsätzen*. On its influence, see George R. Collins and Christiane Crasemann Collins, *Camilo Sitte: The Birth of Modern City Planning* (New York: Rizzoli, 1986).

terrain." And he added, "nothing was more logical, in front of this imperturbable plan, than to carry out the work with the simplest and most basic expression: the straight grid."[7]

The hegemony of urban picturesque models at the beginning of the century (which consisted mostly of Camillo Sitte's book reduced to a few principles converted into common clichés) did not permit considering the gridded extension as a public plan, but to the contrary valued it as the clear evidence of its absence.[8] It was a paradox difficult to admit because, for the first time, the city could be proud to show a European face. The fully operational port, the modernization of the center with large public buildings, the impressive bourgeois residences, and the innovative network of public walks or *paseos* north of the traditional city (from Plaza San Martín to Recoleta), all were recognized by visitors to the celebrations of the centenary (1910 marked the centenary of the liberation from Spanish rule) as typically European. In fact, at that time, travelers started a saga of comparisons: the Avenida de Mayo resembled Paris, with its spacious sidewalks and cafés; the narrow streets of the financial sector resembled the City of London; the Park of Palermo resembled the Bois de Boulogne; the district of La Boca resembled Genoa in Italy; and so on. But these "European quotes" were found only in the center; around them, the threatening growth of the American extension continued.

This double-faced image of the metropolis produced paradoxical results in the discipline of urban planning. The primary reaction was to respond with a radicalization of the traditional model of the concentrated city, insisting on the representation of a small city that renovates and densifies itself while rejecting the very concept of expansion. The professional debate during the first two decades focused mostly on the center, claiming its modernization in terms of functional and aesthetic adjustment of the plan: extensions of avenues, new plazas and monumental ensembles, and, particularly, diagonal boulevards; in brief, everything that allowed the development of "picturesque" perspectives, absent in the homogeneous square-based grid or *cuadrícula*.

It is in this context that the proposal of Joseph Bouvard, the French urban planner recruited by the municipality in 1907 to realize the "Centenary Plan," must be understood. For the city center Bouvard formulated a Paris-like system of avenues and diagonals, which eventually resulted in failure: only two short diagonal segments from the Plaza de Mayo were implemented, and one of them was never finished. Yet, if one leaves the center and focuses on Bouvard's proposals for urban expansion, his plan loses the utopian character of the Haussmannian intervention attributed by his contemporaries and posterior historiography.[9] For the periphery he projected a series of apparently incoherent patterns of streets; they were in fact intended to reform the uniform grid that the plan of 1889–1904—designed by municipal engineer Carlos María Morales and Bouvard's main advisor—had "abstractly" imposed upon the future extension in the Pampas. In this way, Bouvard projected one abstraction over another: the new avenues and diagonals, which in the original European models were designed to open dense sectors of compact and historical cities, were considered, in Buenos Aires, as rural paths to be developed later. With his system of *avenidas* (often diagonal) throughout the new territories he tried, with great accuracy and realism, to favor communication between the centers of population that were starting to disseminate in the squared uniformity.

BARRIO, SOCCER, AND TANGO

In the following decade, while the profession of urban planning stayed focused on its debates about the center, the suburbs became—vertiginously but unnoticed—the great social and urban laboratory, which give birth to the creation of the barrio, one of the most characteristic parts of modern Buenos Aires. The barrio was a social and cultural creation that transformed urban expansion into a new public space incorporating popular sectors. To this end, several urban aspects were combined: the uniformity of the grid with its promises of urban and social integration; the development of the parks, which became civic hearts of the new popular barrios; the associations for the promotion of the neighborhood, organized by the residents of the barrios in order to request urban improvements from the municipality, which appeared in the heterogeneous alluvial society as active cores of civil society; and the soccer clubs, which had a great capacity to create popular territorial identities (Buenos Aires is one of the few cities in the world that has a soccer team in each barrio, with a stadium and its own installations). Last but not least, the barrio was also the birthplace of the popular music par excellence, the tango, offering the foundational myths needed for cultural identity. Soccer and tango were

9. As the official expert in the logic of Buenos Aires, Morales was totally aware that the diagonals or other *percées* were almost impossible to build within the city center: the opening of the Avenida de Mayo had been delayed fifteen years, and its construction became extremely expensive due to the lack of adequate tools. However, Morales saw in the Bouvard Plan the possibility to adjust the "abstract" grid of 1898–1904 to the effective expansion that was taking place in the periphery.

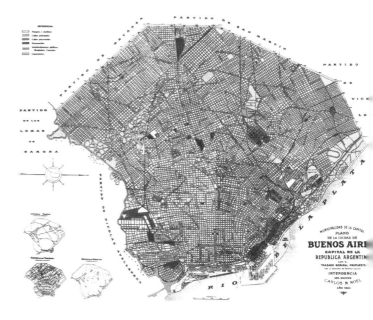

surely the most common and symbolic examples of the intense cultural effervescence of the new suburban society—a genuine melting pot where, in a few years, an original urban identity would emerge from its initial marginality to take cultural control over the whole city.

In fact, during the 1920s, the suburbs advanced in status over the established city to become the new centers that made Buenos Aires alive, thus reverting the balance of the centenary. From then on, urban traditions were reformulated and the controversy between concentration and expansion acquired a clear ideological character: the conflict between urban and political conservatism and reformism. Conservatives insisted on concentrating public investments in modernizing the traditional center, thus reinforcing the breach between center and periphery. Reformists (those socialists and radicals who gained importance by representing barrios) suggested the dissolution of any possible trace of that breach: that is, completing the suburban infrastructure and qualifying it with new civic centers, as well as transferring the old city center to the geographical center of the extended municipality.

All the urban controversy of the 1920s revolved around this "search for the center" of the divided city: the modernized traditional city and the new expanding city. This was the context of the *Proyecto Orgánico de Urbanización del Municipio* of 1925 (Organic Project of Urbanization of the Municipality, known as the Noel

Plan), in which Frenchman Jean Claude Nicolas Forestier (1861–1930) took part as landscape architect. The plan aimed at consolidating the new urban figure in the reformist direction, with new civic centers in the barrio parks and new avenues connecting the periphery. It is in this context that one can interpret the ideological role of two famous foreign visitors: Le Corbusier and Werner Hegemann (1881–1936).[10]

On the one hand, in 1929, Le Corbusier embraced the local conservatism, discovering its most deep-rooted urban myths. This explains his project for the "Cité des Affaires," the platform of skyscrapers on the river that tried to rebalance the de-centered city by inventing a new city on the river, one able to give centrality to the traditional heart and recreate the spirit of the legendary colonial city. In this plan, Buenos Aires would be modernized around its historical center, thereby freeing the surrounding territory and restoring it to the Pampas, that mysterious landscape from ancient times. In his visit in 1931, Hegemann, on the other hand, associated with the socialist and reformist leaders, sharing the belief that the new Buenos Aires should be built "going to its almost virginal center." In that plan, the squared expansion was accepted as the American way to produce public space, but it had to be improved by long-term regional planning that would integrate the urban growth that already started to project the city beyond its new fixed limits of 1887. At the beginning of 1930, this was the challenge offered by reformism: thanks to the grid, the capital city was already unifying the center with the periphery of the first expansion. Now, using improved urban criteria, the second expansion had to be integrated in a metropolitan region.

Alberto Prebisch, Cine Gran Rex, Suipacha 871, Buenos Aires, 1937. Photo Manuel Gómez Piñeiro.

THE 1920S: BORGES, THE GRID, AND THE PAMPAS

The decisive and complex role of the artistic avant-garde in defining the form of metropolitan Buenos Aires during the 1920s and the 1930s can only be understood in relation to the political, cultural, and urban controversy between expansion and concentration. Its action must thus be analyzed in two distinct phases. During the first one—the 1920s—the avant-garde was instrumental in setting up the new periphery as the prime urban protagonist. Its actors saw in the new edges of the city the place for the "re-foundation" of an essential Buenos Aires (in reference to the famous 1926 poem of Jorge Luis Borges, *Fundación mitólogica de Buenos Aires*). During the next decade, however, the position of the avant-garde would shift radically in favor of the conservative project of reevaluating the traditional center.

Contrary to some classic avant-gardes, the movement in Buenos Aires lacked political radicalism, and its aesthetical program was focused on the elitist task of building the myths of a local culture corrupted by the massive presence of overseas immigration. In this context, the early avant-garde embarked upon regaining and reevaluating the Pampas as an essential symbol of Creole culture. Buenos Aires was the setting for creating a language that would produce, simultaneously, its tradition and its future, thus "re-encountering" the evasive face of national identity. Therefore, this movement can be described using an oxymoron: "urban Creole of avant-garde."[11] Jorge Luis Borges (1899–1986) was the spokesperson, the key figure per excellence, whose work epitomized the complexities and contradictions of the decade. There were many other important artists, including the photographer Horacio Cóppola (1906–) and the painter Xul Solar, also creator of a "neo-Creole" lexicon.[12]

As opposed to the conservative vision of the city, for which Buenos Aires was only the center, which released modernizing energy, and the periphery a mere provisional excrescence, and as opposed to the reformist vision, which reverted this equation and situated in the periphery the new political and social meaning of

10. *Proyecto orgánico para la urbanización del municipio. El plano regulador y de reforma de la Capital Federal* (Buenos Aires: Talleres Peuser, 1925); also see Christiane Crasemann Collins, "Urban Interchange in the Southern Cone: Le Corbusier and Werner Hegemann in Argentina," *Journal of the Society of Architectural Historians*, vol. 54, no. 2 (June 1995): 208–27.

11. See Beatriz Sarlo, *Una modernidad periférica: Buenos Aires, 1920 y 1930* (Buenos Aires: Nueva Visión, 1988); and Beatriz Sarlo, *Jorge Luis Borges: a Writer on the Edge* (London: Verso, 1993).

12. *Xul Solar (1887–1963): Collection of the Art Works in the Museum* (Buenos Aires: Pan Klub Foundation/Xul Solar Museum, 1990); *Xul Solar: The Architectures* (London: Courtauld Institute Galleries, 1994). The painter and artist Xul Solar was an intimate friend of Jorge Luis Borges, and he illustrated some of his works. His "neo-Creole" lexicon was based upon the Spanish language and enriched with neologisms and monosyllabic English words.

13. Jorge Luis Borges, "La Fundación mitológica de Buenos Aires," *Cuaderno San Martín* (Buenos Aires: Proa, 1929).

Alberto Prebisch, Original sketch for the Obelisk on Avenida de 9 de Julio, c. 1935. © Archivo Alberto Prebisch, Buenos Aires.

Alberto Prebisch, Obelisk on the Avenida de 9 de Julio, Buenos Aires, 1930s. Postcard, private collection, Brussels.

modernization, this avant-garde was situated in a completely different place. It chose indeed the suburban landscape, the territory that was changing so fast with the pace of expansion, in order to find the answers to its double search for synthesis: between tradition and modernity, and between the city and the Pampas. The simple white houses with straight and blind walls and the paving that rebuilds the imaginary line of unfinished streets lost in the immensity of the plain—these bits and pieces of the city mixed with the Pampas to provide the "urban Creole of the avant-garde" with answers to the anguished questions about the identity of Buenos Aires that had surfaced during the nineteenth century. Where could one establish the character of a city determined to change day after day? What could one identify as its founding core? How could one characterize such an overwhelmingly monotonous, plain, and homogeneous city without historical or natural picturesque beauties, the fulminating result of a modernization "without quality"?

The Creole avant-garde responded with classical ambition. Since "frivolous" time is what passes by most rapidly in countries without history, as Borges says, one has to attach oneself to the thing that remains once time has gone by: an essential order. This is a counter-progressive aspiration that rescues from the modern city the vestiges of an archaic time: the slow cart in the middle of traffic on the avenue or the square of the Pampas in the patio behind a wall. However, what is really remarkable, and what adds ideological ambiguity, is the fact that the counter-progressive aspiration was installed in the suburb, the most progressive region. As a result, the suburbs were ignored and rejected from the image of the city by the traditionalist sectors.

What remains essential in Buenos Aires apart from the passage of time? The most traditional aspects—in fact, the most modern aspects—including the harmonious balance of suburban houses (which in their simplicity announced a "spontaneous cubism"), the abstraction of the Pampas, and above all, the structure that embodied it: the urban grid. There is nothing more essential than that abstract structure, as abstract as the Pampas itself. Borges observed the same thing that all the large local tradition observed with fear: the absolute identification between the grid and the Pampas. However, he reverted its negative connotations, claiming the incarnation of the plain in the straight lines of the plan to the extent that he suggested the "mythological foundation of Buenos Aires" to be a *manzana* (square block) in the middle of the Pampas:

una manzana entera pero en mitad del campo / presenciada de auroras y lluvias y sudestadas / la manzana pareja que persiste en mi barrio."[13] (A full city block, yet in the middle of the country / witness of dawns, rains, and southeast winds / the very block that lives on in my neighborhood.)

The imaginary idea of the "white city" appeared this way in the 1920s: Creole and basic, and able to assume in its essential structure the whirl of expansion. It was an imaginary concept that, without considering reformist programs, claimed as foundational the square-gridded expansion that, at that precise time, was producing the most complete integration of the popular sectors in the city. During the 1930s, however, the Creole and classical avant-garde reversed their urban objective and returned to the center, offering the formula to give new significance to the traditional city through the promise of a harmonious modernization process that would reestablish an essential "meaning."

Widening of Avenida Corrientes, with the Obelisk under construction, Buenos Aires, c. 1935. © Collection Dirección de Paseos, Museo de la Ciudad, Buenos Aires.

THE 1930S: THE WHITE CITY OF ALBERTO PREBISCH

After the military coup of 1930, Buenos Aires was ruled by a conservative coalition that found in the figure of Governor Mariano de Vedia y Mitre (1932–38) an extraordinary vehicle for their program to reestablish the meaning of urban modernization. During his term, all central avenues transversal to the river were widened, the two diagonals were finished, the Avenida Costanera was completed, the Avenida Nueve de Julio was initiated, the underground network was completed; the last water streams crossing the city were canalized, the neighborhoods structure was consolidated and completed with infrastructure; the Avenida General Paz (the Ring of 1887) was built as a landscaped parkway. But, while the capital city was being completed, the political debate about the need to expand the city by incorporating the new suburbs that were already growing beyond its borders was interrupted. Whereas the reformist sectors in natural continuity with the search for the center were making proposals to create the Great Buenos Aires and incorporate public policies within the whole metropolis in expansion, the conservative side enshrined the urban figure formed in 1887, thus closing the city on itself. The Avenida General Paz became the limit between the modern and European city and the new suburbs that would multiply from then on without any system of integration. By consolidating the existing public space, the debate about the needed extension of a public metropolitan space was closed in the 1930s.

For the success of this series of projects, the symbolic re-foundation of the center was essential, and so was appropriating the image of the white city, which the avant-garde had used in the suburbs in the 1920s. The basis for the production of such counter-progressive representations came not from literature or art, but from modern architecture, with the Obelisk constructed by Alberto Prebisch (1899–1970) in 1936 becoming the defining emblem.[14] The counter-symbol to the classical avant-garde was the eclectic Avenida de Mayo and its uncontested icon, the Palacio Barolo (1921), a literal Tower of Babel of stylistic languages, designed by Italian Mario Palanti (1885–1979). In the 1920s, while the Creole was projected in popular little white houses and in the square grid connecting between colonial tradition and avant-garde, Prebisch defended the need for a new classicism in his controversial interventions in the avant-garde magazine *Martín Fierro* (1924–27):

14. See *Alberto Prebisch, une vanguardia con tradición* (Buenos Aires: Fundación CEDODAL, 1999).

15. Alberto Prebisch, Martin Fierro, nos. 5–6 (May 15–June 15, 1924), in *Revista Martí Fierro 1924–1927. Edición Facsimilar* (Buenos Aires: Fondo Nacional de Las Artes, 1995), 35.

16. Antonio U. Vilar, "Arquitectura contemporánea. Carta del Ing. Antonio U. Vilar," *Nuestra Arquitectura* (Buenos Aires, August 1931).

17. I follow the hypothesis by Jorge Liernur about the "discreet" architectural modernism of Buenos Aires. See Jorge Liernur, *Arquitectura argentina en el siglo XX. La construcción de la modernidad* (Buenos Aires: Fondo Nacional de las Artes, 2001).

Each epoch searches for its balance. [. . .] Our epoch searches for that agreement, that balance, it searches for a classicism, its classicism.[15]

When one looks at the work of the main modernist artists of Buenos Aires in the 1930s, such as Antonio Vilar or Jorge Kalanay, it becomes evident that the most locally successful version of modernism was the classical-modern: Vilar himself said in 1931 that "the healthy trends of contemporary architecture" should not be named "modern style" but "classical school of the twentieth century."[16] The search for expressive sobriety and simple masses were the traits that dominated the widespread diffusion of modernist architecture during that decade. A rare exception was the modernizing effect of telescopic projection achieved at the Safico (Walter Moll, 1932), and at the Kavanagh (Sánchez, Lagos y de la Torre, 1935).

The leader of the classical-modern avant-garde was Alberto Prebisch; its manifesto the Gran Rex Cinema he built in 1937. Its sober vitreous facade submits all technological display to the aspiration of a prevailing order, contrasting its "silence" with the "noisy" immediate context, the elaborate Art Deco of the other theaters of Corrientes Street. Likewise, at the urban level, Prebisch's drawings for a square around the Obelisk were the most ambitious proposal to translate this classiccal version of modernist architecture into the public realm.[17] Here the white city of Prebisch broke down the ambiguity that urban precariousness gave to the white city of Borges. It postulated an impressive and homogeneous urban frame that continued in the whole area surrounding the Obelisk the sober lines of the Diagonal Norte: continuous plain and white facades, with regularly spaced windows, a basic plinth at ground level, and a simple cornice. In the center was the Obelisk, its pure form connecting the modern city with the universal culture and, most of all, with national history since it established an immediate dialogue with the old Pyramid of May (the monument to the founding of independent Argentina) located in the historical Plaza de Mayo at the other end of the Diagonal. In the middle of the confusion created by the "vulgar" languages of the modern metropolis, this special version of modernism managed to produce, finally, the act of recognition that the cultural elite had looked for.

This was the end of a cycle, in the city and in the culture, where the productive tension of the 1920s found an official channel to solve the dilemmas of the established culture. The "modern Buenos Aires" assumed its definitive appearance at the end of the 1930s through an architectonical avant-garde that looked for an elitist and nostalgic return to order, denying the metropolitan expansion that would continue nonstop throughout the Pampas. ∎

Sánchez, Lagos y de la Torre, Building Kavanagh, Buenos Aires, 1933.
Postcard, private collection, Brussels.

Walter Moll, Building Safico on Avenida Corrientes, Buenos Aires, 1932.
Postcard, private collection, Brussels.

WHEN BRAZIL WAS MODERN: FROM RIO DE JANEIRO TO BRASILIA

LAURO CAVALCANTI

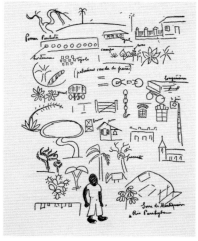

Tarsila do Amaral, Page from Blaise Cendrars, *Feuille de route* (Paris: Au sans pareil, 1924). © Bibliothèque royale de Belgique.

Modernism belongs to the small group of early twentieth-century movements that strove to assert their own universality. For the European modernists, regional cultures and local "ethos" had to be left behind in favor of a new transcontinental culture that would break away from tradition and national chauvinism, and would be put in place for a generation of *hommes nouveaux*.[1]

In the case of Brazil, a peripheral country in the southern hemisphere, the equation was more complex. "Brazilians, and of their time," proposed the *Manifiesto antropófago* (Cannibal manifesto) of 1928.[2] In this seminal text, Oswald de Andrade (1890–1954) advocated that the future cultural production be both cosmopolitan and Brazilian. Through the metaphor of the Indian cannibal who ingested the flesh of his enemies, not only to nourish himself but also to "absorb" their own qualities, Andrade proposed to devour and to regurgitate the influences of the European avant-gardes. A dual movement was therefore necessary, one that provided for the construction of both modernity and nationality. On the one hand, a new art was to accompany the economic transformation of the country and, particularly, the accelerated development of industrialization. On the other hand, the need for broadening the population's access to industrialized goods need not conflict with and could incorporate specific traditions and cultures. Thus, the uniqueness of Brazilian modernism resided in the concomitant and dialectical action of intellectuals in their desire for the utopian construction of a past, and of a future for art and for the country itself. To achieve these goals, it was necessary to "re-discover Brazil" at a time where local traditions and crafts were either unknown or scorned in favor of fantasy-based and superficial interpretations of styles imported from Europe and North America.

The theoretical basis for the re-translation of values in order to form a new national identity in architecture was set forth by Lúcio Costa (1902–1998) in harmony with the modern postulates established by the literary vanguards of the time—including Oswald de Andrade and Mario de Andrade (1893–1945), who militantly espoused the idea of uniting an erudite vanguard with traditional and popular elements. Modernism was not thought of as a style, but rather as a rational evolution of anterior phases and as an ethical and aesthetic solution for the new industrial society.[3]

From today's point of view, the enchantment created by the modernist, multiple and cosmopolitan, production in Brazil between 1920 and 1960 remains strong. But it is now paired with the intellectual desire to better understand it through analysis and scholarship that avoid the two fundamental traps of historiography. The first would be to blindly adopt the points of view of the movement itself, forged as victorious strategies in the battle against the academic and neo-colonial competitors for the control of the Brazilian

1. This essay is adapted from Lauro Cavalcanti, *Introductions to Quando o Brasil era Moderno* (Guia de Arquitectura 1928–1960) and *Quando o Brasil era Moderno* (Artes Plásticas no Rio de Janeiro 1905–1960 (Rio de Janeiro: Paço Imperial, Aeroplano Editora, 2001).

2. Oswald de Andrade, "Manifiesto antropófago" in *Revista de Antropofagia*, no. 1, *Diário de São Paulo*, São Paulo, 1928. Republished in *Brasil: De la Antropofagia a Brasilia 1920–1950* (Valencia: IVAM Centro Julio González, 2001), 591–92 (English translation). See also Eduardo Subirats, *A penúltima visão do paraíso: ensaios sobre memória e globalização* (São Paulo: Studio Nobel, 2001).

3. For more on Lúcio Costa, see the essay by Carlos Eduardo Comas in this book .

Left page
Ismael Nery, *Botafogo Bay, Rio de Janeiro*, watercolor on paper, undated, c. 1930. © Acervo do Centro de Estudos Murilo Mendes, Universidade Federal de juiz de Fora, Minais Gerais.

Avenida Beira Mar, Rio de Janeiro, c. 1906. Photo Gilberto Ferrez. © Instituto Moreira Salles, São Paulo.

4. During those years, also under the impulse of Mayor Pereira Passos (1836–1913), the conquest of new land in the bay and the subsequent construction of the Avenida Beira Mar along the bay radically modified the image of the former colonial city. It must be noted that, at the time, eclecticism was seen as a sign of "international" modernity in contrast to the "retrograde" image of the colonial past. This interpretation was to be reversed during the 1920s–1930s.

Angelo Bruhns and José Cortez, Ecole Normale (today, Institute of Education), sketch of the interior patio, Rio de Janeiro, 1926–30. From Aracy Amaral, *Arquitectura neo-colonial: América Latina, Caribe, Estados Unidos* (São Paulo: Memorial, FCE, 1994).

architectural scene in the 1930s and 1940s. Most of the architectural history books fall into this error, reducing all other currents and styles to the specific viewpoint of modernism. The second risk, common in post-modernist approaches, is to analyze the oeuvre and the protagonists of modernism from a contemporary perspective, without setting them or their interlocutors of the time into context. Such studies make for intelligent and spirited arguments at the price of an easy and superficial criticism that often makes the actions of the group in question an anachronism. In contrast, the study of modernism in Brazil during the four decades in question should simultaneously follow two paths: to associate the study of art with an examination of the aesthetic and social transformations of architecture and urbanism; and to admit the existence of a diversity of modernisms.

Likewise, it is important to remember that, at the beginning of the twentieth century, architecture was taught within the School of Fine Arts in Rio from the third year onward, as one of the specializations—the others being engraving and design of medals. Artists and architects populated the same universe, had the same basic initial training, and thought of art and architecture in a very integrated way.

From 1900 to 1950, Rio de Janeiro was the principal territory for modernization and innovation in Brazil, and the inaugural moment appears to have been the opening, in 1905, of the Avenida Central throughout the historic colonial center. It was a radical operation that swept away thousands of small constructions for the sake of urbanism and sanitation, the obvious model being the Parisian reform of Baron Haussmann from 1853 to 1870. In spite of the eclecticism of the first generation of buildings that lined it, the avenue was seen as a gesture of modernity that coincided with the first innovative trends in the visual arts.[4] When the painter Eliseu Visconti (1866–1944) returned from Europe in 1900, he held an exhibition of decorative art that launched the foundation for industrial processes for art. In some of his works that were strictly for artistic use, he introduced a break with the most rigid academic canons, particularly in the use of angles and colors. Reis Netto and Belmiro de Almeida were two other contemporary artists who, having received a strictly academic education, started to explore new themes and palettes. In the field of caricature, experimentation with freer drawing began to develop, most notably by J. Carlos (1884–1950) and Emiliano di Cavalcanti (1897–1976). One of the grand buildings on Avenida Central, the eclectic Hotel Palace, became a genuine Museum of Modern Art *avant-la-*

lettre: there, Lasar Segall (1891–1957), Cândido Portinari (1903–1962), and Tarsila do Amaral (1886–1973) held their first individual exhibitions.[5]

THE NEO-COLONIAL AND THE NATIONALIST REVIVAL

As in many other Latin American countries, the neo-colonial movement rose to prominence in Brazil during the 1910s. It appeared as a national style that no longer looked to Europe, but rather to the history of the American continent for past references for a new architecture. This pan-American style coincided with the growth of nationalist movements around the world—reflected in architecture in the national-romantic trends—and with the tremendous difficulties in the import of goods from a Europe plunged into World War I.[6] Rejecting the aesthetic codes of eclecticism, the architects of the neo-colonial style questioned the very principles of the Beaux-Arts system and put it into crisis: the white surfaces, increasingly planar, the reduction of ornament, and the pronounced asymmetry of composition in plan and volume prepared the way for the more radical vision of the modern movement.

In Rio de Janeiro, the neo-colonial style found its most ardent defender in José Mariano. Medical doctor, art critic, and professor at the School of Fine Arts, he possessed a large personal fortune, which he placed at the disposal of the new style. In 1921, he created the Heitor de Mello Prize—in recognition of the owner of the most important office in Rio de Janeiro and professor of composition at the School of Fine Arts—that aimed at "creating a type of national architecture inspired directly by the style of the sacred and civil constructions built in Brazil during the colonial period."[7] He led a series of young architects, to whom he gave scholarships to study in the colonial cities of Minas Gerais. It is under his auspices that the young Lúcio Costa spent some time studying in Diamantina: his very first projects clearly bear the mark of this experience. Furthermore, Mariano held a series of small contests between these architects to design various sections of his mansion: Solar Monjope, built in the Botanical Garden neighborhood, brought together the contributions of several winners. From 1926 to 1930, he also promoted what would become the largest neo-colonial work in Rio, the Ecole Normale, designed by Angelo Bruhns and José Cortez and inspired by the old Jesuit colleges and the convents in Pernambuco.

At the Centennial Exposition in 1922, the neo-colonial style had its great opportunity to affirm itself. It was adopted in almost all the buildings, and, on the occasion of the one hundredth anniversary of political emancipation, it was declared to be the style of national aesthetic emancipation. The government decreed the neo-colonial as the national style par excellence, making its use mandatory for representing the country abroad. Despite the naiveté of its conceptual framework and the significant loss of aesthetical quality when applied to large-scale buildings—for instance, at the Ecole Normale (1926–30) and at the National Historical Museum (1919–22)—the neo-colonial style was responsible for much of the good, anonymous, residential architecture that can still be found in the residential areas of various capital cities in Brazil. Other neo-colonial works that are

5. On the period discussed in this essay, see the English version of the book *Quando o Brasil era Moderno*: Lauro Cavalcanti, *When Brazil Was Modern: Guide to Architecture 1928–1960* (New York: Princeton Architectural Press, 2003). Also see the reference book *Brasil: De la Antropofagia a Brasilia 1920–1950* (Valencia: IVAM Centro Julio González, 2001).

6. See Aracy Amaral, *Arquitectura neo-colonial: América Latina, Caribe, Estados Unidos* (São Paulo: Memorial, FCE, 1994).

7. Lauro Cavalcanti, Introduction to *Modernistas na Repartição* (Rio de Janeiro: Editora UFRJ, Paço Imperial, 1993).

Avenida Central, Rio de Janeiro, c. 1907. Photo Gilberto Ferrez. © Instituto Moreira Salles, São Paulo.

Flávio do Carvalho, Competition entry for the monument-lighthouse to Christopher Columbus in Santo Domingo (international competition of 1930-31). From Albert Kelsey, *Program and rules for the second competition for the selection of an architect for the monumental lighthouse...to the memory of Christopher Columbus* (Washington: Pan-American Union, 1931).

8. See for instance *Guia de arquitetura Art Deco no Rio de Janeiro* (Rio de Janeiro: Prefeitura da Cidade do Rio de Janeiro, 1996).

9. Lúcio Costa, *Registro de uma vivência* (São Paulo: Empresa das Artes, 1995). It is obvious that the contemporary interpretation of the period has fundamentally changed. Let us mention, as single example, the futurist-like train station of Mairinque (1906–8) in São Paulo by French architect Victor Dubrugas.

worth mentioning include the schools built in this style during the 1920s by the local government of the Federal District. Yet, at the end of the decade, the neo-colonial movement, which was born to oppose the formalism of the Beaux-Arts system, had become the new "academy" that the modernists intended to uproot.

Imported from Europe and the United States, the Art Deco movement was the logical, albeit less radical, evolution of the modernizing principles of the neo-colonial. Along with the construction of the Avenida Beira Mar and the opening of the tunnels linking Copacabana to the city center, high-rise residential and commercial buildings began to be constructed throughout the southern neighborhoods of Rio—the same phenomenon happened in the heart of São Paulo. On the waterfront of Glória, Flamengo, and Copacabana, Art Deco—sometimes called "modern style" or "Manhattan style"—became the style of choice for the upper middle class that was attracted by its classical modernity, the modern and hygienic white facades, the elegant proportions, the spacious interior spaces, and the sumptuous entrance lobbies. The most renowned architects of the style in Rio were Mário Freire, and Robert Prentice working in association with Floderer.[8]

In spite of its modernity, Art Deco only added to the stylistic confusion. The building boom of the 1900s–1930s had hastened the dominance of design and construction offices (Heitor de Mello, Archimedes Memória, Prentice & Floderer, Riedlinger and Santos Maia in Rio de Janeiro; Ramos de Azevedo, Pucci, and the Sociedade Comercial Construtora in São Paulo) over the studios run by individual architects. The eclectic practice of these large-scale firms, capable of designing high-quality projects for small and large programs in a variety of styles, awakened a negative unanimity amid the modernist and nationalist intelligentsia. Mario de Andrade described São Paulo as a "wedding cake city." Monteiro Lobato deplored the absence of genuine national elements and referred to it as an "architectural esperanto," a "carnival," or even, a "Maori make-up." Likewise, Lúcio Costa described the period as a "hiatus in the history of art" that had produced nothing but "pseudo-architecture."[9]

THE INVENTION OF BRAZILIAN MODERNISM

10. *Warchavchik, Pilon, Rino Levi: três momentos da arquitetura paulista* (São Paulo: FUNARTE, Museu Lasar Segall, 1983).

11. Flávio de Carvalho was an engineer, a painter, and a *provocateur* avant-garde artist. He designed many projects for buildings, wrote avant-garde plays, and produced many provocative performance works: Flávio de Rezende Carvalho and Luiz Camillo Osorio, *Flávio de Carvalho* (São Paulo: Cosac & Naify, 2000).

12. David Underwood, *Oscar Niemeyer and the Architecture of Brazil* (New York: Rizzoli, 1994); Yves Bruand, *L'architecture contemporaine au Brésil* (Paris: Université de Paris IV, 1971).

As in other countries of the New World, modernism came to Brazil following the immigration or the visit of European professionals, the return of Brazilians who studied in Europe, and mainly, the enthusiasm for a new style on the part of the younger generation of architects. The movement was born in São Paulo. The year of 1925 was marked there by the publication of two manifestos, with an Italian accent, in favor of the new style: *Acerca da Arquitetura Moderna* (On modern architecture) by Gregori Warchavchik (1896–1972), a Russian-born architect who had studied and worked with Marcello Piacentini (1881–1960) in Rome, and a letter sent by Rino Levi (1901–1965) while he was still a student, defending the renewal of Brazilian architecture and urbanism.[10]

In the first days of the modernists, the daring proposals of Flávio de Carvalho (1899–1973) were also important.[11] Modernist architecture left the drawing board in 1928—shyly and without yet exploring the plastic possibilities of the new materials—at Gregori Warchavchik's house in São Paulo. One year later, this pioneer built the beautiful cubist house on Itápolis Street, a presage of the force the movement would acquire a few years later. Until the mid-1930s, modern architecture in Brazil held no real surprise; it was applied with correctness and timidity in the tropical climes. It appeared to be merely a new import, different in form but similar in spirit to so many others in previous centuries. This context was radically altered, starting in 1936, via the contacts of Le Corbusier with the Brazilian team—directed by Lúcio Costa—in charge of the design of the new Ministry of

Left
Lasar Segall, *Geometric Landscape*, watercolor and ink on paper, 1924. © Museu Lasar Segall, São Paulo.

Right
Tarsila do Amaral, *City–A Street*, oil on canvas, 1929. © Coleção Paula e Jones Bergamin, Rio de Janeiro. All rights reserved.

Tarsila do Amaral, *Rio de Janeiro, Sugarloaf*, oil on canvas, 1923. © Acervo da Fundação Cultural Ema Gordon Klabin, São Paulo. All rights reserved.

13. Henrique Mindlin, *Modern Architecture in Brazil* (Paris: Vincent, Fréal et Cie, 1956).

14. Carlos Drummond de Andrade was the main Brazilian poet of the twentieth century. As cabinet chief of Prime Minister Capanema, he helped promote the new modern architecture. Mário de Andrade, poet and novelist, collaborated in the creation of the Institute of the National Historic and Artistic Heritage. The anthropologist Gilberto Freyre wrote *Casa Grande e Senzala* (in English: *The Masters and the Slaves: A Study in the Development of Brazilian Civilization*, Berkeley: University of California Press, 1986) and *Sobrados e Mocambos* (1972), two fundamental works for the intellectual formation of Brazil as a modern nation.

15. Getúlio Vargas (1882–1954) led the revolution of 1930 and was president of Brazil until 1945. He was elected for a second term and governed the country again from 1950 to his death by suicide in 1954. More was built in Rio de Janeiro in the 1930s and 1940s than in Brasília in the 1950s and 1960s. See John Dulles, *Vargas of Brazil: A Political Biography* (Austin: University of Texas Press, 1967).

Gregori Warchavchik, Modernist house, rua Itápolis, São Paulo, 1930. From *Guia de Arquitetura 1928–1960 (Quando o Brasil era Moderno)* (Rio de Janeiro: Aeroplano, 2001).

16. Frank Lloyd Wright resided in Rio for three months in 1931: he was a member of the jury for the Christopher Columbus Lighthouse Memorial competition in Santo Domingo.

Education and Health. For this building, conceived and built between 1936 and 1943, modernism was used for the first time on the grand scale of a "palace," proving its feasibility beyond the temperate European climate and the "less noble" program of pavilions, factories, and train stations. There, Lúcio Costa formulated the as-yet-unheard-of theoretical principles for Brazilian modernism, articulating tradition and avant-garde. In this way, the headquarters of the Brazilian ministry helped affirm modernism as a movement for wide application and worldwide reach. For the first time, the architects of a peripheral country challenged the European and North American monopoly on modernism: the Ministry of Education was Brazil's first major contribution to the history of architecture in the twentieth century. Oscar Niemeyer's Pampulha complex (1942–43) followed immediately. There, Niemeyer broke with the existing consensual understanding of modern rationalism and experimented with new formal possibilities and marriages between architecture and structure.[12]

What were the conditions that permitted such changes? How could a remote country, until then known mainly for its exotic nature, landscape, and people, contribute to the international language of modern architecture, a domain that involved new technology, high costs of construction, and sophistication of management?

Henrique Mindlin opened his important book, *Arquitetura moderna no Brasil* (Modern architecture in Brazil) by stating that the history of modern architecture was intertwined with that of a handful of young architects.[13] He could have added that the story of these architects was intimately linked to that of young intellectuals, like Carlos Drummond de Andrade (1902–1987), Mário de Andrade, and Gilberto Freyre (1900–1987), who had decided to operate within the gaps of the cultural apparatus of the *Estado Novo* (New State), trying to change the country by putting into practice the vanguard ideas launched in the previous decade.[14]

During the 1930s, Brazil entered into a favorable economic phase. The new government of Getulio Vargas embarked on the accelerated "modernization" of the country. On the architectural front, it wanted to set its mark on the development of the federal capital and elected as one of its priorities the construction of palaces to house the headquarters of the ministries and the new administration.[15] The architectural atmosphere was still very agitated in Brazil, with the dispute between the modernist, neo-colonialist, and academic architects over the privilege of defining the forms of the new public buildings in Rio de Janeiro. The conquest of the state market was absolutely fundamental in a country where elite and private companies adopted a style only after it had been tried and proven in public works. Unsurprisingly, when Lúcio Costa was nominated director of the School of Fine Arts in 1930, he called the pioneer modernist architect Gregori Warchavchik to teach design. One year later, Costa was "deposed" by the academicians in the faculty: this political move resulted in the blockade of the main avenue of Rio de Janeiro by a student march in his favor—a march Frank Lloyd Wright, who was visiting Rio at the time, participated in.[16]

BRAZIL / EUROPE / USA

To be understood, the history of Brazilian modernist architecture must be related to the international architectural milieu to which it was intimately linked. The lack of opportunities in the stratified and conservative field of European architecture—aggravated by the economic crisis related to World War II—forced many architects to act as theorists and writers for the architectural vanguard. Other professionals like Le Corbusier, Donat-Alfred Agache, and Marcello Piacentini saw the opportunity to carry out their ideas in the emerging Brazilian state market, establishing contacts and alliances to build in Rio de Janeiro or São Paulo. Their combined influence was considerable, even if their built achievements were few. Moreover, contrary to what happened in the United States during the same period, no European with an established reputation—of the likes of Mies van der Rohe, Walter Gropius, or Marcel Breuer—settled in Brazil.

Two axes of international contact structured the beginnings of the Brazilian modernist movement: first, the axis of Brazil/Europe, dominated by France since the arrival of Grandjean de Montigny at the head of the *Mission française* in 1816; second, the axis of Brazil/USA. At the end of the 1930s and the beginning of the 1940s, the Brazilian political scene was, indeed, as much in turmoil as the architectural one: the Vargas government oscillated between remaining neutral or entering the war on the side of the Axis powers or of the Allies. In response, the United States intensified the Good Neighbor Policy that Franklin D. Roosevelt had initiated in 1933 following decades of American interventionism in the South. This strategy was aimed at increasing the North American political, economic, and cultural influence in Latin America, with special attention to countries such as Argentina and Brazil that had strong trade ties with Germany and Italy.

A Gallup survey at the time revealed that a major obstacle to the success of the Good Neighbor Policy was the mutual prejudice that existed between the people of North and South America. Various cultural actions were thus promoted to improve the reciprocal image and bring the people closer together. In the case of Brazil, they included the promotion of the Hollywood career of Carmen Miranda (1909–1955) and the two-week visit by Walt Disney in Rio de Janeiro: the result were three films for the actress (*That Night in Rio; Week-End in Havana; Springtime in the Rockies*); and a new animated character, Zé Carioca, a stylized parrot who appeared next to Donald Duck as a "good neighbor." In 1943, and on a more erudite level, Orson Welles (1915–1985) also journeyed to Brazil, where he started to shoot a full-feature documentary for RKO Pictures, *It's All True.*[17] The same year, under the auspices of the same program, the Museum of Modern Art in New York (MoMA) inaugurated a traveling show, *Brazil Builds: An Exhibition of Colonial and Modern Architecture*. In order to prepare this broad panorama of the new Brazilian architecture, Philip Goodwin, co-designer of MoMA's building, and G. E. Kidder Smith, an American photographer of architecture, spent six months of 1942 in Brazil, visiting buildings and interviewing the new generation of architects. Fascinated by Brazilian modernism, they were the first to capture the singular link between the revolutionary forms and the discovery and preservation of historical buildings.[18]

The success of *Brazil Builds* accelerated the victory of the modernists over the partisans of the competing styles. The show traveled for three years across forty-eight cities of the continent, and its catalogue was internationally distributed. For the first time, international critics and architects turned their attention to the sophisticated production of a country whose image had more often than not been associated with tropical folklore.

Affonso Reidy, Housing complex Pedregulho, São Cristóvão, view of the back facade, Rio de Janeiro, 1947–52. © Arquivo Carmen Portinho.

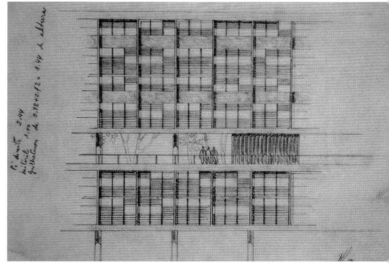

Affonso Reidy, Detail of the facade, housing complex Pedregulho, São Cristóvão, Rio de Janeiro, 1947–52. © Arquivo do Grupo de Perquisa em Habitação e Urbanismo da EESC, Universidade de São Paulo.

17. The film *It's All True* was never completed, as the American producers abandoned the project. A reconstructed version that closely reflects Welles's original concept was released in 1993.

Lasar Segall, *Rua del Mangue* (red lights cistrict), etching, 1926. © Museu Lasar Segall, São Paulo.

The New York World's Fair of 1939 was another event that promoted the Brazilian modernist movement. In line with its "World of Tomorrow" theme, the organizers limited the use of old-fashioned styles to buildings representing the North American states, and decided that the pavilions of foreign nations should be in a modern style. The government of Brazil had to suspend its decree of 1922, which made the neo-colonial style obligatory for buildings constructed to represent the country abroad. A contest was held between the modern architects, with Lúcio Costa and Oscar Niemeyer emerging as winners.[19]

They spent nearly a year in New York, coming in contact with the American and international scene, producing one of the best works both of the fair and of modernism in the first half of the twentieth century. The Brazilian Pavilion used the basic principles of Le Corbusier; yet, the freedom of the ramp, the flexibility of volumes, the solar protection provided with fixed architectonic pieces, the use of curves as expressive elements, and a lack of distinction between internal and external spaces anticipated future trends. The establishment of a peculiar Brazilian idiom, independent and autonomous from the European sources, began with this project. Along with the pavilion of Finland by Alvar Aalto, Costa and Niemeyer's building enthused prestigious critics. Sigfried Giedion wrote:

It is extremely important that our civilization no longer be developed from a single center and that creative works emanate from countries thought provincial, such as Finland and Brazil.[20]

Brazil Builds and the New York World's Fair pavilion strengthened the position of Brazilian modernists in the local architectural field, giving them world recognition and publicity, and encouraging them to maintain their distance from the European canons and to create their own standards. According to Henry-Russell Hitchcock Jr., "the last years have seen the creation of a new national idiom within the international language of modern architecture."[21]

The skirmishes to conquer the dominion of the national scene were fought on two other important terrains: the popular dwelling and the preservation of the past. During the 1930s, the design of low-cost housing projects and the concomitant advocacy for a national housing policy became central points of the modernist discourse and strategy. In doing so, the modern architects were able to take the discussion with their neo-colonial and academic opponents away from the aesthetic domain into the ethical realm. The modern style, besides being superior in its forms, would be the one that would bring, with the simplification and mass production of the construction, a solution to a problem that afflicted everyone: how to create housing to accommodate the enormous numbers of poor people who were moving to the cities during this intense period of industrialization. Although it had more to show in theory than in bricks, the modernist movement produced some very good works designed for popular housing: among those, the Proletarian Apartments (1931–32) by Lúcio Costa and Gregori Warchavchik; the Pedregulho Complex (1947–52) by Affonso Reidy; and the Paquetá Complex (1947–52) by Francisco Bolonha.

Everyone was surprised by the fact that the modernists also supplanted the historicists in caring for the national heritage. Under the intellectual leadership of Lúcio Costa, and quite contrary to the tenets of

18. Philip L. Goodwin and Kidder Smith, *Brazil Builds: Architecture New and Old 1652–1942* (New York: Museum of Modern Art, 1943); also see Zilah Quezado Deckker, *Brazil Built: the Architecture of the Modern Movement in Brazil* (London: Spon Press, 2001).

19. Lúcio Costa won the competition but, recognizing the qualities of Oscar Niemeyer's entry (classified second), he invited the latter to collaborate in the development of the final project.

20. Siegfried Giedon, "Brazil and the Comtemporary Architecture," in Henrique Mindlin, *Modern Architecture.*

21. Henry-Russell Hitchcock Jr., *Latin American Architecture since 1945* (New York: Museum of Modern Art, 1955).

international modernism, a dialectical bridge was established between the past and the future: the emphasis was on the structural likeness between the vernacular architecture of the 1700s, made of wood, stone, and lime, and the new modern buildings. The modernists were able to argue that their historical and artistic interpretation was the most suitable, and helped establish the *Serviço do Patrimônio* (National Heritage Department), responsible for the constitution of a "national symbolic capital" through the selection and protection of works considered to be national monuments. At the same time, they became sole arbiters of the sacralization of the Brazilian historic assets, deciding what could be discarded and what should be preserved for posterity. They acquired enormous symbolic and practical power. As arbiters of the national monuments, they began to express their opinions on the grounds surrounding the protected assets, which in practice granted them the powers of urban planners and the control over the features of the "historical" towns and the centers of the most important cities.[22]

FROM PAMPULHA TO BRASILIA

Just as important as the conquest of the state market in the Vargas era was the adoption of modernism, in the person of Oscar Niemeyer, by Juscelino Kubitschek (1902–1976). From the 1940s to the 1960s, Kubitschek held the offices of mayor of Belo Horizonte, governor of the State of Minas Gerais, and president of Brazil. Few politicians joined with such intensity the objectives of political and architectural renovation. The construction of a new aesthetic would symbolize the Brazilian technical autonomy; its management would mark an exemplary path for the future development of the country.[23]

In architectural terms, this trajectory permitted the appearance of revolutionary projects like Pampulha and Brasilia, which became the symbols of urban and architectonic modernity in Brazil. The construction of this "Brazilianism" paid no tribute whatsoever to the "folklorizing" reductions, frequent in the international image of the country; on the contrary, this new language, at once national and universal, was born from the synthesis of new technologies and unrestricted creative imagination. Brasilia was the only modern foundation, which showed a perfect harmonization between urban design (Lúcio Costa), architecture (Oscar Niemeyer), landscape design (Roberto Burle Marx), and the artists (here invited to produce the public sculptures). In doing so, the conception of the making of Brasilia reached the modernist ideal of making no distinctions between architecture and urbanism, landscaping and plastic arts. Niemeyer had the opportunity in Brasilia to consolidate, on a large scale, the personal language he had been outlining in isolated projects for almost two decades, with structures so light they seemed at times to float above the ground.

The inauguration of Brasilia in 1960 was celebrated as something much larger than the mere construction of a new capital. It evoked pride and expressed, in stone, concrete, and steel, the national objective to achieve progress and a better future. The politicians in power were now eager to build in this Brazilian modern style to symbolize the refinement and efficiency of their administrations. The success of the new architecture crossed over regions and social classes. The elite adhered to the new forms, as did the laypersons and the construction workmen on the outskirts of the cities and in the interior of the country, causing fortunate copies of a stylized modernism to proliferate.

22. See Guilherme Wisnik, *Lúcio Costa* (São Paulo: Cosac & Naify, 2001).

23. See Oscar Niemeyer, *The Curves of Time: The Memoirs of Oscar Niemeyer* (London: Phaidon, 2000); Laurent Vidal, *De Nova Lisboa à Brasilia: l'invention d'une capitale, XIXè-XXè siècles* (Paris: IHEAL, 2002); James Holston, *The Modernist City: An Anthropological Critique of Brasilia* (Chicago: University of Chicago Press, 1989).

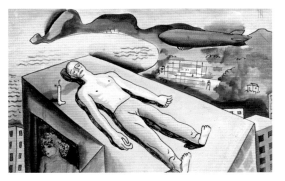

Ismael Nery, *Death of Ismael Nery*, watercolor on paper, December 1930. © Coleção Marcos Marcondes, São Paulo.

Oscar Niemeyer and Roberto Burle Marx (gardens), Itamaraty Palace, Brasilia, 1959–67. Photo Marcel Gautherot. © Institut Moreira Salles, São Paulo.

24. *L'architecture d'aujourd'hui*, 1947, special issue "Brésil," under the direction of Alexandre Persitz.

Oscar Niemeyer, Arcades in the gardens of the Ballroom, Pampulha, Belo Horizonte, 1942. Photo Marcel Gautherot. © Institut Moreira Salles, São Paulo.

The public, at first suspicious and a bit ironic, learned to like the new forms and incorporate them into its day-to-day repertoire. A Brazilian modernist language—whose grammar integrated the new concepts of free space, free structure, independent facades, and the inclusion of unique architectural elements to protect the inner rooms and their occupants from the heat and the excessive light of a tropical country—was being consolidated step by step. The strict modernism that Brazil had imported twenty years earlier from Europe became in the 1950s a more pluralist style, crossing the Atlantic Ocean in the opposite direction. As Europe recovered from the impact of war and entered into a phase of urban reconstruction, the European periodicals published extensive reports on Brazilian architecture. In 1947, *L'architecture d'aujourd'hui* published a special edition dedicated to Brazil, which would have a great impact on European professionals. The second generation of modernists now had Brazil in general, and Oscar Niemeyer in particular, as one of its strongest references.[24]

Paradoxically, the inauguration of Brasilia coincided with a major shift in the international critical view. The International Style had come back in full force in the United States, particularly as the new urban and suburban corporate image. A new orthodoxy was on the rise, which rejected the "inventive" character of the Brazilian model.

Four decades later, at the end of the twentieth century, the renewed interest among the new generation of architects and critics demonstrates that the formal freedom of Brazilian architects between 1930 and 1960 anticipated by three decades, with greater repercussions than what the postmodern movement would eventually produce, the perception that rational functionalism had exhausted itself. If time has undertaken to extinguish the dream of the transforming power of modernist architecture, it has left a legacy in a vigorous, beautiful, and original range of buildings. ∎

Oscar Niemeyer, Dome of the National Congress Building, Brasilia, c. 1962–67. Photo Marcel Gautherot. © Institut Moreira Salles, São Paulo.

REPORT FROM BRAZIL

CARLOS E. COMAS

Lúcio Costa & Oscar Niemeyer, Brazilian Pavilion, International Exposition of New York, 1939. © Casa Lúcio Costa, Rio de Janeiro.

Le Corbusier took notice. While in São Paulo in 1929, he listened to Oswald de Andrade's (1890–1954) theories about anthropophagy as a metaphor for cultural exchange. He describes it in his book *Précisions* as a religious ceremony, implicating both the parricide and sacrifice of heroes:

Anthropophagy was not a habit born out of gluttony; it was an esoteric rite, a communion with the best forces. The meal was meager, one or five hundred partaking the flesh of the captured warrior. This warrior was valiant; his virtues were assimilated; moreover, this warrior had once eaten the flesh of the tribe's own warriors. Thus, the very flesh of one's own ancestors was assimilated by eating his flesh.[1]

Whatever his virtues, the Native American Oswald alluded to in his "Manifiesto antropófago" of 1928 was not a noble savage.[2] Since the discovery of real cannibals in the Amazon at the beginning of the century, the idealized Indian was an object of derision. Likewise, the plot is fantastic and the ambiance rather crude in *Macunaíma: o herói sem nenhum caráter*, a novel also published in 1928 by another de Andrade, Mario (1893–1945). Alternately white, black, yellow, red, man, and woman, Macunaíma is a tropical and barbarian Orlando, as well as the development of the taciturn, indolent, half-white and half-Indian peasant that Monteiro Lobato had sarcastically proposed as the personification of nationhood in *Urupês* of 1915.[3]

Change, cruelty, and crudity are facts of life. Nature is rarely a friend; man is the wolf of man. Lobato reacts against latter-day romantic sentimentalism and symbolist preciousness by promoting a straightforward style. The Andrades parade a kaleidoscopic kind of writing. Analyzing the compositional devices of modernist poetry, Mario stresses the role of polyphony, the multiplicity of superimposed ideas corresponding to the simultaneity of facts and sensations in life. Oswald defends the shaping of a modernist language, born out of mixing the Portuguese with the contributions of other languages immigrated among us and yet tending toward a construction of Latin simplicity. Both assert a right to draw on and add to the whole of the Western culture. Brazilians cannot escape being part of it, by genetics, acculturation, or transculturation. It does not matter if they are bastards, or of mixed blood. Others, like Gilberto Freyre (1900–1987), will not hesitate to attribute the Portuguese capacity for tropical colonization to a mixed cultural heritage made up of Romans, Goths, Arabs, and Jews.

1. Le Corbusier, *Precisions on the Present State of Architecture and Town Planning* [1930] (Cambridge: MIT Press, 1991).

2. Oswald de Andrade, "Manifiesto antropófago" in *Revista de Antropofagia, no. 1, Diário de São Paulo* (São Paulo, 1928). Republished in *Brasil: De la Antropofagia a Brasilia 1920–1950* (Valencia: IVAM Centro Julio González, 2001), 591–92 (English translation).

3. Mário de Andrade, *Macunaíma: The Hero with No Character* [1928] (New York: Random House, 1984); José Bento Monteiro Lobato, *Urupês* [1919] (São Paulo: Brasiliense, 1994).

Left page
Lúcio Costa, Oscar Niemeyer, Affonso Reidy, Jorge Moreira et al., Le Corbusier (consultant), Ministry of Education and Public Health (now Palacio Capanema), main facade with entry portico, 1936–45. Photo Marcel Gautherot. © Institut Moreira Salles, São Paulo.

PUBERTY

4. See Guilherme Wisnik, *Lúcio Costa* (São Pau.o: Cosac & Naify Edições, 2001); Lúcio Costa, *Lúcio Costa: registro de uma vivência* (São Paulo: Empresa das Artes, 1995).

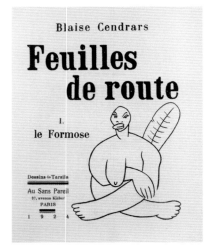

Tarsila do Amara., Cover of Blaise Cendrars, *Feuilles de route* (Paris: Au sans pareil, 1924.. © Bibliothèque royale de Belgique.

Theodor de Bry, *The American Savages Cook the Flesh of Their Prisoners*, in *Americae Tertiae Pars (Memorabile provinciae Brasil'ae Historiam…)* (Frankfurt: M. Becker, 1599). © Special Collections, University of Miami Richter Library.

Educated at the Escola Nacional de Belas Artes in Rio de Janeiro, which was founded in 1826 following the model of the French Ecole des Beaux-Arts, Lúcio Costa (1902–1998) was, in the 1920s, an architect of the neo-colonial persuasion. The project for the Fontes mansion of 1930 was his first modern design, which he presented in airy renderings displaying Palladian and Corbusian themes. A two-story box with a central hall is expanded symmetrically by protruding volumes on stilts. The glazed panes protected by climactically responsive wood blinds assimilate the horizontal window to a characteristic element of colonial and imperial Brazilian houses. Flat ceilings, wood-clad walls, and slender pipe columns provide a foil for Baroque and contemporary furniture.[4] Costa then designed a series of townhouses on narrow urban plots, the company town of Monlevade for the Belgo-minière Company, and the three villas of the Coelho Duarte Estate. These unbuilt projects widen and deepen a line of research where the achievements of Frank Lloyd Wright, Auguste Perret, the Anglo-American residential architecture of the 1910s, and the continental avant-garde of the 1920s are examined in the light of a sound, prized academic training and a heightened consciousness of the Iberian architectural heritage. In the process, the oriental affinities of the *Five Points of Architecture* (1926) are tacitly acknowledged. Was not Le Corbusier's Cité Pessac scorned by many as "the Arab Quarter"?

At that point in time, Costa's efforts definitely converge with contemporary modernist research. Mies van der Rohe explores luxury in Barcelona; Le Corbusier qualifies his mechanomorphism in Rio, where, smitten by the voluptuousness of the landscape, he evokes a meandering river, a serpentine trail, and a Georgian crescent in a curvilinear inhabitable viaduct.[5] Scarce resources and remote sites justify handcraft in the Errazuriz and Mandrot houses. In Paris, the Beistegui apartment, the Swiss Pavilion, and the Porte Molitor Building show the master condoning Surrealist paradoxes and a technological syncretism. The thermal failures of the Salvation Army glazing lead him to sketch shutters for Barcelona and jalousies for Algiers, which he shrewdly christens *brise-soleil*—Juan O'Gorman used them earlier at the Rivera-Kahlo studios in Mexico City (1931), where he added cacti hedges and vibrant colors to constructivist industrial iconography. The Italian Rationalists stress the affinities between *architettura minore* of the past and the modern spirit, while Alvar Aalto's Villa Mairea incorporates farm reminiscences.[6]

In the first half of the 1930s, vernacular architecture becomes a formal source as authoritative in terms of inspiration and composition potential as modern construction, engineering, industry, or painting. Modern architecture is no longer a breakthrough of new technologies and materials, but of linguistics. The economic depression undermines unconditional beliefs in the virtues of the machine and underlines the split between the presumed internationalism of modern architecture and the reality of its (mostly) German and Russian bases. The alliance of modern architecture with industrialization has to be qualified, and the claim of an essential opposition between nationalism and modernity discarded—after all, the constitution of the modern nation and industrialization are historically associated phenomena. As the Italian Rationalists suggested in 1927, a national modern architecture was a real possibility: given the strong classical substrate, symmetry would distinguish Italian modern architecture.[7]

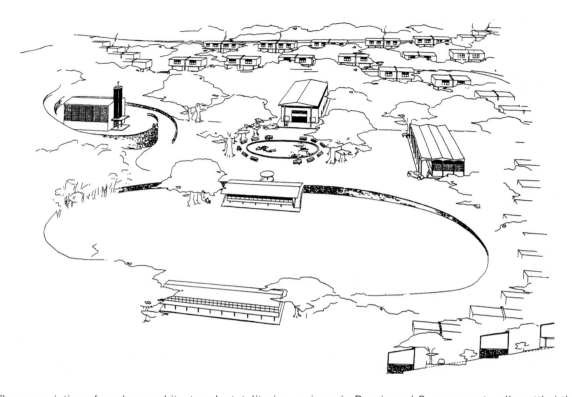

Lúcio Costa, Project for the industrial company town of Monlevade for the Compagnie Belgo-Minière, Minas Gerais, 1939. © Casa Lúcio Costa, Rio de Janeiro.

5. Yannis Tsiomis, *Le Corbusier: Rio de Janeiro 1929, 1936* (Paris: Centro de Arquitectura e Urbanismo do Rio de Janeiro, 1998).

6. See Il Gruppo 7 (Ubaldo, Castagnoli, Figini, Frette, Larco, Pollini, Rava, Terragni), "Architecture" and "The Foreigners," in *Oppositions* no. 6 (Fall 1976): 89–102.

7. See Richard Etlin, M*odernism in Italian Architecture, 1980–1940* (Cambridge: MIT Press, 1991).

8. Julien Guadet, *Eléments et théorie de l'architecture* (Paris: Librairie de la construction moderne, 1909); Quatremère de Quincy (edited by Samir Younés), *The True, the Fictive, and the Real: The Historical Dictionary of Architecture of Quatremere de Quincy* (London: A. Papadakis, 1999); Henry Russell Hitchcock and Philip Johnson, *The International Style* (New York: MoMA, 1932). On Teige, see Eric Dluhosh and Rostislav Svácha, eds., *Karel Teige, 1900–1951: L'enfant terrible of the Czech Modernist Avant-garde* (Cambridge: MIT Press, 1999). The comparison of the Palazzo della Cancelleria in Rome and the Louvre by Guadet has already indicated that a national architecture could be a question of characteristic or representative attributes and elements within the same style, instead of a characteristic style.

The proscription of modern architecture by totalitarian regimes in Russia and Germany naturally settled the 1928 polemic between Le Corbusier and Karel Teige. The Czech architect and artist condemned the concept of modern monumentality (represented by projects like Le Corbusier's Mundaneum). In the manner of Durand, Teige believed in an "automatic" architectural characterization prompted by need and economy against the "deliberate" characterization backed by Quatremère de Quincy (1755–1849) and Julien Guadet (1834–1908).[8] The "International Style" exhibition at the Museum of Modern Art in New York (1931) was thus like a swan song. Overcoming it became a matter of survival for modern architecture.

In 1935, Le Corbusier visited New York, where he attempted to persuade potential patrons that modernism was capable of dealing with any program and any physical and cultural climate. Yet his recent projects were not sufficient in quantity and quality to prove that modern architecture could cope with diversity without losing the uniformity that is the basis of a true style. Indeed, maturity must succeed childhood, and both birth and puberty are awesome thresholds.

POSITION

Modernization did not develop homogeneously in time and space. The degree of industrialization of the Brazilian south in the 1920s was probably as high as that of the Italian north, whereas other regions in both countries remained in a relative state of underdevelopment. Accelerating the modernization of Brazil was one of the goals of the October 1930 revolution led by Gétulio Vargas.

In 1934, following the consolidation of the régime and the appointment of modernist intellectual Gustavo Capanema as Minister of Education, Lúcio Costa wrote *Razões da nova arquitectura* (Reasons for the New Architecture).[9] In this seminal text, Costa defended the alignment with Le Corbusier, which he saw as the "new Brunelleschi." Considering that the structural skeleton was the normative condition of twentieth-century

9. Costa, *Lúcio Costa*; Lúcio Costa, *Razones de la nueva arquitectura y otros ensayos* (Lima: Embajada del Brasil, 1986).

10. On this period, see Carlos Eduardo Comás and Miquel Adriá, *La casa latinoamericana moderna: 20 paradigmas de mediados de siglo XX* (Naucalpán, Mexico: Gustavo Gili, 2003).

11. On the projects for the University City, see Rogerio de Castro Oliveira, "Dos proyectos, Una Ciudad Universitaria: las 'Modernidades Electivas' de Le Corbusier y Lúcio Costa," in Fernando Perez Oyarzún, ed., *Le Corbusier y Sudamerica: viajes y proyectos* (Santiago de Chile: Pontificia Universidad Católica de Chile, 1991), 128–41.

Lúcio Costa, Museum of Jesuit Missions (Guaraní Indians), São Miguel, Brazil, 1937–40. © Casa Lúcio Costa, Rio de Janeiro.

12. See Carlos Eduardo Comas's doctorate thesis, from which this essay is adapted: *Précisions brésiliennes sur un état passé de l'architecture et de l'urbanisme moderne d'après les projets et les œuvres de Lúcio Costa, Oscar Niemeyer, MMM Roberto, Affonso Reidy, Jorge Moreira & Cie, 1936–45* (Paris: Université de Paris VIII, 2002). On the Ministry of Education, also see Carlos Eduardo Comas, "Prototipo, Monumento, Un Ministerio, El Ministerio" in Oyarzún, *Le Corbusier y Sudamerica,* 114–27.

13. Philip L. Goodwin and G. E. Kidder Smith, *Brazil Builds: Architecture New and Old, 1652–1942* (New York: Museum of Modern Art, 1943).

building and that architecture was in fact construction, he argued that a special kind of frame was to be the normative condition of the new architecture. Cantilevered parallel slabs would permit a free plan and facade, which would show off the independence between supports and walls. Modern architecture according to Le Corbusier implied a return to composition, a position validated by sociocultural and technological change; it was the legitimate heir to the academic tradition. To speak of a rupture with the history of the discipline was thus senseless. Like the Renaissance born in Florence and then spread to Europe, modern architecture was a Mediterranean expression on its way to becoming international; it was not to be an international expression going local. Costa praised Walter Gropius and Mies van der Rohe, but condemned both expressionism and constructivism as barbarian. At the same time, he now ignored Perret—although Notre-Dame-du-Raincy (1923) had been a source of inspiration for the church he planned at Monlevade—and the Italian Rationalists.[10] Le Corbusier returned to Rio in 1936 as a consultant for the projects of the University City and the Ministry of Education. Costa cheered his involvement but quickly issued sharp criticism of his proposals. After the master's departure, Costa—with Oscar Niemeyer, Affonso Reidy, Jorge Moreira, and others—worked out alternative designs for the ministry: they contained the same constitutive elements, but the concepts differed radically. Likewise, in the description of the new project for the University City, Costa changed direction and rehabilitated the stances that he had despised in *Reasons for the New Architecture*. He went on affirming that two opposed conceptions meet and complement each other in modern architecture: the Greco-Roman crystalline rationalism (as in his 1936 proposal for the Rectorate, a monolithic structure framed by a portico pointing to Giorgio de Chirico and Marcello Piacentini), and Gothic-Oriental organic expressiveness (as in his version of the Aula Magna based upon the auditorium designed by Le Corbusier in his Palace of the Soviets competition entry of 1931). Moreover, if modern architecture was intrinsically international because new technology knew no borders, it was able to acquire a local character through the particularities of the plans, the choice of materials, and appropriate vegetation. It was a genuine paraphrase of the "characterization" strategies once described by Quatremère de Quincy.[11]

ACTION

The University City and Ministry of Education in Rio by Lúcio Costa and his team were but two of the many projects that shaped the corpus of Brazilian modern architecture from 1936 to 1945.[12] Programs included institutional headquarters and office buildings; educational, health, and recreational facilities; transportation terminals, warehouses, and factories. Apartments were few yet striking in the case of both the luxury condominium and the low-income housing estate. Most projects were mid-rise, completing or covering a whole urban block. Public gardens and squares usually surrounded low-rise leisure facilities, but civic plazas were a rare occurrence. Sites went from rural to metropolitan, often facing prestigious old buildings and parks. Overall, 60 percent of the projects were built and duly published by the specialized press. The year 1942 marked the success of *Brazil Builds: New and Old, 1652–1942*, a show and catalogue produced by the Museum of Modern Art in New York.[13]

Most projects were commissions by the federal government, yet the deposition of Vargas in 1945 did not hamper the consolidation of the Rio-based school, whose most prestigious names were Costa, Niemeyer, the Roberto Brothers, Reidy, and Moreira. The school's hegemony, established by 1950, would not be challenged

until the early 1960s, when the architects of São Paulo embraced the New Brutalism movement, and Juscelino Kubitschek inaugurated Brasilia.[14]

COMPOSITION

The early and precocious Brazilian contribution to modern architecture was to render palpable what was only a sketch, a much more complex task than historians usually assume. Le Corbusier may have foreshadowed the pure prism with blind end-walls and glazed, long facades, doubled—on one or two sides—by sun-breakers or *brise-soleil*. But he never actually built one, much less designed anything like the giant Venetian blinds of the Ministry of Education, the framed vertical slats rising from the solid edges of a virtual prism at the Brazilian Press Association building (M.M.M. Roberto, ABI, 1936–38), or the screens of the Guinle Park apartments (Lúcio Costa, 1948–54)—where the actualization of the *moucharaby* involved a change of material, scale, and mode of fabrication.[15] Le Corbusier never constructed a serpentine slab block as Affonso Reidy did at the Pedregulho housing estate (1947–52); likewise, the building conceived as a "chest of drawers" was already made reality at the Brazilian Insurance Institute headquarters (M.M.M. Roberto, 1941) long before it became a metaphor in the Unité d'habitation of Marseilles (1945–52).

Alone or combined with vaults and sloping surfaces, the "butterfly roof" that Le Corbusier imagined for the Errazuriz House in 1929, soon became a cliché interpreted in many ways. On the other hand, there was no literal precedent in his work for the combination of a blind attic story with a recessed, stepped, two-storied rounded superstructure visible at the ABI Building by the Roberto Brothers, let alone the sculptural, "Gaudi-esque," ship-like, binuclear superstructure of the roof of the Ministry of Education, the unrecognized forerunner of the celebrated roofline at the Unité d'habitation. All of these efforts fit into a larger endeavor: the systematic, though covert, exploration of the "Domino" potential extrapolated from Le Corbusier's Domino House of 1914, aiming at the multiplication of moves in the architectural game and the intensification of the architectural debate that paralleled it. As exceptions that confirm the norm, bearing walls would be used for many small buildings, alone or in combination with columns; parabolic vaults and arches sprang from the earth at Niemeyer's Pampulha Chapel of São Francesco de Assis (1943) or at the SOTRE showroom (M.M.M. Roberto, 1944–49). Almost ironically, a transposition into wood of the reinforced concrete Domino frame appeared at the Park Hotel of Novo Friburgo, another seminal work of Lúcio Costa in 1944.

Marcelo, Milton & Mauricio (M.M.M.) Roberto with Roberto Burle Marx, Santos Dumont Airport, facade on the park, Rio de Janeiro, 1937. From Philip L. Goodwin and G. E. Kidder Smith, *Brazil Builds: Architecture New and Old, 1652–1942* (New York: Museum of Modern Art, 1943).

Lúcio Costa, Sketch for the residential complex of Parque Guinle, Rio de Janeiro, 1948–54. © Casa Lúcio Costa, Rio de Janeiro.

Developments regarding the body of the building—such as the cantilevered block—also included instances of real hybridization, like the combination of curvilinear and straight wings at the Brazilian Pavilion of the New York World's Fair of 1939, the superimposed prisms of the Ouro Preto Hotel (Oscar Niemeyer, 1942), or the virtual crescent made up of pure prismatic volumes at the Guinle Park (Lúcio Costa, 1948–54), a clever manifestation of ambivalence topped by floating pergolas over boxy penthouses. In these projects, the ground floors reiterate a taste for "both-and" rather than "either-or." Those contained within the projection of the pilotis are neither massive nor voided. An intermediary condition is preferred, semi-voided or semi-massive, as in the ground-floor volumes of the Bristol and the Nova Cintra at the Guinle Park. In either case, they appear as recessive, porous, or a combination of both: the gradation ranges from an almost massive base filled with shops (facing the outside street) to the voided, almost nonexistent faces that stand facing the interior street and the park. Porosity presupposes a void between two solids, whether opaque, translucent, or transparent. Sometimes the void is just an indentation, as at the SOTRE; more often than not, it appears as a "hole" that cuts across the building and may constitute a public route.

In those cases, the central void acts as open vestibule that permits the cars to enter at the Press Association Building; as portico and hypostyle hall linking similar forecourts at the Ministry of Education; as front and back porches screened by a panel of hollow blocks at the Ouro Preto Hotel; and as city and landing strip at the Santos Dumont airport (M.M.M. Roberto, 1937). It is a recurring motif in many guises, as can be seen in a public or garden situation, such as the casino, yacht club, dance hall, and chapel at Pampulha (1943). When not made up of independent wings, the expanded building bases are often perforated by patios as well as indented at their borders, displaying either concave or convex dihedral angles. The bound ground plane is always an element of the composition. Its pavement defines an expanded plinth of minimal depth, while planted parterres may look like vestigial wings. Virtual volumetric subtraction interacts and intensifies volumetric exuberance.

Both contained and expanded bases at times display a colossal order, following an early lead by Auguste Perret. The colossal order unifies the ground floor and the mezzanine in office buildings and in the street facade of the Santos Dumont airport; they reach even higher at the garden elevation of the New York Pavilion or the landing strip facade of the airport. The colossal order also qualifies as majestic extroversion of the free plan mechanism. The most spectacular instance of such an extroversion is the street facade of the Ouro Preto Hotel: under the bedrooms' cantilevered balcony, walls mask supports and then indent to reappear behind them; slabs project and recede, truncating columns or emphasizing their total height in a multilevel space. The contrast between the two opposite facades is quite extreme, colossal order versus cantilevered block, and frame versus indented silhouette and honeycombed texture. The recurring ambivalence is the by-product of an impulse that exaggerates stasis and dynamism, immodesty and conventional decorum, a classical substrate and a Baroque impulse, as Lúcio Costa would say. Compositional interest is anchored in dualities whose terms do not fuse but juxtapose themselves as in a polyphony.

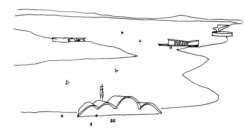

Oscar Niemeyer, Sketch for the development of the lake in Pampulha, Belo Horizonte, c. 1942. © Foundation Oscar Niemeyer, Rio de Janeiro.

CHARACTER

Composition is one of the tools of characterization; material definition is the other. Character is the legitimate source of variety in architecture, according to an academic tradition explicitly acknowledged by Costa and company. Typological or programmatic characterization is the tool that can support and control the quest for multiplicity within unity. Like any other kind of characterization, it will proceed by evoking relevant formal precedents and recalling a proper mood.

Characterization of the zeitgeist in the 1920s relied on construction, engineering, industry, painting, and jazz. Characterization of the genius loci in the 1930s relied on a particular architectural history and a certain geography. But the zeitgeist and the genius loci are elusive entities, the more so if consensus is rare, authority is diffuse or tolerant. Sticking to qualified construction as the foundation for compositional renewal was really a masterstroke. Characterization of type or program (and its emplacement) can then be a much more concentrated, direct, and controllable affair.

Ambivalence now assumes a new tint. In the report he wrote about the New York Pavilion (1939), Costa himself made explicit the connection between a polyphony of curves and a rather womanly Ionic grace and elegance, if not a Dionysian, Baroque frenzy. The straight, virile severity is said to be Doric, if not Apollonian and classical. The Roberto Brothers were the first to associate the colossal order with institutional headquarters supported by rental offices and shops at the Press Association building; moreover, they had conflated the colossal order with a symmetrical void between two solids. In their footsteps, the architects of the Ministry of Education adjusted the mix to suit the monumental agenda and more generous budget. The Ministry of Education set the frame of reference for a correspondence between the colossal order and the public domain of the palace, where several kinds of commerce may go on, from shops to assembly rooms. Almost at the same time, the single order was associated with the ground floor of the apartment building or of utilitarian kinds of buildings.

The feeling for contrast and nuance had manifested itself very early in the two programs where representation of the nation was of the essence. The ephemeral structure of the Brazilian Pavilion in New York (founded upon

Oscar Niemeyer, Hotel in Ouro Preto, Brazil, 1940. From Alberto Sartoris, *Encyclopédie de l'architecture nouvelle—Ordre et climat américains* (Milan: Enrico Hoepli, 1954)

Oscar Niemeyer, with Roberto Burle Marx, Church of São Francisco, seen from the lake, Pampulha, Belo Horizonte, 1943. Photo Marcel Gautherot. © Institut Moreira Salles, São Paulo.

both manor and chapel) descended directly from the Roman villa, whereas, in the ministry as modern monument, the pilotis, transformed into a propylaeum, evoked the forecourts of the Roman Capitol and Versailles. At the pavilion, the grillwork of fixed straight pieces, a modern *moucharaby* hiding the administrative suite, compensated for the abstract and amoeboid biomorphism of the omnipresent curves; at the Ministry of Education, the grille of mobile, curvilinear louvers stood for the figurative mechanomorphism of the episodic curves. Almost palatial, the ministry displayed a "Greco-Roman spirit"; almost domestic, the pavilion showed a "Gothic-Oriental spirit."

Characterization also has an urban side. For Costa and his colleagues, ambivalence has a part in it too. There is the suggestion of a city of business—where, by and large, the traditional block dominates—and of a residential city that also included the garden suburb. As a rule, in the business block, the body of the building will be parallel to one frontage. If the block is square, the base will be expanded, coverage varying from almost total to minimal, from regular to irregular. The original proposal of Ildefons Cerdà for the Ensanche of Barcelona (1859) comes to mind, as well as the typology of parallel bars found in various projects of Gropius and Hilberseimer in 1920s. In fact, there is nothing from Le Corbusier's tenets in the streets that continue to be corridors, or in the urban squares and blocks that remain almost closed. The city is not in the park. As in the past, the park is in the city, and the concepts of enclosure and openness persist on another scale.

UTOPIA

Etymologically, *utopia* means "nowhere." A first meaning is that of an ideally perfect place, especially in its social, political, and moral aspects, or in a work of fiction describing one. A second is that of a chimera, an impossible or absurd fantasy.

In contrast, a movement of architecture that accepts being called "Brazilian Modern" adds a consciousness of place and milieu to a consciousness of contemporaneity. It is thus, by definition, unconcerned with utopian thought and feeling, because perfection is not of this world. It has to accept the world almost as it is. "Almost" means that it is, perhaps, perfectible but that change, cruelty, and crudity will never be eradicated from it; likewise, there is no escape from culture. This theoretical attitude was both mature and cultivated, yet maturity and cultivation have never had really good press in modern times. At best they are considered to be the agents of a conservative modernization and thus scorned.

All this being said, many hints suggest that Lúcio Costa and his group did entertain a "fantasy" in the generative stage of Brazilian modern architecture. Unlike Macunaíma, who had no character and no goal, they wanted to cooperate in the shaping of an inclusive modern architectural language imbued with a classic authority, in the sense that Julien Guadet gave to the expression—the "capacity of withstanding time." They did achieve their goal, though its authority is now almost forgotten. Their fantasy lay in their thinking that eclecticism, in the sense of kitsch, could and would be eradicated by literate consensus. Things did not turn out that way, and very few architects really seem to care. ■

Lúcio Costa, Park Hotel, São Clemente, Novo Friburgo, Brazil, 1944. © Casa Lúcio Costa, Rio de Janeiro.

Jorge Machado Moreira with Roberto Burle Marx, Tapir Building, Rio de Janeiro, 1939–41. From Jorge Czajkowski, ed., *Jorge Machado Moreira* (Rio de Janeiro: Prefeitura do Rio de Janeiro, 1999).

Oscar Niemeyer, Copan Building, São Paulo, 1950. Photo Marcel Gautherot. © Institut Moreira Salles, São Paulo.

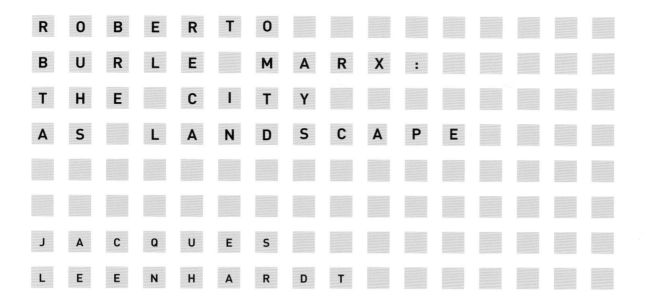

ROBERTO BURLE MARX: THE CITY AS LANDSCAPE

JACQUES LEENHARDT

The painter who wishes for a certain place in his painting to be green places a tree there, and says something more than what he wished to say in the beginning. He adds to his work all the ideas which derive from the idea of a tree and which cannot be reduced to that which is merely just enough. He cannot separate color from any being.[1]

1. Paul Valéry, *Eupalinos ou l'architecte* (1922) in *The Collected Works*, vol. 4 (Princeton: Princeton University Press, 1956) (Author's translation).

It is tempting to recount the life of Roberto Burle Marx (1909–1994) by starting with what appears to be the most exterior aspect of his persona: Brazil. Burle Marx is the son of a country that has given its name to *Haematoxylum Brasiletto*, a tree whose trunk is the color of glowing embers, sought after since antiquity and, since the Middle Ages, imported into Europe from Asia. The Portuguese were overjoyed to find the tree growing in abundance when they disembarked on the coast of South America. The story of Burle Marx, like that of Brazil, is closely linked to that of wood, forests, and plants such as coffee and hevea, which would be the making and unmaking of the country's economic and social destiny, and to the very nature, luxuriance, and biodiversity which is now threatened.

Roberto Burle Marx, *Plan of Square Senator Salgado Filho* (Santos Dumont Airport), Rio de Janeiro, 1938. © Burle Marx & Cia Ltda, photo Haruyoshi Ono.

And yet nothing in this confrontation with his native land and exceptional flora should be taken for granted. At the time of Burle Marx's birth in São Paulo, Brazil was still marked by considerable cultural dependency. Everything that was good and beautiful came from Europe, including manners, taste, and styles. For those who wanted to maintain their place in society in Rio de Janeiro or São Paolo, what Brazil produced was best not discussed. It therefore never occurred to anyone that native plants could be used for embellishing the gardens of the aristocracy, even though Dom João VI, fleeing Portugal when Napoleon appeared, had planted in 1808 the magnificent Botanical Garden of Rio de Janeiro, still the pride of the Cariocas (residents of Rio de Janeiro). Botanical scientists alone were allowed to be interested in native plants while the floral decoration of private or public gardens could only include roses, carnations, and gladioli imported from Europe. Other incentives than those from the local environment would be needed for Burle Marx to discover the incredibly varied vegetation of the various regions of Brazil.

Burle Marx's father was a recent German immigrant while his mother's family, of French and Dutch origin, had been established for some time in Pernambuco, in the northeastern region of Brazil. Burle Marx was therefore a son of the old Europe. A family journey to Berlin in 1928 gave him the opportunity to discover what his eyes could not see in a Brazil that was too familiar and ordinary: the beauty and wealth of tropical flora. The encounter took place at the botanical gardens of Dahlem, which had an abundant collection of rare Brazilian

Left page
Roberto Burle Marx and Affonso Reidy, View of Flamengo Park (Aterro do Flamengo), Rio de Janeiro, c. 1962. Photo Marcel Gautherot. © Institut Moreira Salles, São Paulo.

Roberto Burle Marx, Drawing of a pithecolobium tortum (*jacaré*). From P. M. Bardi, *The Tropical Gardens of Burle Marx* (New York: Reinhold, 1964). © Burle Marx & Cia Ltda, photo Haruyoshi Ono.

Jacaré. Photo Marcel Gautherot. From P .M. Bardi, *The Tropical Gardens of Burle Marx* (New York: Reinhold, 1964).

2. On Burle Marx's multifaceted career, see Rossana Vaccarino and William Howard Adams, eds., *Roberto Burle Marx: Landscapes Reflected* (New York: Princeton Architectural Press, 2000); Jacques Leenhardt, *Dans les jardins de Roberto Burle Marx* (Arles: Crestet Centre d'art, Actes Sud, 1994).

flowers and plants. They must have appeared doubly exotic to him: first as an explosion of colors and shapes exposed far from his native land; second, as a botanical litany expertly displayed in Prussian greenhouses where the shadow of the great Alexander von Humboldt (1769–1859) still lingered—a ghostly presence that in this location took on a paradoxical aura.

Returning to Rio after a year and a half in Germany to paint and study singing, Burle Marx registered in the Fine Arts Academy and started a genuine career in painting. While music and literature would always be an integral part of his work, painting would undoubtedly play the greatest role in influencing the design of his parks and gardens. From the 1920s until the end of his life, he never stopped painting. Knowledge of his pictorial work is thus critical in helping us understand his landscape projects and realizations.[2]

MODERNISM, PAINTING, AND LANDSCAPE

The Brazilian artistic scene of the era revolved around various modernist artists who—in spite of their differences—were driven by the same need to rediscover what was typically Brazilian: among the painters were Lasar Segall, Vicente do Rego Monteiro, Emiliano Di Cavalcanti, Candido Portinari, and Tarsila do Amaral. Indian traditions, the "national" landscape, the common people, and the rich repertoire of images and traditions in music and poetry became the subjects of renewed attention. This new approach, which spread throughout the entire Brazilian society, did not attempt to eradicate the past but, on the contrary, tried to appropriate it to create a culture that was intrinsically Brazilian. Likewise, Roberto Burle Marx took on a realist pictorial expression that strongly related to the urban setting and its human characters; he aimed at capturing the local color but stayed away, like his contemporary Cícero Dias (1907–2003), from any folklore.[3]

The cultural vivacity of this period was such that all artistic disciplines were seized by an urgent need for renewal; concurrently, they showed a strong tendency toward cross-fertilization and interpenetration. Burle Marx showed, for instance, a deep interest in modern music and, especially, literature. He delved into the work of Euclides da Cunha (1866–1909), *Os Sertões*, which gave him a picture of his country of which he was mainly ignorant, a literary and sociological portrait of an entire region, the *sertão*, with its uncompromising climate, flora, and poor and tough people living in the interior of northeastern Brazil. This work, brimming over with an entirely new experience in literature, no doubt acted as a reminder of the whole range of theories on the "ecological park" developed in Germany by Adolf Engler (1844–1930), whom

3. See for instance Cícero Dias et al., *Cícero Dias: uma vida pela pintura* (Curitiba: Simões de Assis Galeria de Arte, 2002); Philippe Dagen, *Cícero Dias: Images au centre du songe; aquarelles et dessins des années vingt* (Paris: Galerie Marwan Hoss, 1994).

Burle Marx got to know while in Berlin. Da Cunha's work revealed within the perspective of both Darwin (1731–1802) and Taine (1828–1893), a style of life that is typically *sertāo*, entirely integrated into the rhythms of nature.[4]

In spite of his association with the modernist movement, Burle Marx's painting remained relatively distant from the formalist radicalization that followed the Modern Art Week of São Paulo in 1922. His own modernist manner was the result of many complex influences and would eventually give emphasis to the drawing of shapes and forms, both on canvas and in his landscape designs. Later, he would abandon the celebration of the object or the figure characteristic of his early work to follow the logic of composition with which he experimented in his many still lives. The lessons he received from the post-cubist movement and his concern for organizing space would directly inspire the pictorial work that he developed for the benefit of the design of his parks and gardens.

In the late 1920s, Burle Marx started to study landscapes and gardens. His first sketches for a landscape project—a tropical garden in Recife ("Study for a Garden," 1929)—clearly show that he attempted to create a new aesthetic effect by making full use of the system of links and repetitions between structures, colors, and materials that he experimented with in his painting. This can be seen, for example, in this and many other drawings where fountains and palm trees are pictured as analog shapes. Likewise, the vertical lines and the horizontal planes appear as constitutive dimensions of the axes of human vision: massifs of trees and plinths of concrete, sky and walls made of bricks or *azulejos* (geometrically patterned ceramic tiles traditionally used in Portugal and Brazil). These systems of opposition, as they multiply the signs of the presence of human artifacts in the natural realm, constantly reaffirm the presence of art in the poetic universe of the garden. The art of painting and the art of designing urban and natural space mixed together, right from his early years of practising as a landscape architect, to create an oeuvre that would incorporate the garden into modernity.

At the other end of his career, this organic link was reinvented in the guise of the landscape designer exercising his influence on painting. Curvilinear shapes made their appearance in his painted works of the 1970s, printed on canvas using the technique of silkscreen printing. These curves originated from his plans for parks and gardens (see, for instance, his scheme for the Parque del Este in Caracas), from graphic depictions of traffic routes, and other layouts defined by their boundaries. It is based on these designs, sometimes printed on top of each other, that his painting style developed in its second phase. By drawing a distinction between silkscreen printing and the unbound work of the paintbrush, the hand, and the body, the idea emerges that Burle Marx transferred his experience of the garden to his painting, an experience simultaneously marked by the constraint of movement and the freedom of the human gaze to deviate.[5]

4. For the English translation of *Os Sertões* (1902), see Euclides da Cunha, *Rebellion in the Backlands* (London: Picador, 1994).

5. On Burle Marx's painting, see Lélia Coelho Frota et al., *Roberto Burle Marx: uma poética da modernidade* (Minais Gerais: Grupo Itaminas, 1989).

Auguste François Marie Glaziou, Campo de Sant'Ana, Rio de Janeiro, c. 1885. Photo Marc Ferrez. © Instituto Moreira Salles, São Paulo.

GARDENS IN RIO DE JANEIRO

6. Louis Van Houtte, *Flore des serres et des jardins de l'Europe* (Gand, 1845–83). On the Mission française see: *Grandjean de Montigny, 1776–1850: un architecte français à Rio* (Boulogne-Billancourt: Bibliothèque Marmottan, 1988).

7. Carlos Gonçalves Terra, *O jardim no Brasil no século XIX: Glaziou revisitado* (Rio de Janeiro: Universidade Federal do Rio de Janeiro, 2000).

8. Charles Adolphe Alphand, *Les promenades de Paris* (Princeton, N.J.: Princeton Architectural Press, 1984). Alphand bestowed a new character to the French tradition as witnessed, precisely, in his design for the Buttes Chaumont.

Since the start of the nineteenth century, Rio de Janeiro had been the scene of intense urban upheaval. Shortly after his arrival from Portugal, Dom Pedro II invited a group of scientists, engineers, and French artists to come to the country. At the head of the *Mission française*, the architect Grandjean de Montigny (1776–1850) imported neo-classicism in architecture, while the art of gardens continued to mimic European models in both shape and choice of plants and trees. Parterres arranged in the French manner co-existed with romantic gardens in the English picturesque style. The Court, which set up residence in Petropolis amid the spectacular mountains that overlook Rio in the distance, aspired to add the aura of civility of English roses and European conifers to its nobility at a time when, paradoxically, Europe believed it could add some colonial glory to its own civilization by bringing exotic plants into its greenhouses and winter gardens. This trend was well reflected in the book by Louis Van Houtte, *Flore des serres et des jardins de l'Europe.*[6]

In 1858, Auguste François Marie Glaziou (1828–1906) arrived in Rio de Janeiro. His work as a hydraulics engineer took him all over the country, enabling him to discover the Brazilian flora in all its unique diversity. Brimming over with enthusiasm, he organized trip after trip into the interior and collected no less than 24,000 species for his herbarium. This drew the attention of Dom Pedro II, who soon made him director of parks and gardens for the city of Rio, a position that he held from 1869 to 1897.[7]

In terms of use of space, Glaziou represents an original synthesis of two great traditions in vogue in Europe: the picturesque nature of the English garden and the formalism of the French garden, the evocativeness of form and nature's right to exuberance. Steeped in the teachings of Jean-Charles Adolphe Alphand (1817–1891), designer of the parks and promenades of Paris under Baron Haussmann, Glaziou designed broad avenues for the gardens of Rio, girding generously cut-out clumps of trees. The garden he created for the Campo Sant'Ana (Praça da Republica) could be called a French version of an English garden, or possibly vice versa. The focus was on making the whole design transparent, further enhancing it by great expanses of green or elevations of huge rocks, for which Glaziou no doubt found inspiration by ambling through Alphand's Buttes Chaumont.[8]

From this rich heritage, Roberto Burle Marx managed to synthesize and create an extremely personal body of work in which he combined art and color, geometry and botany, paying special attention to the human use made of such spaces. His ambition was not just to compose beautiful gardens for private individuals but even more so, in a manner that recalled the social utopias of the Bauhaus, to work for the common good and consequently for and in the city and its public spaces. In this perspective, the encounter with Lúcio Costa (1902–1998), who would remain a friend throughout his life, was a determining factor.

Burle Marx, who had just come back from Recife after designing a dozen gardens and parks while director of the parks department, was commissioned by Costa to design two gardens for the Ministry of Education and Public Health (1936)—one at ground level, by rearranging the approach and the entrance to the building, and the other as a terrace on top of the lower wing containing the auditorium and its adjacent spaces. For the first

Roberto Burle Marx, Gardens of Casa Forte, axial perspective, Recife, Brazil, c. 1935. © Burle Marx & Cia Ltda, photo Haruyoshi Ono.

Roberto Burle Marx, Garden Cavanelas, Pétropolis, Rio de Janeiro, with the house built by Oscar Niemeyer, 1954. Photo Marcel Gautherot. © Institut Moreira Salles, São Paulo.

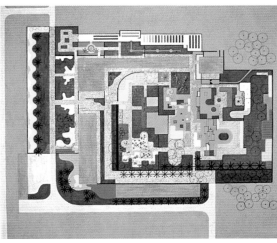

Roberto Burle Marx, Plan of the Fazenda (plantation) Vargem Grande, Areias, São Paulo, 1979. © Burle Marx & Cia Ltda, photo Haruyoshi Ono.

Roberto Burle Marx, Plan of the roof gardens, Ministry of Education and Public Health (now, Palacio Capanema), Rio de Janeiro, 1937. © Burle Marx & Cia Ltda., photo Haruyoshi Ono.

time, he designed a composition of rounded shapes imbricated into one another, like a great organic puzzle whose every element, in turn, consisted of new combinations, obtained at this scale not by the play of shapes but by the selection of the planted species themselves. The gouache drawing, which bears witness to Burle Marx's original intention, cannot but surprise by its quasi-complete absence of green. The artist seemingly intended to offer users of the ministry building a real abstract painting, a painting that can actually be stepped into and walked around in. During the following years he developed this strategy for the design of the Salgado Filho Park, a new entrance to the city for the visitors stepping out of the recently completed Santos Dumont Airport (M.M.M. Roberto, 1937–44).

Burle Marx's method of constructing a double aesthetic experience in space, the experience of the body that feels the winds and smells the fragrances and that of visual and formal perception, no doubt represents one of the most salient features of his vision of a garden. The value of the aesthetic experience of a promenader implies that, in his or her spiritual and physical being, the various levels of perception are continually colliding. As in a theater, he or she has to feel an integral part of the spectacle, to be alive among living beings while retaining the feeling that he is "being entertained," confronted with an event that is happening outside himself. This double experience of vision and physical experience thus represents, in its paradoxical nature, the very basis of a true aesthetic appreciation of landscape and garden.[9]

9. For an inventory of Burle Marx's main projects see Marta Iris Montero, *Roberto Burle Marx: The Lyrical Landscape* (Berkeley: University of California Press, 2001); Vera Beatriz Siqueira, *Burle Marx* (São Paulo: Cosac & Naify, 2001); P. M. Bardi, *The Tropical Gardens of Burle Marx* (New York: Reinhold, 1964).

LAND ART, LANDSCAPE, AND ARTE POVERA

Brazil inherited the tradition of the *azulejos* from Portugal—blue-colored tiles often integrated into architecture. An artist like Candído Portinari made extensive use of them on the outside walls of the Ministry of Education building and, with Oscar Niemeyer, used them again for the chapel of São Francis de Assis in Pampulha (1942). Burle Marx learned the technique and designed a variety of tiled walls, mixing the old traditions of rural handicraft with modern aesthetics. The *azulejos* he designed for Affonso Reidy's Pedregulho housing complex in Rio constitute one of his best creations (1947–52).

In the manner of the follies that adorned parks and gardens in the eighteenth century, walls, pergolas, even sculptures were for him reference points for the eye, which established humanly proportioned spaces.

These follies in a new style were also meant to awaken the viewer's gaze, surprising it by means of a radically unusual element. Burle Marx went very far in this logic. For instance, he purchased the fragments of the granite facade of a demolished bank building in the center of Rio, and he installed them in his own estate of Guaratíba (known as Sitio Burle Marx south of Rio)—an extreme example of his desire to make us notice the beauty of the site through an unusual element. The same applied to the river pebbles—visible, for instance, in the gardens of the Museum of Modern Art—that he collected and placed in strict enclosures that provided a violent contrast. These contrasts distance the local aspects of the landscape, often giving them their own dramatic content in order to support the natural power emanating from the environment. The use of natural, rough materials such as rocks, the simple masses that he sculpted himself (like at the Ministry of the Armed Forces in Brasilia, 1970), or even the recycled objects and ready-made sculptures, establish an unexpected link with the land art movement and the minimalism of the 1960s. Generally speaking, these artists of the 1960s treated natural space as an essential challenge, with the garden as the limiting framework. With Burle Marx, nature became an artistic space bearing witness to the network of aesthetic relationships that gradually evolved, far removed from him, between Arte Povera, land art, and landscape design.[10]

The visitor or user of his parks and gardens gets the exciting yet always unstable feeling that he or she walks at once within nature and a work of art. It is surprising to note that Burle Marx was not afraid of destroying what could appear to be the "harmonious disorder" of his gardens with the introduction of brutally geometric lines or forms. There is certainly nothing systematic in his method. However, it appears that he found in these disparities a way of demarcating, in often extremely limited spaces, the force of order within the force of nature. His desire to put the mark of artifice onto the natural character of the garden also took on other forms. An example is the bromegrass garden for which a special space was set aside within the general layout of the vast Fazenda Vargem Grande. The plants growing there are set out like a display shelf, and the constructions of local stone resemble hewn and shaped rockery. This enabled Burle Marx to create concentric flowerbeds, somewhat like pyramids with circular sections, providing an impressive visual spectacle. Furthermore, thanks to these assemblages often rising to 10 feet, he was able to block out less interesting views in the distance by emphasizing an exceptional collection of his favorite plant: the *Vriesea imperialis*.

URBANISM, PROMENADE, AND TIME

The dimension of time is part of the art of the garden. Initially the garden evolves to the rhythm of the growth of the vegetation while the link established at the beginning with the vegetal material is but an incomplete foreshadowing of what the garden will be like when fully grown. It is therefore difficult to speak of a definitive state of a garden since the life expectancy of every species is different, and pruning, cutting, and replanting never ceases.

However, it is the walker who experiences the most crucial aspect of time regarding the garden and the landscape. The spatial layout mainly serves to give rhythm to the promenade by alternating walking and resting, strolling and stopping, with benches dotted about providing a well-earned rest. The structure of the garden anticipates the walker's sequential experience. The walks will therefore be constructed "in real

10. *Concept Art, Minimal, Arte Povera, Land Art: Collection Marzona* (Stuttgart-Kunsthalle Bielefeld: Editions Cantz, 1990).

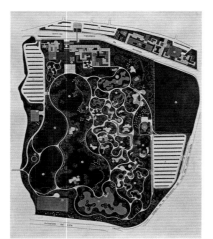

Roberto Burle Marx, Parque del Este, plan, Caracas, 1961. © Burle Marx & Cia Ltda., photo Haruyoshi Ono.

Roberto Burle Marx, Square Burle Marx, Museum of Modern Art, Rio de Janeiro, c. 1962. Photo Marcel Gautherot. © Instituto Moreira Salles, São Paulo.

time," by alternating structured perceptions of the chosen viewpoints and the unwinding of the visual sequences at constantly changing angles.

The first impression that the visitor may form is the general layout of the park, indicated by a plan at the entrance like at the Parque del Este in Caracas. Likewise, the geography may provide a panoramic overview. Due to its topography, the Fazenda Vargem Grande allows for a plunging view that provides a sweeping panorama of the garden area.

The second level of perception is linked to the arrangement of the viewpoints that divide or frame the landscape according to favorable angles. The visitor who takes a break elects a specific arrangement of forms and colors, near or far, whichever is most pleasing. The promenader composes his or her own landscape, a highly aesthetic and independent game, which is, if not the work of the landscaper, then at least of the insistent invitation emanating from the bench deliberately placed in that location.

The third concept, and possibly the most important, is what the walker experiences when moving. Perhaps "concept" is the wrong word in this case as the walker is submitted entirely to the experience provided by

Roberto Burle Marx, Gardens of the Museum of Modern Art, Park of Flamengo, Rio de Janeiro, 1961. © Burle Marx & Cia Ltda., photo Haruyoshi Ono.

Roberto Burle Marx, Avenida Atlántica, Copacabana, Rio de Janeiro, c. 1972. Photo Marcel Gautherot. © Instituto Moreira Salles, São Paulo.

the immediate surroundings. Yet, this sensorial experience or perception is, in fact, the conscious work of the designer. The time taken for the walk has been integrated into this concept, like the time taken for the spectator to move through a kinetic work of art.

Burle Marx paid special attention to these dynamic aspects of perception. The sequence of elements that constitute the sensation was essential to the extent that he knew that designing a garden was not simply creating a picture frame. The dynamic aspect of the walk meant that the painter had to become a film-director. Like the cineast, the landscape architect must be able to conceive, in real time, the articulation of the fixed plans and their very succession. He must move the walker along so that one element can be played off against the other. The dialectic of the walk is thus based on two elements: the images of the landscape, always framed and more or less fixed, whose construction marks a culmination of previous experiences, and a sequence of mobile elements that are difficult to control. These elements are for the walker significant and pertinent aspects that affect his or her consciousness. They may emanate from memory or from the movements of one's own body. A particular shape, perceived in a flash, a particular flower or tree,

11. On the collaboration with Reidy see Nabil Georges Bonduki et al., *Affonso Eduardo Reidy* (São Paulo: Ed. Blau-Instituto Lina Bo Bardi, 2000). The Gloria Hotel, at the edge of the bay at the time of Le Corbusier's sojourn in Rio, was one cf the buildings that were isolated from the sea following the construction of the Aterro do Flamengo.

thus acquire, in an instant engendered by the awakening of the mind and the senses, an autonomy and singularity that removes them momentarily from the overall view.

The development of the vast waterfront park on reclaimed land (between 1953 and 1965), running from the Santos Dumont Airport to the edge of Botafógo, enabled Burle Marx to put all his training and experience into practice. The idea was to guide residents and visitors from the city to the sea. Between history and nature, an enigmatic space would open up which the senses would have to rearrange. Expressing the stratified temporality of the architectural constructions overlooking the city, in perpetual revolution since Rio de Janeiro became the capital of the empire and then of the republic, and in complete contrast with the eternal nature of the tireless sea, was a real challenge. At the beginning of the twentieth century, under the administration of Pereira Passos, the construction of the Avenida Beira Mar city had initiated the "conquest" of the Guanabara Bay. Constructed along the historical center in direction of the church of Glória, cadenced with a series of squares in the French manner, the avenue put the city and the landscape into synchronic movement. During the next two decades, Rio was submitted to a demiurgic urbanism that, opposite the Flamengo district, denied the reality of nature and geography to enter into modernity: the historic hill of the Castelo was razed to the ground to give way to a new business district at the center of which Lúcio Costa and his team were to build the Ministry of Education of Public Health. The removed soil was thrown into the sea to form the Santos Dumont Airport.

In 1961, a design team was established to develop the urbanization master plan of the Aterro do Flamengo—four hundred acres of reclaimed land along the shore in the 1950s. The project included a linear park, dotted with various cultural and sport infrastructures; it integrated, in a great modernist vision, a ribbon-like sinuous expressway that would have separated, for the first time in its history, the city from the sea. The project took place at a time of booming population growth, accompanied—particularly during the subsequent military dictatorship—by ruthless demolitions of the city fabric to create new and large traffic arteries. In these conditions, the park itself would act as a link, not only between buildings and water, a major symbolic contrast, but also between the various poor harbor districts, the former bourgeois center, and the rich and modern districts of Flamengo and Copacabana to the south.[11] Architects Affonso Reidy and Jorge Moreira were in charge of the general plan and the conception of its infrastructure; Burle Marx was commissioned to design the parks, gardens, sport areas, beach, and promenades.

The large-scale project, which was a magnificent collective dream, was accomplished entirely as planned, and it is to its discipline that the city still owes, forty years later, its exceptional link with its maritime setting. The Salgado Filho Park and the gardens of the Museum of Modern Art, which Burle Marx had designed earlier with Affonso Reidy, were extended for a couple of miles with strictly geometric parterres and sinusoid-shaped lawns. The beddings, the groves of trees, and the sport areas such as the soccer fields were constrained within a repertoire of primary forms, circles, ovals, or squares; vividly colored planes and imposing lawns effected the horizontal line while vertical palm trees invited the sky down to earth.

Eventually, Burle Marx gave this pharaonic layout the quality of a work of art. Nature would submit itself to art to accompany the architecture to the sea. The rigid volumes of the city would be morphed into undulating masses of vegetation along the traffic lanes, and would gradually be absorbed by the changing reflections of the bay, right up to the shoreline. Along the pedestrian walks, the bike lanes and the express road itself (which eventually blends in with the park rather than divides it), the city became landscape; the landscape became architecture.

Between 1969 and 1972, the City of Rio invited the landscape architect to further study the relationship between city and nature by redesigning the beachfront avenue in Copacabana. Here also, a wide, three-mile long strip of land was reclaimed from the ocean. Both the existing beach and avenue were relocated toward the water and widened to accommodate the intense pedestrian and vehicular traffic. On the city side, Burle Marx designed a 100-foot wide sidewalk along which he installed a series of "islands" for rest and social interaction,

Roberto Burle Marx, Park of Flamengo, perspective, Rio de Janeiro, 1961.
© Burle Marx & Cia Ltda., photo Haruyoshi Ono.

protected from the sun by a thick canopy. In doing so, he abandoned the traditional concept of continuous alignments of trees in favor of a more complex and picturesque composition. To maintain the visual continuity, he reinterpreted the Portuguese tradition, well known in Rio, of paving the sidewalks with black and white mosaic pieces: here, they undulate like ocean waves. At eye level, or, better, from the seafront terraces of the hotels and apartment buildings, the pavement of Avenida Atlántica appears as a gigantic canvas, a colorful ground "painted" with abstract and organic motifs. In the words of Edgardo Mario Ruiz :

With his solid plastic education, Burle Marx invented, from "modernism" and the use of abstraction, a new style of communication between the various forms of culture and landscape in Brazil. The indigenous flora, the coconut trees that feed the native populations, the pre-Columbian figures, the Portuguese technique, all become elements of a genuine Indo-African-Lusitanian syncretism that resonates in this natural and man-made landscape, and on the sidewalks. Here one could interpret the colors of the ground—black, white and red—as the representation of the three races that constitute the Brazilian culture and people. The sidewalks of Copacabana have become a collective symbol, the "ocean waves" through which the residents identify within the city, as Cariocas. Copacabana is a rare and unique meeting place between popular forms of expression, the natural environment, and the art of an artist: the created landscape represents all the cultures that make the culture of the country. It is Brazil.[12] ∎

12. Edgardo Mario Ruiz, "Brasil en las veredas de Copacabana," Internet http://www.jornaldapaisagem.com.br /artigos/art_ruiz01_esp.htm.

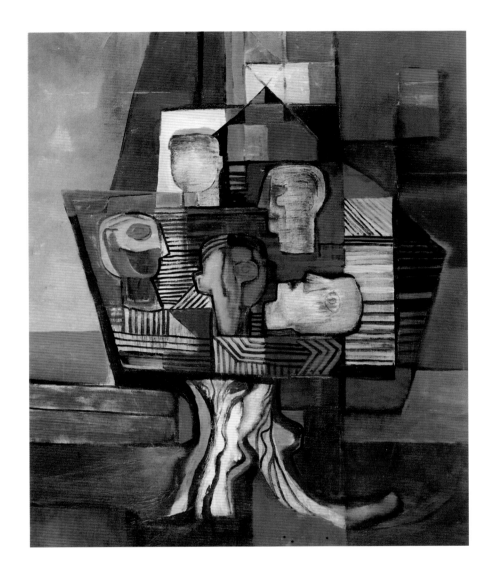

Roberto Burle Marx, *Ex-Votos 2*, acrylic paint on canvas, 1964. © Burle Marx & Cia Ltda., photo Haruyoshi Ono.

Roberto Burle Marx, *Fishes*, oil on canvas, 1951. © Burle Marx & Cia Ltda., photo Haruyoshi Ono.

Roberto Burle Marx, *Landscape with Ex-Votos, Mannequins, and a Rooster*, oil on canvas, 1946. © Burle Marx & Cia Ltda., photo Haruyoshi Ono.

LINA BO BARDI: TOWARD AN ARCHITECTURE WITHOUT BORDERS

OLÍVIA DE OLIVEIRA

For those arriving by sea, the Ministry of Education and Health drew near like a great blue-and-white ship against the sky. It was the first message of peace after the flood of World War II.... In the period immediately post-war, it was like a lighthouse shining over a field of death...It was a marvelous thing.... The fascination for an unimaginable country that had no middle class, only two great aristocracies: that of the Land, Coffee, Sugarcane and...that of the People.[1]

The work of Lina Bo Bardi (1914–1992), absent from most histories of architecture, remained unknown outside Brazil until a very few years ago, when a traveling exposition, organized soon after her death in 1992, awakened a growing interest in the various countries where it was shown. This successful tour confirmed the expressive force and up-to-date nature of a multifaceted body of work that dissolved the limits between the disciplines of architecture, thought, art, and landscape. As a woman, a foreigner—even though a naturalized Brazilian—and a survivor of World War II, Lina Bo Bardi was particularly sensitive to questions linked to the different forms of segregation, barriers, and borders. Her architecture witnesses the search to overcome every type of bipolarity, showing us the possibilities of hybrid models without borders, coherent and crossbred.

Born in Rome, Lina Bo received her degree in architecture in 1939 and worked in Milan from 1940 to 1946 in association with Carlo Pagani, editing and illustrating for various Italian periodicals, including *Illustrazione Italiana, Vetrina, Cordelia, Tempo, Europeo, Corriere De la Sera*, and *Grazia*. In 1944 she and her partner took over the assistant directorship of the magazine *Domus, la casa dell'uomo*. She participated in the main editorial groups and architectural associations in the Milan area, as well as in the group of young architects *Architetti Associati* that formed the basis for the MSA (*Movimento di Studi per l'Architettura*), where a profound theoretical reflection was developed seeking to reestablish contact with the CIAM (Congrès international d'architecture moderne). In this environment, Lina Bo made contact with various colleagues, artists, and intellectuals, among them Franco Albini, Giancarlo Palanti, Luigi Figini, Marco Zanuso, Luciano Canella, Raffaelle Carrieri, Gió Ponti, Giorgio De Chirico, Elio Vittorini, Giancarlo De Carlo, and Ernesto Rogers. During this intense period of struggle, reflection, and introspection, Lina Bo sympathized particularly with many of the ideas defended by architect—and founding member of the group BPPR in 1932—Ernesto Nathan Rogers (1909–1969).[2] At that time Rogers and his collaborators were questioning the Rationalist vision of the

1. Lina Bo Bardi, "Curriculum Literário," in Marcelo Carvalho Ferraz, ed., *Lina Bo Bardi* (São Paulo: Instituto Lina Bo e P. M. Bardi, 1993), 12.

2. See Ezio Bonfanti and Mario Porta, *Città, museo e architettura. Il gruppo BPPR nelle cultura architettonica italiana, 1932–1970* (Florence: Vallechi, 1973).

Left page
Lina Bo Bardi, Leisure and Culture Center SESC Pompéia, view of the sport towers, São Paulo, 1977.
Photo Jean-François Lejeune.

Lina Bo Bardi, Bowl-chair Bardi, study, watercolor, 1951. © Instituto Lina Bo e P. M. Bardi, São Paulo, photo Nelson Kon.

3. Quoted in Manfredo Tafuri and Francesco Dal Co, *Architettura Contemporanea, Modern Architecture* (New York: Electa/Rizzoli, 1986), 333.

4. Antonio Gramsci, *Il materialismo storico e la filosofia de Benedetto Croce* (Rome: Editori Riuniti, 1977).

prewar period and discussing a new strategy of dialogue with tradition. A continuity of the modernist ideals was proposed through their updating and contextualization, which implied rethinking the relationship with the past, the popular tradition, as well as the pre-existing conditions of the environment, whether natural or constructed. Ernesto Rogers's phrase "to weld the cultured tradition and the popular tradition" adequately suggested the state of mind of many Italian intellectuals of the 1950s.[3] It did not mean to Lina Bo a negation of the rationalist postulates in favor of a regionalism of a national-popular nature but rather the search for a balance between the rational and the empirical, between the real and the imaginary. This tie to the past was in no way an act of nostalgia or of stylistic formalism; it meant the search for a method. Whether for Rogers or for Bo, the role of the intellectual coincided with Antonio Gramsci's postulate: to establish a bridge and a balance between tradition and modernity. This is one of the foundations of the work that Lina Bo Bardi would develop over the course of her American career.[4]

Lina Bo Bardi (curator), Exhibition NORDESTE, *bonecos*, or cotton puppets, hand-sewn in Caruaru, Pernambuco, 1963. © Instituto Lina Bo e P. M. Bardi, São Paulo, photo Luiz Hossaka.

OFF TO AMERICA, IN SEARCH OF ANOTHER WAY OF LIFE

In 1946, at the age of 32, Lina Bo arrived in Brazil with her husband and art collector, Pietro Maria Bardi (1900–1999), an important and polemic figure in the Italian Rationalist movement. Brazil was merely the first stop on a long journey, but their immediate enchantment with Rio de Janeiro as well as the possibility of immediate work—the creation of a representative museum in São Paulo—led the couple to remain in the country. Brazil would be, in the eyes of Bo Bardi, like "an unimaginable country, where everything was possible," a place to try out and mature the reflections first contemplated in Italy.[5]

During the first part of her life in Brazil, she settled down in São Paulo and, along with her fellow countryman, architect Giancarlo Palanti, established *Studio d'Arte Palma*, a studio dedicated to architecture and industrial design. Then she became a naturalized Brazilian and, with Pietro Maria Bardi, she founded *Habitat*, a magazine of art, architecture, and culture, from whose pages she launched various criticisms of the architecture produced at that time in Brazil and adulated by international critics. At the same time, she used the opportunity to pay homage to the vernacular architecture and the local popular wisdom.

The capacity of popular culture to improvise, simplify, and invent permeated the architecture of Bo Bardi. For her and for a whole generation of intellectuals and artists of the post–World War II era, it was important to come back into contact with what was "vital, primary, and anti-crystallized in man."[6] This is where the limits between the culture of the elite and the popular culture started to disappear in the production of various artists working

5. About Pietro Maria Bardi, see Riccardo Mariani, *Razionalismo e Architettura Moderna. Storia di una polemica* (Milan: Comunità, 1989). The quote is from: Lina Bo Bardi, "1a Lezione," manuscript for *1a Aula de Teoria e Filosofia da Arquitetura*, Escola de Belas Artes de Bahia, August 11, 1958.

6. Ibid.

Lina Bo Bardi (curator), Exhibition NORDESTE, series of *canecas*, or cups made out of oil and lubricant cans, at the Feira de Santana, Salvador de Bahía, 1963. © Instituto Lina Bo e P. M. Bardi, São Paulo, photo Luiz Hossaka.

7. As regards Reyner Banham, I am referring in particular to the essays published in *The Architectural Review* at the end of the 1950s.

8. Aldo Van Eyck, "Team 10 primer: Otterlo Meeting," in Alison Smithson, ed., *Team 10 primer* (London: Studio Vista, 1968), 22; first published in *Architectural Design* (December 1962).

9. Peter Smithson in "Le Corbusier Exhibition, February 1959," in Alison Smithson, *Team 10 primer*, 32.

10. The *neoconcretista* group was originally made up of Ligia Clark, Amilcar de Castro, Reinaldo Jardim, Lygia Pape, Theon Spanudis, and Franz Weissmann. See "Manifesto Neoconcreto" in Ronaldo Brito, *Neoconcretismo. vértice e ruptura do projeto construtivo brasileiro* (Rio de Janeiro: FUNARTE, 1985), 12–13.

11. Raquel Gerber, "Glauber Rocha e a Experiência Inacabada do Cinema Novo," *Glauber Rocha* (Rio de Janeiro: Paz e Terra, 1977), 23.

around historian and critic Reyner Banham (1922–1988). Bo Bardi's work entered into a dialogue with the polemic writings of Banham, Joseph Rykwert, and above all with the ideas produced by the architects of Team 10—Alison Smithson (1923–1993), Peter Smithson (1923–2003), and Aldo Van Eyck (1918–1999)—who were demanding a conscientious consideration of psychological, emotional, and anthropological factors in architecture and argued for a reconciliation of man with his environment.[7] It was the so-called emotional revolution promoted by Aldo Van Eyck.[8] All these architects had in common a respect for the work and the ideals formulated by Le Corbusier, reserving for him a special place for having "breathed the breath of life" into them.[9]

At the end of the 1950s, Bo Bardi moved to Salvador da Bahía, in the northeast of Brazil, to create and direct the Museum of Art of Bahía. Her work established an intimate relation with that of several young artists who at the time were working on the frontier between the rational and the instinctive. This was a generation that sought to free the imagination and work with what was at hand, following the example of the "super-sensible" objects of Ligia Clark and Helio Oiticica (1937–1980) or the irreverent films of Glauber Rocha (1938–1981), creator of the *Cinema Novo* (New cinema). "We live by adversity," Helio Oiticica would say, followed by Rocha who produced his *Estética da Fome* (Aesthetics of hunger). In the same way, the work *Cultura posta em questão* (Culture called in question) by the poet Ferreira Gullar, leader of the Neoconcretist group, broke ties with any premise of transcendental order to propose a culture that participated in the Brazilian problems that flourished at the time.[10] Conversely, Rocha found in Bo Bardi a master teacher and ally, and he exemplified her work at the head of the Museum of Art of Bahia as a true "war against the province":

The war that the new generations should make against the province should be immediate: the cultural activity of the University and the Museum of Modern Art are two battle tanks . . . , the clarions of battle resounded for the grand exhibitions of the Museum of Modern Art and by the staging of Brecht's "The Threepenny Opera," which provoked great excitement in the petit-bourgeois thinking. . . . Against intellectual elitism, oratory, the mythology of the public square, against the tie and the moustache. . . . The province is being defeated in the very province itself: defeated in its conventional language, in its taboo against the freedom to love, in its social rules of dress, in its laws against the revolution.[11]

In her restoration scheme for the old complex of Solar do Unhão—to house jointly the permanent headquarters of both the Museum of Modern Art and the Museum of Popular Art—Bo Bardi literally removed the distance between the modern and the popular forms of expression. At the inauguration in 1963, she curated a huge exposition entitled *Civilização do Nordeste* (Civilization of the northeast), containing more than a thousand pieces from the artisans of the northeast region of the country—objects made from practically nothing. As Lina explained:

Raw material, trash. Burned out light bulbs, pieces cut from textiles, oil cans, old boxes and newspapers. Each object delineates the limits of the "nothing" of misery. That limit and the continuous hammering of the "useful" and "necessary" is what constitute the value of this production, the poetry of non-gratuitous human things, things non-created out of sheer fantasy. It is in this sense of modernist reality that we critically present this exhibition. As an example of direct simplification of forms full of vital electricity. . . . This exhibition is intended to be an invitation to young people to consider the problem of simplification (not of indigence) in the world today; it is a necessary road to find poetry within technical humanism. It is an accusation. A non-humble accusation that confronts the degrading conditions imposed by men with a desperate effort of culture.[12]

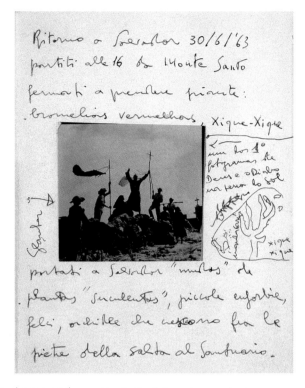

The search for simplification was for Bo Bardi a synonym for humanization and modesty. Against the myth of the originality and the autonomy of the official modernist architecture produced in Brazil in the 1950s, she would produce an architecture that—just as the objects in this exhibition—would make use of the unforeseen, the misfortunes, the precariousness, and the lack of means. Poverty impelled her toward the construction of an alternative language, toward an art of combination inseparable from an art of utilization—very close to kitsch, which operates on the essentiality of means to obtain the maximum expression—capable of proposing an experience distinct from the absurd richness of the real. From her opus arises a powerful criticism of the society deteriorated through consumption; her work is "tactical" inasmuch as it operates by moving within the enemy's camp to attack him where he least expects it. It is in these marginal aspects that resides the power of her architecture, which literally undoes every type of bipolarity between large and small, past and present, figure and background, global and local, natural and artificial, order and chaos, modernist and vernacular architecture, between dream and reason. This consistency reveals an attitude as political as it is ethical, civic, and ecological.

The museum in Bahía was also to house a Popular University to train master workmen and designers to prompt the natural conversion of artisan work into industrial design. This project was abruptly interrupted amid the political turmoil created by the military overthrow of the government in 1964. The exhibition *Civilization of the Northeast* headed the year after for Rome, where it was to be shown at the Gallery of Modern Art: it was scandalously censured and forbidden to open a couple of days prior to its inauguration.

THE WORK AS A MANIFESTO

The oeuvre of Bo Bardi is not only a manifesto against heroic and universal architecture but also against the idea of development associated with progress—which invaded Brazil in the 1950s giving way to mass industrialization—and against the optimism and the promise of an El Dorado that had its emblematic image in the creation of Brasilia. Bo Bardi broke with the hegemonic idea of progress, with the Western model of homogeneous and irreversible linear historical time, always pointed toward the future. She herself explains:

But linear time is an invention of the West, time is not linear, it is a marvelous intricacy where, at any moment, points can be chosen and solutions invented, without beginning and without end.[13]

At the Museum of Art of São Paulo (MASP, or Museu de Arte de São Paulo), designed and built between 1959 and 1968, this concept was developed to the extreme—a "musée hors des limites" (a museum out of the limits).[14] Pietro Bardi described it as such for its important dimensions and its sophisticated structural

12. Lina Bo Bardi, "Nordeste" in: *Mirante das Artes*, no. 6 (Nov.–Dec. 1967).

13. Marcelo Carvalho Ferraz, ed., *Lina Bo Bardi* (São Paulo: Instituto Lina Bo e P. M. Bardi, 1993).

14. Expression used by Pietro Maria Bardi, founder and director of MASP, in his article: "Musées hors des limites," *Habitat*, no. 4 (1951): 50.

15. Ibid.

system that makes it possible to free practically all of the interior of supports and to exhibit *"n'importe quel objet, un machine, un produit, un aéroplane, ou même un cirque"* (any object, a machine, a product, an airplane, or even a circus). He also hinted at the very conception of the art gallery.[15]

In the art gallery or Pinacotheque, the structure dematerializes, reduced to the minimum. Not only does the architecture levitate, but the objects do as well: time and space are in suspension. The MASP breaks with the concept of museum as a continuous, unidirectional, and linear space, such as the Mundaneum project

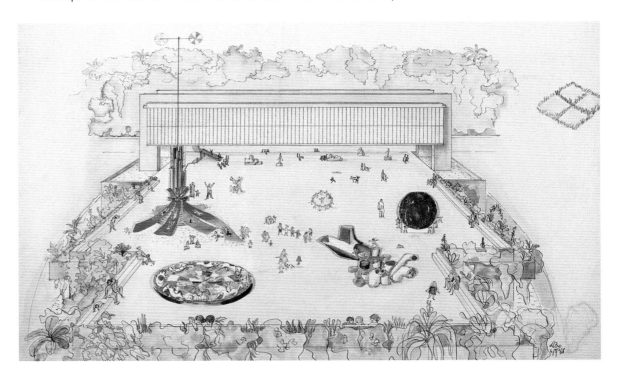

Lina Bo Bardi, São Paulo Art Museum (MASP), study for the urban belvedere, watercolor and collage on paper, São Paulo, 1957–68. © Instituto Lina Bo e P. M. Bardi, São Paulo.

Lina Bo Bardi, São Paulo Art Museum (MASP), perspective under the museum-bridge, watercolor and pencil on paper, São Paulo, 1957–68. © Instituto Lina Bo e P. M. Bardi, São Paulo.

Lina Bo Bardi, São Paulo Art Museum (MASP), interior view of the art gallery, São Paulo, 1957–68. © Instituto Lina Bo e P. M. Bardi, São Paulo, photo Pedro Ribeiro.

by Le Corbusier or the Guggenheim Museum in New York by Frank Lloyd Wright: both of these transmit a notion of continually amplified and progressive time, and the building and the visitor seem to advance together with the passage of time. Here Bo Bardi compressed all time to offer it as one single instant of infinite duration.[16] In this immense lightbox, the paintings of different eras and styles floated with no sort of systematization. They were presented on transparent glass panels supported by a concrete cubic base. Lina believed that the paintings should "return to the air," that is, to the easel, to the very moment in which they were being painted. With this attitude, she promoted a dual subversion of the idea of progress, both because she introduced the notion of the reversibility of time, and because, with it, the creative moment when the painting was still in full dialogue with the painter was re-established. The idea here is to keep time activated at that instant to re-present it to the visitor, who with his or her presence will again have a dialogue with the painting and give it life. The paintings left the walls to seek the company of the public. They mixed with the public, and, due to the transparency, they created a fusion and an overlaying of events. Paintings and visitors were freed from all barriers of periods and predefined interpretations. As though at a ball, the visitor was free to choose the painting with which he would begin the dance.

Bo Bardi conceived her architecture from the movement of the body, not as an absentminded stroll, but as a ritual dance choreographed by the man and the woman who, with their dance, inaugurate a unique time and place. Her buildings, as "organisms suited to life," are open mechanisms that set in motion only when solicited; in other words, when someone explores them, invades them, penetrates them, travels through them, and in his or her journey, invents the place. Against the functional routine, she proposed an architectural form that would sharpen the senses and the imagination, a place for the dance, able to "*déclencher le moment poétique*" (to kick off the poetic instant), Le Corbusier would say.[17]

16. This was the impression that a visitor could experience at the time. Unfortunately Lina's work has been dramatically altered and the experience of the space and the art in the space totally denatured. See Olívia de Oliveira's introduction to *2G*, no. 23/24, Barcelona (December 2002). It is a special issue dedicated to Bo Bardi's built works.

17. Willy Boesiger and Oskar Stonorov, eds, *Le Corbusier et Pierre Jeanneret. Oeuvre Complète 1952–1957* (Zurich: Artemis, 1984), 11.

Lina Bo Bardi, São Paulo Art Museum (MASP), view from Avenida Paulista, São Paulo, 1957–68. © Instituto Lina Bo e P. M. Bardi, São Paulo, photo Flieg.

Lina Bo Bardi, Glass House (Casa de Vidro), São Paulo, 1951. © Instituto Lina Bo e P. M. Bardi, São Paulo, photo Peter C. Scheir.

Lina Bo Bardi, Glass House (Casa de Vidro), entry staircase, São Paulo, 1951. © Instituto Lina Bo e P. M. Bardi, São Paulo, photo Pedro Ribeiro.

THE HYBRID CONDITION

Bo Bardi's affinity for tradition and popular knowledge can already be seen in her early American works: they make evident the interference and crossbreeding of the erudite with the popular, the modernist with the vernacular, the universal with the local. In them there is no place for a dichotomy between elements considered to be antithetic. Here the opposites are no longer seen as contradictions, and they cohabit jointly at the same time and in the same place. This notion is present in the furnishings produced at the end of the 1940s by Studio de Arte Palma, as well as in the articles she wrote for the magazine *Habitat*, where popular techniques of construction, materials, and ways of life of the local population intersected with the best paradigms of contemporary architecture and design. One example was her design for chairs, inspired by objects and situations of Brazilian day-to-day life, such as hammocks, or based upon the squatting or horseback riding positions so common to the rural population. This crossbred, hybrid, indeterminate yet unstratified characteristic would be present in all her oeuvre.

Her own residence in São Paulo (1951) is a demonstration of this hybrid condition. Although most photographs feature only one facade of this building, the Casa de Vidro (House of Glass), as it came to be known, is clearly composed of two bodies: the first, in front, where the social areas of the house are located, is crystalline, floating, supported on thin metallic columns, very close to a modernist language. The second preserves the private portion of the house, walled in and set on the ground, set back and constructed with traditional techniques and materials. In this house, Bo Bardi already achieved a keen, up-to-date, and singular interpretation of the work of the modernist masters. On the various occasions when she published articles on the work of Le Corbusier, Frank Lloyd Wright, or Mies van der Rohe, she emphasized above all the sensations the visitor ought to have upon penetrating these architectural forms. This concern is clearly present in Casa de Vidro, where the visitor is taken into the interior along a precise, controlled route, accentuating the relation of the house to nature and the landscape.[18] The visitor passes literally under the house raised on pilotis to climb a surprising open-air staircase that serves as first belvedere over the city and reveals the suspended patio at the center of which grow trees. Having arrived in the completely transparent living room, the visitor rediscovers the panorama, filtered this time through the colonial furniture and traditional objects that furnish the space.

Here the glass no longer has the strict sense of the liberating transparency that it had in the 1920s and that often legitimized an inquisitive and terrifying character, being capable of use as an instrument for surveillance, accusation, and punishment. In the Glass House, only the social parts of the house are transparent. The private rooms are protected from unwanted eyes by a white wall that passes through the house from one side to the other. This is the true facade of the house, functioning like the doors on a cupboard, just as Peter Smithson would propose, years later, in his text "In Praise of Cupboard Doors."[19] This wall guarantees needed privacy, putting forward Bo Bardi's concern about day-to-day life lived within the intimate spaces.

In contrast, the glass here is seen as a film on which nature stamps its marks. It is a device that captures its surroundings and in turn projects their reflections on the house. This ephemeral, mutant, ambiguous aspect of glass is what interests Bo Bardi. The house remains camouflaged in the middle of nature, in the same way that the very thin metallic columns, only five inches in diameter, are painted a greenish-gray color to more easily blend in with the vegetation.

Lina Bo Bardi, Glass House (Casa de Vidro), view of the back of the house, São Paulo, 1951. © Instituto Lina Bo e P. M. Bardi, São Paulo.

18. [Editor's note: see Felipe Hernandez's essay in this book.]

19. Published in *ILAUD—International Laboratory of Architecture and Urban Design* (Urbino: Signus and Insights, Annual Report, 1979), 40–41.

Lina Bo Bardi, New City Hall of São Paulo, drawing of the great wall with vertical gardens, watercolor, 1990–92. © Instituto Lina Bo e P. M. Bardi, São Paulo.

The vegetable world permeates the architecture of Bo Bardi. From her first drafts, the green element is generally included. The garden is always a part of her architecture; trees literally pass through her buildings; mosses and flowers grow from the walls; structures mimic and even assume vegetable forms. This approximation of architecture and nature reached its height in the project for the new city hall in São Paulo (built in the renovated Palace of Industry of 1924), where a splendid vertical garden stretches across a wall 650 feet long. The sensuality of these gardens, as well as the overcoming of the traditional antithesis between artificial and natural, designed nature versus wild nature, that these architectural forms vindicate, are obvious references to the works of Roberto Burle Marx.

PLACES OPEN TO THE INDEFINITE

20. Aldo Van Eyck, "Otterlo Meeting—1959," in Alison Smithson, 43.

21. See: Eduardo Subirats, "Fourier o el mundo como voluptuosidad" in *Utopía y subversión* (Barcelona: Anagrama, 1975), 11–46. Fourier was a French social theorist who advocated a reconstruction of society based on communal associations of producers known as phalanges.

The reconciliation between antithetic elements is exalted in the architecture of Bo Bardi through pronounced open voids, expanded passageways, and significant elements for gathering, circulating, and passing through. They help understand the need for a joint cohabitation between two apparently opposing parts. Such places of transition assume an ambiguous meaning, being at the same time one thing and another, above and below, large and small, past and present, natural and artificial. An equality is established, a reciprocity, a reconciliation, and an exchange between conflicting polarities, exactly as in the beginning of the *gemelliparité* observed by Aldo Van Eyck among the Dogon people, where reality is always produced in complementary planes that balance one another.[20] This principle is what Bo Bardi constantly evokes in dramatizing these places of transition and passage. They are used as mechanisms to space out the time of entry or exit from a place. With this, the sense of passing from one place to another is increased; the threshold is no longer just a mark or a line but an interval, a place where things happen. This is the role of the "patio of the roses" in the Casa de Vidro, of the impressive interspace span of MASP, of the multiple aerial walkways that tie together the two buildings of the sports complex of the SESC Pompéia, and of the innumerable stairways that dot her architectural forms.

Lina Bo Bardi, Leisure and Culture Center SESC Pompéia, watercolor illustrating the "possible future of SESC," São Paulo, 1977. © Instituto Lina Bo e P. M. Bardi, São Paulo.

Within the best Surrealist spirit, the nuclear motif of Bo Bardi's work—the void as an intermediary element—is the place where no impulse is repressed. Bo Bardi liked to quote John Cage (1912–1992), who, upon encountering the huge span of MASP, exclaimed, "This is the architecture of freedom!" As a matter of fact, the free span of MASP is an exact silent interval in the music of John Cage; a place to listen to another, open to the indefinite. It is not by chance that silence is, likewise, a nuclear motif in Charles Fourier's (1772–1837) theories. Silence configures a subterranean level of reality, of that which is oppressed but not suppressed. It subsists alongside the imprisoned desire. Exactly like music, silence is the reverse, the other, that which is merely hidden.[21]

The SESC Pompéia (1977–82) is perhaps the best example within Bo Bardi's oeuvre to speak about this Fourierist appeal to the whole body, fragmented by Western civilization. Called upon to design a community leisure center for culture and sports for company workers and residents in an old industrial zone, the architect encountered an abandoned factory doomed to be demolished along with all the others in the neighborhood. Her decision to preserve the existing building, as well as the materials and elements that would help recall the memory and the existence of a factory in this location, was not at all a matter of nostalgia. She preserved the image of the factory in order to subvert it. Here, work was transformed into an ally of pleasure and no longer its adversary, a strategy that reflected her own way of working. The disagreeable, repressive, violent, and laborious character of industrial work gave way to sensitivity, freedom, imagination, and libido. Such a concurrence lies not only in the Situationist thought but also in the atmosphere evoked by Fourier's "phalansteries," "immanent fields in which desire is developed," and the "organizing molecules of harmony."[22] The game here takes on a productive dimension, and desire is conceived of as a force capable of inverting the moral order of work and civilization, not only transgressing its law but disarticulating it and subverting it. The logotype designed by Lina for the new complex, with the chimney spewing forth flowers instead of smoke, was the perfect translation of this idea.

Her decision to maintain and reuse the factory transformed the available site into a long, narrow strip of land, the middle of which was traversed by a rainwater runoff area considered unsuitable for construction purposes. The design of the new complex was born out of these two conditioning factors. The image of the new building, entirely made of exposed concrete, reaffirms the idea of a factory, with its direct reference to industrial buildings. The solution was to design two vertical blocks connected by elevated walkways that cross over the drainage area, itself restored as a solarium; as a result, the aerial "expressionist" catwalks connecting the two dissonant towers became the most expressive elements of the complex. The wider tower houses the swimming pool and the four stacked gymnasiums. The narrower one contains the rest of the

Lina Bo Bardi (curator), Exhibition *Caipiras, capiaus: pau-a-pique*, Center SESC Pompeía, forest of *paus-mastro* at the entry of the exhibition, São Paulo, 1984. © Instituto Lina Bo e P. M. Bardi, São Paulo.

22. Ibid. On Situationist thought, see Simon Sadler, *The Situationist City* (Cambridge: MIT Press, 1998); Patrick Mosconi, ed., *Internationale Situationniste* (Paris: Librairie Arthème Fayard, 1997).

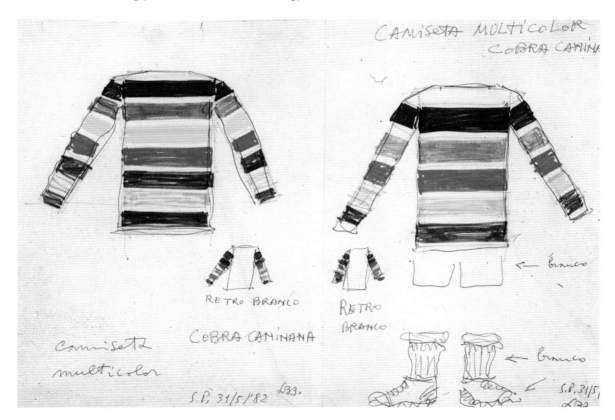

Lina Bo Bardi, Drawing for a soccer shirt (SESC Pompeía), watercolor and pencil on paper, São Paulo, 1982. © Instituto Lina Bo e P. M. Bardi, São Paulo.

Lina Bo Bardi, Center SESC Pompeía, view across a window in the sports tower, São Paulo. © Instituto Lina Bo e P. M. Bardi, São Paulo.

program as well as the services and all vertical circulations; to access any of the sport rooms, one has to cross an aerial bridge. The result are two absolutely united blocks. One is the complement while appearing to be the antonym of the other, which is also expressed in the differences in the treatments of the openings in the facades: regularly aligned amoeba-shaped holes in the pool and gymnasia tower, and a disorderly pattern of square-shaped orders of organic-shaped windows in the service tower. Bo Bardi summarized the relationship with a poetic image: an embrace.[23]

Bo Bardi called the SESC complex a "cultural citadel." For her, the word *citadel* had a double meaning, signifying both a fortress for the defense of a city and a place of attack. It is a "goal," a point scored against the adversary's net, taking on the exact Situationist meaning as a criticism and subversion of the bourgeois ideas of pleasure. In fact, the reference to soccer, the national sport, was present from the first drafts for SESC, and the architect did render a genuine homage to the sport with this project. The soccer evoked by Bo Bardi is that happy and healthy sport that expresses the freedom of the body, as in a "ballroom dance," played with enthusiasm. It is not the "mechanical" soccer, whose objective is merely not to lose, but a "magical" soccer like that played by Mané Garrincha, who turned the field into a circus ring, the ball into a tamed animal, and the game into an invitation to a party.[24] Garrincha's soccer is also a metaphor for the art of combat within the camp of the oppressor, the art of dribbling and the thousand ways to play and undo the game of the other, astutely freeing himself from the network of forces and established representations. This is a parable of the entire SESC, which pays homage to the common people, the forgotten, the losers, and the "ugly," as well as a powerful criticism of a world that punishes failure. Bo Bardi herself made it clear:

I want SESC to be even uglier than MASP![25]

■

23. Lina Bo Bardi, "Na Pompéia. O Bloco Esportivo," in *Casa Vogue* (Nov.–Dec. 1986): 134.

24. Eduardo Galeano, *El Futbol a sol y sombra* (Madrid: Siglo XXI de España, 1995), 118. Mané Garrincha was a mythical player in Brazilian soccer, famous for his "dribble." He had both feet angled toward the left: as a result, he was nicknamed "the angel with distorted feet" (*O Anjo das pernas tortas*). He was twice World Champion with the Brazilian team; in 1962 he was voted best player in the world.

25. So explain Bo Bardi's collaborators. On this theme, also see the introduction to the exhibition *O "Belo" e o direito ao feio—The "Beautiful" and the Right to the Ugly*, which Lina organized at the SESC Pompeia, October 24–30, 1982.

Lina Bo Bardi, Centre SESC Pompeía, Study for the renovation of the interior street, São Paulo, 1977. © Instituto Lina Bo e P. M. Bardi, São Paulo.

Lina Bo Bardi, Center SESC Pompeía, study for a bar, watercolor and pencil on paper, São Paulo, 1977. © Instituto Lina Bo e P. M. Bardi, São Paulo.

MODERNITY AND NATIONALISM: JUAN O'GORMAN AND POST-REVOLUTIONARY ARCHITECTURE IN MEXICO, 1920–1960

EDWARD R. BURIAN

Diego Rivera, in his conversation, speeches, and lectures, in public or elsewhere, attempted to teach the Mexicans what was Mexico. He was one of the greatest twentieth-century "discoverers" of Mexico. It is through his voice that, for the first time, I heard of the importance of popular art and its unknown artists. Of the painters of pulquerías . . . of Hermenegildo Busto . . . of his master José Guadalupe Posada, the engraver and lithographer with incomparable talent. . . . Before Rivera's arrival in Mexico City, pre-Hispanic art was considered mere archeology. . . . He was the first public person to inculcate in the Mexican people the comprehension of their glorious pre-Columbian past; he made them understand the grandiose tradition of a magnificent art. [1]

MODERNITY AND NATIONALISM

After achieving independence from Spain in 1821, the concept of modernity arrived in Mexico as an idea imported from France. It came within the particular nineteenth-century post-colonial Mexican context that encompassed the influence of Jesuit thought, the liberal reforms of Benito Juárez, the separation of church and state, and the ongoing struggle to form a national identity.[2] However, this notion of modernity also pursued an international agenda—one that could generally be characterized by an orientation toward the future, by technical rationalism, and an obsession with progress. As in much of Latin America, the simultaneous emergence of Mexico as a nation and its embracing of modernity resulted in a dichotomic quest that concurrently sought to be part of the cosmopolitan, international avant-garde, and to define itself as nativist and nationalist.

During the first half of the nineteenth century, the design of modern building types in Mexico reflected the post-Enlightenment concerns of French architectural theorist Jean Nicolas Louis Durand, professor of architecture at the new École Polytechnique. Durand ushered in the modernist dogma of rational functionalism with his attempts to codify the ideal of utilitarian functionalism and, as a consequence, make architectural theory both international and scientific. In his landmark *Précis et leçons d'architecture* (1802–5), he stated, "One should not strive to make a building pleasing, since if one concerns oneself solely with the fulfillment of practical requirements, it is impossible that it should not be pleasing."[3] His theory of rationalism was reflected in the idealized gridded organization of rooms, corridors, and courtyards of neo-classical buildings, such as the Hospicio Cabanas in Guadalajara of 1812 by Manuel Tolsa, as well as a series of idealized, geometricized prison and hospital projects in the early nineteenth century.[4]

1. Antonio Luna Arroyo, *Juan O'Gorman, Autobiografía, antología, juicios críticos y documentación exhaustiva de su obra* (Mexico City: Cuadernos Populares de Pintura Mexicana Moderna, 1973). Quoted by Víctor Jiménez in *Juan O'Gorman—Principio y fin del camino* (Mexico City.: Círculo de Arte, 1997), 7–8.

2. Antonio Méndez-Vigatá, "Politics and Architectural Language: Post Revolutionary Regimes and Their Influence on Mexican Public Architecture, 1920–1952," in Edward Burian, ed., *Modernity and the Architecture of Mexico* (Austin: University of Texas Press, 1997), 61–89.

3. Quoted by John Fleming, Hugh Honour, and Nikolaus Pevsner, *A Dictionary of Architecture* (New York: Penguin Books, 1980), 98.

4. See *Catalogo edificios públicos del siglo XIX, Mapoteca Manuel Orozco y Berra*, 1995, 14, plate 7.

Left page
Juan O'Gorman, *Multiple Self-Portrait*, tempera on masonite, 1950.
© Museo de Arte Moderno, Mexico City, / INBA.

5. Alan Colqhoun, "The Concept of Regionalism," in G. B. Nalbantoglu and Wong Chong Thai, eds., *Postcolonial Space(s)* (New York: Princeton Architectural Press, 1997), 13–23.

6. Jean Charlot, *Mexican Art and the Academy of San Carlos, 1785–1915* (Austin: University of Texas Press, 1962).

7. Víctor Jiménez and Alexandrina Escudero, *El Palacio de Belles Artes: construcción y historia* (Mexico City: Consejo nacional para la Cultura y las Artes, 1994). Eagle Knights were pre-Columbian Aztec warriors who covered themselves in eagle masks and feathers on the arms and body during battle.

Pyramid of Tenayuca (Chichimec period, twelfth century), near Mexico City. Photo Juan Rulfo. © Juan Rulfo & Carla Aparicio de Rulfo, bajo custodía de la Fundación Juan Rulfo.

The concept of nationalism has played a defining and critical role in architectural history, particularly from the nineteenth century onward. Recent architectural discourses in response to the phenomena of globalization have also brought the elusive notion of regionalism to the forefront of discussions of contemporary culture. Significantly, regionalism as an intellectual proposition arose as a nineteenth-century nationalistic German and British reaction to the international and cultural dominance of France.[5] As in many European and American countries, the national ideals and yearnings also appeared in works of art, music, literature and architecture in nineteenth-century Mexico.[6] Under the reign of Mexican dictator Porfirio Diáz from 1876 to 1910, the Academy of San Carlos—the propagation center of French architectural design and culture—started to espouse an idealized pre-Columbian iconography in architecture, urban design, and the visual arts. Mythologized heroes such as Cuahtemoc, Tlahicole, and others, appeared in sculptures, paintings, and in the public spaces of the city. On the Avenida de la Reforma in Mexico City, modeled on the Champs Elysées in Paris, a major intersection featured the Monument to Cuahtemoc, the last Aztec emperor, erected by Jiménez and Noreña between 1878 and 1887. In the Palacio de Bellas Artes, begun in 1904 by Italian architect Mario Boari (also author of the Central Post Office) and completed three decades later by Federico Mariscal, the sculptural decoration of the facade portrayed Aztec Eagle Knights.[7] In the years just prior to the Revolution, radical breaks from painting classical models took place in the

Carlos Obregón Santacilia, Perspective and plan of the Monument to the Revolution and the Plaza de la República, ink and pencil on paper, undated [1932–33], Mexico City. © Instituto Nacional de Belles Artes (INBA)/Acervo Santacilia.

"open air schools" at the Academy of San Carlos, where local people, landscapes, and urban life were advocated as subject matter. Painters like Santurnino Herrán portrayed Impressionist portraits with nationalist themes. Likewise in landscape painting, the vast, heroic Mexican landscapes of José María Velasco (1840–1912), Joaquín Clausell (1866–1935) and, later, Gerardo Murillo (alias Dr. Atl) (1875–1964), inspired a national pride of place that would find its creative outlet after the Revolution.

José Vasconcelos (1882–1959), the philosopher, intellectual, and post-revolutionary minister of education from 1920 to 1924, officialized those pre-1910 trends and became the driving force behind the Mexican mural movement. In his writings of the 1920s, he advocated the notions of "Americanism" and idealized the Native Americans in the context of Mexico's agrarian revolution and cultural nationalism. Vasconcelos claimed that Latin America could become the cradle of a future man, of a universal civilization whose development, aided by racial mingling, would result in a "cosmic race."[8] In this perspective, the Mexican mural movement—led from the 1920s to the 1960s by the "big three," Diego Rivera (1886–1957), José Clemente Orozco (1883–1949), and David Siqueiros (1896–1974)—offered a coherent, unifying rationale and justification for the sacrifices of the masses who fought during the revolution for widely divergent reasons. In creating an official government art of racial and cultural affirmation that idealized the indigenous and largely mestizo population, which was still largely illiterate in the 1920s, various post-revolutionary regimes were able to transcend the suffering of the masses.[9] In government-sponsored post-1920 architecture, the murals by Rivera, Orozco,

Vue de Chichén-Itza, Temple of the Warriors, c. 1935. Photo Germaine Wenziner. © Musée Royaux d'Art et d'Histoire, Cinquantenaire, Brussels, IAM 87.1.3.

PERSPECTIVA: EDIFICIO · GUARDIOLA · C·OBREGON·SANTACILIA·ARQUITECTO· ·FEDERICO·RAMOS·INGENIERO·CIVIL·

8. José Vasconcelos, *La raza cósmica: misión de la raza iberoamericana* (Paris: Agencia mundial de librería, 1920–29); in English: *The Cosmic Race* (Baltimore: John Hopkins University Press, 1979). For a discussion of the modern search for national Mexican identity see Henry Schmidt, *The Roots of Lo Mexicano: Self and Society in Mexican Thought, 1900–1934* (College Station: Texas A&M Press, 1978).

9. Méndez-Vigatá, "Politics and Architectural Language," 61–89.

Carlos Obregón Santacilia, Perspective of the final project for the Guardiola Building and its surroundings, ink and pencil on paper, undated [1942], Mexico City. © Instituto Nacional de Belles Artes (INBA)/Acervo Santacilia.

10. See, for instance, Leonard Folgarait, *Mural Painting and Social Revolution in Mexico, 1920–1940: Art of the New Order* (Cambridge: Cambridge University Press, 1998).

Siqueiros, and others acted as "billboards" from the scale of an individual room to the collective scale of an entire site. They served to both nationalize and localize existing buildings and new works of modernist architecture. In the University City (1950–52) directed by Mario Pani and Enrique del Moral—one of the last grand urban projects of the twentieth century—murals served an exemplary and didactic purpose of racial affirmation.[10]

MODERN ARCHITECTURE IN POST-REVOLUTIONARY MEXICO

Prior to the revolution, Mexico was ruled with an iron hand by dictator Porfirio Díaz (1830–1915). While Díaz had modernized the country in terms of technological advances—with the introduction of electricity and telegraphs to major cities, the construction of railroads and bridges to link the various regions, and the leasing of land to foreigners for mining and oil production—the majority of Mexicans lived in appalling conditions.[11] Rebuilding Mexico, a country torn apart following ten years of civil war in which over a million people perished and millions were displaced, was a daunting task, to say the least.

Post-revolutionary governments became the official sponsors of most public architecture as succeeding administrations rapidly constructed schools, clinics, hospitals, and public housing. However, contrary to the "official" history of Mexican architecture, architects in the early 1920s worked eclectically in both revivalist and modernist modes of composition. Little discussed were a series of buildings produced for international exhibitions such as the Pavilion of Mexico for the Rio de Janeiro Exhibition of 1923. The Benito Juárez School

11. The average life expectancy of the general population in Mexico in 1910 was 27 years and the infant mortality rate was 25 percent. Most of the population was malnourished; only 20 percent was literate. The majority of Native Americans were landless farmers tied to the haciendas for life because of their debts to hacienda owners in a feudal-like system. While some Mexicans were amassing fortunes under the Díaz regime, foreigners were making even more money, as their enterprises were largely unregulated and exempt from most taxation. Mexico was the third-largest producer of oil in the world by the turn of the century, but the oil industry was almost entirely a monopoly of British and U.S. businesses.

12. Víctor Jímenez, *Carlos Obregón Santacilia: Pionero de la Arquitectura Mexicana* (Mexico City: Instituto Nacional de Bellas Artes, 2001). For the Monument to the Revolution, Santacilia reused and completed the structure that had been originally destined to become the Presidential Palace. Also see Méndez-Vigatá, "Politics and Architectural Language," 77.

13. Probably the most blatant was the catalogue for the international exhibition of 1963, *4000 años de arquitectura en México*, published by the Secretary of Public Education: the colonial and Porfirian eras were barely mentioned and all the eclectic work of the 1910–1930 was omitted.

Statue of the Caballito, Paseo de la Reforma, Mexico City. Photo Juan Rulfo. © Juan Rulfo & Carla Aparicio de Rulfo, bajo custodia de la Fundación Juan Rulfo.

(1923–25) of Carlos Obregón Santacilia utilized a colonial vocabulary and courtyard organization, whereas Ángel Bachini's Casa de Pueblo in Mérida (1926) and Manuel Amáblis's Mexico Pavilion at the Ibero-American Exhibition (1929) adopted a neo-Mayan style. In the case of Amáblis's work, the central plan was derived from the Natuatl nahui ollin symbol.

Carlos Obregón Santacilia (1896–1961), recalling George Howe in the United States, worked in diverse modes of composition.[12] His later works included the Monument to the Revolution (1933–38), where stylized Art Deco sculpture and classical architecture merged in what was termed *integracíon plástica*, the Deco Guardiola Building (1938–41), the streamlined Hotel Prado (1933–46), and the resolutely modernist Instituto Mexicano del Seguro of 1940. José Villagrán García (1901–1982), who has often been described as the "father of modern architecture in Mexico," also produced little discussed traditional work such as the Estadio Nacional and the Tuberculosis Sanitorium, both in 1929. Only his modernist work was portrayed in official nationalistic books on Mexican architecture in what appears to be selective editing of the concept of modernity for political purposes.[13]

Many have referred to the 1930s and 1940s as a Golden Age of modern work in Mexico, particularly in the cinema. Many undervalued works of architecture from this period sought to represent an emerging industrial age with equivalent images of speed and movement, paralleling the Art Deco movement and the growing influence of kinetic and cinematic images. At the same time, abstracted classical and neo-vernacular systems of ornament sought to "nationalize" these works of architecture by utilizing both pre-Columbian and colonial imagery. Particularly noteworthy in this regard were the works of Juan Segura (1898–1989) including his Ermita Building completed in 1931. This socially motivated, multi-use building on a narrow triangular site combined shops and a movie theater on the ground floor with housing above. A large skylight provided light to an upper-level courtyard for the housing units. This multi-use building, with its complex section, in some respects prefigured Le Corbusier's projects for the Unité d'habitation of the 1950s. Another architect, Francisco Serrano (1900–1982), designed a series of memorable housing projects in Mexico City. One of his least known and most remarkable buildings is the Cine Encanto theater of the late 1930s. His composition of movement and light expressed in a taut, streamlined skin vividly reflected a heroic optimism about the possibilities of the cinema, technical rationalism, modernity, and progress.

Parallel to this development, the international modernism that emerged in the Americas and around the world was best represented in Mexico with the work of the "new generation" of architects: Enrique de la Mora y Palomar (1907–1978), Vladimir Kaspé, Max Cetto (1903–1980), Enrique Landa, Enrique del Moral (1906–1987), and Juan Sordo Maldaleno (1916–1985). Enrique de la Mora's apartment building on Calle Strausburgo (1934) was one of the best works of the period. This small building in the middle of the capital was tightly organized on a narrow site and designed for the use of business people. A staircase gave access

Mario Boari and Federico Mariscal, Palacio de Belles Artes, view of the atrium, Mexico City, 1904–34. Photo Enrique Bostelman, all rights reserved. Downstairs center, Rufino Tamayo, *The Birth of our Nation*, 1952; upstairs center, Diego Rivera, *The Man at the Crossroad*, 1934 ; upstairs right, David Siqueiros, *The Torture of Cuauhtemoc*, 1951.

Enrique de la Mora and José Creixell, Apartment Building, Calle Estrasburgo, Mexico City, 1934. Photo Esther Born. From Esther Born, *The New Architecture in Mexico* (New York: Architectural Record, 1937).

Juan Segura, Ermita Building, Mexico City, 1930–31. Photo Edward R. Burian. © The Edward R. Burian Collection of the Art and Architecture of the American Southwest and Mexico.

The house-studio for the painters Diego Rivera and Frida Kahlo, San Angél, Mexico City, 1931. Photo Guillermo Kahlo. © Museo Casa Estudio Diego Rivera Frida Kahlo / INBA.

Road, cactus, and church. Photo Juan Rulfo. © Juan Rulfo & Carla Aparicio de Rulfo, bajo custodía de la Fundación Juan Rulfo.

Juan O'Gorman, House-studio for the painter Diego Rivera, ink and pencil on paper, San Angél, Mexico City, 1931. © Museo Casa Estudio Diego Rivera Frida Kahlo / INBA.
Left: south facade; right: north facade.

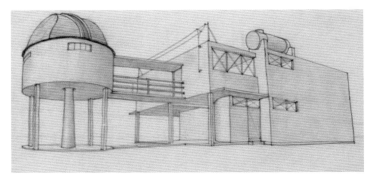

Juan O'Gorman, Residence and astronomy laboratory for Luis Enrique Erro, pencil on paper, Mexico City, 1932. © Colección Juan O'Gorman, Coordinación Servicios de Información Universidad Autónoma Metropolitana, Azcapotzalco.

Juan O'Gorman, Project for a building, pencil and watercolor on paper, Mexico City, 1933. © Colección Juan O'Gorman, Coordinación Servicios de Información Universidad Autónoma Metropolitana, Azcapotzalco.

to five compact, stacked studio units with a shaded outdoor roof terrace on the top floor. The living area of each of the three middle units was expressed as a protruding mass above the street while strip windows provided ample light in each unit.

Likewise, a large program for public housing projects was established: they were to be modern, national symbols in terms of their social organization and response to local climate, materials, and labor practices. Murals and bas-relief sculptures by José Clemente Orozco, Carlos Mérida, and others promoted racial affirmation and pride. Among the most prominent were a series of multi-family ensembles designed by Mario Pani (1911–1993), including his Nonoalco-Tlateloloco Urban Housing Project of 1964.[14]

14. On all those mentioned works, see Edward Burian, *Modernity and the Architecture of Mexico*. Also see Keith Eggener's essay in this book.

15. Ida Rodríguez Prampolini, *Juan O'Gorman: arquitecto y pintor* (Mexico City: Universidad Nacional Autónoma de México, 1982); *Las casas de Juan O'Gorman para Diego y Frida* (Mexico City: Casa Estudio Rivera & Kahlo, 2001; Werner Kleinerüschkamp, *Hannes Meyer, 1889–1954: Architekt, Urbanist, Lehrer* (Berlin: Ernst, 1989).

JUAN O'GORMAN: THE HOUSE-STUDIO RIVERA-KAHLO

Born in Coyacán in the suburbs of Mexico City, Juan O'Gorman quickly abandoned his medical studies to embark upon architecture. Early in his career, he became an advocate for rational functionalism in Mexico. Like his mentor, Villagrán García, he embraced selected aspects of Le Corbusier's theories such as engineering, social programs, workers' housing, and the political nature of architecture. In the 1930s, he was appointed chief architect of the Department of School Construction of the Ministry of Education. There he designed and built thirty primary schools and technical schools and also produced socially driven housing projects. During this period he became the director of the Polytechnic School of Architecture with German architect Hannes Meyer, who came to Mexico as a refugee from the Bauhaus in Germany and was responsible for several, mostly unsuccessful, planning projects between 1939 and 1949.[15]

From 1928 to 1937, O'Gorman designed a series of twelve functionalist homes, including a residence for Dr. Luis Erro (1932), whose observatory suggested a helmeted pre-Columbian figure recalling monumental Olmec sculpture, and a house for the noted American anthropologist Frances Toor (1934). Unlike the earlier houses, the project was more nativist and "mexicanized," with the appearance of strong local colors to contrast with the modernist white. Yet, his best-known and most influential work was the house and studio designed for the noted painters Diego Rivera and Frida Kahlo (1907–1954) in 1931. The program—two independent houses-studios—was clearly expressed by the two separate cubic volumes, linked together by a catwalk bridging over the courtyard. Utilizing such Corbusian principles as the open plan, free section and facade, concrete frame, strip window, and roof terrace, the complex recalls Le Corbusier's Ozenfant Studio in Paris of 1922; however, it took an obvious national and local expression. Instead of merely siting the house as a freestanding object, O'Gorman planted a wall of local cordon cactus at the street edge in the traditional Mexican manner, and, in doing so, created a series of plaza-like outdoor rooms.

The exterior colors were Indian red and deep blue, while the interior colors were yellow and parrot green.[16] The Indian red wall recalled the traditional tezontle volcanic stone, traditional to Mexico City from the pre-Columbian and colonial eras. It was, in Octavio Paz's words, the "color of dried blood." The terrazzo floor in the Rivera studio was a riot of color utilizing colored stone chips and expressed as a distinct element from the walls. Glazing consisted of steel industrialized windows; all steel fenestration and metal work were painted orange vermilion. The traditional vernacular colors utilized in the exterior facades related the architecture to the culture of the place. O'Gorman's interest in making an architecture concerned with progress, universality,

16. The deep blue color was similar to that Kahlo used in her own house in Coyoacán, a deep matte blue traditionally used in Mexican houses to ward off evil spirits. Víctor Jiménez et al., *Las casas de Juan O'Gorman para Frida Kahlo y Diego Rivera* (Mexico City: Ministerio de Fomento, 1999).

Juan O'Gorman, Interior patio of house-studio for Diego Rivera and Frida Kahlo, San Angél, Mexico City, 1931. Photo Arturo Osorno. © Museo Casa Estudio Diego Rivera Frida Kahlo / INBA, courtesy Víctor Jiménez.

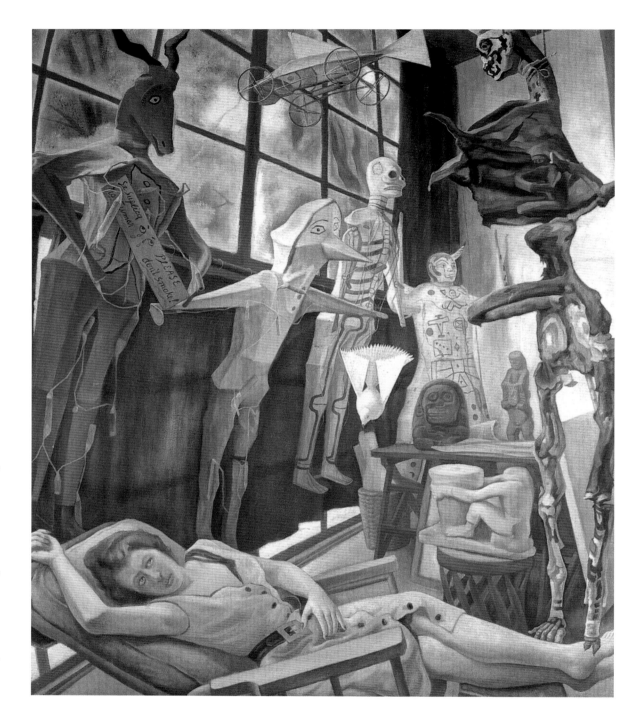

Diego Rivera, *The Artist Studio*, oil on canvas, 1954. © Acervo Patrimonial Secretaría de Hacienda y Crédito Público, all rights reserved. For the Judas, also see p. 128.

Diego Rivera was an enthusiastic collector of pre-Columbian and popular art. His collection included many Judas of paper, of which many examples can still be found in his house-studio.

For their construction the artisans used techniques of construction with *carrizo* (a type of bamboo) and painting with lime and anilines. The Judas were related to the treason of Judas Iscariot. They also represented death (often, with a head-skull and a body-skeleton) and appeared as symbols or caricatures of the history of Latin America: the priest, the conquistador, the dictator, and other political figures. They were burnt on Holy Saturday before Easter.

technological rationalism, and abstraction, was thus enriched by the encounter with the vernacular Mexican tradition—here expressed in the bright colors and the cactus fence.

The influence of Le Corbusier's works was manifest, yet O'Gorman's treatment of the interiors was more radical. Photographs of houses such as Villa Savoye showed industrial objects, modern appliances, views to landscapes, and cubist paintings to project an image of modernity, physical well-being, and a controlled sense of order; interior surfaces were smooth and uninterrupted with concealed wiring and plumbing. In contrast, in the studios of the Kahlo/Rivera residence, the mechanical and electrical systems were exposed as distinct, separate elements; all pipes were visible, and electrical power runs and connections were used as expressive compositional elements, reminiscent of veins and arteries. The "machines" of the house—the showers for instance—were proudly displayed to aid in health and cleansing. Ironically, although machine technology was utilized as an expressive device, the building was produced by inexpensive hand labor. This dichotomy presented itself often in the history of modern architecture in Mexico, in the sense that the representation of industrialized systems of construction did not correspond to the realities of handcraft technology.

The installation of Rivera's studio was striking and surreal. Both Rivera and Kahlo were avid collectors of indigenous art. Huge and brightly colored Judas figures hung inside the interiors. These served to create a surrealist sense of dislocation, yet were deeply rooted in the universe of the vernacular traditions of Mexico. Rivera's painting *The Painter's Studio* (1954) shows the studio's interior in all its ambiguity: a reclining woman turns provocatively toward the viewer with eyes cast upward in the seemingly limitless extension of the gridded ceiling. Dominating her on all sides are Judas, skeletons, half-human figures, pre-Columbian art, and an animal-like machine. Architecturally, the studio space acts as a hooded camera lens and framing device for capturing and categorizing views of the landscape, with its cantilevered window wall gestured toward the city. As seen in the painting, the glazing system also allowed the possibility for curtains to be closed across the lower portion of the window wall. As with a camera lens, both human and inanimate objects could be selectively placed in focus.[17]

Juan O'Gorman, *Portrait of Diego Rivera*, tempera on triplex, 1958. © El Colegio Nacional, Mexico.

PAINTINGS AND UNIVERSITY CITY

In the mid-1930s, O'Gorman became disenchanted with architectural practice. He believed that developers who wanted to build the least for maximum profit were corrupting functionalist architecture in Mexico. He claimed that this evolution led to an architecture of negligible qualities for the user and for the country. As a result, O'Gorman stopped practicing and devoted himself to easel and mural painting from approximately 1936 to the late 1940s. It is during that time that he produced works such as *La ciudad de México* (The City of Mexico, 1942–49) or *Los mitos paganos* (The Pagan Myths, 1944), where his interest in the integration of the "organic" and the "mechanic" became explicit.

O'Gorman returned to architecture—more precisely to the "synthesis of the arts into architecture"—as one of a series of architects who participated in the design of the Ciudad Universitaria (University City) in Mexico City from 1950 to 1952. Planned by Enrique del Moral and Mario Pani, the campus employed both modernist

17. See Beatriz Colomina, *Privacy and Publicity: Modern Architecture as Mass Media* (Cambridge: MIT Press, 1994). As Colomina has pointed out, in the work of Le Corbusier, the window wall acted as a camera lens for capturing and categorizing the landscape.

Juan O'Gorman, Library and Murals, University City, Mexico City, 1951. From Clive Bamford Smith, *Builders in the Sun: Five Mexican Architects* (New York: Architectural Books Publishing, 1967), all rights reserved.

18. His original scheme was a pre-Columbian type of pyramid. However, this proposal was rejected as unacceptable to the campus architects because of the abstract, International Style vocabulary of the rest of the new campus. See Mario Pani and Enrique del Moral, *La construcción de la ciudad universitaria del Pedregal* (Mexico City: Universidad Nacional Autónoma de México, 1979).

compositional principles derived from Le Corbusier's *Five Points of Modern Architecture*, and native strategies, such as terracing reminiscent of pre-Columbian urbanism and a series of large-scale, billboard-like murals espousing racial pride, technological progress, and respect for pre-Columbian ancestors. The murals portrayed straining, heroic, Native American and mestizo figures struggling against the forces of colonial exploitation and Porfirian dictatorship, as well as the technology of an emerging, progressive future merged with the grandeur of a mythic pre-Columbian past. The suggestion was that Mexico was back on course after being sidetracked in the colonial and post-colonial eras, implying a sense of legitimization of the present. Pani and del Moral's own modernist Rectorate Tower of 1951 acquired a "national" dimension with the use of local materials, large murals, and tri-dimensional works by Davíd Alfaro Siqueiros.

In 1951 O'Gorman collaborated with Gustavo Saavedra and Juan Martínez de Velasco on the design of the Central Library at the University City. The original scheme in the form of a pyramid was modified into a practically windowless stack tower sitting on a plinth containing the catalogues and reading rooms.[18] The library utilized both hybrid handcraft and industrialized technology. The native stone was set by hand into a modular concrete panel, which was hoisted in place by machines. The building had few figural and sculptural gestures in its massing, and the allegorical layering of the facade was reduced to a wall plane, akin to a canvas for representation. O'Gorman's mural represented a shift to a didactic, symbolic, allegorical architecture as well as mythological imagery and occasionally compositional devices from pre-Columbian culture. Masks and anthropomorphic relationships appeared at a variety of scales in the composition of the library's mosaic facades, including a Tlaloc-like (god of rain) goggle-eyed figure with a short, centralized strip of corridor for a nose facing west, and numerous superimposed masks and figures on a smaller scale, whose overall pattern told the story of Mexican and world history. In one of the landmark symbols of modern Mexican architecture, O'Gorman—architect and painter—was able to reconnect to a mythical past for political and racial purposes. The very scale of the facade and its centralized position near the center of the campus suggested the ritualistic function of both witnessing and suggesting collective activities of the student body.

O'Gorman's use of pre-Columbian imagery became more overt in the design of a studio/gallery/tomb for and with Diego Rivera, the Anahuacalli of 1944, and his own home of 1951. Designed to house Rivera's collection of pre-Columbian art, the Anahuacalli rose on top of a small hill near the eastern edge of Luis Barragán's residential development, the Gardens of El Pedregal.[19] The profile of this stone-walled and corbel arched building was inspired by various pre-Columbian cultures, including the talud and tablero of Zapaotec pyramids, feathered serpent sculptures from Teotihuacan, and other Mayan sources. For his own "underground" home, he used hand-laid stone covered by stone mosaic and modern industrialized glazing. Its style recalled the "grotesque" architecture and gardens of the Italian Renaissance as well as the pre-Columbian use of monumental masks in architecture. The siting in the Pedregal area was particularly meaningful: the eye-shaped window in the tower faced toward Popocatepl and Ixtaccihuatl, the two sacred volcanoes, male and female, of the ancient Mexican mythology.

Over the course of his entire career O'Gorman's work represented an immense struggle to produce an authentic Mexican architecture. Both his painting and architecture reflected the tension between seemingly opposed dichotomies: the cosmopolitan and the nativist, the mechanic and the organic, abstraction and figuration, and technology and representation. He embraced the pre-Columbian past in an attempt to reclaim an embedded lost consciousness—a national resource with the potential to be unlocked in the psyche of the people. It was analogous in many respects to the ideas being explored by the Surrealist movement. Ultimately, O'Gorman's extraordinary corpus formed a critical point of departure in the development of modern architecture in Mexico: by questioning the nature of orthodox modernism in Mexico, he opened the door for many architects who would follow him.

Juan O'Gorman, Personal house, El Pedregal, Mexico City, 1951. From Clive Bamford Smith, *Builders in the Sun: Five Mexican Architects* (New York: Architectural Books Publishing, 1967), all rights reserved. Also see illustration p. 113.

19. *Anahuacalli: Museo Diego Rivera* (Mexico city: Artes de México, 1965); Keith Eggener, *Luis Barragán's Gardens of El Pedregal* (New York: Princeton Architectural Press, 2001). See illustration in Eduardo Subirats's essay, 95.

20. See George Kubler, *The Shape of Time: Remarks on the History of Things* (New Haven: Yale University Press, 1962).

GLOBALIZATION

Too often there is the sense of viewing the United States and Mexico as simply paired opposites: industrialized versus handcraft, pragmatic versus romantic, Protestant and secular as opposed to Catholic and mystical. However, examining the phenomena of the intermixture of cultures, especially along the border between the two nations, reveals unexpected insights and defies simple stereotypes. The notion of different design and ideas pollinating one another through architects working across continents is certainly not a new idea or phenomenon. In the case of Mexico, the historic adaptation of "outsiders" aesthetics and technologies existed in the pre-Columbian era as well as in the mestizo culture of the colonial period.[20] Some have even argued that modernism was embraced with a special fervor in the context of Mexican *mestizaje*. Even the simplistic notion of modern architecture originating in Europe and then making its way around the world needs to be reexamined.[21]

Can we still talk about local cultures in a post-industrial, electronic culture?[22] Contrary to the simplistic stereotypes of the popular media, Mexico is extremely diverse in terms of bio-regions, climate, geography, and culture—from the dry expanses of deserts in the north, to high valleys with a temperate climate in the middle of the country, and the rain forests along the coasts and in the south. This varied geography, the historically limited development of the country's transportation network, the distance to the capital of Mexico City, and even the emphasis placed on the family, has led to a strong regional identification and a preference for local practices and local initiatives. One can only imagine what an architecture might be like that engages the

21. Historian William Curtis has commented on the development of modern architecture simultaneously occurring at various places around the world, including Mexico; see his *Modern Architecture Since 1900* (London: Phaidon, 1996).

22. This conclusion addresses a complex issue in the post-industrial twenty-first-century electronic age. Even "local cultures" in Mexico, such as the Aztec culture, borrowed many beliefs and cultural influences from other pre-Columbian groups in both art and architecture. During the colonial era in Mexico, the influences came not only from Spain, but also from Arabic countries, England, France, Germany, and even China.

Juan O'Gorman, Study for the mosaic of the south facade, University Library, Mexico City, watercolor, 1952. © Colección Patrimonio Universitario Universidad Nacional Autónoma de México (UNAM).

23 The cultural dominance of Mexico City is overwhelming, even more so than the art and architectural media centers of New York and Los Angeles in the United States. Many comment about the lack of recognition for work produced outside of Mexico City, not only in architecture, but also in literature, painting, music, theater, and cinema. It is an understatement to say that if we take the time to look outside of Mexico City, many other architects, across the ages, have produced quality works of architecture during the pre-Columbian, colonial, and modern eras. I will only mention a series of twentieth-century Wrightian houses in Monterrey, N.L., which have been virtually ignored in the discourse of modern architecture in Mexico. As a result we think too often about Mexico—and the United States as well—as monolithic cultures with homogenous conditions.

contemporary conditions of place and the possibilities of a post-industrial age within the specific conditions of the country. Perhaps the most serious issue that affects the majority of Mexican citizens is the relationship between architectural form making, materials and their assembly, and labor practices. The excess of labor in Mexico is obvious to anyone who is even a casual visitor to the country, and the question arises whether industrialized components make sense in Mexico, where much of the population is underemployed and heavy equipment for building is sometimes scarce and expensive. In this perspective, the re-examination of the undervalued architecture of Mexico from 1920 to 1960 offers many potential lessons about the creation of an architecture that enhances the experience of place and the qualities of materials by all human senses.[23] ∎

Carlos Obregón Santacilia and Diego Rivera, Secretary of Public Health, view of the Council chamber, Mexico City, 1929. Photo Jorge Pablo de Aguinaco. All rights reserved.

SETTINGS FOR HISTORY AND OBLIVION IN MODERN MEXICO 1942-1958

KEITH L. EGGENER

When the revolution wins we're going to clean it up. We'll make a new city, bigger and better than the one across the river.[1]

Juan O'Gorman's painting *La Ciudad de México* of 1942 and the concrete towers designed in 1957–58 by Mathias Goeritz and Luis Barragán for Mario Pani's Satellite City are iconic images of Mexico City in the modern era. Together, they bracket a period of remarkable urban transformation. Between 1940 and 1960, national and international investment in Mexico, and with these industrial and economic growth—all focused on the capital city—rose precipitously. Legions of displaced peasants, vast numbers of Mexico's rising middle and entrepreneurial classes, European expatriates fleeing the war and its aftermath, North Americans leaving behind the anti-communist hysteria of the early 1950s: these and many others flooded into the city seeking employment, opportunity, and escape. During this twenty-year period the metropolitan area's population surged from 1.7 million to 5.4 million. Cultural production flourished, as did all varieties of congestion and environmental degradation.[2] Construction boomed. Up went vast public markets and soaring office and hotel towers, cultural, governmental, educational, and industrial complexes, medical and transportation facilities, and expansive residential projects for all classes of citizen.[3] A geographically contained, pedestrian-scaled city of stone walls, belfries, plazas, and gardens, became a sprawling metropolis of glass-clad skyscrapers, subdivisions, highways, and shantytowns. Like Paris in the mid-nineteenth century or New York in the first decades of the twentieth, Mexico City around 1950 endured a "crucial upheaval that both irrevocably altered its physical structure and established a pattern for future change."[4]

It was during this same period that Mexico's agrarian populist Revolution of 1910–20—the central event of the nation's history in the twentieth century and the catalyst for much of its subsequent modernization and reform—began fading from lived memory and realpolitik. A related dissolution took place within the realm of architecture and urban planning. Established by the early 1930s as both an expression and an agent of progressive social and political reform, modern architecture in Mexico after World War II became gradually distanced from earlier revolutionary aims, while increasingly privatized in its ownership and indirect in its messages. Four crucial artifacts—the painted city of O'Gorman (1942); the University City, campus for the National Autonomous University of Mexico (UNAM, 1947–52); the Gardens of El Pedregal, a residential

1. Worker Neftalí Amador, looking north across the Rio Grande, as quoted by Martín Luis Guzmán in *The Eagle and the Serpent* (New York: Alfred A. Knopf, 1930), 4. The book was first published in Madrid in 1928; this statement would have been made around 1914.

2. Gilbert Joseph, Anne Rubinstein, and Eric Zolov, eds., *Fragments of a Golden Age: The Politics of Culture since 1940* (Durham: Duke University Press, 2001).

3. Max L. Cetto, *Modern Architecture in Mexico* (New York: Frederick A. Praeger, 1961).

4. Donald Olsen, *The City as a Work of Art: London, Paris, Vienna* (New Haven: Yale University Press, 1986), ix. On planning in Mexico City prior to 1940 see Carol McMichael Reese, "Urban Development in Mexico City, 1850–1930," in Arturo Almandoz Marte, ed., *Planning Latin American Capital Cities, 1850–1930* (London: Routledge, 2002).

Left page
Luis Barragán, Barragán House, living room with photomontage of the Gardens of the Pedregal, Ramírez 14, Mexico City, 1947–48. Photo Armando Salas Portugal © Foundation Barragán, Birsfelden.

Juan O'Gorman, *La ciudad de México*,
tempera on agglomerate, 1942–49.
© Museo de Arte Moderno, México
D.F./INBA.

5. Carlos Fuentes, *Where the Air Is Clear* (New York: Ivan Obolensky 1960), 5.

subdivision that opened in 1949; and the Towers of the Satellite City (1957–58)—allow us to chart this development. Taken as a sequence of events, these four projects represent a city shifting its constructive energies from center to periphery, revolution to commodification, history to nostalgia—a place, in words used by native son Carlos Fuentes in 1958, "ancient in light...cradled among birds of omen," becoming a "city woven by amnesiacs."[5]

VIVA MÉXICO

6. On the Uppsala map of Tenochtitlán/México, see Richard Kagan, *Urban Images of the Hispanic World, 1493–1793* (London: Yale University Press, 2000), 54–55.

In the foreground of O'Gorman's *La ciudad de México*, two hands hold up a map. It is a reproduction of the Uppsala Map—now in Sweden and dated from about 1550—which is generally acknowledged to have been drawn by native Indians at the Colegio Imperial de Santa Cruz de Tlatelolco, under the auspices of Viceroy Antonio de Mendoza. The map displays the old island city of Tenochtitlán, surrounded by Lake Texcoco, and connected to the mainland by causeways.[6] Near the map and looking toward it is a bricklayer with patched overalls and distinctly Indian features. In one hand he holds a trowel, in the other a blueprint. Immediately behind him stands a partly built brick and reinforced concrete frame wall; this is matched on the scene's other side by a rubble masonry wall of the sort made in ancient times by the local Aztecs. Beyond these is the modern city that the bricklayer and others like him are building. Old structures mix with new ones here. Domes, towers, and no less than four partly built, steel-framed skyscrapers punctuate the skyline. A wide street to the left of center, visible between the map and the bricklayer and dotted with people and cars, leads to the center of the city, the historic Plaza Mayor or Zócalo. Beyond this are water, foothills, and

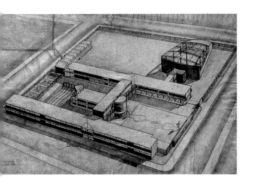

Juan O'Gorman, Secondary School Type B, ink and pencil on paper, c. 1932. © Colección O'Gorman, Coordinación Servicios de Información Universidad Autónoma Metropolitana, Azcapotzalco.

Mario Pani, Enrique del Moral et al., Aerial view of the University City of Mexico, November 14, 1952. © Archivo fotográfico of IIE-UNAM, Colección Katy Horna.

distant snow-capped peaks. Floating in the sky overhead, defying the rather flat realism ruling the rest of the image, are four figures: a plumed serpent, an eagle clutching a scroll, and two partially draped women—one dark, one lighter—holding aloft a banner reading *Viva México*. Along the painting's bottom edge, beneath the map, a trompe l'oeil scroll says in Spanish, "Here is represented the heart of Mexico City as it can be seen from the top of the Monument to the Revolution in the eastern direction." This is signed by O'Gorman and dated 1942.

The hands holding the map reach into the painting from just outside—or just in front— of it. They become stand-ins for our own as we regard this scene from precisely their owner's (O'Gorman's?) position. The domed revolutionary monument we stand on actually predates the revolution. Begun in 1900 by the French architect Émile Bernard, it was to have been the legislative palace for the government of Porfirio Díaz. For several years during and after the revolution it stood unfinished. Finally, between 1933 and 1938 it was converted to its present form and use by architect Carlos Obregón Santacilia and sculptor Oliverio Martínez. Its great round arches and its placement at the western end of Avenida de la Revolución, at what was once the city's western edge, make it a kind of gateway to the central city. Its construction history makes it a bridge between the periods immediately before and after the civil war. From its top we see the revolution as a *fait accompli*, as the modern capital of a nation renewed rises in triumph.[7]

Alberto T. Arai, Paseo de los Frontones (promenade of the frontons), University City of Mexico, 1952. © Archivo fotográfico of IIE-UNAM, Colección Katy Horna.

O'Gorman (1905–1982) had been an important contributor to this renewal. During the 1930s he headed both the new School of Industrial Techniques and the Architectural Office of the Federal Ministry of Public Education. At that time he designed more than twenty public schools and many houses for clients such as Diego Rivera and folklorist Frances Toor. Like the offices, housing, hospitals, schools, and factories of other progressive Mexican architects of the day—Enrique Yañez, Juan Legarreta, and Alvaro Aburto among them—O'Gorman's buildings were stripped-down affairs made of reinforced concrete, brick, and glass, based largely on the work of Le Corbusier. Many of these projects were funded by the post-revolutionary Calles and Cárdenas administrations, each of which used the new buildings to conduct its programs and effectively support its claims to political legitimacy and progressiveness. Architecture like O'Gorman's appealed on both economic and ideological grounds. Compared to the Beaux-Arts classical and Spanish colonial-revival style buildings favored by earlier administrations, the new architecture was efficient, cheap, and easy to build and maintain. It was also free of the unwanted historical and political baggage carried by revival styles like the Spanish colonial. Its associations were reformist, technological, egalitarian, and moral.[8] "Architecture or Revolution," Le Corbusier had warned in 1923—in *Vers Une Architecture*, a book that O'Gorman knew well. Mexico had found room for both.

The juxtaposition in *La ciudad de México* of old map and new city compels us to compare these: over time the one has become the other. What is less immediately clear is whether we are to see this process as one of continuity or rupture. Many of the contemporary city's buildings and other features are readily identifiable in the painting. We see, for instance, the colonial-era House of Tiles, the Metropolitan Cathedral, and the Alameda, as well as the neoclassical Palace of Fine Arts and the modern National Lottery and National Insurance towers. We see no pre-Columbian structures, however. The most direct explanation for this is

7. Luis E. Carranza, "The Struggle for Form: Cultural Production in the Mexico of Luis Barragán," in Federica Zanco, ed., *Luis Barragán: The Quiet Revolution* (Milan: Skira, 2001), 262; Carlos G. Mijares Bracho, "The Architecture of Carlos Obregón Santacilia," in Edward R. Burian, ed., *Modernity and the Architecture of Mexico* (Austin: University of Texas Press, 1997), 151–61.

8. For good overviews of the architecture of this period, see Burian, ed., *Modernity and the Architecture of Mexico*; Valerie Fraser, *Building the New World: Studies in the Modern Architecture of Latin America, 1930–1960* (London: Verso, 2000), 22–86.

Luis Barragán and Mathias Goeritz, *The Animal of the Pedregal*, Plaza de las Fuentes, Gardens of El Pedregal, Mexico City, 1950. Photo Armando Salas Portugal. © Foundation Barragán, Birsfelden.

Luis Barragán, Plaza de las Fuentes (Square of the Fountains), Gardens of El Pedregal, Mexico City, 1948–49. Photo Armando Salas Portugal. © Foundation Barragán, Birsfelden.

9. See also "Encuesta Espacios: Arquitecto Juan O'Gorman," *Espacios 25* (June 1955): 23; and Keith Eggener, "Contrasting Images of Identity in the Post-War Mexican Architecture of Luis Barragán and Juan O'Gorman," *Journal of Latin American Cultural Studies* (March 2000): 32–33.

10. Octavio Paz, *The Labyrinth of Solitude* (New York: Grove Widenfeld, 1985), 195.

11. It was an optimism that O'Gorman would lose. He grew increasingly bitter and eventually committed suicide in 1982. See Esther McCoy, "The Death of Juan O'Gorman," *Arts and Architecture, New Series 1:3* (1982): 36–40.

12. For an alternate reading, see Oriana Baddeley and Valerie Fraser, *Drawing the Line: Art and Cultural Identity in Contemporary Latin America* (London: Verso, 1989), 44–45.

that none were visible from our vantage point, most traces of the old Aztec city having long since been destroyed by the Spanish. This absence also points to a theme underlying the painting and much Mexican political and cultural discourse during the 1940s. For O'Gorman and for many Mexicans, the Conquest was now seen as a breaking point, an invasion that forced underground the country's "real" culture—pre-Hispanic culture, "the one and only tradition of Mexico," O'Gorman called it.[9] But if the Aztec city had indeed been obliterated, at least now the spirit that built it could resurface. This spirit was alive and well, O'Gorman tells us, in myth, imagination, and in the bloodlines and actions of such people as the bricklayer. The mythical plumed serpent Quetzalcóatl (inventor of medicine, agriculture, and astronomy), the eagle guiding the Aztecs to found Tenochtitlán, the allegorical figures of the Indian and the *mestiza*: these have returned to watch over the city and urge its people from above. The map too is not simply an antique, a point of comparison, but a spiritual road plan of renewed potential.

"To live," said Octavio Paz in 1950, "is to be separated from what we were in order to approach what we are going to be in the mysterious future."[10] O'Gorman's painting embodies this view. The realism of its style is matched by the realism of the painter's outlook: cautious yet hopeful.[11] The distant past is itself intangible, unreachable, yet its memory, its values, and its spiritual force remain to guide the builders of a reinvigorated nation. So the native bricklayer, liberated from peonage by the revolution, builds his wall. It is a structure that when completed will never be seamless. Its two halves, the modern brick and concrete and the ancient stone, will always be distinct. And yet the man keeps at his task, knowing that the only way to complete it is to try to fill the void.[12]

A PLACE MARKED BY DESTINY

If *La ciudad de México* showed the developing promise of the revolution, the University City—the campus for the National Autonomous University of Mexico—was to be its architectural realization. The University City was a classic utopian modernist scheme: architecture and planning intended to accommodate and effect fundamental social change, in this case to help prepare "the new Mexican."[13] It was, further, "a showpiece of the Mexican government's achievements in modernizing the country since the Revolution."[14] In scale and ambition it was—almost—what its name advertised: a city unto itself.

By the 1940s, the 400-year-old University of Mexico's outmoded facilities lay scattered across the old city center. Between 1943 and 1947 the federal government acquired 1,730 acres of land in the wild, 2000-year-old Pedregal lava field at the city's southern edge. Some 200 million pesos were allocated for the design and construction of a new, integrated campus for 25,000 to 30,000 students—there are by now ten times that many. Architects Mario Pani (1911–1993), Enrique del Moral (1906–1987), and Mauricio Campos (who died unexpectedly in the early stages of the project) were commissioned to develop the overall plan and conduct competitions for the individual buildings. In 1950 Carlos Lazo was appointed director-general of the project and made responsible for coordinating the efforts of the more than 150 architects, engineers, and artists, and 7,000 workmen. Ground was broken for the first buildings that year, and by November 20, 1952, when Mexican President Miguel Alemán officially dedicated the complex, it was 80 percent complete. Classes began the following year.

The site chosen for the new university was partly a matter of expediency, that is, the Pedregal was ample, available, accessible, inexpensive, seismically stable land. Before 1945 its permanent population consisted mainly of insects, wild animals, and criminals in hiding. But painters, poets, and nature lovers had also been venturing there for some time, for the place was one of highly peculiar form and rich historical associations. The Pedregal was a volcanic landscape in a country where volcanoes had long held profound cosmological and cultural significance. It was the home of rare plant and animal species, and of ancient Mexicans who once built their houses and temples there. A later generation of native Mexicans had sought refuge there from the Spanish; later still, in the twentieth century, peasant revolutionaries hid there from the forces they finally overthrew. This was a site left undeveloped and untainted by European imperialism. Forbidding though the Pedregal was, by the mid-twentieth century it was seen by many as the ancient heart of Mexico, Eden rediscovered. "The new University City," said University Rector Luis Garrido in 1952, "is rising in a place marked by destiny. It was the seat of an ancient civilization and now it will be the seat of the culture of the future."[15]

The University City's urban planning and architecture expressed this same melding of historical reference and futurist idealism. The overall axiality of the plan, the terraces, and the large, open courts evoked ancient Mexican cities such as Monte Albán and Teotihuacán. A more recent source of interpretation was found in CIAM's (Congrès Internationaux d'Architecture Moderne) *Charter of Athens* of 1933. The widely read document advocated the importance for city planners of attending to topography, local resources and economic considerations, sociological needs and spiritual values, functional analysis, green space, and zoning and traffic circulation—all suggestions that Pani and del Moral followed scrupulously. Open space was amply provided and gave the students and other users of the campus a variety of intimate and collective

13. Celia Ester Arredondo Zambrano, "Modernity in Mexico," in Burian, ed., *Modernity and the Architecture of Mexico*, 92.

14. Fraser, *Building the New World*, 62. Other sources include: *Ciudad Universitaria 1952–2002* (Mexico City: UNAM, 2002); Mario Pani and Enrique del Moral, *La construcción de la Ciudad Universitaria del Pedregal* (Mexico City: UNAM, 1979); José Rogelio Alvarez Noguera, ed., *La Arquitectura de la Ciudad Universitaria* (Mexico City: UNAM, 1994).

15. Luis Garrido, *"El Destino de la Ciudad Universitaria, Arquitectura México 39* (Sept. 1952), 198. For a brief history of the Pedregal site, see Keith Eggener, *Luis Barragán's Gardens of El Pedregal* (New York: Princeton Architectural Press, 2001), 106–10.

Augusto Pérez Palacios, Jorge Bravo, and Raúl Salinas, Aerial view of the Olympic Stadium and the Paseo de los Frontones in construction, University City of Mexico, January 26, 1951. © Archivo fotográfico of IIE-UNAM, Colección Katy Horna.

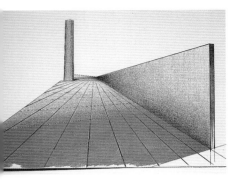

Luis Barragán, Project for the Plaza del Cigarro (Square of the Cigar), Gardens of El Pedregal, Mexico City, 1956. Photo Armando Salas Portugal. © Foundation Barragán, Birsfelden.

meeting places. Housing, work, and recreation were accommodated in separate but well-linked areas. In the northwest section was the Olympic Stadium, to the northeast the main campus with its facilities for teaching and administration. Student housing and sports and recreation facilities filled the southeast section, while the southwest area was designated for faculty housing. Individual buildings—low-lying, Mies van der Rohe–inspired boxes of brick and reinforced concrete and "Corbusian" steel and glass slabs—were accented by volcanic stone and translucent obsidian; local materials and traditional construction techniques were used whenever possible. The forms of some structures suggested volcanoes (the Olympic Stadium), pre-Columbian pyramids (the *frontones*, or jai alai courts), or colonial-era religious buildings (the School of Engineering).[16] As had been the case with government buildings during the 1920s and 1930s, interior and exterior walls were adorned with figurative, didactic, large-scale murals, mosaics, and bas-reliefs. Produced by such prominent artists as Diego Rivera, David Alfaro Siqueiros, and Juan O'Gorman, the subjects of these included "The Right to Learning," "The Conquest of Energy," the "History of Ideas in Mexico," and "Pre-Columbian Sport."[17] According to Carlos Lazo, all of this was to provide a setting for the fulfillment of Mexico's "highest and most intimate destiny," a place in which "to integrate the individual with the noblest desires of the community."[18] Here the ultimate goals of the revolution would be attained. Mexico's children—*la Raza Cósmica,* as Education Minister José Vasconcelos had called them in the 1920s—would come here to absorb the lessons of their nation's long and glorious past, and prepare for an even more brilliant future.

Of course, the University City was no more a full-fledged city than O'Gorman's painted *Ciudad de México.* Clean, orderly, unified, efficient and fully modern, contained yet spacious, the university stood in contrast to and removed from the crowded, cluttered, chaotic, old city that it served. It was a model, paradigmatic city, subject to controls on its form and operation that could never be applied to the capital as a whole. In this respect it was rather less like a real city than that of O'Gorman's painting. The University City had a single landlord (the federal government) and, in effect, a single function (providing higher education). The residential components of its plan were never fully realized and thus few people ever lived there; they commuted instead. Connected to the rest of Mexico City by Avenida Insurgentes, the university stood several miles south of the center, well outside the city's 1950s boundaries.

Depending upon one's perspective, and quite possibly by design, this removal of the university from the city center presented either a significant advantage or a substantial hindrance. In his book *The Mexican University and the State: Student Conflicts, 1910–1971,* historian Donald J. Mabry suggests that the University City's isolation served government interests by "making effective demonstrations more difficult," thus causing a "decline of university-state conflicts in the 1950s. To reach [the centers of government] from the campus, students had to travel over ten miles by city bus in a system that was not as well developed as it would become by the end of the decade." For this and other reasons, in 1954 many students tried, unsuccessfully, to boycott the new campus. "This issue of isolation," Mabry writes, "often disguised as protests over the bus system, was the most volatile issue for UNAM in the 1950s."[19] The revolution won, those in power now sought to celebrate and mythologize its legacy, while moving to the margins any possibility of continued debate and dissent. Not until the following decade would they try to erase these altogether.

16. Cetto, *Modern Architecture in Mexico,* 66–93.

17. See Esther McCoy, "Mosaics of Juan O'Gorman," *Arts and Architecture* 69 (February 1964): 36–38.

18. Carlos Lazo, *Pensamiento y Destino de la Ciudad Universitaria* (Mexico City: UNAM, 1952), 10, 45. José Vasconcelos, *La raza cósmica: misión de la raza iberoamericana* (Paris, 1920–29); in English: *The Cosmic Race* (Baltimore: John Hopkins University Press, 1979).

19. Donald J. Mabry, *The Mexican University and the State: Student Conflicts, 1910–1971* (College Station: Texas A+M University Press, 1982), 207.

Isolation of a different sort is central to the work of Mexico's most famous modern architect, Luis Barragán. In two of his rare published writings, Barragán lamented the increasingly fast-paced, public character of modern life. He presented his architecture as an antidote to this, one geared toward refuge, privacy, solitude, and meditation.[20] Subdivisions such as his Gardens of El Pedregal (1945) and Los Clubes (1963–64) were located well away from the central city, protected by distance, gates, and uniformed private security, their houses hidden behind high walls. Individual houses such as his own in the Tacubaya neighborhood of Mexico City (1948), or those he built for Antonio Gálvez (1955) and Francisco Gilardi (1977), seem almost fortress-like from the street. Walls and doors are solid, defensive, and utterly lacking in ornament or invitation. Windows are few or absent altogether; some project from the buildings like monitors, and all are barred, high-placed, or both. Bright exterior colors—the hot pink of the Gilardi House, usually described as festive or tropical—might almost be taken as a note of warning, like those on a venomous snake or insect. Inside all is cool and quiet, protectively labyrinthine in layout, reservedly luxurious, coddled in filtered light. This was, in short, an architecture of withdrawal and seclusion, and it was obviously beyond the means of many. His day's work done, O'Gorman's bricklayer would have been promptly shown the exit.

Barragán (1902–1988) moved to Mexico City from his native Guadalajara in 1936. Mexico City was then undergoing a real estate boom, and over the next four years Barragán built about thirty houses and apartment buildings there. Like much of the architecture then going up in the city, his thin-walled, glass and concrete buildings, with their roof terraces and factory windows, borrowed heavily from Le Corbusier's work of the 1920s. Most were speculative ventures that Barragán financed himself, and he profited handsomely by them. By 1940 he could afford to slacken his professional pace. He spent his time designing private gardens on his land in Tacubaya (acquired in 1943) and on property he bought in the Pedregal, just west of the University City site. This last provided the setting for his 865-acre Gardens of Pedregal. There Barragán and his associates—city planner Carlos Contreras, architect Max Cetto, artists Mathias Goeritz and Jesús "Chucho" Reyes, realtor José Alberto Bustamante, and photographer Armando Salas Portugal—designed roads and water systems, walls and gates, public plazas and sculptures, demonstration houses and gardens, and an extensive print and broadcast advertising campaign. A building code—first outlined by Diego Rivera and supposedly backed by the authority of President Alemán, who toured the site with Barragán—was formulated to protect the distinctive native landscape and regulate its architectural development away from neo-colonial and other pastiche models. Gently curving roadways were made to follow the lay of the land. Flat-roofed modern houses were set amidst the native rocks and vegetation. Many of Mexico's best-known modern architects—Francisco Artigas, Enrique del Moral, and Félix Candela among them—built houses there. The project was a huge commercial and critical success—along with the University City it was the most widely published Mexican architectural project of the period. And though it has changed much over time, it remains one of the capital's most desirable neighborhoods, home to movie stars and ex-presidents.

A comprehensively planned subdivision at the urban fringe, intended for upscale automobile commuters and high-grade houses and gardens of modern (i.e., non-historicist) design, El Pedregal was like nothing

20. See Barragán's two published lectures: "Gardens for Environment—Jardines del Pedregal," *Journal of the American Institute of Architects* 17 (April 1952): 167–72; and "Barragán on Barragán," *Archetype 2: 1* (1980): 30–31. Also see Eggener, *Luis Barragán's Gardens of El Pedregal,* 28–30, 85–86.

Luis Barragán and Max Cetto, Demonstration House, 140 Fuentes, Gardens of El Pedregal, Mexico City, 1949. Photo Armando Salas Portugal. © Foundation Barragán, Birsfelden.

21. Luis Barragán, "Gardens for Environment," 169.

22. For more on real estate considerations, see Eggener, *Gardens of Pedregal*, 21–24, 57–58, 82–86.

23. Carlos Fuentes, *Where the Air Is Clear*, 142–43.

else in Mexico at the time. Yet for all its modernity of form and concept, the development was something of a throwback to nineteenth-century, quasi-utopian, upper-class suburban schemes such as Riverside, Illinois, and Llewellyn Park, New Jersey, in the United States. Made possible by the automobile, in a country where automobile ownership was still a luxury, the Gardens of El Pedregal appealed to a small, privileged class that wanted and could afford to remove itself from the city and its problems, including crime, pollution, traffic, and crowding—even today the subway stop nearest El Pedregal is at least two miles away. At a time of breakneck urban growth, El Pedregal's distance from the maddening crowd appealed to those who could afford it. Barragán alluded to this aspect of urban flight when he said that the place was intended to promote "the peace and serenity that every man should have every day and especially in present times."[21] High stone walls and private security ensured homeowners' "peace and serenity," just as high prices assured the "right" kind of resident, and building regulations secured—or were supposed to secure—the "right" kind of architecture. A resident commercial center and private primary schools were established so that El Pedregal's children and homemakers need never leave the garden, even if its breadwinners must daily venture out into a less well-composed and well-protected realm.

Real estate advertisements for El Pedregal make clear how Barragán wanted the project to be seen and toward whom it was directed. It was expressly marketed as a haven from Mexico City's relentless growth and mounting social and environmental ills (such as crime, crowding, costs, pollution, and seismic instability). Advertisements emphasized its exclusivity and security, abundant open spaces and lush vegetation, clean air and healthful, relaxing ambiance, and its easy access by automobile to the city center and to business, cultural, and shopping areas. One group of ads billed it as "The Most Beautiful and Exclusive Subdivision in Mexico City." Another called it "The Residential Zone of the Most Brilliant Future." Yet another called it "The Ideal Place to Live."[22] Like the classic nineteenth-century elite suburbs of London and New York, El Pedregal was an idealized setting, a "city" where no one worked. Or to be more precise, no one who worked there lived there, apart from live-in domestics; and in the days before telecommuting, no one who lived there worked there. El Pedregal offered a refuge from the real city, an ideal space where life was refined and secure, filled with beauty and promise, where the air was clear.

In his novel of 1958, *La región más transparente* (Where the air is clear), Carlos Fuentes includes a character named Federico Robles. Like Barragán, Robles had been a real estate speculator working in Mexico City during the late 1930s and 1940s. "He was one of the first to build apartment buildings," recalls Librado Ibarra, an embittered bureaucrat who had known Robles years before in law school. "In nineteen hundred thirty-six [the year Barragán arrived in the capital] there was no one to stop him.... The city grew and grew, and he grew with it."[23] Ibarra becomes rancorous as he compares Robles's success with his own failure—one that is equated here with the larger failure of the revolution, a loss of nerve, if not a moral bankruptcy, that made possible the success of a project like El Pedregal:

That was rural education, and I was supposed to do something about it. So, the same beginning, you see, a great opportunity, great promise, everything for which the Revolution had been fought, land reform, labor, now education. And

Luis Barragán, Sketch for the Fuente de los Amantes (Fountain of the Lovers), Las Arboledas, Mexico City, 1958. Photo Armando Salas Portugal. © Foundation Barragán, Birsfelden.

you observe what my experience has been. What was sure was something else, and Federico Robles got it. So it follows that what Federico Robles got was what the Revolution was fought for. That there might be more subdivisions in Mexico City.[24]

CITY WOVEN BY AMNESIACS

A few years later, in another part of the city, Barragán became involved with another subdivision. Backed by former president Alemán and other powerful investors, the Satellite City was the project of Mario Pani.[25] Begun in 1954, this covered over 2,000 acres and was intended to house some 200,000 people. It was obviously much less exclusive than El Pedregal, but still decidedly middle-class and automotive in orientation. Fresh off his success at El Pedregal, Barragán was invited to design a promotional symbol for the project. He in turn invited his friend, the German émigré artist Mathias Goeritz (1915–1990), to collaborate. The Towers of Satellite City were designed and built in 1957–58.[26]

Drawing on the *Charter of Athens* and on recent satellite projects in Europe, Pani's Satellite City was one of many housing developments built at that time to ease Mexico City's growing pains. It was located alongside the city's main northbound highway, almost ten miles northwest of the Zócalo. According to Pani, the Satellite City when completed would be "absolutely self-sufficient...a truly autonomous urban entity."[27] Its various sectors and super-blocks were carefully zoned to provide areas for habitation, recreation, education, civic and commercial functions, and parking and transportation. If these last took up a seemingly disproportionate share of the development's space, Pani said it was because this was "the epoch of the automobile," and the Satellite City was "a city of the epoch." He called it "a truly modern city...a city of the future, a city of tomorrow that we are beginning to build today."[28] In all of this the project was comparable to the University City, but if its functions were more genuinely diverse, its architectural forms were notably more homogeneous. According to one observer of the 1980s:

Probably no section of the capital seems less identifiably Mexican than the endless sprawling neighborhoods of characterless middle-class homes in Satellite City to the north. The zone is a monument both to the middle-class Mexican's desire to own his home and to his fascination with the American way of life. Beside the multi-lane highways are huge shopping malls that are reachable only by car. The architecture of most houses could be described as modern utilitarian, although wealthier families have followed the American example of building homes around the golf courses and private clubs.[29]

The towers designed by Barragán and Goeritz stand on a traffic island at the development's southern edge, surrounded by twelve lanes of blacktop. They are five in number and wedged-shaped, with their sharpest angles pointing back toward the city center. Made of reinforced concrete, hollow inside, they rise from a flat

Luis Barragán, Paseo de los Gigantes (Promenade of the Giants), Las Arboledas, Mexico City, 1957–63. Photo Armando Salas Portugal. © Foundation Barragán, Birsfelden.

24. Ibid., 143.

25. Louise Noelle Merles, "The Architecture and Urbanism of Mario Pani," in Burian, ed., *Modernity and the Architecture of Mexico*, 177–89; and *Mario Pani: la visión urbana de la arquitectura* (Mexico City: UNAM, 2000).

26. G. Nesbit, "The Towers of Satellite City," *Arts and Architecture 75* (May 1958), 22–23; and Vittorio Magnago Lampugnani, "Luis Barragán: Urban Design and Speculation," in Zanco, ed., *Luis Barragán: The Quiet Revolution*, 158–59, 252.

27. Mario Pani, "México: Un Problema, Una Solución," *Arquitectura México 60* (December 1957), 217.

28. Ibid., 222, 225

29. Alan Riding, *Distant Neighbors: A Portrait of the Mexicans* (New York: Vintage Books, 1986), 388–89.

concrete-paved plaza, from 111 to 177 feet high, but as their site slopes downward toward the city, they seem taller when approached from the south. Originally they were to have been much taller, as high as 600 to 1,000 feet, and accompanied by two additional towers. One was to have been used as an observatory, the others as water tanks. The ground was to be terraced and landscaped with steps, lawns, and a fountain or reflecting pool; the design was scaled back for economic reasons. According to the original scheme, two were left neutral in color and three were painted with plastic paints: one red, one yellow, one blue. Collectively they look like a somewhat miniaturized skyscraper city, or a vastly oversized model of one, but either way they read as evident representations of buildings rather than buildings themselves. They share this aspect—the representation of modern urban architecture—with O'Gorman's painted *Ciudad de México*, but there the comparison ends. Where O'Gorman placed at the center of his painting a wide boulevard filled with people and cars, the Towers of Satellite City present a peculiarly lifeless and abstract face. The space immediately around them is almost always empty. They are a quiet and all but inaccessible center hemmed in by billboards and speeding cars, not a distinct place so much as a sign or symbol of something beyond themselves.

According to Pani, the towers stood for "man's untamable urge to transcend to great things . . . the spirit and the dignity of human works."[30] Goeritz called them a "plastic prayer."[31] More prosaically, they were advertisements. At El Pedregal Barragán had demonstrated his ability to turn otherwise undesirable land into valuable real estate and this, along with his friendship with Alemán, seems to have been the main reason for his having been invited to participate here. The towers—unavoidable elements of verticality and dash in an otherwise almost unrelentingly flat, monotonous landscape—beckoned would-be exurbanites to come, to stop and imagine the possibilities of life in a newer, cleaner, safer, more exclusive city outside the city. They were, in effect, advertisements for urban flight.

In the chapter on "critical regionalism" in his book *Modern Architecture: A Critical History*, Kenneth Frampton illustrated the work of Barragán with just one image: the Towers of Satellite City.[32] One would be hard-pressed to find a less regionalistic, less inherently Mexican design in Barragán's oeuvre. The towers grew from earlier projects by Goeritz that were themselves inspired by the medieval towers of San Gimignano, Italy, and by the modern ones of Manhattan. Barragán contributed his fascination for the haunting plazas of Italian painter Giorgio De Chirico, and his interest in Corbusian tower blocks.[33] At El Pedregal he had showcased the native landscape; he echoed it there in the rambling, abstract, cubic forms of the houses that he built on his own and with Max Cetto. Patios, open-beamed ceilings, and rough stone walls referred discreetly to the site and to Mexican architecture of the colonial past. None of this sort of historical or geographical situating enters into the Satellite City project. Its five faceless concrete towers could be almost anywhere, anytime. What they evoke is not so much the dynamism of the modern city but an obscure reminiscence of a city of the past, or many cities, seen through the filter of memory and the flickering of the mind's eye. They are, say, New York in the 1920s, when Barragán saw it for the first time. They are the city left behind.

"Nostalgia," said Barragán, "is the poetic awareness of our personal past, and since the artist's own past is the mainspring of his creative potential, the architect must listen and heed his nostalgic revelations."[34] With the Towers of Satellite City there is no longer that sense of history—of specific shared experience, of justifiable violence, hard work, and future promise—that fueled O'Gorman's painting. There is instead a

Mario Pani, Housing neighborhood of Tlatelolco (with Banobras Tower in the background), 1964. From Clive Bamford Smith, *Builders in the Sun: Five Mexican Architects* (New York: Architectural Books Publishing, 1967), all rights reserved.

30. Pani, "México: Un Problema, Una Solución," 225.

31. Federico Morais, *Mathias Goeritz* (Mexico City: UNAM, 1982), 37.

32. Kenneth Frampton, *Modern Architecture: A Critical History* (New York: Thames and Hudson, 1992), 318–20.

33. Luis Barragán, "Como Deben Desarrollarse Las Grandes Ciudades Modernas: El Crecimiento de la Ciudad de México," in *Luis Barragán: Escritos y conversaciones* (Madrid, 2000), 50–53. On his interest in De Chirico see Eggener, *Luis Barragán Gardens of El Pedregal*, 77–81.

34. Barragán, "Barragán on Barragán," 31.

vague nostalgia: history with all pain (save the poetic variety) removed; in other words, a kind of forgetting, a flight from the tough truths of present and past, and a failure to imagine—or a disinterest in engaging— the future.[35] Approaching the towers from the south, seeing them in all of their miniaturized mock urban splendor, one might not be amiss in thinking of another towered structure of the 1950s: Snow White's palace at Disneyland near Los Angeles. Both are castles in the air, icons of escape from cities growing recklessly.

35. This definition of nostalgia comes from David Lowenthal, *The Past Is a Foreign Country* (Cambridge: Cambridge University Press, 1985), 8.

AFTERMATH: THE FORGOTTEN ONES

I'm not looking for applause from the people, from the rabble, and I don't want to go down in the annals of history. To hell with the people and to hell with history.[36]

In 1950 director Luis Buñuel released his controversial film *Los Olvidados*. Set in contemporary Mexico City, this depicts a group of boys, abandoned by their families and society, struggling to survive on the city's streets. Modern architecture is a distinct feature of the film, and it is used in a most peculiar way. Almost every scene of violence, real or implied—a threat, an argument, a mugging, a murder, or a police shooting—takes place before an otherwise vacant building site. The skeletons of modern steel and reinforced-concrete frame buildings bear silent witness to these events, and they evoke the remains of the three boys murdered during the course of the film. These dead boys and their associates are the forgotten ones, the ones the revolution failed most cruelly, left to rot while the city rises all around them.

Luis Buñuel, Scene from the film *Los Olivados* (The Young and the Damned), 1950. Courtesy Cinémathèque de Belgique, Brussels.

Buñuel's use of Mexican modern architecture as a backdrop for brutality was prophetic. Between 1962 and 1964, there arose near central Mexico City the Nonoalco-Tlatelolco complex, Mario Pani's largest and most ambitious public housing project. Its 198-acre site would accommodate 100,000 people in 101 buildings ranging from four to twenty-two stories (at a density of 505 persons per acre), plus parks, clinics, schools, parking, and facilities for sports, recreation, entertainment, socializing, and shopping. This again was to be a self-contained city of the future, one also that made an attraction of its local past. At the development's center was the *Plaza de las Tres Culturas* (Square of the three cultures) where could be seen, along with Pani's modern tower blocks, the ruins of an Aztec ceremonial site and a sixteenth-century Spanish-colonial church. On the evening of October 2, 1968, ten days before the opening of the Mexico City Olympics, 10,000 people gathered to demonstrate in the plaza.[37] This was one of the smaller of a series of student-led protests ongoing in the capital since July. As was by now the custom, government troops and armed cars ringed the square during the event. Police helicopters circled overhead. The largely middle-class protesters were demanding a public dialogue with the authorities, an end to oppression by the military and police, and a renewed government commitment to democracy, education, and basic human rights—the goals of the revolution updated. As the meeting was drawing to a close, a flare was dropped from one of the helicopters; shots were fired from the perimeter; the troops moved in. As reporters were barred from the site, to this day no one knows how many died before it ended, probably more than three hundred. Many more were wounded or arrested and jailed without trial. By morning the plaza was empty, the bodies had been carted off, the blood washed away.

36. Mexican President Gustavo Díaz Ordaz (1964–70), speaking to a colleague near the end of his term in office. Quoted in Nick Caistor, *Mexico City: A Cultural and Literary Companion* (New York: Interlink Books, 2000), 136.

37. For accounts of this event see Caistor, *Mexico City*, 131–38; Elena Poniatowska, *La Noche de Tlatelolco* (Mexico City.: Ediciones Era, 1971).

38. Caistor, *Mexico City*, 135.

The events at Tlatelolco recalled the urban violence of the revolution, only now that violence served no purpose save that of perpetuating an entrenched, remote, and notoriously corrupt establishment. No official explanation of the massacre was offered, and few of the city's newspapers even mentioned it. Soon after, however, responding to international criticism in a speech before the nation, President Díaz Ordaz offered what might seem in this context like a cruel parody of the optimism once expressed by O'Gorman and others. "Tomorrow the sun will shine again," he said. "Life in the city, in the country, the life of millions of Mexicans will follow its normal course."[38] (He did not need to add "or else" for this to sound like a threat.) One would be hard pressed to find a better example of official obliviousness, or a clearer indication that the revolution was finally dead and buried.

Modern architecture did not cause this terrible sequence of events. Modern architecture and its associated artworks had once been a part of the peoples' cause for hope, vehicles by which to realize the promises of the revolution. That is what O'Gorman's painting shows. But over time those promises became hollow and the architecture remote—not emptied of meaning so much as possessed of meanings too delicate or oblique to represent communal experience or inspire collective good will. For all practical purposes, place became mere space, ambivalent, ready and waiting to be filled by whatever actions and ideas pushed the hardest, shouted the loudest, or paid the highest price. And history's tough lessons were traded for the dubious comforts of a selective amnesia. ■

Luis Barragán, Study for the development of the valley of Mexico, c.1960. © Foundation Barragán, Birsfelden. One of Barragán's paintings that illustrate his concepts for the development of the metropolis, it recalls Dr. Atl's (1875–1964) aerial views of volcanoes and landscapes (*aeropaisajes*). Barragán's view shows Mexico City from the south; to the southeast, the snowy peaks of the sacred volcanoes, Popocatépetl and the Iztaccíhuatl; to the east, Texcoco, the most important Aztec city on the edge of the lakes that surrounded Tenochtitlán. Barragán's vision protects what is left of them on both side of the straight parkway; to the northeast, the site of Teotihuacán; to the north, the plains in direction of Tula; to the northwest, Sattelite City and the five colored towers marking the entrance; the central districts of Mexico City with a dense grouping of skyscrapers around the historic center and near the Paseo de la Reforma; to the south, the aera of El Pedregal and the canals of Xochimilco. (Editor's note.)

Luis Barragán and Mathias Goeritz,
Towers of Satellite City, Mexico City,
1957–58. Photo Armando Salas Portugal.
© Foundation Barragán, Birsfelden.

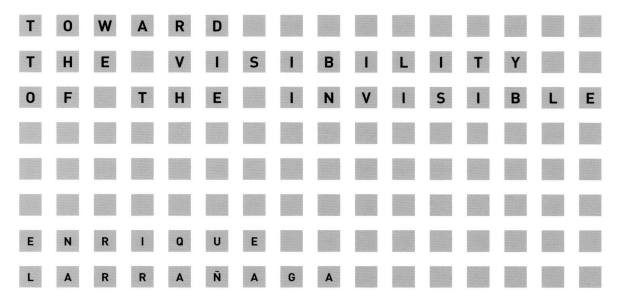

TOWARD THE VISIBILITY OF THE INVISIBLE

ENRIQUE LARRAÑAGA

I returned to the source and discovered that modernity is not outside but within us.[1]

1. Octavio Paz, *In Search of the Present: Nobel Lecture, 1990* (San Diego: Harcourt Brace Jovanovich, 1990), 33.

Trapped in the heavy traffic of Caracas while trying to reach the tentacular suburbs that extend far away from the Guaire River valley, it is hard to believe that this extremely modern city, with a population of more than four million, was a small town of just over 100,000 people only seventy years ago.

For some three hundred years, Caracas kept almost the same urban framework and extension it had achieved by the early seventeenth century, and, with fluctuations marked by riots and diseases, about the same population. The small capital of a poor colony based on modest coffee and cocoa exports, its most opulent public buildings and affluent houses would have looked impecunious when compared to similar buildings in other Latin American capitals. While surprisingly refined and avant-garde, Caracas was just a modest settlement where revolutions and leaders succeeded one another as division and despair became the norm.

The beginning of the twentieth century brought changes that would substantially alter this condition. A viscose, dark matter, called *mene* by aboriginal people, good for lighting up lamps and caulking ships and noticed by the Spaniards very early in the colony, suddenly became a major force. The discovery of quite a few important oil fields and, chiefly, the daily burst of some 565,000 cubic feet of oil at Los Barrosos II, launched a completely new phase in the life, pace, nerve, demographical and urban armature, and historical sense of the country. The poor land, often ignored by travelers for whom it was only a brief stop in transit toward other more promising scenarios, conceived and even enacted by its people as a circular, almost inescapable cycle of iterations, suddenly discovered opportunity and assumed it as a virtually mandatory duty. After decades of poverty and neglect, Caracas began enjoying political and economic stability for the first time due to its international worth as a reliable oil supplier. As a result, the city underwent a series of changes so profound and so deep they seemed impossible to cope with. As important, it found itself the capital of a redefined country and, therefore, felt the urge to redefine itself. The new economy brought new social dynamics and new people to a country that substantially differed from the quiet rural one of only a few years before. New people demanded new facilities; these often implied new uses and generated new programs. The existing city not only proved unsuited for that new life but also provided evidence of the times to be overcome. The possible became not only a dream but a factual need, making adventure a daily reality.

Alexander Calder, *Wire Portrait of Carlos Raúl Villanueva*, 1950s. © Collection Margot de Villanueva, Fundación Carlos Raúl Villanueva.

Left page
Carlos Raúl Villanueva and Alexander Calder, Interior view of the Aula Magna, with the acoustical "clouds," University City of Caracas, 1952–53. Photo Paolo Gasparini. © Fundación Carlos Raúl Villanueva.

2. Others included Carlos Guinand-Sandoz, a graduate from the Technische Hochschule München; Gustavo Wallis, who studied under Albert Kahn; and Cipriano Domínguez, a graduate from the Ecole Spéciale d'Architecture in Paris.

3. In particular, Manuel Mujica Millan and Rafael Bergamin from Spain, Arthur Kahn from Romania, and, later, Don Hatch and Emile Vestuti from the United States.

4. See Marta Vallmitjana, ed., *El Plan Rotival: la Caracas que no fue, 1939-89* (Caracas: Ediciones Instituti de urbanismo, Faculdad de arquitectura y urbanismo, 1991).

Architecture, that costly refinement only a few could afford and even fewer appreciate, suddenly became a leading emblematic and driving force in a process through which society faced its challenges and tried to decipher its rising symbols.

A group of young people, including Carlos Raúl Villanueva (1900–1975) and Luis Malaussena (1900–1958), returned to the country with abilities suddenly appreciated by a society demanding novelty and splendor.[2] In only a few years, they significantly changed the nature and perception of architecture and its role. New technologies allowed for the first tall buildings; the old plantations along the valley were successively and randomly transformed into neighborhoods; and a vigorous public school program was developed. Architects came from abroad, adding to the local energy the solidity of their more consolidated expertise.[3] Amid eclectically displayed styles, young architects, imported professionals, and foreign craftsmen introduced modernism to the general public in an almost subversive manner. Large housing projects, as well as new working and institutional requirements, became opportunities to reshape the city; and joyfully welcoming the opportunity of its reformulation, the city greeted its first major urban project, planned by French urbanist Maurice Rotival (1892–1980) in 1939.[4]

THE PLAN ROTIVAL AND ITS AFTERMATH

5. Many plans have followed and none has been fully pursued. The areas on both sides of the highway were used for projects without any overall strategy, until the design developed in the 1980s by Carlos Gómez de Llarena (Parque Vargas) recovered the avenue and proposed an urban model that, while now questioned and still unfinished, sets a comprehensive plan for the area and its recuperation of its public spaces.

6. Carlos Raúl Villanueva, *Caracas en tres tiempos* (Caracas: Ediciones Comisión Asuntos Culturales del Cuatricentenario de Caracas, 1966).

[Anonymous], *Nuestra Señora de Caracas*, oil on canvas, 1766. © Concejo Municipal del Municipio Libertador, Caracas.

As an overall strategy in the grand Beaux-Arts tradition, the Plan Rotival proposed ordering the urban expansion with a system of straight boulevards, diagonal avenues, and *rond-points* that, superimposed over the colonial grid, would transform the gridded street system into a more dynamic pattern. The central axis of the plan—the only piece that was actually implemented—was Avenida Bolívar, a Paris-inspired boulevard that would slice through the colonial city and introduce cosmopolitan grandeur into the rather humble existing fabric. At its western termination, Rotival proposed a huge forum and modeled the Calvario Hill into a pyramid dedicated to Simon Bolívar—both projects, alien to the character of the city, were unrealized. The demolitions for the new avenue were not yet complete—eventually fourteen blocks were razed—when the scheme was radically being altered. The modern boulevard became a multi-level expressway that created a hostile automobile barrier within the historic center.[5]

Following Rotival's departure for Yale University in 1940, Carlos Raúl Villanueva was commissioned to construct the first section of the avenue at the foot of the hill, now to be redesigned as a public park. There lay the old and dilapidated neighborhood of El Silencio, which President General Isaís Medina Angarita intended to destroy and replace with a "model" housing complex as a joint venture between public and private sectors. In his project of 1942, Villanueva rejected Rotival's monumental plaza and laid out a well-balanced network of urban blocks destined to residential and small-scale commercial uses: seven blocks with interior collective gardens, arcaded streets, and two squares erased all memory of the former, unhealthy district.[6] With courtyards as a typological reference and decorative motifs borrowed directly from vernacular imagery—particularly the arcades and the entrance portals—Villanueva tempered the modernist impact of the operation. "As regards the style," he wrote in 1950, "it was necessary to establish a connection with the colonial city, which was losing every day a little bit more of its old character, and to remember some of its basic elements."[7] Villanueva masterminded the operation, technically very complex, in record time (1942–45). Its academically correct composition of streets, squares, and nodes stood, and still

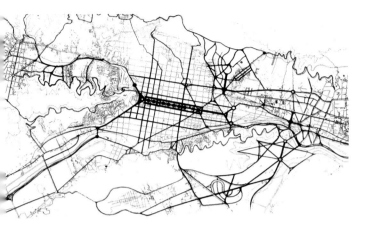

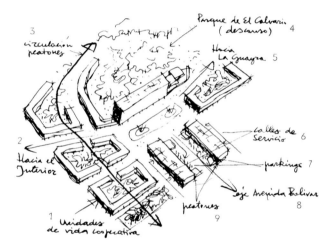

stands sixty years later, as a clearly urban and proper proposal on what the city—and an urban renewal operation—could and should be.

At about the same time (1942–49) and to the very east of Villanueva's new Silencio, Cipriano Domínguez designed what would soon become a city symbol, the Centro Simón Bolívar. The project, which was built on top of Rotival's avenue with traffic passing underneath, organized commercial and office areas in a network of streets, passages, galleries, and buildings that induced a different and innovative perception of the city, its scale, parts, views, territories, and speeds.[8] Although it is often compared to Rockefeller Center in New York, the Centro Simón Bolívar is not as much a place to be in as one to go through. In these terms, and in a very modern manner, the project operates as a system that effectively and precisely intertwines urban situations for both the user and the viewer at both local and urban scales, on both horizontal and vertical dimensions, and with both the ceremonial serenity of symmetry and the charming accidentalness of picturesque sequences.

Both the physical and temporal adjacency of El Silencio's traditional urbanity and Centro Simón Bolívar's metropolitan intensity show the velocity with which explorations and changes occurred in a city so eager to come across its own destiny that it allowed itself almost no time to question other possibilities. Almost overnight, the city of quiet stillness was reinvented as one of communication, which then seemed to surrender to the city of movement. The avenue that was to constitute its spine turned into a spire toward the open horizons awaiting the city to be. This change corresponded to one in urban paradigms induced by cultural references encouraged by economical changes. An increasing American presence in almost all productive operations of the wealthier state infused the "American way of life" into a society that adjusted its referential focus from a nineteenth-century Parisian model to a modern ideal represented by the United States. If in the early 1900s students went to Europe for an education, they were now coming back from the north, where they had studied in the best universities and under the most relevant figures of the times, to realize in this land of opportunities the ground-breaking ideas of those new pioneering paradigms.[9] As new avenues were opened, new neighborhoods populated the valley and bridges, and highways were frenetically built. A hotel standing on top of the mountain, a shopping center carved around a hill, or a glass box planted as a colonizing mark, all displayed their joyful iconography as physical evidence of an all-inclusive modern determination.

7. Villanueva, *Caracas en tres tiempos*.

8. Gustavo Wallis and Carlos Guinand, *Wallis, Domínguez y Guinand: arquitectos pioneros de una época* (Caracas: Galería de Arte Nacional, 1998).

Top left
Maurice Rotival, Plan Rotival, *Revista Municipal del Distrito Federal*, November 1939. From Marta Vallmitjana et al. *El Plan Rotival. La Caracas que no fue* (Caracas: Instituto de Urbanismo, 1991).

Bottom left
Carlos Raúl Villanueva, Sketch for the reconstruction of El Silencio neighborhood, 1941. From Sybil Moholy-Nagy, *Carlos Raúl Villanueva and the Architecture of Venezuela* (New York: Praeger, 1964).

9. Tomás José Sanabria, a student under Gropius and Sert at Harvard, Martín Vegas, a Mies van der Rohe disciple at IIT, and Dirk Bornhorst, a graduate from University of California at Berkeley, can be cited, among others.

Carlos Raúl Villanueva, View of El Silencio Neighborhood, c. 1945. Photo Paolo Gasparini. From Sibyl Moholy-Nagy, *Carlos Raúl Villanueva and the Architecture of Venezuela* (New York: Praeger, 1964).

10. For an overall view, see William Niño Araque et al., *1950: El Espíritú Moderno* (Caracas: Fundacion Corp-Group Centro Cultural, 1998).

The urban and architectural "fireworks" of the 1940s–1950s made of Caracas a city substantially and comprehensively defined by modernity. And as expected, the evidence of this assertion makes the city—its examples and its experiences as complex, problematic, and relative as the very definition of modernity. Almost everywhere—often in conflicting terms—the emerging metropolis displayed visible signs of modernism as well as sensible interpretations of modernity. This might be proven by comparing two contemporary works of the highest urban and symbolic importance, which were designed by two former classmates of the Ecole des Beaux-Arts in Paris: the Military Academy (Academia Militar de Venezuela) by Luis Malaussena and the University City (Ciudad Universitaria de Caracas) by Carlos Raúl Villanueva.[10]

THE URBAN SYSTEM "LA NACIONALIDAD"

11. See Silvia Hernández de Lasala, *Malaussena: arquitectura académica en la Venezuela moderna* (Caracas: Fundación Pampero, 1990).

12. See Richard Etlin, *Modernism in Italian Architecture, 1890–1940* (Cambridge: MIT Press, 1991).

The urban system called "La Nacionalidad" was conceived and implemented between 1942 and 1955 to the south of and separated from the historic center by a chain of hills and mountains. Its east-west axis linked the two poles of a new education system for the country: the military schools to the east, and the new campus of the university to the west. The project of the Military Academy partook of the modernization of the army, a process initiated ten years earlier after the death of military dictator Gómez. The goal was to elevate the intellectual level of the armed forces, to remove them from the moral morass of the dictatorship, and to adapt them to the rapid yet brutal development of civil society. Luis Malaussena began the design in 1945 on a site quite far away from the existing city. In the following years, the project developed into an urban articulation for the military education facilities through a sequence of ceremonial spaces aligned as an urban park linking the Academy and the University in construction.[11]

The three building stages show three different, perhaps complementary and certainly skillful, approaches to the modes, manners, and variants of the modern stylistic palette, wisely utilized by an eclectic architect who precisely adopted and adapted formal options to representative intentions. The stark composition of the Academia Militar—the first phase to the east end of the axis—evoked the austere, classical-modern monumentality of Marcello Piacentini's works in fascist Rome: the symmetrical composition, centered on a large open square, recalls the University of Rome and other urban moments in the EUR district.[12] Designed

Luis Malaussena, Aerial view of the Paseo de los Próceres, the Military Club (left), and the Military Academy (end of axis), Caracas, 1940–50s. From Silvia Hernández de Lasala, *Malaussena, arquitectura académica en la Venezuela moderna* (Caracas: Fundación Pampero, 1990).

in 1950–52, the *Círculo Militar* (Armed Forces Club) assumed the image of a looser, more international modernism. Here the architect adopted an asymmetrical and dynamic parti of horizontal volumes, whose articulation brings to mind Hadrian's Villa in Tivoli and the mature works of Alvar Aalto.

For the third phase Malaussena conceived the Paseo de los Precursores and the Avenida de los Próceres as an impressive parade mall dedicated to national heroes, a reinterpretation of the Invalides transplanted from Paris into the wilderness of the Caracas valley. Along the avenue he located a series of monuments (columns, groups of statues, fountains, etc.) that avoids the traps of academicism while creating a kinetic space for nature and national history. Beyond the Paseo, the axis continued along the soft curves of the topography to connect to the opposite, civil pole of the urban system "La Nacionalidad": the University City.

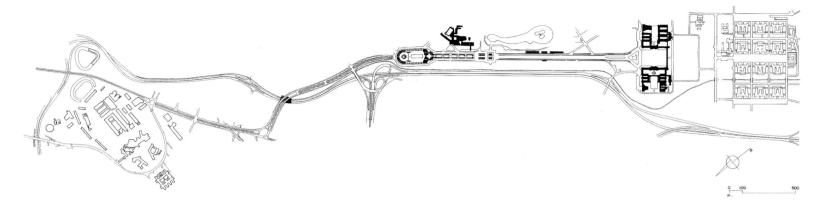

Luis Malaussena and Carlos Raúl Villanueva, Plan of the Military Academy, the Paseo de los Próceres, the Military Club (from right to center), and the University City of Caracas (left). Drawing by Joan Mitjans and Bianca Gruber. From Silvia Hernández de Lasala, *Malaussena, arquitectura académica en la Venezuela moderna* (Caracas: Fundación Pampero, 1990).

THE UNIVERSITY CITY: FIRST PHASE

When he received the commission for the master plan for the new campus of Universidad Central de Venezuela in 1943, Villanueva already enjoyed a good reputation, gained through a few public projects—such as the Fine Arts Museum (1935–38) and the new neighborhood of El Silencio—in which he had skillfully mixed recognizable styles with spaces and articulations of quiet charm and festive luminosity. Eclectically incorporating familiar motifs, his interest in supporting his work with a proper understanding of local architectural traditions might be read as an attempt to root his buildings and his own soul in a place he knew only as the land his parents came from. Son of a Venezuelan diplomat, Villanueva was born in London and remained in Europe until coming to Venezuela for the first time in 1929. With a strong French accent, the critical distance granted by his good sense of humor, and a bohemian attitude that earned him the nickname *El Loco*, Villanueva remained foreign to his own country, a fact that probably allowed for the playful discovery of what for others might just be daily life.

Carlos Raúl Villanueva, University City of Caracas, first master plan, 1944. From Sibyl Moholy-Nagy, *Carlos Raúl Villanueva and the Architecture of Venezuela* (New York: Praeger, 1964).

13. Sibyl Moholy-Nagy, *Carlos Raúl Villanueva and the Architecture of Venezuela* (New York: Praeger, 1964); on the campus, see *Ciudad Universitaria de Caracas: Patrimonio Mondial* (Caracas: UCV, UNESCO, 2002). Built like the Military Academy complex during the years of Marco Jiménez's dictatorship and thus used in a propagandistic way as manifestation of that government's achievements, the university complex continues to transcend the socio-political conditions of its conception. Placed on the UNESCO World Heritage list, it stands as one of the most important urban and architectural ensembles in twentieth-century America.

Carlos Raúl Villanueva, University Hospital, University City of Caracas, 1945–54. Photo Mariano U. De Aldaca. © Archivo Shell/ CIC-UCAB.

Carlos Raúl Villanueva, Olympic Stadium, University City of Caracas, 1949–52. Photo Paolo Gasparini. © Proyecto Ciudad Universitaria de Caracas-Patrimonio.

Villanueva's first proposal for the 500-acre site of Ciudad Universitaria was a highly formalized academic exercise in the Beaux-Arts tradition of the North American campus. A vast oval, set against an irregular site, showed a strong formal presence. Its short and main axis, running between the sports complex on the northeast end of campus and the hospital on the site's southwest edge, organized university life around a central space defined by scholastic buildings organized as symmetrical quadrangles. With minor adaptations, this master plan would prevail for the first years of the process and, to this day, the pentimento of its framework continues to mark the actual experience of Ciudad Universitaria de Caracas and its relationship to the "sublime" landscape that surrounds it.[13]

The first building on campus, the University Hospital, was completed in 1945. The center of this massively symmetrical and frontally set structure—it recalls the principles of Durand and the medical complexes built in New York in the 1930s—was made up of two large courtyards lined with treatment and surgery rooms. On both sides, four seven-story bars of patient rooms—wrapped in balconies and painted in bright blue, red, and yellow under the direction of artist Mateo Manaure—opened on the campus and the mountains in a rare and optimistic interpretation of the program between the individual and the collective. Here Villanueva's hospital transcended the academic scheme of composition and integrated various modernist and rationalist references, such as Giuseppe Terragni's Novocomum in Como (1927–29), the Universum Cinema by Erich Mendelsohn in Berlin (1927–28), or, even more so, the Paimio Sanatorium by Alvar Aalto (1929–33), which used a similar system of ship-like balcony promenades.

In 1949 Villanueva started working on the Sports Complex, built as originally planned on the northeast end of campus and completed by 1951. Considerations of solar orientation suggested a subtle shift that broke the rigidity of the plan's symmetry. However, this compositional adjustment was widely surpassed by the conceptual changes realized during the design and construction of these buildings, changes that would from then on inform Villanueva's work. Influenced by Pier Luigi Nervi's sport complexes in Italy, Villanueva subjugated composition to technique and, in so doing, realized the expressive power of structure as basic to form. Unlike the primarily compositional operations structuring the University Hospital, the beauty of the formal choices made for the Olympic Stadium (1949–51), the Baseball Stadium (1949–51), and the Swimming Pool (1953–60)—a grouping that Sybil Moholy-Nagy later compared to the theater complex in Pompeii—lies in the way in which they manifest truth and, by stating the material veracity of technique, set aesthetics as a question of ethics.[14]

In the Olympic Stadium, the direct correspondence between profile, loads, masses, and forces turns structural evidence into a moving and distinct pleasure. Structural ribs rest on incredibly thin columns; beams hold and cover the seating areas of the main tribune while the general seating area, supported on diagonal concrete poles, opposes gravity and the floating lightness of the tribune. Space flows and reverberates without the mediation of style but through the plain evidence and translucent actuality of materiality. While the building stands on the site as an object, the overwhelming power of the structural ribs

14. Alfredo Rodriguez-Delfino and Blas Lamberti did all original calculations, later revised by Constantin Polidiroff and Anatoli Kravchenko.

Carlos Raúl Villanueva, Covered Square (mural by Mateo Manaure), University City of Caracas, 1952–53. Photo Paolo Gasparini. © Proyecto Ciudad Universitaria de Caracas-Patrimonio.

15. See Enrique Larrañaga, "La Ciudad Universitaria y el Pensamiento Arquitectónico en Venezuela" in *Obras de arte de la ciudad universitaria* (Caracas: Universidad Central de Venezuela, 1991), 43–61.

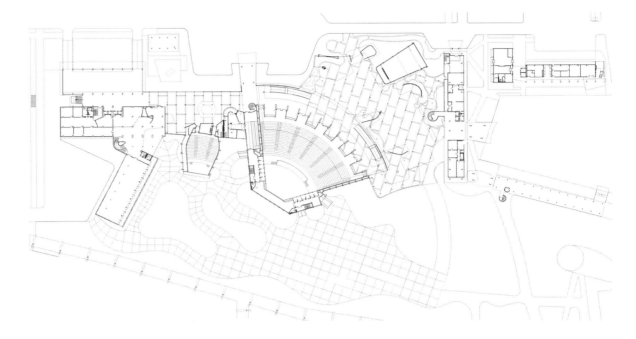

Carlos Raúl Villanueva, Plan of the Covered Square and of the Cultural and Administration Center, University City of Caracas, drawing by David Guzmán and Gabriel Djukic. © University City of Caracas, all rights reserved. The author describes the covered plaza, starting from the right edge of the drawing.

on what could be read as the back of the building are a commanding presence and provide the stadium with its most significant facade. But, as in a project by French architect Boullée, iterating bearing members finally dissolve the object as such into a system that speaks more about the rationality of order than about its specifically visual or compositional characteristics.

THE CAMPUS AS GESAMTKUNSTWERK

Pivotal to this realization, the Cultural and Administrative compound—articulated around its center, the Covered Plaza or Plaza Cubierta (Covered Plaza)—stands midway between the hospital and the sports forum. Comprising the Rectorate, various lecture and concert halls, the university museum, the Aula Magna or main auditorium, and the library, the complex was repeatedly studied by Villanueva between 1943 and 1950: all of his preliminary schemes respectfully followed the longitudinal symmetry of the original master plan.[15]

In the ultimate revision of the project (1951) prior to construction in 1952–53, Villanueva abruptly abandoned the longitudinal axis. First, he turned the overall composition around in a cross-axial organization opposed to the original direction of development. Second, at the very location of the oval void of the first scheme, he conceived a continuous ensemble of buildings and public spaces that he articulated following an apparently chaotic, yet highly structured, organic order. The massiveness of the original grouping of buildings around the elliptical green was broken into pieces of somewhat Bauhaus-like symbolic distinctiveness, liberating the arrangement and its parts from overall constraints and letting their particular characteristics and forces be fully expressed.

Coming from the city center across Plaza Venezuela and the "La Nacionalidad" axis, the administrative complex is reached along a long, concrete arcade that winds parallel to the hill and whose asymmetrical, cantilevered section makes it look as if emerging from it. The twisting clock tower marks the entering turn to the *Plaza del Rectorado* (Court of Honor), on which the stark muteness of the Administration Building conveys a silent monumentality, disturbed only by the playfulness of a concrete canopy and the murals by Armando Barrios and Oswaldo Vigas.

Passing the threshold under the Administrative Building or along the curved arcade leaping over the campus as a detached puzzle piece, the visitor enters the undefined realm of the Plaza Cubierta, a sequence of skewed frames activating a multi-directional game of visual discovery. From this point to its end at the back of the library, the plaza can be read as the endless repetition of Le Corbusier's Maison Domino: columns and beams define a regular, albeit rotated, system of iterative lines that suggest an evident but still mysterious depth. Swirling roof openings, bright murals, colorful vegetation, and alternating shapes of contrasting shadows on shiny floors confront the simplicity of structural lines and their rotation in a seemingly endless switching of direction, light, and core. Constructed of suprisingly intertwined sections, spaces emerge and transform incessantly. Repetition renders structure almost invisible; beam outlines emphasize rotation as contrasted with floor patterns; shadows reformulate centrality; murals accentuate and dilute depth; columns of light subvert flatness as an experiential topography.

Alexander Calder, Sketch for the "Clouds" in the Aula Magna, University City of Caracas, 1952. © Collection Margot de Villanueva, Fundación Carlos Raúl Villanueva.

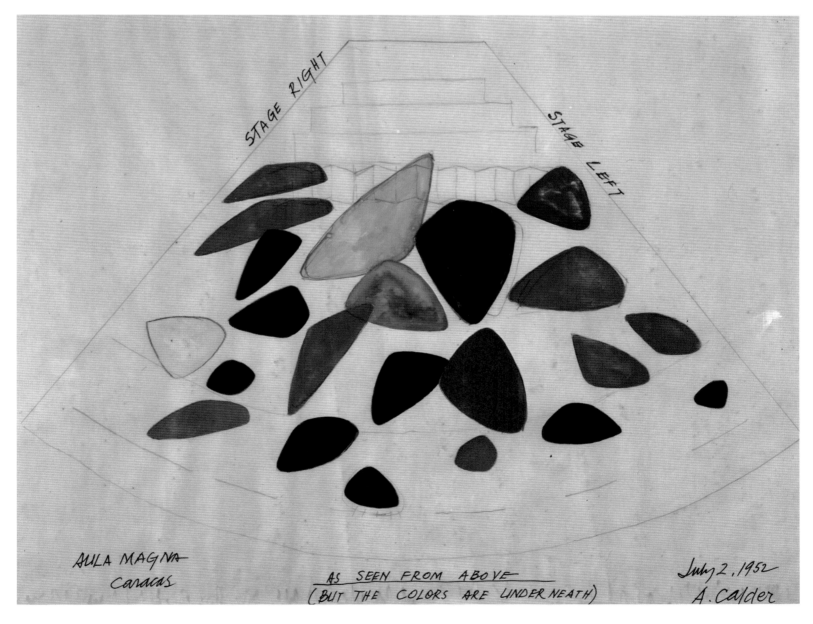

STAGE RIGHT

STAGE LEFT

AULA MAGNA
Caracas

AS SEEN FROM ABOVE
(BUT THE COLORS ARE UNDERNEATH)

July 2, 1952
A. Calder

Martín Vegas and José Miguel Galia,
Torre Polar seen from Plaza Venezuela,
1951–54. © Collection of Archivo Shell/
CIC-UCAB.

16. On the "integration of arts" and the
collection of contemporary art by
Venezuelan and international artists,
see Marina Gasparini, ed., *Obras de
arte de la Ciudad Universitaria de
Caracas.*

17. Martin Heidegger, "Building.
Dwelling. Thinking," *Poetry,
Language and Thought* (New York:
Harper & Row, 1975), 154.

18. Citing Alois Riegl, Herbert Read
defines the term as proper to those
types of art in which form is dictated
by "inward sensation rather than
outward observation": Herbert Read,
"The Vital Image," *Icon and Idea: The
Function of Art in the Development of
Human Consciousness* (Cambridge:
Harvard University Press), 25.

Villanueva invited some of the most important artists of his time to design art works for this magnificent and intriguing succession of spaces—this synthesis, creating art that relates to iarchitectural sequences—is known as the "integration of the arts."[16] Small gardens appear everywhere in the Covered Plaza. Here is Jean Arp's sculpture, the *Cloud Shepherd*; there, to the right, the inflected yellow window of Victor Vasarely's mural *Homage to Malevich*; behind, a flicker of light; ahead, a patch of nature trapped in a place that offers itself as a break in the everlasting passing of continuous space and, in its center, also curved, the *Mural* by Pascual Navarro. Concrete block lattices mediate between an emerging background and a light-dissolved foreground. From here, facing Fernand Léger's *Bimural*, the winding roof profile embraces Henri Laurens's bronze *Amphion*, twisted as an anxious screw holding buttresses and expanded as an open hand. Intertwined and permanently, as well as pertinently, dissolved in light, space transcends form and transforms it into experience. Boundaries, understood "not [as] that at which something stops but...that from which something begins," are here revealed as interactive links through which outward signs allow for the realization of inward beings.[17] As if prying into a side view, accepting an intruding light, deciphering the sky through a shadow moving on the floor, distant spaces are invited into the fragmented continuity of this place to support the compelling power of presences revealed, as what seems to be remembered becomes an object of desire.

As the puzzling regularity of the hypostyle chamber turns into convex balconies of floating bulk, these virtual rooms develop into fluid ascending ramps that seductively lead to the luminous and introspective splash of the Aula Magna. The surfaces of this splendid space wrap around as a cave, blending together floors, walls, and ceilings in a spatial continuity that, with its haptic embrace, expands the room's invigorating breath.[18] Calder's *Clouds* float as passing butterflies. With delicate purity, the balcony glides as a fine leaf separated from the shining shell. Structural ribs span over the hall as if embracing a massive mountain, while the apparently effortless interior forms an open field full of reverberating lights and sounds. A delicate canopy hangs from the ribs and over the vestibule like sheltering trees in a forest. As in a journey toward substance and hoping to transcend the simplistic satisfaction of merely visual clues, the Aula Magna edifies an intensely physical presence in which all senses participate in the realization of a place as suggestive as a possibility behind a translucent veil.

Outside—if such simple categories can still be applied to these entangled spatial interactions—a perforated concrete block wall turns light into sparkles that at sunset spatter the pavement like fish on a liquid surface. Casting bright shadows on another Vasarely mural at the entrance to the Concert Hall with voids framing the distant views, the passage leads to the library entry hall, densely colored by a stained-glass mural by Fernand Léger. A narrow stair ascends to the main reading room, which opens widely onto the main garden, and, through it, onto the whole campus, the city, and the mountain.

From this urban belvedere, the tentacular network of "covered walks" can be best perceived as a comprehensive urban and architectonic laboratory. It traverses the campus and its buildings, blends with

Metropolitan Caracas (the colonial center is at the very center), 1994. © Instituto Geográfico de Venezuela Simón Bolívar.

the palm trees and gardens, protecting students and other residents from tropical sun and rain. The wide covered walks protect food stands, improvised bookstores, and all the ambulatory activities that, in the colonial center of the city, jam the streets and sidewalks; the narrower ones provide open-air classroom and seminar spaces. Manifesting an urban framework that subverts the original preeminence of one single, central space, these "arcades" reverse a traditional solid-void pattern by building up "streets" that project the suave atmosphere of domestic corridors into a new scale, meaning, and role. With their oscillating surfaces, folded planes, tree-like pillars, and harsh textures, these artifacts examine the emotional strength of the materiality of concrete and the articulation of experiential situations through sequences in which delimiting becomes an extremely effective way of linking.

By transposing image into substance, the public spaces of the Ciudad Universitaria give presence to an "aura" that renders visible, or at least experiential, that which is seemingly invisible—or "is not behind, underneath, ahead, beyond or above the visible (but) hidden in the experience of the visible, where it cannot be seen."[19] By means of that experiential imminence, these spaces transform physical limits into situational links that, intervening not just on but in, with, and within the world, act as frames to transpose, interrogate, and confront images that, if reduced to mere visibility would hide the substance experience is trying to unveil.[20] In so doing they promote a process of realization as open, intertwined, and unpredictable as the very experiences those links make possible.[21] With modern inclusiveness, Villanueva combines the spatial transparencies of modern architecture with the deep intermediations of traditional colonial architecture, such as long and dark corridors, the entrance porches or *zaguanes*, the latticed wood windows, and terracotta screens (acting as *rejas* or *moucharaby*). He sets the whole within the exuberance of tropical vegetation and applied bright colors, in a comprehensive though divergent experience that constructs the world through the reconstruction of its sources and the deconstruction of its conventions.

No longer reducing the observer to the passivity of just looking at things, the spaces in and around Plaza Cubierta as well as the inviting ramps at the subsequent School of Humanities, the luminous studio areas at the Architecture School or the kinetic shadows of the entry pergolas at the Dentistry School, dynamically engage the visitor as a working actor looking "for" and "forward to" experiencing a multiplicity of situational links. This interactive rapport, which simultaneously emphasizes and questions reality through the changing perception of the witnessed, the flow of natural elements, the elusive interlocking of forms and, above all, the comprehensive enjoyment of the senses, decidedly, perhaps even naively, aims at the realization of the profound being of place as free from the interfering mediations of convention and the

19. An "appearance of a distance, however close it might be," in Walter Benjamin's words quoted by Luis Pérez Oramas, "Duchamp y la fábula jurásica," *Mirar Furtivo* (Caracas: Consejo Nacional de la Cultura, 1997), 168. The quote is from John Eiderfield, "Irredentas" in *I Simposio International Armando Reverón. Ponencias* (Caracas: Proyecto Armando Reverón, 2002), 44.

20. "The visual in a visual artist is not constrained to the visible within the limits of an image," writes Luis Pérez-Oramas, "Duchamp y la fibula jurásica," 172.

21. "One would like to build an ideal form, without anything useless, so logical and so pure that there would be no noticeable difference among roofs, walls, and natural space": Villanueva, *Caracas en tres tiempos*, 65.

22. Paz, *In Search of the Present*, 17.

deceiving tricks of imagery. Visible clues are reduced to their basic armature and displayed, thus allowing their many variables to affect perception with their multiple or interrelated circumstances. The spaces of the Covered Plaza do not present place as a concluded fact but, through experiential artifacts and emotional lenses, pose it as a developing process through which presence is realized as both awareness and accomplishment of that which is in, with, within, besides, and beyond the world, and supports experience. And there lies precisely the very modernity of these intriguing spaces with their puzzling sequences, invigorating multiplicities, compelling moments, and intertwining allusions. It is a modernity that this city, extended without real growth, saturated by mirages of progress and daily confronted with its own hopeless failure in the aching sight of slums and desertion, could certainly reassume as a task that calls for immediate and urgent action. As intensely as the city of Caracas keeps questioning its evolving identity, the Ciudad Universitaria offers itself as a process that keeps unfolding its questions and options as an endless maze around and toward the construction of place. Each question demands an answer, which soon becomes the source of yet many more questions, the world full of signs, hints, and wills turned into opportunities to further scrutinize it, each actor aiming at deciphering a world constructed and deconstructed by every move, quest, desire and memory of all who enact it. Perhaps still, and hopefully forever:

Modernity is a word in search of its meaning.[22]   ∎

Cipriano Domínguez, Towers of the Centro Bolívar seen from El Silencio, 1990s. Photo Jean-François Lejeune.

Carlos Raúl Villanueva, Covered Square with a Vasarely wall panel in the center, University City of Caracas, 1952–53. Photo Paolo Gasparini. © Fundación Carlos Raúl Villanueva.

Carlos Raúl Villanueva, University City of Caracas, aerial view, c. 1960. Photo Mariano U. De Aldaca. © Archivo Shell/ CIC-UCAB.

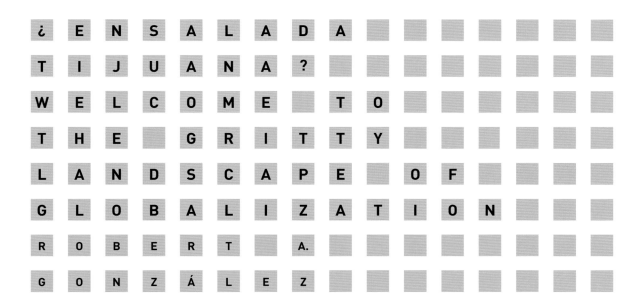

¿ENSALADA TIJUANA? WELCOME TO THE GRITTY LANDSCAPE OF GLOBALIZATION

ROBERT A. GONZÁLEZ

Globalization both ignores borders and alters them, leaving behind a postmodern urban grit that has inspired diverse artistic interpretations worldwide. The concept of townscape as "gritty" is not a felicitous one. But in the case of the twelve metropolitan crossing points on the U.S.–Mexico border, where adjoining cities form border towns, it is precisely a fascination with this disorderly urban residue that has repeatedly brought these divided cities so much attention. This has been the case with Tijuana, which, of all the border towns, is arguably the most legendary, even notorious, and most often studied and discussed. It is also true for the borderland's court jester, the bicultural performance-artist Guillermo Gómez-Peña—a postmodern Romulus/Remus couple who feeds off the teats of culture clash itself.[1] Both the city and the artist in question, however, must be understood as "striations" and not as composites of borderland conditions that reach out beyond city limits and down deeper than cultural clichés. Urban disorderliness of this sort, in fact, extends as far south as Mexico City, and northward to San Antonio, and to East Los Angeles and beyond. It could never be summed up by one single iconic image; such a continuously constructed mega-city is never to be encapsulated.

Many have tried to make sense of this conceptual territory. In the early 1990s, geographer Lawrence Herzog and geographers Daniel Arreola and James Curtis, documented the historical and architectural development of the twelve border cities with studies that concentrated on the 1,200-mile long borderland corridor.[2] Presenting another dimension, writer Gloria Anzaldúa and critical theorist José Saldívar's literary and textual studies helped us to look beyond this corridor to consider multiple forms of cultural practices as a vast hemispheric enterprise.[3] By drawing from James Clifford's theory of ethnography as travel writing and Néstor García Canclini's conception of culture as hybridization, for example, Saldívar reminds us in *Border Matters* of the cultural interpreter's common inability to claim purview to "liminality."[4] This term refers to the ability to convey from experience that which exists between the sensate and the subconscious. A similar concern is conveyed in Renato Rosaldo's thinly veiled criticism in his introduction to García Canclini's *Hybrid Cultures*, where Rosaldo reminds us that the success of border readings still hinges on the tenuous position of the participant-observer. Keeping this in mind when reviewing the art and architecture of the borderlands is important, especially as this cultural landscape—and state of mind— continues to gain the international attention of many who wish to interpret the sensations of the border without subconsciously knowing them.

In this perspective, the subtle social and cultural criticism expressed with the Mexican artist Betsabée Romero's "potpourri car"—a gender-reversal of the typical "macho" low-rider—and the salient homage to

1. Among the extended literature: Guillermo Gómez-Peña, *Codex Espangliensis: From Columbus to the Border Patrol* (San Francisco: City Lights Book, 2000); Glenn Harper, *Interventions and Provocations: Conversations on Art, Culture and Resistance* (Albany: State University of New York Press, 1998).

2. Lawrence A. Herzog, *Where North Meets South: Cities, Space, and Politics on the U.S.-Mexico Border* (Austin: Center for Mexican American Studies Book, 1990); Daniel D. Arreola and James R. Curtis, *The Mexican Border Cities: Landscape Anatomy and Place Personality* (Tucson: University of Arizona Press, 1993); Lawrence A. Herzog, *From Aztec to High Tech: Architecture and Landscape across the Mexico-United States Border* (Baltimore: John Hopkins University Press, 1999).

3. Gloria Anzaldúa and Cherríe Moraga, *This Bridge Called My Back: Writings by Radical Women of Color* (New York: Kitchen Table, Women of Color Press, 1983); also see "Tijuana Calling: Travel Writing, Autoethnography, and Video Art," in José David Saldívar, *Border Matters: Remapping American Cultural Studies* (Berkeley: University of California Press, 1997).

4. Néstor García Canclini, *Hybrid Cultures: Strategies for Entering and Leaving Modernity* (Minneapolis: University of Minnesota Press, 1995); José David Saldívar, *Border Matters*.

Left page
Betsabée Romero, inSITE97, *Ayate Car*, 1997. Photo Philipp Scholz/Rittermann. © inSITE97.

Pablo Vargas Lugo, inSITE97, *Kiosko Esotérico*, Centro Cultural Tijuana, Tijuana, Mexico. © inSITE97.

5. ERRE, quoted in Néstor García Canclini, "InSITE: Art at the U.S.-Mexico Border," *Aula* 1 (1999): 81–91.

6. Canclini, ibid.

hypocrisy expressed with the Tijuana artist Marcos Ramírez ERRE's double-headed Trojan Horse ("we already know all their intentions towards us, and they know our intentions towards them") respond to the everyday concerns of those who live on the border.[5] However, an increasingly international line-up of artists whose work has recently been making the artistic circuits, including prominent figures like Polish-born Krzysztof Wodiczko and Belgian filmmaker Chantal Akerman, present new interpretations of the globalized state of the U.S.–Mexico border. The challenge is to see to what extent their work provides us with useful interpretations of what it means to live and breathe in the borderlands of *Las Américas*, the belly of globalization.

The San Diego, California–based art program inSITE, which began in 1992, has been a notably forthcoming vehicle for promoting interpretations of the border, not simply as a regional condition but as a phenomenon of globalization. Organized every three to four years by its director, Michael Krichman, who works with a pan-American curatorial team, inSITE has provided us with almost a decade of public art projects that illuminate the everyday border experience with architectural and urban installations outside the limits of the gallery space. As an institution, inSITE has indeed established the borderlands as a regional art laboratory, making it the "ironic," "postmodern," and "intercultural" laboratory that García Canclini talks about, one where we can locate the "uncertainty generated by the bilingual, bicultural, and bi-national oscillations" of the city.[6]

The diverse body of work that the umbrella organization has produced emphasizes the contrast between modernity's orderly programs and the recent globally oriented artistic approaches that decidedly zoom in on every case of urban disorientation, where artists make sense and nonsense of the borderland phenomenon. Numerous artists have interpreted the borderlands as junctures where the designs of local and international architects confront the organic textures of tourism and globalization on a daily basis. The extent to which border readings can surpass the neo-imperial tendencies of globalization and attain the perspective of the liminal observer, however, led the program's director to consider ways of bringing artists closer to their subjects. If works of art begin to function like travel writing that will eventually be exported, how can one assure that a state of liminality will be achieved? Moreover, if most of the projects are meant to be experienced in situ, how can we understand them when they travel outside of the borderlands?

IN-SITE AND WODICZKO

In 2000, Krzysztof Wodiczko's projections of "self," a much larger version of his earlier "Alien Staff" project, marked an important moment in the inSITE program.[7] This evening performance attempted to humanize Tijuana's central urban icon, the Centro Cultural de Tijuana (CECUT), with distorted facial projections. The spherical structure, which was built in 1982 by Mexican architects Manuel Rosen and Pedro Ramírez Vázquez, is located in one of the most important vortices of the borderland corridor. Among the well-known metropolitan architects few have built in the borderlands; Ramírez Vázquez is one of them. His most famous building, one of his rare non-circular-based projects, is Mexico City's Museum of Anthropology (1964). This building complex harkens back to the rectilinear, pre-Columbian urban center of nearby Teotihuacán. The museum's immense pre-Columbian–like forecourt, which makes a spatial rather than a stylistic reference, is partially sheltered by an inverted pyramid, a whimsical play on the past that surprises the visitor with its lively rainwater funnel.[8]

In the Tijuana superstructure, however, the architects offered the city a generous plaza and decided to express the border's fluid condition in the interior of the building. The exterior cascading stairs, on which the superstructure sits, do give the platonic centerpiece a dynamic foundation, but the building nevertheless seems to have been "parachuted in." Ironically, the artist ERRE, who gained his fame through inSITE, produced an early installation in 1994 where he symbolically resurrected on CECUT's plaza a one-room Mexican shanty he called "Century 21," representative of the kind of dwelling that had been destroyed (and would someday reappear) in the early 1980s to make room for CECUT. Another artist, Pedro Vargas Lugo, commented on the commercialism of this ominous urban icon with his project *Kiosko Esotérico*, built for inSITE1997.

In most cases inSITE brings together almost an equal percentage of regional and international artists. To resolve the situation of the artist who is not local, inSITE began to require a residency of one hundred days. During such a period, Polish-born Wodiczko became involved with the labor rights organization Factor X, a group that assists *maquiladora*-workers, mostly women, who were the subjects of his eventual display.[9] The women's images were transmitted onto CECUT's round surface. At first glance one might claim that Wodiczko's performance demoralizingly exposed the pained faces of abused Mexican women—survivors of rape, employment abuse, and incest—transforming the CECUT plaza into a real-life hour of *Cristina*, the Spanish-language version of Oprah Winfrey's talk show. The transformed iconic structure, resembling an

7. Canclini, "InSITE"; Susan Buck-Morss et al., *InSITE1997, Private Time in Public Space: San Diego/Tijuana* (San Diego: Installation Gallery, 1998).

8. See Pedro Ramírez Vázquez, *The National Museum of Anthropology, Mexico City: Art, Architecture, Archaeology, Anthropology* (New York: Harry N. Abrams, 1968).

9. Krzysztof Wodiczko is internationally renowned for his large-format projections (slides and videos) on urban facades and monuments. Since the end of the 1980s, he developed a series of "nomadic" instruments for the homeless and migrant workers. These instruments are designed for survival, communication, self-confidence, and health. See Krzysztof Wodiczko, *Critical Vehicles: Writings, Projects, Interviews* (Cambridge: MIT Press, 1999). *Maquiladoras* are factory workers in Tijuana and other border towns.

10. Perhaps the effect in the foreign European land was too far removed from the border to convey the subconscious sense of place, but it was sensational nevertheless. Chantal Akerman later criticized the installation in Kassel as technically inappropriate and incomplete: the presentation at the CIVA in Brussels (May 22–October 5, 2003) followed her exact requirements. [Editor's note.]

odd-looking, disembodied head, brought public irony to Tijuana's public realm, especially when considering the building's intended use for rock concerts and cultural programs. In a darkened city, projections of Wodiczko's real-life performers eerily cloaked the modern urban structure, which sustained a heroic image by day, transforming it into a morbid confessional by night, the very act de-materializing the strongholds of the nationalist project itself.

This highly effective technique of awesome projections, which is Wodiczko's signature move, was later documented in a film that replays the making of the original projections. This film shows a close-up of each woman struggling as she comes to terms with her pending public confession and as she gathers the courage to read into a microphone under the artificial light of an apparatus uncomfortably attached to her head. The apparatus both illuminates her and transmits her image. The contraption was designed by MIT Visual Arts students, who worked hastily to construct this mediating tool while the artist worked to convince Factor X's recipients to perform for inSITE. Interestingly, almost the exact reverse of this real-life strategy was used by filmmaker Chantal Akerman with her film *From the Other Side*, about border crossings near Douglas, Arizona (2002). The artist reconceived the film as a video and film installation for the exhibition *Dokumenta* 11 in Kassel, Germany. In this interior installation, which was simultaneously broadcast along the border itself, human subjects were shown in the dangerous plights of the border's wastelands.[10]

At a later date, the communication that Wodiczko initiated with the geographers and sociologists of the Colegio de la Frontera in Tijuana resulted in a true laboratory interaction and transformed what would otherwise be called another performance produced "for art's sake" into a long-term project. Now, concerned Tijuana residents are working with Factor X to repeat the ritual of public *testimonio* as public therapy, bringing a well-known Latin American ritual, by way of a Polish-American artist, to the border. Similar kinds of female public

Meyer Vaisman, inSITE2000, *Tijuana.*
© InSITE2000.

protest occurred in Buenos Aires with the "Mothers of the Plaza de Mayo" during and after the military dictatorship, and in Santo Domingo after Trujillo's assassination in 1965. Those who saw the live performance doubt whether CECUT can ever be experienced the same way again. The global border city is, of course, simultaneously visible and invisible, and "borderlandia" can thus be imagined as an invisible mega-city (composed of multiple cities) that is best detected when its randomly located icons are brought to light. Wodiczko's illuminated globe in turn lit globalization's gritty textures, making the global city visible, if only for one night.

ANTI-MONUMENTS TO GLOBALIZATION

The colorful tower designed by Mexican architect Ricardo Legoretta in Los Angeles's Pershing Square, or even Luis Barragán and Mathias Goeritz's towers of Satellite City in Mexico City, may be considered as "borderland" monuments.[11] Yet, it is the less obvious and sublime anti-monuments that serve as the best representations of globalization. In Tijuana, this includes the "zones of tolerance," or prostitution mini-cities where gynecological and security services are often combined with nightclubs and sleeping quarters. This border city's urban spine, of course, is the dangerous, razor-sharp metallic wall constructed by the U.S. Army Corps of Engineers, the modern builders of this symbol of intolerance. As for its business and industrial core, it is surrounded by *maquiladoras* and *cartonlandias*—the imposing factories and spontaneous corrugated company towns that are ironically made of the same packaging materials used to export First World–ready goods. This is the building cycle of globalization.

As a child, I remember the *cartoneros* peddling their jerry-rigged rickshaws in my own Texas border town barrio, each man collecting from trash heaps any piece of material that could be reused across the border, only blocks from where it was originally produced, to patch up or add to his humble home. The architecture of

11. For a different interpretation of Barragán and Goeritz's project, see Keith Eggener's essay in this book. [Editor's note.]

Marcos Ramírez, ERRE, *Toy a Horse*, inSite1997. Photo Jimmy Fluker. © inSITE97.

12. This essay is dedicated to the memory of John Thomas Redfield. I'd like to thank Michael Krichman and the staff at inSITE, Stella Nair, Laura Elisa Pérez, and Stephen Redfield for their assistance.

globalization in the Americas is indeed one of mobile laboratories that continuously construct new towns. How do we begin to evaluate exportations of borderland art, representations that speak to distinct global conditions, while considering the exposure they get in the art world, part of a social and cultural milieu that has historically ignored this very border condition? Furthermore, what do we make of border architecture that is transformed by local artists to better encapsulate the condition of the present-day economic forces distorting Latin American cities? When these representations leave town, in whatever shape or form, do we even know where they came from when they do not carry an overt border stamp?

Moments of borderland integration into the mainstream, as in the case of the famous Caesar salad—originally concocted in Tijuana's Hotel Caesar—give us a gauge with which to evaluate outside perceptions of border exportations. One cannot help but ask if the salad would have enjoyed the same popularity if it had been called a Tijuana Salad, a name that more readily references the pickled sausages one finds at U.S. convenience stores ("Tijuana Mama" is my favorite), not to mention the *mercados* that fill Tijuana's streets. The building cycles of globalization know no borders in the end, and sadly, they involve the work of as many makers of landfills as builders of notable cultural landscapes.[12] ∎

David doesn't know how his mother could have survived, but she did. Or how she wound up in Los Angeles. She probably picked up some odd jobs along the way. She probably slept outside, or in barns or in parks. We know she worked at a gas station. In a diner. And often as a cleaning woman. We could follow her trail from city to city. And even a little in Los Angeles. In Los Angeles, after a while, we lost her because, after a while, the money orders and the letters stopped coming. That's why David crossed the line himself, to try and find her. She was a waitress. One day she didn't show up. She was a cleaning woman. One day she didn't show up. She spoke little, did her job. She was polite but somber, someone said. She was missed when she left, especially by the children. She never stole.

The landlady told David, She lived here. She left. She left her coat behind. I kept it, just in case ... but she never came back for it. She must have gone back to Mexico. It's been four months since she left already, and, I don't know why, but I couldn't rent her room again. Sometimes I think it's her fault. She must have left some kind of atmosphere in the room, or a spell.

I really have nothing against her, and I don't see what she could have against me or the room. Why she left I have no idea, no idea at all. She left the rent money on the table, and her jacket. No letter, nothing. She didn't have much. I wasn't here when she left. She must have used the occasion. I don't have much to say about her. We weren't close at all. And I'm easy to get close to. But she ... she didn't see anyone, men or women. One time, I wanted to go down to Mexico on vacation, and I asked her what were some good places. She shrugged. She sort of murmured something, and I didn't really catch it; then she went up to her room. There's really nothing to say about her. She always left at the same time and came back at the same time. She hardly ever went out again. Sometimes on Sunday she must have gone to the beach, I think. I think so because on Sunday sometimes there was a little sand on the steps. Sometimes she stepped out a few minutes to smoke. I don't like people smoking inside. So she would wander down the block a little, smoking. She looked like she was thinking. But about what I can't tell you. She was always very neat. You could tell she ironed her clothes. Down the cellar, there's a washing machine and a dryer. The tenants are allowed to use them so she used them. But she must have ironed in the room. When she ironed, she would turn on the radio. I could hear it. Once she blew out the fuses. I told her not to listen to the radio and leave the lights on and iron. But it probably wasn't her fault. Because a radio uses practically nothing. Anyway, a little while after that she left. I wonder if she's in Mexico or somewhere else. Sometimes I think she's dead. But that's because lots of times I have these black thoughts. She isn't dead. She's in Mexico or somewhere else, but I can't tell you where. I never saw her around the neighborhood again. Well, I thought I did ... but I'm not sure it was her.... It was right nearby ... where the street crosses the boulevard. There's lots of Mexicans down there. I was in my car but when I got up there, there was nobody there. I must have been hallucinating.

Chantal Akerman, *From the Other Side* (2002), voiceover at the end of the film.

Chantal Akerman, Triptych from the film-installation *From the Other Side*, 2002. © Chantal Akerman; Galerie Marian Goodman (Paris); Firststreet Gallery (London). Coproduction Chemah IS, Corto Pacific, Centre Georges Pompidou; courtesy of Arte France, AMIP, RTBF.